WORLD OF LANGUAGE

Nancy Nickell Ragno   Marian Davies Toth   Betty G. Gray

Contributing Author – Primary   Elfrieda Hiebert
Contributing Author – Vocabulary   Richard E. Hodges
Contributing Author – Poetry   Myra Cohn Livingston

Consulting Author – Thinking Skills   David N. Perkins

SILVER BURDETT GINN

NEEDHAM, MA   PARSIPPANY, NJ

Atlanta, GA   Irving, TX   Deerfield, IL   Santa Clara, CA

Acknowledgments

Cover: Sid Evans

Contributing Writers: Sandra Breuer, Judy Brim, Wendy Davis, Anne Maley, Marcia Miller, Anne Ryle, Gerry Tomlinson

Contributing artists: Laurel Aiello, Ernest Albanese, Victor Ambrus, Lori Anderson, Esther Baran, Howard Berelson, Lisa Bonforte, Vince Caputo, Chi Chung, Virginia Claus, Floyd Cooper, Laura Cornell, Jack Crane, Jim Cummins, Fred Daunno, Susan David, Helen Davie, Betsy Day, Kees de Kiefte, Pat and Robin DeWit, Susan Dodge, Eldon Doty, John Dyess, Len Ebert, Alan Eitzen, Marlene Eckman, Grace Goldberg, Lydia Halverson, John Holder, Robert Jackson, Jan Naimo Jones, Barbara Lanza, Robert J. Lee, Vickie Lerner, Gary Lippincott, Michael McDermott, Diana Magnuson, Claude Martinot, Yoshi Miyake, Kim Mulkey, Nancy Munger, Stella Ormai, Vida Pavesich, Steve Petruccio, A. and M. Provensen, Sandy Rabinowitz, John Rice, David Rickman, Vera Rosenberry, Sally Schaedler, Steve Shindler, Dick Smolinski, Scott Snow, Joel Snyder, Susan Spellman, Sandra Spiedel, Barbara Steadman, Sharon Steuer, Susan Swan, Tom Tierney, George Ulrich, Richard Walz, Fred Winkowski

Handwriting models: Michele Epstein

Picture credits: All photographs by Silver Burdett & Ginn (SB&G) unless otherwise noted.

Unit 1: 5: *t.* Jonathon A. Meyers/Amwest; *b.* © 1990 Gabe Palmer/The Stock Market. 36: All by Dan DeWilde for SB&G. 40: Peter A. Silva/Picture Group. 41: *A Very Young Dancer* by Jill Krementz. Used by permission of Dell Books (A division of Bantam, Doubleday, Dell Publishing Group, Inc.). **Unit 2:** 58: L.S. Williams/H. Armstrong Roberts. 59: The Granger Collection. 61: *Samuel Adams* by John Singleton Copely, American, 1738–1815. Oil on canvas, 50 x 40¼ in. 62: Historical Pictures Service, Chicago. 94: All by Dan DeWilde for SB&G. 98: *Lost Drummer Boy,* painting by Percy Moran. Courtesy Petersen Galleries, Beverly Hills. 99: *What's the Big Idea, Ben Franklin* by Jean Fritz. Illustrations by Margot Tomes. Reprinted by permission of the Putman Publishing Group. **Unit 3:** 110: Photograph by Ansel Adams. Courtesy of the Trustees of the Ansel Adams Publishing Rights Trust. All rights reserved. 114: Tom Hollyman/Photo Researchers, Inc. 117: Roger Tory Peterson/Photo Researchers, Inc. 118: Courtesy Gale Research Company. 130: Courtesy of the Trustees of the Ansel Adams Publishing Rights Trust. All rights reserved. 131: Courtesy of the Wynn and Edna Bullock Trust. 132: From *Camera Work,* April 1910. The Metropolitan Museum of Art, Alfred Stieglitz Collection.

133: *t.* © Gerry Ellis/Ellis Wildlife Collection, 1990; *m.l.* Animals Animals/Anthony Bannister; *b.* Peter Menzel/Stock, Boston. 140: Photograph by Wynn Bullock. Courtesy of the Wynn and Edna Bullock Trust. 144: All by Dan DeWilde for SB&G. 148: Bob Schlosser/The Huntington Library. 149: *Words with Wrinkled Knees* by Barbara Juster Ebensen. Jacket art copyright © 1986 by John Stadler. Reprinted by permission of Harper & Row Publishers, Inc. **Unit 4:** 158: Bob Connell. 161: *t.* Copyright © 1973, Grandma Moses Properties Co., New York. 162: All by Chris Arend/Alaska Photo. 164: Permit courtesy of Sculpture Placement, Ltd. of Washington D.C. 180: William E. Ferguson. 181: *t.* Judy Cutchins; *b.* Bob Connell. 187: Courtesy of Wheaton Historical Society, Millville, New Jersey. 190: All by Dan DeWilde for SB&G. 196: All by Dan DeWilde for SB&G. 200: *The Table* by Georges Braque, photo by Superstock. 201: *Sketching Outdoors in Spring* by Jim Arnosky, copyright © 1987. Illustrations copyright © 1987 by Jim Arnosky. Reprinted by permission of Lothrop, Lee & Shepard Books (A division of William Morrow and Company, Inc.). **Unit 5:** 256: All by Dan DeWilde for SB&G. 261: *Voice of Black Hope: Mary McLeod Bethune* by Milton Meltzer. Illustrations copyright © by Stephen Marchesi. All rights reserved. Reprinted by permission of Viking Penguin, Inc. **Unit 6:** 272: Jim Hamilton. 276: Jeff Foott. 277: *l.* Herb Lanks/Shostal Associates; *r.* © Gerry Ellis/Ellis Wildlife Collection, 1990. 280: *l.* Philip John Bailey/The Picture Cube; *r.* Nancy Dudley/Stock, Boston. 301: *t.* Frank Jensen/The Stock Solution; *m.l.* Roy Kaltschmidt/Wild Images; *b.* Tom Till. 308. All by Dan DeWilde for SB&G. 313: *Ko-Hoh: The Call of the Trumpeter Swan,* copyright © 1986 by Jay Featherly. Used by permission of Carolrhoda Books, Inc., 241 First Ave. N., Minneapolis, MN 55401. **Unit 7:** 358: All by Dan DeWilde for SB&G. 362: George Hunter/TSW-Click/Chicago, Ltd. 363: *Fables* by Arnold Lobel. Copyright © 1981 by Arnold Lobel. Reprinted by permission of Harper & Row, Publishers, Inc. **Unit 8:** 372: Jeff Rotman. 375: Douglas Peebles. 378: *b.l.* Karales/Peter Arnold, Inc; *inset* Joel W. Rogers/Aperture Photobank. 396: Jeff Rotman. 397: All by Douglas Faulkner. 398: Charles Seaborn/Odyssey Productions. 399: Al Grotell. 402: *l.* Scott Kraus/New England Aquarium; *r.* Reed Kaestner/ Nawrocki Stock Photo. 403: *l.* Jeff Rotman; *r.* F.H. Barnwell, University of Minnesota. 405: *l.* © 1990 Tongass N.F. Alaska/The Stock Market; *r.* Jeff Foott/Tom Stack & Associates. 406: *l.* Charles Seaborn/Odyssey Productions; *r.* Douglas Faulkner. 410: All by Dan DeWilde for SB&G. 415: *Night Dive* by Ann McGovern. Cover photograph copyright © Martin Scheiner. 439: Bob and Clara Calhoun/ Bruce Coleman. **Dictionary:** 442: *r.* Erich Hartmann/Magnum Photos. 444: *l.* John R. MacGregor/Peter Arnold, Inc.; *r.* Illustrations from *The World Book Encyclopedia,* © 1988 World Book, Inc. 446: *r.* L.L.T. Rhodes/TSW-Click/Chicago, Ltd. 447: Sisse Brimberg/Woodfin Camp & Associates. 448: *l.* Massachusetts Historical Society; *r.* Private collection. 450: Denise Tackett/Tom Stack & Associates. 451: Brown Brothers. Every effort has been made to locate the original sources. If any errors have occurred the publisher can be notified and corrections will be made.

CONTENTS

INTRODUCTORY UNIT

UNIT 1 USING LANGUAGE TO NARRATE

PART 1 LANGUAGE AWARENESS ◆ SENTENCES

PART 2 A REASON FOR WRITING ◆ NARRATING

UNIT 2   USING LANGUAGE TO PERSUADE

PART 1   LANGUAGE AWARENESS ◆ NOUNS

PART 2   A REASON FOR WRITING ◆ PERSUADING

UNIT 3   USING LANGUAGE TO CREATE

PART 1   LANGUAGE AWARENESS ◆ PRONOUNS

PART 2   A REASON FOR WRITING ◆ CREATING

UNIT 4   USING LANGUAGE TO INFORM

PART 1   LANGUAGE AWARENESS ◆ VERBS

PART 2   A REASON FOR WRITING ◆ INFORMING

UNIT THEME: Artists at Work

Literature Model: Are Those Animals Real? How Museums Prepare Wildlife Exhibits

UNIT 5   USING LANGUAGE TO RESEARCH

PART 1   LANGUAGE AWARENESS ◆ VERBS

PART 2   A REASON FOR WRITING ◆ RESEARCHING

UNIT 6   USING LANGUAGE TO DESCRIBE

PART 1   LANGUAGE AWARENESS ◆ ADJECTIVES

PART 2   A REASON FOR WRITING ◆ DESCRIBING

UNIT 7   USING LANGUAGE TO IMAGINE

PART 1   LANGUAGE AWARENESS ◆ ADVERBS

PART 2   A REASON FOR WRITING ◆ IMAGINING

Literature Model: The Dragon King/
The Crow and the Pitcher

UNIT THEME: Fables

UNIT 8   USING LANGUAGE TO CLASSIFY

PART 1 LANGUAGE AWARENESS ◆ SENTENCES

PART 2 A REASON FOR WRITING ◆ CLASSIFYING

WRITER'S REFERENCE BOOK

AWARD **LITERATURE** WINNING

AMERICAN
LIBRARY
ASSOCIATION
NOTABLE
BOOK

The Best Bad Thing
by Yoshiko Uchida

AWARD
WINNING
AUTHOR

Why Don't You Get a Horse, Sam Adams?
by Jean Fritz

AWARD
WINNING
AUTHOR

Mary McLeod Bethune
by Eloise Greenfield

AMERICAN
LIBRARY
ASSOCIATION
NOTABLE
BOOK

The Trumpet of the Swan
by E. B. White

AWARD
WINNING
ILLUSTRATOR

"The Crow and the Pitcher"
selected and adapted by Louis Untermeyer
illustrations by A. and M. Provensen

IRA/CBC
CHILDREN'S
CHOICE
1986

Where the Waves Break: Life at the Edge of the Sea
by Anita Malnig

— from *Aesop's Fables*

Selected and Adapted by
Louis Untermeyer   Illustrated by
A. and M. Provensen

The Crow and the Pitcher

Dying of thirst, a Crow ⟨...⟩ ave a cry of pleasure.
"Caw⟨...⟩er! A pitcher of

⟨...⟩e was water in it.
⟨...⟩ter left in it was
⟨...⟩ot reach down far

⟨...⟩ push it over,
⟨...⟩ould have no

school became a college, and Mrs. Bethune ⟨...⟩
president. Mary McLeod Bethune then fou⟨...⟩
to work for the education of black childr⟨...⟩
speeches all over the United States. Wh⟨...⟩
1955, Mrs. Bethune's work had chang⟨...⟩

Mary McLeod Bethune's love fo⟨...⟩
when she was a child in South Car⟨...⟩
true story of Mary's childhood.

Mary was born in the log cab⟨...⟩
1875. She was the fifteenth chil⟨...⟩
were born later. Mary loved th⟨...⟩
was very small, her father le⟨...⟩
of Old Bush, the mule with⟨...⟩
the plow. When she was a⟨...⟩

LITERATURE

from

The Trumpet of the Swan

by E. B. White

Every spring, Sam Beaver and his father took a trip to their wilderness camp in Canada. Sam's father liked to fish there, and Sam enjoyed exploring. It was while he was exploring, early one morning, that Sam made a wonderful discovery. He found a small, still pond where two great trumpeter swans had built their nest.

LITERATURE: Story

Introductory Unit

Literature in Your World

In the *World of Language* literature is a key. Literature unlocks your imagination. It opens your mind to the world of ideas. Through literature you can enter any time and any place. You can experience many different adventures. You can meet people you would never meet and share ideas with the greatest minds. Literature is indeed a key. It is a key to enlarging your world. It is the key to enriching your world of language.

Writing in Your World

Writing is a way to reach out to your world. When you write, you write *to* someone. You write to be read. Writing is also a way to find out about yourself. It is a way to explore your ideas, feelings, and dreams. Sometimes you write for others and sometimes you write just for yourself. Sometimes you write to explore ideas.

Writing is creating, and you are its creator. Writing is thinking, and it is discovering what you think. Writing is a way of finding out about your world. Writing is a way to change it! That is a powerful thought. Writing *is* powerful. It is a powerful tool in your world and in the wonderful world of language.

What Is a Writer?

A writer is anyone who writes. *You* are a writer. You already do a lot of writing. Sometimes you write for your readers. Other times, though, you write just for yourself. Here are three kinds of writing you can do.

Writing to Inform ✦ Writing can help you get something done in the world. You might write a report about clean air to let people know how important it is.

Writing to Create ✦ You can use your imagination to write a poem or a story.

Writing to Express Yourself ✦ You can write to express what you think or feel — to explore your ideas. This writing is a kind of talking to yourself.

Many writers use a journal when they write just for themselves. This is a good idea for you, too. After all, you are a writer!

Journal Writing

A journal is a writer's best friend. Carry one with you. Then you will be ready to

- jot down an idea
- practice and experiment with writing
- express yourself in words
- write your opinion of a book, a movie, a song
- record your impressions — of a late summer thunderstorm, a baseball game, a kitten

A journal can be a special notebook or a section of another notebook. It can be a homemade notebook made by stapling paper in a folder. Once you have your journal, use it right away. You will find many ideas for journal writing throughout this book.

Introducing the Writing Process

Sometimes you want to write something, make it really good, polish it, and then share it with other people. Using the writing process will help you achieve your goal.

Using the writing process simply means going through the process of writing step by step. You do not expect to write a perfect paper right away. Instead, you take time—time to think, to plan, to get ideas. Later you review what you have written. You make changes and corrections.

With each stage of the writing process, you are given *strategies*, or ways of working. You are given ways to get ideas, ways to get started and keep going, ways to improve your writing and to share it.

Think, Read, Speak, Listen, Write

At the end of each unit, you will use the writing process. You will write something to share with others. Will this be difficult? Not at all, for you will be well prepared by the lessons in that unit.

- ◆ A **Thinking Skill** lesson gives a strategy to use in reading and writing.
- ◆ A **Literature** lesson gives you a model for the writing you will do.
- ◆ A **Speaking and Listening** lesson helps you develop skills for using language orally.
- ◆ **Writing** lessons focus on the kinds of writing you will be doing as you use the writing process.
- ◆ Two **Connection** lessons help you use what you learned in grammar and literature in your writing.

Using the Writing Process

WRITER'S HINT

As you write, think about these things.

1. Purpose Why are you writing? To tell a story? To describe something? To give information?

2. Audience Who will read what you write? Someone your own age? Someone younger? An adult?

Write a Description

On the next four pages you will preview the five stages of the writing process. You will try each one. The stages are: *prewriting, writing, revising, proofreading,* and *publishing*.

Writers often start by prewriting and end by publishing. They may, however, go back and forth between the other stages. As you become more familiar with the stages, you will feel more comfortable moving back and forth. With each stage there is an activity for you.

Read the Writer's Hint. For your description your *purpose* is to describe an object so well your classmates can "see" it. Your classmates are your *audience*.

1 Prewriting ♦ Getting ready to write

Have you ever said, "I don't know what to write about" or "I don't know what to say"? Don't worry. Most writers feel that way before they start writing. There are lots of ways to get the ideas you need. Here are a few: brainstorm, draw an idea cluster, keep a journal, or interview someone.

PREWRITING IDEA

Using Your Senses

Choose an interesting object to describe, something you can see in your classroom. Don't tell anyone what it is. Observe the object carefully for several minutes. What do you see? Does it make a sound if you move it? What does it feel like? Does it have a smell? Take notes on what you observe. Your notes can be just words.

2 Writing ◆ Putting your ideas on paper

You have your writing topic. You have your notes. A blank page is staring at you. How can you get started?

The important thing is just to start writing. Don't worry if your ideas are out of order. Don't worry about spelling, either. You can make changes later to improve and correct your writing.

WRITING IDEA

Starting with a Question

Put your prewriting notes in front of you and begin. You might begin with a question such as *Have you ever really looked at our pencil sharpener?* Next use your notes to describe the object. Do not write everything on your list, though. Choose the best details. Write on every other line to leave room to make changes.

Finally, add an ending sentence, such as *Our pencil sharpener is old and very noisy, but it works fine!*

3 Revising ♦ Making changes to improve your writing

Reading to yourself is the first thing to do when you revise your writing. First think about your *purpose*. Did you stick to your purpose of describing an object? Or did you forget to describe and start telling a story? Then think about your *audience*. Will your classmates understand what you wrote?

Next read your writing aloud to a partner. When you finish, ask your partner to make suggestions and ask questions. Think about your partner's comments. Then make the changes *you* feel are important.

REVISING IDEA

Read to Yourself and Read to a Partner

First read your description to yourself. Think about your purpose and audience. Did you really write a description? Will your classmates be able to "see" what you describe? Make changes to improve your description. You can cross out words and write in new words. You can draw arrows to show where to move words or sentences.

Your writing may look very messy at this point. That is all right.

Next read your description to a partner. Ask, *"What part did you like best? Is there any part that you would like to know more about?"* Listen to the answers. Then make the changes you think will improve your description.

4 Proofreading ◆ Looking for and fixing errors

After you have made sure your writing says what you want it to say, proofread it. Look for errors. Check capital letters and punctuation, indenting, and spelling. Then make a clean copy in your best handwriting.

5 Publishing ◆ Sharing your writing with others

There are many ways to share your writing. You may read it aloud to others. You may record it with a tape recorder or post it on a bulletin board. One of the best parts of writing is hearing or seeing your audience's response.

USING LANGUAGE TO NARRATE

PART ONE

Unit Theme *Hobbies*

Language Awareness Sentences

PART TWO

Literature *The Best Bad Thing* by Yoshiko Uchida

A Reason for Writing Narrating

Writing
IN YOUR JOURNAL

WRITER'S WARM-UP ◆ What hobbies interest you? Do you like to collect things, like coins or stamps? Maybe you prefer an active hobby, like skating or gymnastics. Some people build models or sew or cook. Other people like bird-watching or photography. Write in your journal. Tell about a hobby you have or one you would like to have.

GETTING STARTED

Have a Sentence Marathon. Take turns completing this sentence: *I really enjoy _____.*

1 Writing Sentences

Knowing how to form sentences can make your writing clear and effective. Read the three sentences below. They are about people and their hobbies. Notice that each sentence tells a complete thought.

1. A hobby can give you hours of fun.
2. You can develop any special interest into a hobby.
3. People of all ages enjoy hobbies.

Read the two groups of words below. They are not sentences. Neither group tells a complete thought.

4. Building model rockets.
5. A large collection of seashells.

> **Summary** ◆ A **sentence** is a group of words that expresses a complete thought. When you write, use sentences that express your thoughts clearly.

Guided Practice

Tell which of these groups of words are sentences and which are not sentences.

1. Puppetry is a popular hobby.
2. Giving puppet shows for friends.
3. Some people make their own puppets.
4. My aunt created and operated marionettes.
5. A puppet with strings.

Practice

A. Read the groups of words below. Write *sentence* or *not a sentence* for each one.

  6. Some people like making things.
  7. Made the clay elephant for our circus.
  8. Others like collecting things.
  9. Ann has a large autograph collection.
10. Interesting hobbies in music and art.
11. Todd is writing the music for our school play.
12. Victoria is painting the scenery.
13. Many different kinds of sports.
14. The bobsled flashed down the track.
15. The soccer ball whirled into the net.
16. A photo story about our new school.
17. Won a blue ribbon at the hobby show.
18. The class was proud of its awards.

B. Make complete sentences by adding words to each group of words.

19. ____ seems like an interesting hobby.
20. I especially enjoy ____.
21. Dancing is ____.
22. ____ to play the bass drum.
23. Perhaps I could collect ____.
24. ____ tropical fish.
25. Of course, I like ____.
26. ____ drawing and painting.
27. ____ building model ships.
28. Someday I want to ____.

Apply ◆ Think and Write

From Your Writing ◆ Did you use complete sentences to express your thoughts in the Writer's Warm-up? Rewrite any incomplete sentences.

✎ **Remember**
to use complete sentences to express your ideas.

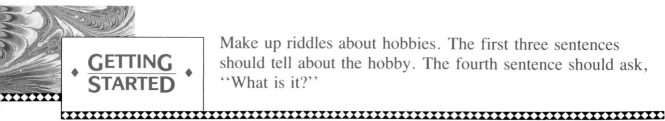

♦ GETTING ♦
STARTED

Make up riddles about hobbies. The first three sentences should tell about the hobby. The fourth sentence should ask, "What is it?"

2 Declarative and Interrogative Sentences

If a sentence tells something, it is declarative. If a sentence asks something, it is interrogative.

Declarative: Hobbies are important in people's lives.
People enjoy having special projects.

Interrogative: What is your hobby?
Do you have more than one?

A declarative sentence makes a statement and ends with a period. An interrogative sentence asks a question and ends with a question mark. All sentences begin with capital letters.

> **Summary** ♦ A **declarative sentence** makes a statement. When you write this kind of sentence, end it with a period (**.**).
> An **interrogative sentence** asks a question. When you write this kind of sentence, end it with a question mark (**?**).

Guided Practice

Tell whether each sentence is declarative or interrogative.

1. What are you doing with that loom?
2. I am weaving a rug.
3. Do you like my design?
4. I designed the pattern myself.
5. It certainly is bright and bold.

Practice

A. Read each sentence below. Write *declarative* or *interrogative* to tell what kind of sentence each is.

6. Hobbies help people increase their knowledge.
7. Did you already know that?
8. A fossil collection is a good example.
9. The collector learns something new with each fossil.
10. Isn't that a fine way to gain knowledge?
11. How else do hobbies help people?
12. Many people join hobby clubs.
13. Hobbies can help build friendships.

B. Write each sentence. Begin each with a capital letter. Use periods and question marks correctly.

14. do you belong to a hobby club
15. would you like to visit my hiking club
16. this hobby show is a very busy place
17. have you seen the model planes
18. isn't this an interesting camping exhibit
19. the kite exhibit is across the room
20. the coin collection is valuable

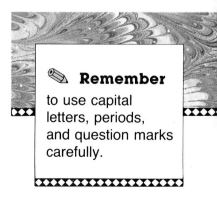

C. Change each sentence to the kind named in parentheses ( ).

21. Have you noticed the video cameras? (declarative)
22. Is this computer game very difficult? (declarative)
23. These wood carvings are really unusual. (interrogative)
24. Are you getting hungry? (declarative)
25. We should look for the cafeteria. (interrogative)

Apply ◆ Think and Write

Forming Questions ◆ Write three interrogative sentences about what the children on this page are doing. Ask a classmate to write three statements that answer your questions.

> ✎ **Remember**
> to use capital letters, periods, and question marks carefully.

Suppose you were in charge of a kite contest. What commands would you give to the people in the contest?

3 Imperative and Exclamatory Sentences

Read each sentence below.

■ **1. Please get your kite ready.**   **2. Wait for the signal.**

Sentence **1** politely tells someone to do something. It is a request. Sentence **2** also tells someone to do something. It is a command. Both sentences are imperative sentences. They end with periods.

■ **3. That kite will crash!**   **4. The wind is too strong!**

Sentences **3** and **4** show strong feeling or excitement. Both sentences are exclamatory sentences. They end with exclamation marks.

> **Summary** ♦ An **imperative sentence** gives a command or makes a request. When you write this kind of sentence, end it with a period (.).
>
> An **exclamatory sentence** expresses strong feeling. When you write this kind of sentence, end it with an exclamation mark (!).

Guided Practice

Read these sentences about flying a kite. Tell which sentences are imperative and which are exclamatory.

1. Please keep your kite away from the others.
2. Your kite is taking a nosedive!
3. That was a close call!
4. Tell me how you did that.

Practice

A. Here are some more sentences about kites. Read each sentence. Write *imperative* or *exclamatory* to tell what kind of sentence it is.

5. Give your kite more string.
6. That is all the string I have!
7. Pull back quickly.
8. This kite refuses to fly!
9. Please don't give up.

B. Write each sentence. Begin each with a capital letter. Use periods and exclamation marks correctly.

10. i am really upset about my kite
11. please calm down now
12. get your kite ready to try again
13. you are stepping on the tail of my kite
14. excuse me

C. Add words to each group of words below. Write imperative or exclamatory sentences.

15. Please keep your _____.
16. Look at _____.
17. What an exciting _____!
18. Watch me _____.
19. Bring your _____.
20. How high _____!
21. The winner is _____!

Apply ♦ Think and Write

Creative Writing ♦ Imagine that you entered a kite-flying contest. Write three imperative and three exclamatory sentences about your experience, but do not punctuate them. Trade papers with a friend and add the end marks to each other's sentences.

✎ **Remember** to use different kinds of sentences to express your ideas.

◆ GETTING ◆
STARTED

Use your school subjects as subjects of sentences. How many sentences can you make up?

EXAMPLE: *Math begins at ten o'clock.*

4 Subjects and Predicates

When you write, your sentence needs two parts to express a complete thought.

1. Kites   come in almost every shape and size imaginable.
2. These high fliers   are fun to build and fly.
3. Kite lovers from many lands   agree.

The part of the sentence in blue is the subject. It names someone or something. The subject may be one word, as in sentence **1**. It may also be many words, as in sentences **2** and **3**.

The part of the sentence in green is the predicate. It tells what the subject is or does. The predicate may be one word, as in sentence **3**. It may also be many words, as in sentences **1** and **2**.

> **Summary** ◆ A sentence has two parts. The **subject** names someone or something. The **predicate** tells what the subject is or does. Use complete sentences when you write so that you will communicate clearly to your reader.

Guided Practice

One part of each sentence below is underlined. Tell whether the underlined part is the subject or the predicate.

1. Kites <u>have a long and interesting history</u>.
2. <u>The people of China</u> invented kites long ago.
3. Chinese kites <u>were the very first type of aircraft</u>.
4. <u>Some early kites</u> were made of silk.
5. Today kite manufacturers <u>use a wide variety of materials</u>.

Practice

A. Read each sentence. Write *subject* or *predicate* to identify
the underlined part of the sentence.

 6. Kites <u>had many different uses in the past</u>.
 7. <u>The people of Samoa</u> used kites to pull their canoes.
 8. <u>People in Korea</u> used kites for fishing.
 9. A large kite <u>behaved like a sail in the wind</u>.
 10. <u>Some Japanese kites</u> were sixty-five feet tall.

B. Write each sentence. Draw one line under the subject.
Draw two lines under the predicate.

 11. Benjamin Franklin is the most famous kite flyer.
 12. His experiment proved something about electricity.
 13. Engineers used a kite once for building a bridge.
 14. The kite pulled a cable across the Niagara River.
 15. Kites of years ago measured the weather for us.

C. Add the missing subject or predicate to each sentence part.

 16. Kite festivals _____ .
 17. A dragon kite _____ .
 18. _____ are soaring over the treetops.
 19. They _____ .
 20. I _____ .
 21. _____ glides gracefully in the air.
 22. The string _____ .
 23. _____ became difficult to manage.
 24. _____ crashed in the field.
 25. _____ was surprised to hear the news.

Apply ◆ Think and Write

Dictionary of Knowledge ◆ The Wright brothers studied
kites before they built their plane. Read about these inventors
in the Dictionary of Knowledge. Write some sentences about
their interest in flying.

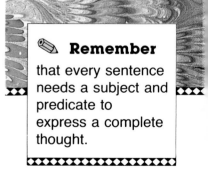

✎ **Remember**
that every sentence
needs a subject and
predicate to
express a complete
thought.

Ken likes to fly kites. He has one that's big and one that's small. What other words meaning *big* and *small* could you use to describe the kites?

VOCABULARY ◆
Using the Thesaurus

To find the meaning of a word, you often look in a dictionary. Sometimes you know a word's meaning, but the word isn't quite right for what you want to say. Suppose you want to describe an insect that is very little. You could use *little*, but the insect is even smaller than little. In this case, use a thesaurus.

A **thesaurus** contains lists of synonyms—words with similar meanings, and antonyms—words with opposite meanings. You will learn more about synonyms and antonyms in Unit 7.

Like a dictionary, a thesaurus lists entry words in alphabetical order. Writers can look up a word and find a list of synonyms and antonyms for that word. Writers can then choose words that make their writing more interesting.

Study the thesaurus entry below.

	Part of Speech	Meaning

Entry word — **throw** (v) to release and use force to send through the air.

Example sentence — Jackie threw the football to her teammate.

Synonyms —
cast—to throw forcefully with a jerk. The fisherman cast his line into the water.
fling—to throw with force. Jodi flung her coat on the chair and rushed up the stairs.
heave—to lift and throw. The trash collectors heaved the large bags into the truck.
hurl—to throw powerfully. The strong athlete hurled the shotput.
pitch—to throw something at a target. We pitched horseshoes in the backyard.
toss—to throw lightly with the palm of the hand upward. See if you can toss the beanbag so it lands in the circle.

Antonym — ANTONYM: **catch** (v)

Building Your Vocabulary

Choose synonyms from the thesaurus entry on page 12 to replace *throw* or *threw* in these sentences. Use a different synonym in each sentence.

1. Thompson <u>threw</u> the pitch with great strength.
2. He <u>threw</u> it straight into the catcher's glove.
3. <u>Throw</u> me that pencil, please.
4. The sailors <u>threw</u> the anchor over the side of the ship.

Practice

A. Use the entry on page 12 to answer these questions.

1. What is the entry word? Its part of speech?
2. What are six different synonyms for *throw*?

B. Find *yell* in the Thesaurus that begins on page 452. For each sentence, replace *yelled* with an interesting synonym.

3. Ken <u>yelled</u>, "Watch the tricks my kite can do!"
4. We all <u>yelled</u> when he finished each trick.
5. "That one was really neat!" Lynn <u>yelled</u>.

C. Use the Thesaurus to answer the questions below. Look up the entry words given in parentheses ( ).

6. Is <u>furious</u> angrier than <u>annoyed</u>? (angry)
7. Which is more crooked, <u>curved</u> or <u>zigzag</u>? (crooked)
8. Should a marching band <u>strut</u> or <u>trudge</u>? (walk)

LANGUAGE CORNER ◆ Pictographs

A **pictograph** is a picture or symbol that stands for a word or an idea.

What might the pictographs on the right stand for? Make up some pictographs of your own.

How to Combine Sentences

Sentences that repeat words can be combined, or joined, into one sentence. You can combine sentences that repeat subjects or predicates. Read the sentences below. In example **1**, is the subject or the predicate repeated?

1. Lisa collects stamps.   Lisa saves them in an album.
2. Lisa collects stamps and saves them in an album.

Lisa is the subject of both sentences in example **1**. The sentences tell about two things Lisa did. Example **2** uses the word *and* to combine the sentences into one strong sentence.

You can also use the word *and* to join sentences that have the same predicate. Which example below do you prefer?

3. Lisa arranged a display of stamps.
   Dieter arranged a display of stamps.
4. Lisa and Dieter arranged a display of stamps.

The Grammar Game ✦ Join each pair of sentences into one strong sentence. What word will you add to each pair?

♦ Ella saved an avocado pit.
  Ella sprouted it in a glass of water.
♦ My cousins grow herbs in the kitchen.
  I grow herbs in the kitchen.

Working Together

See how combining sentences can keep you from repeating words too often. Work as a group on activities **A** and **B**.

A. Use the word *and* to combine each pair of sentences into one longer sentence. Then combine different sentence pairs to make new sentences. How many new combinations can you write?

> **1.** We recycle bottles. We save stacks of newspapers.
> **2.** We clean the playground. We use containers for trash.
> **3.** We pick up aluminum cans. We reuse paper bags.

B. Choose two names of group members for each sentence. Then use *and* to join the sentences together.

> **EXAMPLE:** <u>Cal</u> waited patiently.　<u>Lee</u> waited patiently.
> <u>Cal and Lee</u> waited patiently.

> **4.** ____ took swimming lessons in July.
> **5.** ____ earned money by delivering newspapers.
> **6.** ____ washed cars and dogs for the neighbors.
> **7.** ____ camped in a national park.
> **8.** ____ visited a zoo and a museum.
> **9.** ____ entered a spelling contest.
> **10.** ____ went to the arts-and-crafts festival.

WRITERS' CORNER ♦ Sentence Variety

Using different kinds of sentences makes writing more interesting. What kinds of sentences are in this paragraph?

Have you ever tried developing your own photographs? Many beginners have great results. Ask your librarian about classes. It's fun!

Read what you wrote for the Writer's Warm-up. What kinds of sentences did you use? Is there variety?

USING LANGUAGE
TO
NARRATE

=== **PART TWO** ===

Literature *The Best Bad Thing* by Yoshiko Uchida

A Reason for Writing Narrating

CREATIVE
Writing

FINE ARTS ◆ Did you know that every stamp has a story? Look at the image on each stamp. What made it special enough to be featured on a stamp? Imagine that one of the images comes to life. It is whispering its story in your ear. Write the story the stamp has to tell.

CRITICAL THINKING ♦
A Strategy for Narrating

A CONCLUSION SENTENCE

Telling a story is often called **narrating.** After this lesson you will read part of *The Best Bad Thing* by Yoshiko Uchida. In it the storyteller is a girl named Rinko. Rinko uses the words *I* and *me* to narrate an experience she had. Later you will write a narrative about an experience you have had.

Here is part of Rinko's story. What does Rinko think about what happened in this part of the story?

One evening when I was washing the supper dishes, the old man came to the back door with two of his kites. . . .
"Anybody interested in flying these before it gets dark?" he asked.
"Yeah, me!" Zenny yelled. . . .
I noticed right away that the old man had only two kites. He's leaving me out again, I thought. . . .

Rinko saw that there were three people and two kites. She had been left out before. She drew the conclusion that she would be left out again. You may draw a conclusion about something that happened or about something you read, saw, or heard.

Sometimes people reach the same conclusion. When people know the same facts, they might conclude the same thing. Sometimes people draw different conclusions. This happens when people know different facts or have different experiences.

Learning the Strategy

You often draw conclusions. For example, suppose your neighbors are packing their van with fishing rods and bicycles. What might your conclusion be? Imagine that a boy finds a valuable watch. He tries to find out who lost it. What kind of person might you think he is? Suppose you go to camp. You hardly sleep. What might you conclude about camp?

Writing a conclusion sentence can help you decide what you think. Perhaps you want to write a funny story about going to camp. At the end you want to tell what you thought about the experience. First write what happened. Then write a conclusion sentence that tells what you think. Read the conclusion sentence at the bottom of the sample at the right. Would you draw the same conclusion?

> *What happened at camp:*
>
> *The roof leaked.*
>
> *Raccoons ate my brownies.*
>
> *I couldn't sleep.*
>
> *I heard strange noises.*

> *I think camp is a lot of fun.*

Using the Strategy

A. Think of a "first" in your life. It might be the first time you tried to skate. Write what happened. Then write a conclusion sentence that starts with the words *I think*.

B. *The Best Bad Thing* tells about kite-flying. Before you read it, write everything you know about kites. Then add a conclusion sentence about kites or kite-flying. Begin your conclusion sentence with *I think*.

Applying the Strategy

♦ Suppose you draw a conclusion about someone or something. Can your conclusion ever change? Explain why or why not.

♦ When do you draw conclusions? Think of three situations.

LITERATURE

from

The Best Bad Thing

by Yoshiko Uchida

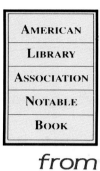

The month Rinko spent on Mrs. Hata's farm one summer was filled with surprises. Auntie Hata and her sons, Zenny and Abu, were much nicer than Rinko had expected. The old man living in Mrs. Hata's barn turned out to be a master kite maker from Japan.

Rinko was amazed when she first walked into the barn and saw the colorful kites hanging from the walls and rafters. She watched in wonder while the old man painted a samurai kite with the glaring eyes of a warrior's face. As he worked, the old man told Rinko about the magic of kite flying. He said that flying a kite lets you become part of the sky. "You become the kite and the sky and the universe itself," the old man told her, "and then we are all one and the same."

That day, Rinko wasn't sure what the old man meant about the kite and the sky and the universe. Yet one day she understood his meaning. Here is Rinko's story of how it happened.

One evening
when I was washing
the supper dishes, the old
man came to the back door
with two of his kites. One was
the diamond kite with the cross-eyed
samurai who looked as if he'd just swallowed
some of Dr. Oniki's awful brown medicine for
stomach flu. The other was the yellow-and-black
butterfly I'd seen hanging from the rafters of the barn.
"Anybody interested in flying these before it gets dark?"
he asked.

"Yeah, me!" Zenny yelled, and I saw the life suddenly come
back to his face.

I noticed right away that the old man had only two kites.
He's leaving me out again, I thought. But the old man thrust
the butterfly kite toward me and said, "Well, come on, Rinko.
Hurry up and dry your hands. I'll help you get this one up."

"Me?"

"Yes, you!"

I shook the suds from my hands, wiped them on my skirt,
and ran out into the fields with Zenny and the old man. The
sun had bleached the weeds so they seemed almost white, and
the breeze was making them rustle, as if they were whispering
to each other. Auntie Hata probably would have said that was
exactly what they were doing.

The old man held the samurai kite high over his head, angling
it to catch the breeze, while Zenny held the spool with the
flying line and backed away from him.

"Now," the old man shouted, and Zenny gave the kite a sharp tug. The samurai kite darted around for a while as if it weren't sure which way to go, and then it began to climb.

I could hardly wait to get my hands on the butterfly kite, but I watched as the old man stood with his back to the breeze and tossed it into the air. The wind lifted it right up as though it belonged in the sky, and pretty soon the butterfly was climbing.

Finally the old man handed me the spool. "Hold the line taut," he said, "and if the butterfly asks for more, feed it to her a little at a time. Understand?"

"Yes, OK," I said, turning to him.

But the old man was watching the kite. "Keep your eyes on the kite, Rinko," he said. "Listen to what it tells you."

Pretty soon I could feel the butterfly tugging at my line like a living thing, telling me it wanted to climb. So I fed out the line little by little and my butterfly soared higher and higher, its tail dancing, until it was a small black speck in the sky.

All of a sudden I understood what the old man meant that day he was making his samurai kite. I really felt as though I was the butterfly up there and it was *me* flying in the sky. I felt like I was part of the sky and part of the entire universe.

Library Link ♦ *Read about Rinko's other adventures on Auntie Hata's farm in* The Best Bad Thing *by Yoshiko Uchida.*

Reader's Response

Would you like the old man to teach you to fly a kite? Why or why not?

The Best Bad Thing

 ## Responding to Literature

1. Rinko told us about her first kite-flying experience. Do you remember doing something special for the first time? Tell about that first time.

2. The old man said, "Listen to what the kite tells you." What did he mean? How can a kite talk to you?

3. What is your favorite scene from the story? Draw a picture of that scene. Write a sentence for your picture to tell what is happening.

Writing to Learn

Think and Decide ♦ Rinko wanted to try kite flying. She thought she would like it. What would you like to try doing? Make a chart like the one below. Write what you know about the hobby you will try. Then write a conclusion sentence.

I think

Conclusion Sentence

Write ♦ Write about what you want to try doing. At the end tell why you think you would or would not like it.

SPEAKING and LISTENING ◆
Telling About an Event

Everyone likes to hear a good story—especially if it is told well. In this lesson you will find some tips on how to tell about an event. You will also practice listening well so that you will remember what you hear.

Telling about just any everyday event may not interest your listeners. Choose an event that is funny or exciting. Everyone enjoys listening to a well-told story.

How to Tell About an Event	1. Plan your story. Tell its details in order. Build suspense. Some stories have a surprise at the end. Just before you come to the surprise, pause. Always include how you felt about the event. 2. Practice, practice, practice. Say your story out loud before you tell it. Close your eyes and listen to yourself. If possible, tape-record your story. 3. Look at your audience. Take a deep breath. Smile. 4. Talk slowly and clearly. Make sure everyone can hear you. 5. Speak with feeling. Think of yourself as an actor on stage.
How to Be an Active Listener	1. Be alert. Pay attention to the storyteller. 2. As you listen, try to predict how the story will end. 3. As the story is being told, picture it in your mind. You might even picture it as a movie on a giant screen. 4. Later review the story step by step. Tell it to yourself.

Summary ◆ When you tell about an event, tell the details in order. Build suspense. When you listen, picture the story in your mind. Then review the story to remember it.

Guided Practice

Practice your speaking and listening skills. Tell about one of the events below.

1. making a new friend
2. a funny thing that happened on a field trip you took
3. the nicest surprise your class has had this year

Practice

A. Work with a classmate. Pretend you are taking a trip into space. The first person can tell how you got there and what you saw. The second person can tell how you returned and how you felt after the adventure.

B. Work with a classmate. Take turns putting yourself in one of the situations below. Tell the story as if it had happened to you. Add an ending and tell how you felt. As the listener, try to predict how the story will end.

> You climbed a mountain. You got to the top.
>
> You were riding a horse. Ahead of you was a hedge.
>
> You were flying an airplane. Suddenly you were surrounded by fog.

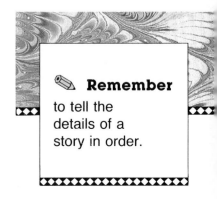

C. Think about a story you recently read. Tell the story to a classmate. As the listener, put yourself in the story that your partner tells. Together, comment on the ending of the story. Would you change the ending if you could?

Apply ◆ Think and Write

Retelling a Story ◆ Did someone in your class tell a story that you liked? Think about why it was your favorite. Review the story step by step. Make some notes to yourself so that you will be able to retell the story.

✎ **Remember** to tell the details of a story in order.

For each of these times, tell something that could or did happen: *yesterday*, *next year*, *suddenly*, *never*, *pretty soon*, *before long*, *in a hundred years*.

WRITING ♦ Time Order

Think about time for a moment. Time gives order to life. Everything that happens takes place at a certain time and for a certain length of time. That time may be in the past. It may be sometime in the future, or it may be right now!

Time order may be used to talk or write about things that happen. Just start at the beginning and give the details as they happen. Words like the ones below make the time order of events clear.

Time-Order Words				
first	then	now	at last	meanwhile
second	soon	once	immediately	all of a sudden
next	later	until	right away	at five o'clock
last	finally	before	after a while	at the same time

Read this paragraph about kite flying. Notice that the underlined words tell about time order.

Kite flying began <u>long ago</u>. For <u>thousands of years</u> people have sent kites soaring into the sky. <u>Recently</u>, kite flying has become popular. <u>Today</u> hobby shops sell many kinds of kites. Are you ready <u>now</u> to try this sport? <u>At first</u> you may feel clumsy. <u>Before long</u> you will gain skill. <u>Soon</u> you will learn to control a kite. <u>Someday</u> you may even enter kite-flying contests.

> **Summary** ♦ **Time order** is the order in which things happen in time. Words such as *first*, *next*, and *last* tell about time order.

Guided Practice

Read these sentences about *The Best Bad Thing*. Find the time-order words.

1. At last I could feel the butterfly tug at my line.
2. My butterfly immediately soared higher and higher.
3. Its tail danced until it was a small speck in the sky.
4. After a while the kite was towering in the sky.
5. All of a sudden I felt the joy of kite flying.
6. Now the old man decided to leave this country.
7. He would soon return to Japan.
8. First Rinko looked in the barn for the butterfly kite.
9. Then she found the kite hanging on the wall.
10. Finally Rinko carried it back to her room.

Practice

A. Write the sentences below as a paragraph. Use the time-order words to discover how the story goes.

11. At first I felt annoyed.
12. One day my sister told me to go fly a kite!
13. I next asked my sister to help me make a kite.
14. Finally she agreed to do it.
15. Then when I thought about it, I said, ''Why not?''

B. Would you like to try a hobby like kite flying? Scuba diving? Rock collecting? Stargazing? Skiing? Photographing gorillas in the wilds of Africa? Use your imagination. Then write some sentences about your hobby. Use a time-order word in each one.

Apply ♦ Think and Write

Dictionary of Knowledge ♦ Read about Benjamin Franklin and his famous experiment with a kite. Then in your own words, tell how the experiment was done. List the time words you use to help retell the story in the right order.

> ✎ **Remember**
> to use time-order words to make your writing clear to your reader.

◆ **GETTING STARTED** ◆

You probably know the two-letter abbreviation for the name of the state you live in. Take turns telling the two-letter abbreviations for the names of <u>other</u> states.

WRITING ◆
A Friendly Letter

Heading → 4172 Castro Street
Harrisonburg, Virginia 22807
September 29, 1991

Greeting → Dear Mama,

Body → I had a great treat yesterday. I flew a beautiful butterfly kite. It climbed and soared like a real butterfly. For a moment I felt like I was up there myself. It was a wonderful feeling.

Closing → Your daughter,

Signature → Kim

This friendly letter starts with a heading to tell the writer's address and the date. Notice the commas between the city and the state, and between the date and the year.

The first word of the greeting begins with a capital letter. The name of the person receiving the letter is followed by a comma.

The message of a letter is called the body. The first word is indented because the body of the letter is a paragraph.

The first word of the closing begins with a capital letter. The closing ends with a comma. The last part of the letter is the signature. It tells who wrote the letter. Notice how the closing and signature line up with the heading.

> **Summary** ◆ A **friendly letter** has five parts: the heading, greeting, body, closing, and signature.

Guided Practice

Name the letter part in which each item belongs.

1. Yours truly,
2. June 7, 1991
3. Chico, California 95926
4. Jenny
5. 6 Elm Road
6. Dear Dr. Oniki,

Practice

A. Write each letter part below correctly. Remember commas.

7. july 4 1989
8. dear papa
9. your friend
10. marion virginia 24352
11. dear mr. watkins
12. march 4 1990
13. sincerely
14. ogden utah 84402
15. love
16. yours truly

B. The letter parts below are not in order. Write the letter by arranging the parts correctly.

17. Thanks for the kite kit. I will put it together on Saturday. It looks like it may be hard, but I love building things. Come help me fly it when I finish!
18. Your cousin,
19. Dear Pablo,
20. 29 Samter Place
    Berea, Kentucky 40403
    May 3, 1991
21. Carmen

Apply ♦ Think and Write

A Friendly Invitation ♦ Write a friendly letter to someone you know. Invite that person to join you for a special event. Be creative. Make the person really want to say yes. Before you mail your letter, turn to page 473 to find out how to address an envelope.

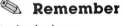 **Remember**
to include a heading so the person who gets your letter can write back.

Focus on the Narrator

Every story needs a storyteller, or **narrator**. Often, the author has the main character tell his or her own story.

Yoshiko Uchida does this in *The Best Bad Thing,* which you read earlier. Rinko, the main character, is also the narrator.

Rinko speaks of herself as *I* and *me*. For example: "*I* noticed right away . . ." "He's leaving *me* out . . ."

Everything in the story is seen through Rinko's eyes. For example: "I really felt as though I was the butterfly . . ."

The words *I* and *me* tell the reader that this is Rinko's own story. She is telling it. There are a number of advantages in telling a story that way. Here are four of them.

A Story Told by "Me, Myself, and I"

1. The reader gets to know the narrator very well.
2. The reader comes to like the narrator and understand how he or she feels.
3. The reader "lives through" the story with the narrator. Thus, the story seems true-to-life.
4. Telling a story about "I" and "me" is a good way for a young writer to learn how to write a story.

The Writer's Voice ◆ A story told with an "I" and "me" narrator makes the events seem real. Choose a story everyone knows, such as "Goldilocks." Pretend you are one of the characters and tell the story. Start by introducing yourself. For example, "I am baby bear."

Working Together

The main character in a story often tells the story. This kind of "I" and "me" narrator makes the story seem personal and real. As a group, do activities **A** and **B**.

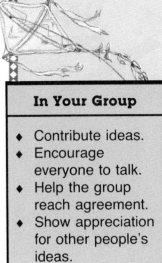

A. Discuss each sentence below. If Rinko is telling her own story in the sentence, answer YES. If Rinko is not telling her own story, answer NO. The group should agree on each answer.

1. I felt the butterfly kite tug at my line.
2. Rinko loved the yellow-and-black kite.
3. She watched the butterfly climb into the sky.
4. Then I understood the old man's words.
5. Finally the old man let me fly the kite.

B. "I" and "me" narration becomes "we" and "us" narration if more than one person is telling the story. Suppose that your group goes on a field trip, or puts on a play, or enters a contest. As a group, write a story about one of these activities. Use a "we" and "us" narrator.

In Your Group

- ◆ Contribute ideas.
- ◆ Encourage everyone to talk.
- ◆ Help the group reach agreement.
- ◆ Show appreciation for other people's ideas.

THESAURUS CORNER ◆ Word Choice

Rewrite each sentence below with an "I" and "me" narrator in place of "Jan." Use the Thesaurus to replace each word in dark type with an appropriate synonym for *good*.

1. Jan thought the weather was **good** for flying a kite.
2. The man gave Jan some **good** tips on kite flying.
3. "Well," Jan said, "the breeze is **good** but not very strong."
4. People told Jan that the man was a **good** kite-maker.
5. Jan knew that some kites are almost too **good** to fly.

Writing a Personal Narrative

A narrative is a story. Stories people tell about themselves are called personal narratives. In personal narratives, the writers call themselves *I* or *me*.

In *The Best Bad Thing*, Rinko narrates a story about herself. She tells about the day she learned to fly a kite. Her words tell the reader what she did and how she felt.

Know Your Purpose and Audience

In this lesson you will write a personal narrative. Like Rinko, your purpose will be to tell about a time when you learned how to do something.

Your audience will be your classmates. Later you and your classmates can display your stories or read them to each other.

MY PURPOSE

MY AUDIENCE

1 Prewriting

Prewriting is getting ready to write. First you need to choose a topic for your personal narrative. Next you can make some notes to help you plan what you will write.

Choose Your Topic ◆ You have learned how to do many things. Make an ''I can'' list. On it, list things that you have learned how to do. Then circle one thing to be the topic of your personal narrative.

Think About It

Think of all the things you have learned how to do. Write down even the smallest things. Then stop to think about each item on your list. Does one thing stand out as your favorite? That one thing will be your topic choice.

Talk About It

Your classmates can help you think of things for your ''I can'' list. With them, talk about what you have learned to do in gym class or in art or music classes. Remember to discuss also the things you do outside of school.

Topic Ideas

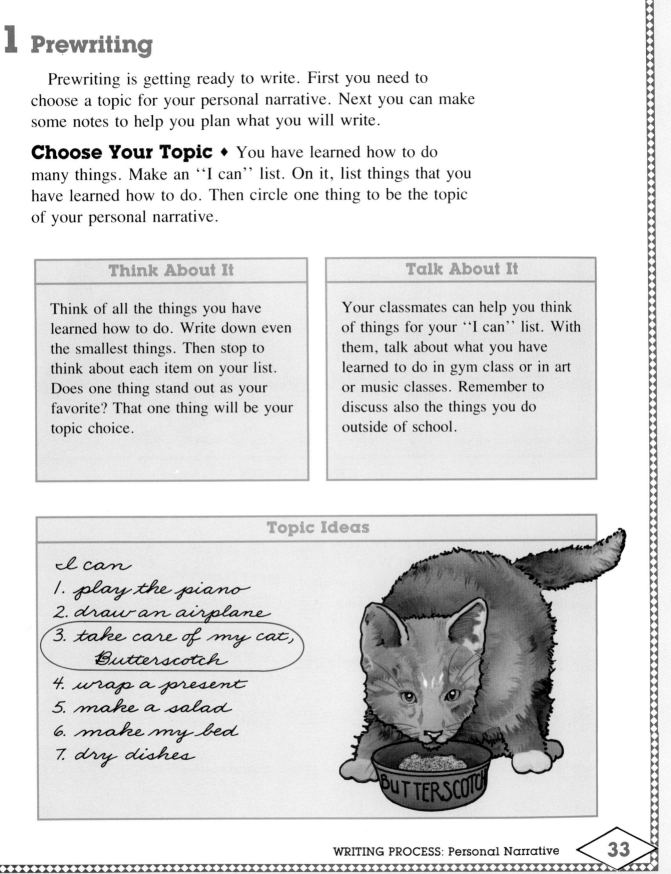

I can
1. play the piano
2. draw an airplane
3. take care of my cat, Butterscotch
4. wrap a present
5. make a salad
6. make my bed
7. dry dishes

BUTTERSCOTCH

Choose Your Strategy ◆ Here are two strategies to help you gather ideas before you write. Read both of them. Then try using one strategy to plan what you will write.

PREWRITING IDEAS

CHOICE ONE

A Conversation   Model

Have a partner ask you questions about what you learned. Did you learn it in steps? Did someone help you? How did you feel while you were learning it? How did you feel when you finally "got it right"? Talking about it should help you remember important details. Write some notes about your conversation.

CHOICE TWO

A Conclusion Sentence   Model

Tell about what you learned how to do. Finish each sentence. Write enough "Then" sentences to show all the steps. Finally, add a conclusion sentence to sum up your feelings or ideas about the experience. Begin your conclusion sentence with the words "I think."

What I Learned _I learned how to take care of my cat._

First _Mother showed me how to feed him._

Then _Mother showed me how to brush him._

Last _Mother said that I should play with him._

I think _taking care of a cat is easy and fun._

2 Writing

Writing is putting your ideas on paper. First, review your conversation notes or your conclusion. Then start to write. You might try a beginning like one of these.

- ♦ I wanted to learn how to ____.
- ♦ One day Uncle Rick said he would teach me to ____.

As you write, don't worry about errors. You can go back later to make changes. Tell your story in time order. Add your conclusion sentence at the end.

Sample First Draft ♦

I wanted to learn how to take care of my cat, Butterscotch. My mother said that she would teach me. Then showed me how to brush his coat. First my mother showed me how to mesure his food. When I brushed softly, Butterscotch rubbed against my leg. Then my mother said I should play with my cat. I made up a Game with a cloth mouse.

I feel good when I take care of Butterscotch. I learned that taking care of a cat is easy and fun.

3 Revising

Revising is making changes to improve your writing. Writers check to make sure their writing says what they meant to say. The idea below may help you.

REVISING IDEA

FIRST Read to Yourself

Think about your purpose. Did you explain your experience clearly? Think about your audience. Will they understand? Make a caret (⌄) where you want to add information.

Focus: Did you use the words *I* and *me* to tell your story?

THEN Share with a Partner

Ask a classmate to be your first audience as you read your personal narrative aloud. Here are some guidelines you might use to help each other.

The Writer

Guidelines: Read aloud slowly and clearly. Listen to your partner's comments.

Sample questions:
- What part did you like best?
- **Focus question:** Did you understand how I felt?

The Writer's Partner

Guidelines: Be honest. Say what you really think. Be kind. Say it politely.

Sample responses:
- The part I liked best was _____.
- How did you feel when _____?

Revising Model ♦ Here is a sample narrative that is being revised. Revising marks don't have to look neat. Use them to show yourself the changes that you want to make.

This sentence needed a subject.

This sentence was out of order.

The writer's partner wanted to know how the writer felt.

Useful and *proud* tell exactly how the writer felt.

I wanted to learn how to take care of my cat, Butterscotch. my mother said that she would teach me. Then, *she* showed me how to brush his coat. ⟨First my mother showed me how to mesure his food.⟩ When I brushed softly, Butterscotch rubbed ~~That made me feel so happy!~~ against my leg. ∧ Then my mother said I should play with my cat. I made up a Game with a cloth mouse. *useful and proud* I feel ~~good~~ when I take care of Butterscotch. I learned that taking care of a cat is easy and fun.

Read the revised sample above. Read it the way the writer has decided it *should* be. Then revise your own narrative.

Grammar Check ♦ Some exclamatory or interrogative sentences may make your story more interesting.

Word Choice ♦ Can you find more exact words for words like *good*? A thesaurus can help you improve word choices.

Revising Checklist

☐ **My purpose:** Did I tell about something I learned to do?

☐ **My audience:** Will they understand?

☐ **Focus:** Did I use the words *I* and *me* to tell my story?

4 Proofreading

Proofreading is looking for and fixing errors. Check for mistakes in spelling, capital letters, and punctuation marks.

Proofreading Model ♦ Here is the sample personal narrative about learning to care for a cat. The writer has added red proofreading marks to fix errors.

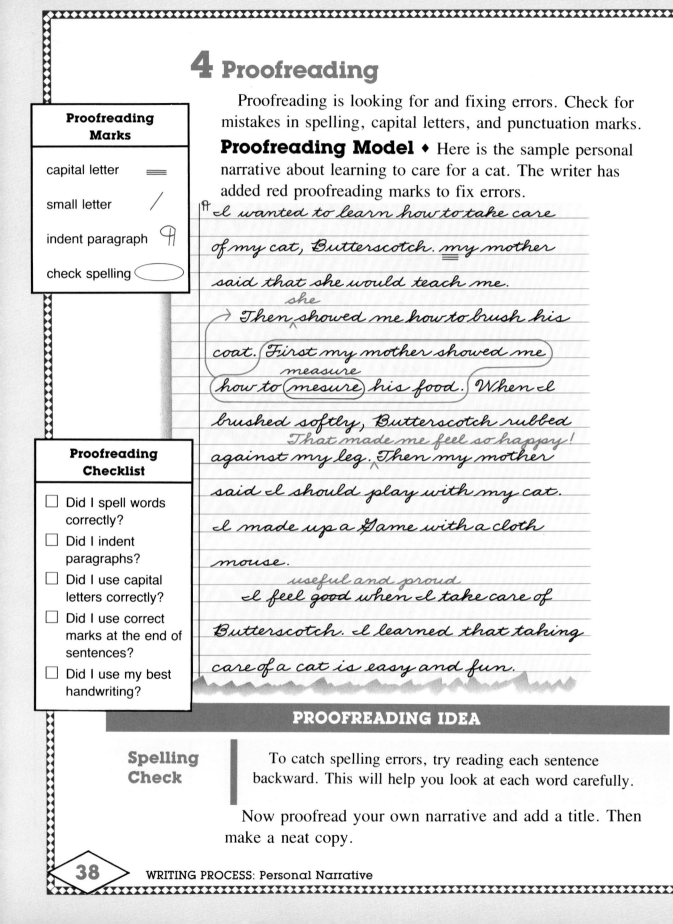

I wanted to learn how to take care

of my cat, Butterscotch. my mother

said that she would teach me.

she
→ Then showed me how to brush his

coat. First my mother showed me

measure
how to mesure his food. When I

brushed softly, Butterscotch rubbed
That made me feel so happy!
against my leg. Then my mother

said I should play with my cat.

I made up a Game with a cloth

mouse.
useful and proud
I feel good when I take care of

Butterscotch. I learned that taking

care of a cat is easy and fun.

Proofreading Checklist

- ☐ Did I spell words correctly?
- ☐ Did I indent paragraphs?
- ☐ Did I use capital letters correctly?
- ☐ Did I use correct marks at the end of sentences?
- ☐ Did I use my best handwriting?

PROOFREADING IDEA

Spelling Check

To catch spelling errors, try reading each sentence backward. This will help you look at each word carefully.

Now proofread your own narrative and add a title. Then make a neat copy.

5 Publishing

Publishing is sharing your writing with others. Try one of the ideas below for sharing your personal narrative.

My Cat, Butterscotch

I wanted to learn how to take care of my cat, Butterscotch. My mother said that she would teach me.

First my mother showed me how to measure his food. Then she showed me how to brush his coat. When I brushed softly, Butterscotch rubbed against my leg. That made me feel so happy! Then my mother said I should play with my cat. I made up a game with a cloth mouse.

I feel useful and proud when I take care of Butterscotch. I learned that taking care of a cat is easy and fun.

PUBLISHING IDEAS

Share Aloud

Would you like to learn what your classmates learned? On three papers, write *3*, *2*, and *1*. Listen as your classmates read their stories. Then hold up *3* if you are very interested in learning what they learned. Hold up *2* if you are somewhat interested. Hold up *1* if you are not interested.

Share in Writing

Use clothespins to hang your personal narrative on a line in your classroom. Read some of your classmates' stories. Tell the writers what you liked about their stories.

CURRICULUM
·CONNECTION·

Writing Across the Curriculum Science

In this unit you wrote about something you learned to do. You wrote the steps carefully. In a similar way, scientists carefully describe how they do their experiments. At the end of their experiments, they write a concluding sentence telling what they learned.

Writing to Learn

Think and Analyze ◆ Study the picture of the scientist below. Think about what he sees.

Conclusion Sentence

Write ◆ Write three facts that you think the scientist might write. Then write a conclusion sentence about what he sees.

Writing in Your Journal

In the Writer's Warm-up you wrote about a hobby. Throughout this unit you read about other hobbies. Did you discover a new hobby? Write in your journal about something you would like to do as a hobby.

BOOKS TO ENJOY

 ## Read More About It

Instant Paper Toys to Pop, Spin, Whirl, and Fly *by E. Richard Churchill*
If you enjoy making things, this book may be for you. All you have to do is follow the instructions to build toys out of ordinary paper. And they really work!

A Very Young Dancer *by Jill Krementz*
Ballet is a hobby that takes training and hard work. This book follows a ten-year-old girl studying to become a ballerina. Share in her excitement when she is chosen to dance in "The Nutcracker Suite."

Book Report Idea   Accordion Book Report

Why not share your next book report like this?

Make an Accordion Book
Start with a long strip of paper. Fold it, accordion style. Write the title and author on the front. On each page, tell something about the book. Tell about the main characters or a favorite scene. Draw a picture. Share your accordion book by displaying it or by reading it aloud.

UNIT REVIEW

Unit 1

Sentences *pages 4–11*

A. Write *sentence* or *not a sentence* for each group of words.

1. Running around the track.
2. This is my first running race.
3. All of the other runners.
4. I have practiced every day.
5. My ankle hurts a little.

B. Write each sentence. Then write *declarative, interrogative, imperative,* or *exclamatory* to show what kind of sentence each one is.

6. A big crowd of fans has arrived.
7. Please show me to my seat.
8. May I have a program?
9. What a hot day for a race!
10. The first runners are lining up.

C. Write *subject* if the subject is underlined. Write predicate if the *predicate* is underlined.

11. A flag signals the start.
12. The runners begin in a group.
13. Everyone is moving fast.
14. One runner stumbles.
15. The crowd watches quietly.

Thesaurus *pages 12–13*

D. Read each thesaurus entry. Write the answer to each question.

neat (adj.) — clean and in order. Our room must be <u>neat</u> before we go outside to play.
orderly — having a regular arrangement.
organized — arranged in some order or pattern.
tidy — neat and in order.
trim — in good condition or order.
well-groomed — neat in appearance.
ANTONYMS: **cluttered, disorderly, disorganized, messy, sloppy, untidy**

16. What is the entry word?
17. What are three synonyms of *neat*?
18. How many antonyms are listed for *neat*?

push (v.) — to move something by using force against it. It will be easier if we <u>push</u> our bikes up the hill.
nudge — to push gently.
poke — to push against with something pointed.
propel — to move or cause to move forward or ahead.
ANTONYMS: **drag, jerk, pull, tow, tug**

19. What is the entry word?
20. What words are synonyms of *push*?
21. How many antonyms are listed for *push*?

Time Order   *pages 26–27*

E. Write each set of sentences below as a paragraph. Use the time-order words to discover how the story goes.

22. Then she dipped the brush in the paint.

23. First she washed off all the dirt.

24. Anne decided to paint the front door a new color.

25. Soon the door looked brand–new.

26. Finally he packed all his clothes.

27. Then he rolled the sleeping bag into a neat sausage shape.

28. First Everett checked to make sure the tent was in good condition.

29. It was time to get ready for the camping trip.

30. He finally had everything ready for the trip.

31. Then he started to look for boots, a compass, and a flashlight.

32. He checked off *tent, sleeping bag,* and *clothes.*

33. Everett looked at the list of things he needed.

34. First they loaded all the big things.

35. Then they stuffed all the little things around the edges.

36. The family carried everything out to the car.

37. At last they climbed in the car and started off.

Friendly Letter   *pages 28–29*

F. Write each letter part below correctly. Use capitals and commas as needed.

38. dear donald

39. 75 hancock road

40. kalamazoo michigan

41. cynthia

42. your nephew

43. dear alison

44. 54 essex street

45. dear uncle frank

46. 4216 nod road

47. october 16 1991

48. your friend

49. carson city nevada

G. The letter parts below are out of order. Arrange the parts in the correct order and write the letter.

50. 266 Parker Drive
Kansas City, Missouri 64108
July 21, 1990

51. Teddy

52. Dear Grandma,

53. Your grandson,

54.   My parents and I really enjoyed our visit with you. Thank you for all the good times and for the special meals you cooked. The guided tour of the underground caves was fascinating. I still can't believe that millions of bats live down there. I'm sure glad I don't live in a cave!

LANGUAGE PUZZLERS

Unit 1 Challenge

Pinwheel Sayings

Write the eight famous sayings in this pinwheel. Begin each with a capital letter and end it with a period. (Hint: For each saying, you will find the subject in one pinwheel spoke and the predicate in another spoke.)

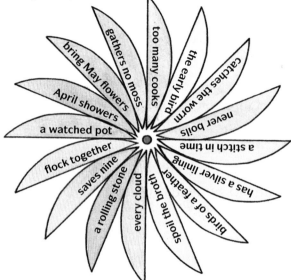

Alphabet Sentences

Try writing these four sentences. (Hint: There is one of each kind—interrogative, declarative, exclamatory, and imperative.) Use capital letters and punctuation where needed.

1. Y R U N LN leaving
2. O I N V U
3. A blueJ with BD I's 8 A P
4. C MLE B4 2morrow

Unit 1 Extra Practice

1 Writing Sentences
p. 4

A. Write *sentence* or *not a sentence* for each group of words.

1. The city of Chicago is on Lake Michigan.
2. Traders bought and sold grain.
3. Nearly 14,000 ships in the port.
4. The city was also a railroad center.
5. Built the Union Stock Yards.
6. A fire almost destroyed the city in 1871.
7. The Chicago Fire began on October 8, 1871.
8. On the west side of the city.
9. No one knows how the fire started.
10. A newspaper story about Mrs. O'Leary's cow.
11. Was made up by a reporter.
12. The weather had been very dry.
13. Many wooden buildings in the neighborhood.
14. The fire should have stopped at the Chicago River.
15. However, a strong wind was blowing that day.
16. Carried the fire across the river.

B. Write the group of words in each pair that is a sentence.

17. **a.** Burned for twenty-seven hours.
    b. The fire destroyed more than 13,500 buildings.
18. **a.** More than 2,000 acres were burned.
    b. Almost 100,000 people without homes.
19. **a.** About one third of the city was destroyed.
    b. Hundreds of millions of dollars damage.
20. **a.** Began to rebuild the city immediately.
    b. People from all over the world sent help.
21. **a.** We remember the Chicago Fire every October.
    b. Learning how to prevent fires all year long.
22. **a.** Often called the Windy City.
    b. Chicago is a thriving city today.

C. Write the group of words in each pair that is a sentence.

23. **a.** Tigers belong to the cat family.
    b. The largest members of the family.
24. **a.** Found in Asia.
    b. Tigers live and hunt in tall grass.
25. **a.** Their stripes blend in with the grass.
    b. Can sneak up without being seen.
26. **a.** There are very few tigers left.
    b. Killed for their beautiful fur.
27. **a.** Live in zoos.
    b. Many laws protect tigers.

2 Declarative and Interrogative Sentences

p. 6

A. Read each sentence below. Write *declarative* or *interrogative* to tell what kind of sentence each is.

1. I would like some pancakes.
2. What kind of pancake would you like?
3. Blueberry pancakes are my favorite.
4. Would you like syrup on them?
5. Are pancakes good for you?
6. They are made with eggs, milk, and flour.
7. Do only Americans eat pancakes?
8. People from many countries eat pancakes.
9. Pancakes are used in many different ways.
10. The Mexicans have pancakes called tortillas.
11. Tortillas are made from cornmeal.
12. How are they eaten?
13. Sometimes they are filled and rolled.
14. Are tacos made from tortillas?
15. Tacos are fried and then filled.
16. The French have thin pancakes called crepes.
17. Can crepes be filled with different foods?
18. They can be a whole meal or just a dessert.

B. Write each sentence. Begin each with a capital letter. Use periods and question marks correctly.

19. the Italians fill thin pancakes with meat or cheese
20. do any Asians eat pancakes
21. the Chinese have pancakes
22. what are they called
23. pancakes in China are called bing
24. they are made from rice flour
25. how are they eaten
26. they are filled with meat and vegetables
27. can you think of any other kinds of pancakes

3 Imperative and Exclamatory Sentences   *p. 8*

A. Read each sentence. Write *imperative* or *exclamatory* to tell what kind of sentence each one is.

1. Please come with us.
2. Be ready at eight.
3. How scary the fun house is!
4. Buy three tickets for the roller coaster.
5. Please ride with us.
6. I'm terrified of heights!
7. Wait for us.
8. Hurry, the ride is about to start!
9. Go to the back of the line.
10. Make sure the seat belt is fastened.
11. Ask the operator how long the ride is.
12. Please hold my hand.
13. I don't like this!
14. I want to get off!
15. How far away the ground looks!
16. Keep your eyes closed.
17. Please go on the next ride with me.
18. What fun that was!

B. Write each sentence. Begin each with a capital letter. Use periods and exclamation points correctly.

19. how dizzy I feel
20. please hold my money for me
21. twelve tacos are too much for anyone to eat
22. tell me when it's eight o'clock
23. take a picture of me with the toys I won
24. how funny you look with that pirate hat on
25. this stuffed animal weighs a ton
26. put a new roll of film in the camera
27. help me wake Terry
28. how tired I am

C. Some of the sentences below are written incorrectly. Write them correctly. If a sentence is correct, write *correct*.

29. Put some nutmeg in the apple pie.
30. The pepper is very hot.
31. Please pass the salt!
32. Put some parsley in the dressing.
33. This is delicious.
34. Put the cloves in the ham.
35. Something smells wonderful.
36. Stir in the onions!
37. I love garlic.
38. Pick some chives from the garden.

4 Subjects and Predicates   *p. 10*

A. One part of each sentence below is underlined. Write whether the underlined part is the subject or the predicate.

1. Sara <u>saw a very old book in the library</u>.
2. <u>The librarian</u> showed her the pictures.
3. The people in the pictures <u>wore long robes</u>.
4. Their homes <u>were large stone houses</u>.
5. <u>The pictures in the book</u> were colorful.

B. Read each sentence. Write *subject* if the subject is underlined. Write *predicate* if the predicate is underlined.

6. Life in the Middle Ages was not like life today.
7. Farm families built their own small cottages.
8. Many people lived under a lord in a great house.
9. The house with high walls was the manor house.
10. The whole village was called a manor.
11. Peasants worked on the large farms.
12. Weavers made cloth for clothing.
13. Other peasants made foods like bread and cheese.
14. The life of a peasant was a very hard one.
15. Women practiced as doctors in the 1400s.

C. Write each sentence below. Draw one line under the subject. Draw two lines under the predicate.

16. The whole family worked hard in the Middle Ages.
17. Children were treated like small adults.
18. Young people did have some time for games.
19. Piggyback games were popular then, too.
20. Reindeer bones were used for skates.
21. These skates were tied on with leather straps.
22. Grown-ups liked to have fun, too.
23. Clowns amused large groups of people in great halls.
24. Royal families enjoyed musical shows.
25. Actors in wagons traveled around the country.

D. Write each sentence. Draw one line under the subject. Draw two lines under the predicate.

26. Benjamin Franklin led a very interesting life.
27. This famous American was born in 1706.
28. He started the first public library in America.
29. This man invented a new type of stove.
30. His discoveries about electricity won him praise.
31. His name is on the Declaration of Independence.

UNIT TWO

USING LANGUAGE TO
PERSUADE

PART ONE

Unit Theme   *Colonial America*

Language Awareness   Nouns

PART TWO

Literature   *Why Don't You Get a Horse, Sam Adams?*
by Jean Fritz

A Reason for Writing   Persuading

Writing
IN YOUR JOURNAL

WRITER'S WARM-UP ◆ What do you know about colonial America? Perhaps your state was one of the original thirteen colonies. Who lived in America over two hundred years ago? What kinds of work did people do then? How did people get their food and clothing? Write in your journal. Tell what you know about life in colonial America.

Pretend you are traveling to a different state or country. Name the place where you are going, a person with whom you would like to go, and something special you would take.

1 Writing with Nouns

Read these sentences about early colonists in America. Notice the underlined words.

The <u>Pilgrims</u> came to <u>America</u> on a <u>ship</u>.
Many <u>colonists</u> built <u>houses</u> near the <u>ocean</u>.

There are three nouns in each sentence. Each noun names a person, place, or thing.

Study the chart below. It shows the six nouns in the sentences. It also shows what each noun names.

Persons	Pilgrims	colonists
Places	America	ocean
Things	ship	houses

Summary ◆ A **noun** names a person, place, or thing. You use nouns in your writing to give information.

Guided Practice

Name the nouns in each sentence below.

1. The colonists came from different countries.
2. Their children also came to this faraway land.
3. Many early settlers arrived from England.
4. The Pilgrims departed from their old homes.
5. These travelers boarded a small ship.
6. The Mayflower sailed across the Atlantic.
7. The vessel arrived safely at Plymouth.
8. The colony of Massachusetts was born.

Practice

A. These sentences tell about Jamestown, the first English settlement in America. Each sentence contains three nouns. Write each sentence. Underline every noun.

9. Three ships sailed from a port in England.
10. Many of the travelers were seeking gold in America.
11. Finally the sailors saw tall trees along the shore.
12. These people had landed on the coast of Virginia.
13. Jamestown would be the first settlement in the colonies.
14. The colonists had little food and no water.
15. Their leader bought corn from local Indians.
16. Powhatan was the chief of the largest tribe.
17. The chief had a daughter named Pocahontas.
18. Pocahontas became a loyal friend to the settlers.

B. Write each sentence. Underline the nouns.

19. The early colonists made new friends.
20. Many of these people worked on farms.
21. Few settlers in the new land were wealthy.
22. England ruled the thirteen colonies.
23. Each colony had its own governor.

C. Complete the sentences. Use at least one more noun in each sentence. Write the sentences.

24. The colonists came to ____ .
25. They arrived on ____ .
26. ____ became friends with the colonists.
27. Together they planted ____ .
28. We learned about the colonies from ____ .

Apply ◆ Think and Write

From Your Writing ◆ Make a list of all the nouns you used in the Writer's Warm-up. Compare your list with a classmate's list.

✏ **Remember**
that nouns can help you create word pictures for your reader.

Make up silly phrases about animals.
EXAMPLES: *an angry antelope*   *one odd octopus*
five fabulous foxes   *some silly seals*

2 Singular Nouns and Plural Nouns

Read these sentences. Notice the underlined nouns.

The <u>farmer</u> paid the <u>workers</u>.
The <u>colony</u> was filled with <u>fields</u>.
The <u>sun</u> beamed down through the <u>trees</u>.

Nouns can be singular or plural. The words *farmer*, *colony*, and *sun* are singular nouns. Each names one person, place, or thing. The words *workers*, *fields*, and *trees* are plural nouns. Each names more than one person, place, or thing.

Study the rules for plural nouns below.

■ **1.** Add *-s* to form the plural of most nouns.

colonist<u>s</u>   river<u>s</u>   grain<u>s</u>   pea<u>s</u>   chicken<u>s</u>

■ **2.** Add *-es* to form the plural of nouns that end in *ch*, *sh*, *s*, *ss*, *x*, or *z*.

bench<u>es</u>   bush<u>es</u>   bus<u>es</u>   class<u>es</u>   tax<u>es</u>

> **Summary** ♦ A **singular noun** names one person, place, or thing. A **plural noun** names more than one person, place, or thing. Use the correct form of each noun in your writing.

Guided Practice

Tell whether each noun is singular or plural.

1. mules   **3.** wagon   **5.** houses   **7.** dress   **9.** lunch
2. shovel   **4.** ax   **6.** lamps   **8.** bottles   **10.** dishes

Practice

A. Write each noun. After each noun write *singular* or *plural*.

11. pumpkin	**21.** carrot
12. boxes	**22.** peaches
13. cabbages	**23.** orange
14. cucumber	**24.** plums
15. fox	**25.** bananas
16. grapes	**26.** bunch
17. glass	**27.** onions
18. horses	**28.** radishes
19. bush	**29.** chicken
20. pumpkins	**30.** bus

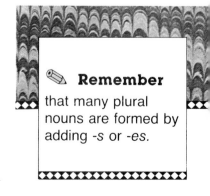

B. Write each sentence about apple growers in colonial times. Use the plural of each word in parentheses ( ).

31. Some (farmer) planted large apple orchards.
32. Workers picked the ripe (apple) in the autumn.
33. Bushels of apples were put into cider (press).
34. (Jug) of cider could be stored all winter.
35. (Box) of apples were also stored in the cool cellar.

C. Think of a plural noun to complete each sentence. Use the word in parentheses ( ) to help you. Write the sentence.

36. Farmers kept the _____ in the barn. (animals)
37. Plantation owners grew _____ in the fields. (vegetables)
38. Some workers helped pick _____ in the orchards. (fruits)
39. _____ ran around the farmyard. (Animals)
40. A rabbit hid behind the tall _____ . (plants)

Apply ◆ Think and Write

Creative Writing ◆ Pretend you live on a farm. (Perhaps you really do!) Write some sentences about your experiences. Underline the singular nouns in your sentences once. Underline the plural nouns twice.

> ✎ **Remember**
> that many plural nouns are formed by adding *-s* or *-es*.

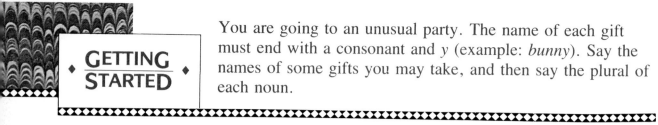

GETTING STARTED

You are going to an unusual party. The name of each gift must end with a consonant and *y* (example: *bunny*). Say the names of some gifts you may take, and then say the plural of each noun.

3 Spelling Plural Nouns

Here are some rules for forming plural nouns in special ways.

Rules for Plural Nouns

1. If a noun ends in a consonant and *y*, change *y* to *i* and add *-es* to form the plural.

Singular	family	cherry	butterfly
Plural	families	cherries	butterflies

2. Some plurals are formed by changing the spelling of the singular noun.

Singular	man	woman	child	ox
Plural	men	women	children	oxen

Singular	foot	tooth	goose	mouse
Plural	feet	teeth	geese	mice

3. A few nouns have the same singular and plural forms.

Singular	elk	moose	deer	sheep
Plural	elk	moose	deer	sheep

Summary ◆ Some plural nouns are formed in special ways. When you write, pay attention to the spelling of plural nouns.

Guided Practice

Spell the plural form of each singular noun below.

1. colony   **2.** tooth   **3.** deer   **4.** party   **5.** child

Practice

A. Write each singular noun below. Then write its plural form.

6.	woman	**16.**	library
7.	foot	**17.**	city
8.	puppy	**18.**	reindeer
9.	baby	**19.**	factory
10.	sheep	**20.**	goose
11.	mouse	**21.**	dictionary
12.	moose	**22.**	grandchild
13.	ox	**23.**	strawberry
14.	man	**24.**	saleswoman
15.	elk	**25.**	canary

B. Each sentence below has two plural nouns. One plural noun is not correct. Write each sentence correctly.

26. The hungry guests ate all the cherrys.
27. Uncle Joe brought toy mouses for the children.
28. Our ponys soaked their tired feet in water.
29. Two families arrived in a cart pulled by oxes.
30. We saw moose and elks near the house.

C. Use a plural noun from the chart in this lesson to complete each sentence. Write the sentences.

31. Horses and ____ grazed in the pasture.
32. ____ scurried through the barn.
33. Hens, chickens, and ____ pecked grain in the barnyard.
34. Men and ____ danced in the ballroom.
35. A man helped the ____ climb up on the pony for a ride.

Apply ◆ Think and Write

Animal Nouns ◆ Write sentences using the singular and plural forms of the names of ten animals. Try to use some names that change from *y* to *ies* when forming the plural. Ask a partner to check your work.

> ✎ **Remember**
> to check the spelling of the plural nouns you use.

4 Common Nouns and Proper Nouns

Read these sentences. Notice the boxed nouns.

A colonist founded the city.
William Penn founded Philadelphia.

The nouns in blue are common nouns. A common noun names any person, place, or thing. The nouns in red are proper nouns. A proper noun names a particular person, place, or thing.

Some proper nouns, such as *William Penn*, have more than one word. Each important word in a proper noun begins with a capital letter.

■ United States of America   Delaware River

> **Summary** ◆ A **common noun** names any person, place, or thing. A **proper noun** names a particular person, place, or thing. Proper nouns can add detail to your writing.

Guided Practice

The nouns are underlined in the sentences below. Tell which are common nouns and which are proper nouns.

1. Many people visit Philadelphia each year.
2. The Declaration of Independence was signed in the city.
3. The Pennsylvania State House was the exact location.
4. That building is now known as Independence Hall.
5. The Liberty Bell hangs one block away.

Practice

A. Read the sentences about early Pennsylvania. Write each underlined noun. Then write *common* or *proper* after each.

    6. <u>William Penn</u> founded the <u>colony</u> of <u>Pennsylvania</u>.
    7. He was given the <u>land</u> by <u>King Charles</u> of <u>England</u>.
    8. <u>Colonists</u> came from many different <u>countries</u> in <u>Europe</u>.
    9. <u>Settlers</u> from <u>Germany</u> were called <u>Pennsylvania Dutch</u>.
    10. The <u>capital</u> of the new <u>colony</u> was named <u>Philadelphia</u>.
    11. <u>Penn</u> founded the <u>city</u> next to the <u>Delaware River</u>.
    12. <u>Delaware Indians</u> had lived in the <u>area</u> for many <u>years</u>.
    13. <u>Philadelphia</u> soon became the busiest <u>port</u> in <u>America</u>.
    14. <u>Goods</u> were shipped to other <u>colonies</u>, to the <u>British West Indies</u>, and to <u>England</u>.

B. Write each sentence below. Draw one line under each common noun. Draw two lines under each proper noun.

    15. The Constitution was signed in Philadelphia.
    16. The city became the first capital of the United States of America.
    17. Its famous people included a woman named Betsy Ross.
    18. The Betsy Ross House is now open to tourists.

C. Write a proper noun for each common noun below. Then write a sentence using the proper noun.

    EXAMPLE: lake
    ANSWER: Lake Erie   We stood on the shore of Lake Erie.

    19. town   **20.** river   **21.** woman   **22.** street

Apply ♦ Think and Write

Dictionary of Knowledge ♦ Read about the Liberty Bell, and write a paragraph about it. Draw one line under the common nouns in your paragraph and two lines under the proper nouns.

✎ **Remember**
that proper nouns add detail to your writing.

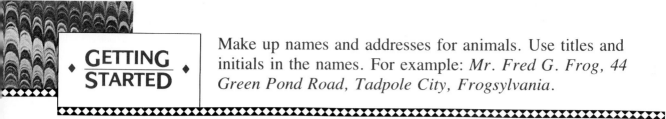

Make up names and addresses for animals. Use titles and initials in the names. For example: *Mr. Fred G. Frog, 44 Green Pond Road, Tadpole City, Frogsylvania.*

5 Using Capitals with Proper Nouns

Here are some rules for capitalizing proper nouns.

1. Capitalize each word in the name of a person or pet.	George Washington Fluffy	
2. Capitalize an **initial** in a name. Put a period after the initial.	Abigail S. Adams J. P. Jones	
3. Capitalize a **title** before a name. If the title is an **abbreviation** (shortened form of a word), put a period after it.	Mr. Bell Miss Lee Dr. Montgomery President Jefferson	Ms. Ryan Mrs. Chu
4. Capitalize every important word in the names of particular places or things.	New York Harbor Ellis Island Statue of Liberty	
5. Capitalize names of days, months, holidays, and special days.	Tuesday April Fourth of July	

Summary ◆ Each important word in a proper noun begins with a capital letter. Initials and titles in names also begin with a capital letter. Initials and titles that are abbreviations are followed by a period.

Guided Practice

Tell what capital letters and periods are needed below.

1. new york   **3.** friday, may 7   **5.** dr lynn s roberts

2. lake george   **4.** w l garrison   **6.** statue of liberty

Practice

A. Write the following nouns. If the noun is a proper noun, use capital letters and periods where they are needed.

7. mercy o warren
8. rhode island
9. lake
10. paul revere
11. rin tin tin
12. monday, june 17
13. doctor
14. dr adam t levy
15. potomac river
16. declaration of independence
17. mr crispus attucks
18. school
19. franklin high school
20. united states of america
21. country
22. thanksgiving day
23. general george washington
24. mrs m washington

SAMUEL ADAMS
painting by John Singleton Copley
Deposited by the City of Boston
Courtesy, Museum of Fine Arts, Boston

B. Write the following sentences about some famous patriots. Use capital letters and periods where they are needed.

25. boston, massachusetts, was a famous colonial city.
26. samuel adams often spoke at town meetings in boston.
27. adams did not like the laws passed by great britain.
28. mr adams was a cousin of president john charles adams.
29. john c adams was the father of president john q adams.

C. Copy and complete the following sentences. Use information about yourself.

30. My name is (initial) (initial) (last name).
31. I live in the state of (state's name).
32. My mother's name is (title) (first name) (last name).
33. My dentist's name is (title) (first name) (last name).
34. I know a dog named (pet's name).
35. My birthday is in (month).

Apply ♦ Think and Write

A Birthday List ♦ Write the full names and birthdays of five classmates. If a person has a middle initial in his or her name, make sure to include it.

✎ **Remember**
to use capital letters for proper nouns, initials, and titles.

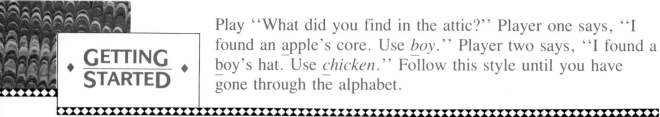

GETTING
STARTED

Play "What did you find in the attic?" Player one says, "I found an apple's core. Use *boy*." Player two says, "I found a boy's hat. Use *chicken*." Follow this style until you have gone through the alphabet.

6 Singular Possessive Nouns

Some forms of nouns show that a person or thing owns something. Read the following sentence.

■ **The lightning rod was this <u>man's</u> invention.**

The word *man's* is a possessive noun. It shows that the man owns the invention.

Now read these sentences.

| <u>Benjamin Franklin's</u> many talents amazed people.
| At age twelve, Benjamin went to work in <u>James's</u> print shop.

The words *Benjamin Franklin's* and *James's* are possessive nouns. Each names one person. An apostrophe (') and *s* was added to *Benjamin Franklin* and *James* to show ownership.

> **Summary** ◆ A **possessive noun** shows ownership. To form the possessive of a singular noun when you write, add an apostrophe and s (**'s**) to the singular noun.

Guided Practice

Spell the possessive form of each singular noun.

1. woman **3.** George **5.** England **7.** colonist
2. Martha **4.** puppy **6.** horse **8.** Dr. Williams

Practice

A. Write the possessive form of each singular noun.

  9. governor

10. Charles

11. Molly Pitcher

12. New Jersey

13. kitten

14. printer

15. Plymouth Rock

16. ship

17. John Alden

18. Priscilla

19. daughter

20. son

B. The sentences below tell about the interesting life of Benjamin Franklin. Write each sentence. Use the possessive form of each singular noun in parentheses ( ).

21. Young (Ben) career began in his (brother) print shop.

22. At seventeen he found a job in (Samuel Kreimer) shop.

23. By 1774 he became (Pennsylvania) chief printer.

24. Franklin published the popular *Poor (Richard) Almanac*.

25. The (almanac) pages contained many clever sayings.

26. In 1731, Franklin started this (country) first library.

27. From 1737 to 1753 he was (Philadelphia) postmaster.

28. Franklin was awarded a science (group) special medal.

29. (Benjamin Franklin) most famous experiment was done with his son William.

30. They used a (kite) wet string and a key to prove that lightning was electricity.

31. Later, Franklin was one of the (Continental Congress) most active members.

32. At the age of 81, Benjamin Franklin was one of the (Constitution) signers.

Apply ◆ Think and Write

Making Decisions ◆ You and your friends have two free hours. How will you amuse yourselves? With Roger's game? With Carla's radio? Write a paragraph telling how you will spend the time. Use at least three singular possessive nouns.

✎ **Remember**
that a singular possessive noun shows that a person or thing owns or has something.

Think of things that people might need to do their jobs. For example: *carpenters' tools, printers' paper, tailors' needles, policemen's whistles*. Can you think of any others?

7 Plural Possessive Nouns

You have studied singular possessive nouns. Those are singular nouns that show ownership.

Plural nouns can also show ownership. Compare the possessive forms of these singular nouns and plural nouns.

Singular Possessive	Plural Possessive
shoemaker's hammer	shoemakers' hammers
blacksmith's forge	blacksmiths' forges
man's hat	men's hats

The plural nouns *shoemakers* and *blacksmiths* end in *s*. An apostrophe is added to form the possessive.

The plural noun *men* does not end in *s*. What is added to form the possessive of *men*?

> **Summary** ◆ To form the possessive of a plural noun ending in *s*, add an apostrophe. To form the possessive of a plural noun that does not end in *s*, add an apostrophe and *s*.

Guided Practice

Spell the possessive form of each plural noun.

1. ladies
2. gentlemen
3. children
4. parents
5. teachers
6. chairs
7. carpenters
8. seamstresses
9. farmers
10. deer

Practice

A. Write the possessive form of each plural noun.

11.	citizens	**17.**	workers
12.	babies	**18.**	dresses
13.	mice	**19.**	women
14.	patriots	**20.**	shopkeepers
15.	feet	**21.**	villages
16.	hands	**22.**	colonies

B. Write the sentences about jobs in colonial times. Use the possessive form of each plural noun in parentheses ( ).

23. Many (workers) skills were needed in village life.
24. The (cabinetmakers) job was to build furniture.
25. Blacksmiths made (horses) shoes.
26. They also repaired (farmers) tools.
27. (Silversmiths) efforts produced silver trays.
28. The (weavers) looms were used to make fabric.

C. Choose the form of the plural noun in parentheses to complete each sentence. Write the sentences.

29. The (colonists, colonists') worked together to survive.
30. Planters bought supplies at the (merchants, merchants') shops in the village.
31. Saddles were (leatherworkers, leatherworkers') specialty.
32. (Glassblowers, Glassblowers') made bottles and jars.
33. Wheels were crafted by (wheelwrights, wheelwrights').
34. (Wagons, Wagons') wheels were made of wood and iron.

Apply ◆ Think and Write

A Historical Paragraph ◆ Children in the colonies often learned a trade from a skilled worker. Write a paragraph telling what trade you would have liked to learn. Use at least three plural possessive nouns in your paragraph.

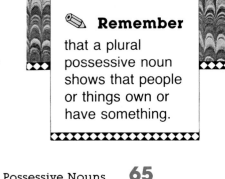

✎ **Remember**
that a plural possessive noun shows that people or things own or have something.

Be a word builder! Build new words by adding *under* to each of these words: *ground*, *foot*, *line*, *shirt*, *water*. Build more words by adding *over* to words you know.

VOCABULARY •
Compounds

Read the sentence below.

■ The <u>caretaker</u> will <u>tiptoe</u> <u>barefoot</u> over the <u>buttercup</u>.

How are the underlined words alike? How many words form each underlined word?

The underlined words are compounds. A **compound** is a single word that is formed from two smaller words. *Caretaker* is formed from the words *care* and *taker*. *Tiptoe* is formed from the words *tip* and *toe*. What words form the compounds *barefoot* and *buttercup*?

The small words in a compound often give a clue to the meaning of the compound.

■ **pony + tail = ponytail   jelly + fish = jellyfish**

Building Your Vocabulary

Below are pictures of things whose names are related. Find the compound that names each picture. What word do all these compounds have in common?

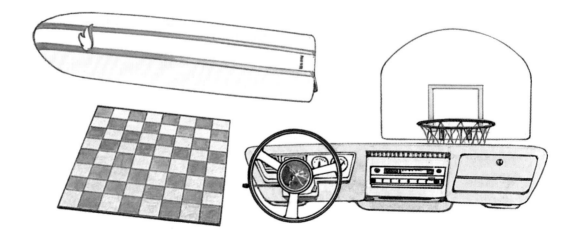

Practice

A. Many sports words are compounds. Write all the compounds that you find in this paragraph about baseball.

    Barbara loves watching baseball at nighttime. She likes to hear the announcer talk over the loudspeaker. At home, Barbara plays softball. She plays both shortstop and in the outfield. Barbara can outrun all of her teammates. After the game they eat popcorn in the dugout. Barbara sometimes wishes that the game could go on until midnight.

B. Write compounds that solve the riddles. Use the words listed below to form the compounds.

cat	cow	horse	dog	butter
fly	fish	hand	shoes	house

1. I work on a ranch with cows and horses.
2. I protect horses' feet.
3. I swim around and have whiskers.
4. I am an insect with beautiful wings.
5. I am a little home for dogs.

C. Form a compound for each meaning below.

6. a boat you can sail   **8.** a walk made of boards
7. a case for books   **9.** a cloth for a table

LANGUAGE CORNER ◆ Blended Words

    Some words are chopped and then blended together to make a new word. For example, *flare* comes from *flame* + *glare*. *Squiggle* comes from *squirm* + *wiggle*.

    Make up some blended words of your own.

SMOKE + FOG = SMOG

How to Revise Sentences with Nouns

You have been using nouns to name persons, places, and things. Choosing nouns carefully in your writing can give readers a clear picture of what you mean. Read the sentences below. Which one gives a clearer picture in your mind?

1. The park ranger spotted the wounded animal.

2. The park ranger spotted the wounded bear.

Both sentences tell us what the ranger saw, but the noun *bear* in sentence **2** gives us more information. The exact noun *bear* also makes the sentence more interesting to read. You can picture exactly what the writer wants you to.

See how changing the exact noun can give you a different picture of what the ranger saw.

■ **3.** The park ranger spotted the wounded owl.

The Grammar Game ◆ Check your noun know-how! Write three exact nouns as quickly as possible to replace each word below. Then compare lists with a classmate. Did you write any of the same exact nouns?

bug   clothing   tool   entertainer   container

Working Together

As your group does activities **A** and **B**, choose exact nouns to give readers a clear picture.

In Your Group

- Give your ideas to the group.
- Ask questions to get people talking.
- Record everyone's ideas on a list.
- Help the group finish on time.

A. Use each group member's name at least once to complete these sentences. Then replace the underlined words with exact nouns of the group's choice.

   1. ____ found a <u>coin</u> on the playground.
   2. ____'s <u>pet</u> does tricks.
   3. ____ plays the <u>instrument</u> in the school band.
   4. The <u>appliance</u> at ____'s house is broken.
   5. ____ has <u>clothing</u> with blue and white stripes.
   6. ____'s <u>relative</u> is coming for a visit tomorrow.

B. Replace each underlined word with an exact noun of the group's choice. Then write the paragraph again, using different exact nouns.

   Our class had a Pioneer's Day <u>meal</u>. We cooked some <u>food</u>. George brought a <u>vegetable</u> salad. Jan's relative baked <u>dessert</u>. After eating, we put on a <u>show</u>. Mary and Eric were famous <u>people</u>. Paul and Chris were <u>workers</u>. Our day was a great success.

WRITERS' CORNER ♦ Collective Nouns

Sometimes specific exact nouns are used to name certain groups of things. Such nouns are called *collective nouns.* Are you familiar with the examples below?

colony of ants	**crowd of people**	**carton of eggs**
fleet of ships	**flock of turkeys**	**gaggle of geese**
swarm of bees	**herd of horses**	**pride of lions**

Can you think of any others? Read what you wrote for the Writer's Warm-up. Could you have used any collective nouns?

THE SPIRIT OF '76
painting by Archibald M. Willard
original painting hangs in the Selectmen's Meeting Room, Abbot Hall, Marblehead, Massachusetts.

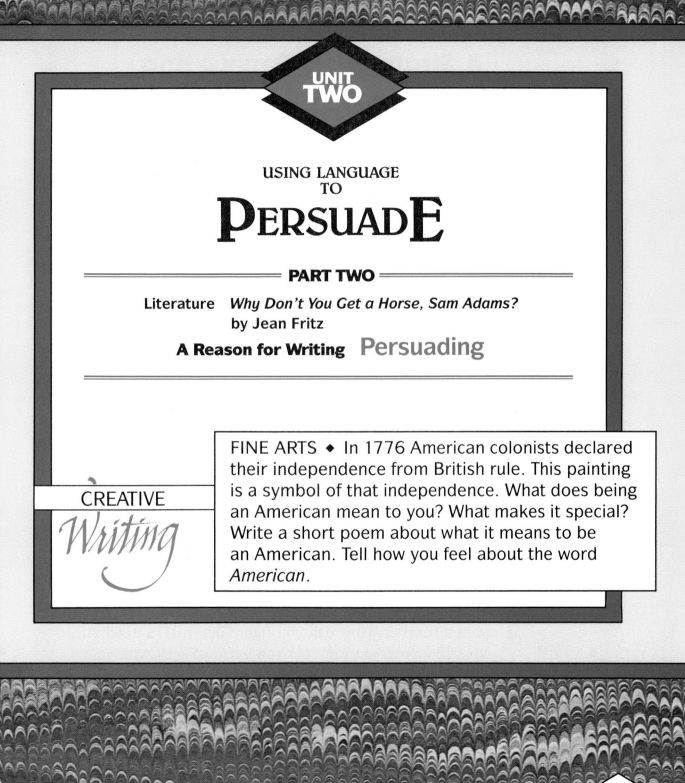

USING LANGUAGE
TO
PERSUADE

PART TWO

Literature *Why Don't You Get a Horse, Sam Adams?*
by Jean Fritz

A Reason for Writing Persuading

CREATIVE
Writing

FINE ARTS ◆ In 1776 American colonists declared
their independence from British rule. This painting
is a symbol of that independence. What does being
an American mean to you? What makes it special?
Write a short poem about what it means to be
an American. Tell how you feel about the word
American.

CREATIVE THINKING ♦
A Strategy for Persuading

A THOUGHT BALLOON

Persuading means getting someone to agree with you. After this lesson you will read part of *Why Don't You Get a Horse, Sam Adams?* In the story, John Adams tries to persuade his cousin that he needs a horse. Later you will write a persuasive argument of your own.

How does John try to persuade Samuel in this scene?

"Riding would be good for your health," he began.
Samuel was not concerned with his health.
Riding was sociable, John suggested. Samuel said walking was sociable . . . .
Well, riding was a more convenient way to get about, John went on. . . .

To persuade his cousin, John put himself in Samuel's place. He tried to look at things as Samuel would. John had the right idea. To persuade someone, first you have to understand that person's point of view.

Learning the Strategy

It is often helpful to understand someone else's point of view. For example, you might want to surprise your friend with a hamster. How can you figure out if it's a good gift to give? Suppose you were playing hide-and-seek with your brother. Why would it be helpful to know how he thinks? Suppose you set up a lemonade stand on a hot day. How could knowing your customers' point of view help you sell lemonade?

How can you understand another person's point of view? Your own experience can help you. Think of the lemonade stand. You might not know all the people passing by. However, you know how *you* feel on a hot summer day. So you can imagine how *they* probably feel.

Making a thought balloon is one way to help imagine someone else's thoughts. The thought balloon below shows what one of your lemonade customers might be thinking. How might this help you write a sign for your stand?

> It's so hot. I'm really thirsty. How much is the lemonade? If it's expensive, I won't buy any.

customer °°°

Using the Strategy

A. Imagine a child named Lee. On the playground everyone else is playing games with friends. Lee is standing at the side watching. What is Lee's point of view? What do you imagine Lee is thinking? Make a thought balloon. In it, write what you imagine Lee is thinking. Then decide how you might act toward Lee if you were there.

B. Sam Adams was a famous person who lived long ago. Everyone rode horses then. However, Sam did not ride a horse. Can you imagine what his reasons were? Make a thought balloon for Sam Adams. In it, write what you imagine he thought about horses. Then read *Why Don't You Get a Horse, Sam Adams?* Find out if you are right.

Applying the Strategy

- How do you figure out how another person feels?
- When might it be important to look at things from someone else's point of view?

AWARD
WINNING
AUTHOR

from # Why don't you get a *horse,*

SAM ADAMS?

by Jean Fritz

In the early days when America still belonged to England, there lived in Boston a man named Samuel Adams. He was a man who had his own ideas about things. While other men rode horseback, Samuel Adams walked around Boston. While others stayed loyal to England, Samuel said that America should break free.

Samuel and his cousin John Adams felt the same way about America's independence. Yet they had different opinions about riding horses. John thought that Samuel should ride a horse like other men did. Samuel argued that walking or riding in a carriage suited him better. Of course, Samuel knew that his escape from British soldiers at Lexington would have been faster on a galloping horse than in a creaking carriage. Even so, Samuel wouldn't learn to ride.

Then in 1775, Samuel and John Adams were traveling to a meeting in Philadelphia. The leaders of the Revolution were deciding what to do. On the way, Samuel and John often stopped at inns to talk things over. It was at one of these inns that they argued about horses one last time.

At a tavern in Grafton, Connecticut, John Adams decided to make one last attempt to get Samuel on a horse.

"Riding would be good for your health," he began.

Samuel was not concerned with his health.

Riding was sociable, John suggested. Samuel said walking was sociable and riding in a chaise could be sociable, too.

Well, riding was a more convenient way to get about, John went on. As a leader of the Revolution, Samuel was a busy man and needed to get about easily.

Samuel was not interested in convenience.

Riding was the fastest way to travel, John observed. In time of war, it was sometimes important to move fast.

Still, Samuel was not convinced. If he thought about his escape at Lexington, he didn't mention it.

John sighed and tried another tack. It was a pity, he said, that early man had gone to such trouble to domesticate an animal, only to have Samuel Adams come along and reject it.

Samuel didn't give two hoots for early man.

Then John Adams sat back in his chair and took a deep breath. He had one more argument. "You should ride a horse for the good of your country," he declared. America would surely be declaring its independence soon, he pointed out; if all went well, they themselves would be signing such a declaration in Philadelphia. Then they would be not just leaders of a revolution; they would be the statesmen of a new nation.

John leaned toward his cousin. "A proud new nation," he said. A great nation. A republic as Rome had been in ancient times. And whoever heard of a great nation with statesmen who could not ride horseback? John listed the heroes of Roman history. He reviewed the names of Roman senators. All were horsemen, he said. And he would not want Americans to be inferior in the least way.

For the first time Samuel looked thoughtful.
After all, he told himself, he had put on silk
stockings and a ruffled shirt so as not to shame
the Commonwealth of Massachusetts at the
meeting in Philadelphia. How could he refuse
to get on a horse if the honor of his country
were at stake? How could he put a stain on
American history—indeed right on the opening
chapter?

Library Link ♦ *John Adams had finally found an argument
that convinced his cousin Samuel to ride a horse. You can learn
more about John and Samuel Adams's historic journey by reading*
Why Don't You Get a Horse, Sam Adams? *by Jean Fritz.*

Reader's Response

What do you think of Sam Adams's reasons for refusing to
ride a horse?

Why don't you get a *horse,* SAM ADAMS?

Responding to Literature

1. Turn the story into a play. Have a Readers Theatre. Different students read the parts of characters. Other students read the parts the characters do not speak. They are the narrators. Decide who will read which parts. When you read, remember to speak clearly.

2. John and Sam are cousins. Do you think they are more alike than different? Tell why.

3. Sam Adams lived long ago. Would you like to have lived in another time? Tell about that time. Tell what you would do.

Writing to Learn

Think and Imagine ♦ Below is a picture of Sam Adams riding a horse for the first time. What might he have been thinking at that moment? Write Sam's thoughts in a thought balloon.

Thought Balloon

Write ♦ Use your thought balloon to write a short letter from Sam to his grandchildren. Be sure Sam tells how he felt when he first got on the horse.

LITERATURE: Historical Fiction · **79**

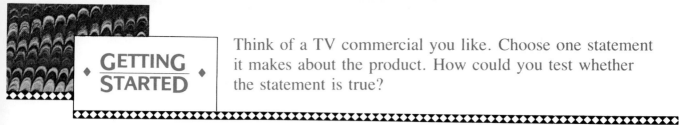

Think of a TV commercial you like. Choose one statement it makes about the product. How could you test whether the statement is true?

SPEAKING and LISTENING ◆
Facts and Opinions

What is the difference between a fact and an opinion? A fact is a statement that can be tested and proved to be true. An opinion is what someone *thinks* or *says* is true. Maybe it is true; maybe it isn't. It is an opinion because no one has proved it or because it cannot be tested.

Both facts and opinions are valuable. However, you need to know how to tell the difference. People believe their own opinions. They often state these opinions as if they were facts. If you can tell a fact from an opinion, you will be likely to question such statements as *Riding is better than walking*. You will think, "Really? Then prove it!"

Here are guidelines to help you separate fact from opinion.

Giving Facts and Opinions	**1.** When you state a fact, offer proof if you can. Tell how you know the fact was proved to be true. **2.** When you state an opinion, use such phrases as *It seems to me*, *I think*, *In my opinion*, *Although others disagree*. **3.** Clearly state the reasons for your opinion.
Being a Critical Listener	**1.** Ask yourself, "Can this statement be proved?" **2.** Ask yourself, "Who says so? Is the person an expert?" **3.** Be careful of statements that say *all*, *everyone*, *never*, or *always*. Such statements are often opinions.

Summary ◆ A **fact** is true information about something. An **opinion** is what a person thinks about something. Separate fact from opinion when you speak and when you listen.

Guided Practice

Tell whether each statement is a fact or an opinion.

1. Newspapers were taxed by England in colonial times.
2. By 1765 there were nearly forty newspapers in the colonies.
3. A newspaper reporter leads an exciting life.
4. Gathering the news is an important part of a reporter's job.
5. Samuel Adams would have been a good newspaper reporter.

Practice

A. Write *fact* or *opinion* for each sentence below.

6. Movies about the Revolutionary War are never dull.
7. Actors always enjoy playing historical roles.
8. In colonial times, town criers called out the news.
9. Today news is often broadcast by satellite.
10. It would have been fun to interview Samuel Adams.
11. On September 17, 1775, John Adams wrote to James Warren.
12. John Adams told how he got his cousin to ride a horse.
13. Author Jean Fritz used facts from John Adams's letter.
14. If Samuel Adams were alive now, he would be on TV.

B. Work with a partner. Take turns stating one fact you know about the topics listed below. Then state one opinion you have about each topic. Give reasons for your opinions. As the listener, listen carefully to separate fact from opinion.

baseball　　　**breakfast**　　　**homework**　　　**snow**

Apply ◆ Think and Write

Dictionary of Knowledge ◆ American colonists had strong opinions. In fact, they once held a tea party to express an opinion. Read about the famous Boston Tea Party in the Dictionary of Knowledge. Write what the colonists thought of the tea tax. Then write your opinion of what they did about it.

> ✎ **Remember**
> to listen
> to separate facts
> from opinions.

Start with this statement: *Many things have changed since George Washington's time.* Take turns telling more about the statement. (Hint: Were there cars or airplanes then?)

WRITING ◆
A Paragraph

You know that words are put together to form a sentence. In the same way, sentences are put together to form a paragraph. Knowing how to build a paragraph is the key to good writing.

A **paragraph** is a group of sentences about one main idea. Since a paragraph is a *group* of sentences, it tells more than a single sentence does. Often the first sentence tells what the paragraph is about. It states the **main idea**. The other sentences tell more about the main idea.

The first sentence of a paragraph begins a little bit to the right. We say that it is **indented**. Indenting tells the reader that a new paragraph is beginning. Here is a sample paragraph.

> Samuel Adams was a leader of the American Revolution. Before the war, Adams gave stirring speeches to the colonists in Boston. His speeches called for independence from England. To protest the British Tea Act of 1773, Adams organized the Boston Tea Party. He later became an important member of the Continental Congress. He was also a signer of the Declaration of Independence.

- ◆ What is the paragraph about?
- ◆ Which sentence tells the main idea?
- ◆ Which sentences tell more about the main idea?
- ◆ What title could you give the paragraph?

Summary ◆ A **paragraph** is a group of sentences about one main idea. Paragraphs help your readers find and follow your main ideas.

Guided Practice

Tell which sentences belong in a paragraph
about taking a ride on horseback.

1. Children often enjoy riding horses.
2. A newborn horse is called a foal.
3. Horses eat large amounts of hay and oats.
4. Horseback riders should wear comfortable clothing.
5. Many riders in the United States use a Western saddle.
6. Most horses live for twenty to thirty years.

Practice

A. Decide which sentences belong in a paragraph about
schools of the Puritans. Write *yes* or *no* for each sentence.

7. In Puritan towns, school was required by law.
8. School was held in the home of a teacher.
9. Some Puritans became better known as Pilgrims.
10. The Pilgrims founded Plymouth Colony in 1620.
11. Puritans believed that everyone should learn to read.
12. Oliver Cromwell was a Puritan leader in England.

B. Choose one of these main ideas. Write it as the first
sentence of a paragraph. Add at least three sentences that
tell more about the main idea to finish the paragraph.

> **Horseback riding is a safe, enjoyable sport.**
> **Horseback riding is a silly, dangerous sport.**
> **It would be fun to live in colonial times.**
> **I am glad I do not live in colonial times.**

Apply ◆ Think and Write

Finding Main Ideas ◆ Finding and writing down the main
idea can give you a better understanding of what you read.
Turn to the chapter you are now studying in your science or
social studies book. Read four paragraphs. Write the main
idea of each one.

> ✎ **Remember**
> to make sure that
> all the sentences
> in a paragraph
> are about
> the main idea.

Begin with this sentence: *Last night I dreamed I lived in colonial America.* Take turns adding sentences that tell more about your dream. For example: *I lived down the street from John Adams. I saw Paul Revere ride by on his horse.*

WRITING ♦
Topic Sentence and Details

You have learned that all of the sentences in a paragraph tell about one main idea. Often the main idea is stated in a single sentence. This sentence is called the topic sentence. All of the other sentences in the paragraph tell more about the topic sentence. These sentences give details about the main idea.

Read the following paragraph. Notice that the topic sentence is underlined. In this case, it is a question.

Topic Sentence

Details

> <u>What was newspaper publishing like in colonial times?</u> First of all, the newspaper was published only once a week. About three hundred copies were printed. Since people shared their copies, however, the newspaper had many readers. Even then, over two hundred years ago, most newspapers had advertisements. Ads for schoolteachers, dance teachers, music teachers, potters, and silversmiths helped to pay the cost of publishing.

- ♦ Tell the main idea of the paragraph.
- ♦ Tell five details that are given that tell more about the topic sentence.
- ♦ Would you expect the paragraph to talk about Samuel Adams? Why or why not?
- ♦ What would be a good title for the paragraph?

Summary ♦ The **topic sentence** states the main idea of a paragraph. The other sentences in the paragraph give details that tell more about the topic sentence.

Guided Practice

Read the following topic sentence and answer the questions.

Growing up in colonial America was difficult at times.

1. What kind of information might the paragraph give?
2. Could the paragraph discuss school and chores?
3. Could it discuss the most common names for boys and girls?

Practice

A. Read the following topic sentence. Then write your answers to the questions that follow.

Samuel Adams and John Adams were cousins, but they were quite different.

4. What kind of information might the paragraph give?
5. Could the paragraph discuss the differences between Samuel Adams and Paul Revere?
6. Could it discuss Samuel Adams's dog, Queue?
7. Could it describe how John and Samuel Adams looked?
8. Could it tell how the personalities of John and Samuel Adams were different?

B. Write a topic sentence for each of these ideas.

9. your favorite school subject
10. a person you would like to read about
11. why dogs are such great pets

C. Write a paragraph. Begin with one of the topic sentences you wrote for **Practice B**. Then add two or more sentences that give details about that topic sentence.

Apply ◆ Think and Write

A "Wonder" Paragraph ◆ Write a paragraph that discusses something you wonder about. Start your topic sentence with *I wonder why*. Then add more sentences about what you wonder.

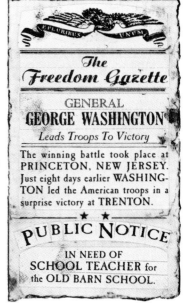

✎ **Remember**
to state the main idea of your paragraph in a topic sentence.

WRITING ◆
A Persuasive Paragraph

You have opinions. You like certain things. You dislike other things. You agree with some ideas. You disagree with others. If you are like most people, you enjoy expressing your opinions. Sometimes you just want to say what you think. Other times you may want to persuade others to agree with you.

Your opinion is valuable. Learn to express it clearly, and you will make your opinion count. A good way to develop a clear organization of your opinion is to write a paragraph. When you write a persuasive paragraph, you put your opinion in writing. You focus your ideas. You choose details that count and discard others.

Read this persuasive paragraph. Notice that the writer's opinion is stated at the two most powerful places in any paragraph—at the beginning, and at the end.

State opinion ▷

Give facts and reasons ▷

Repeat your opinion ▷

Samuel Adams should not have worn such shabby clothes. He was a leader, a representative from Massachusetts. People want to be proud of their leaders. They do not want them to wear frayed coats, scuffed shoes, and darned socks. But this is what Samuel Adams did. Even his friends were embarrassed by his appearance. Although they said nothing, they sent new clothes to his house so he would look nice when he went to Congress in Philadelphia. His friends should not have had to do this. Samuel Adams should have taken care of his clothes himself, since he was a leader of others.

Summary ◆ A **persuasive paragraph** gives the writer's opinion and reasons to support it. Writing a persuasive paragraph will help you organize your thoughts clearly.

Guided Practice

State a topic sentence for each of these opinions. You may use questions for some of your topic sentences.

1. an opinion about birthdays
2. an opinion about your city or town
3. an opinion about a game you like
4. an opinion about a game you don't like

Practice

A. Choose any four of the opinions below. Write a topic sentence for each opinion you chose. You may write some sentences as questions.

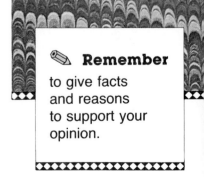

5. an opinion about clothes you like
6. an opinion about clothes you don't like
7. an opinion about a pet
8. an opinion about a movie star
9. an opinion about a rainy day
10. an opinion about music you like
11. an opinion about a rule you agree with
12. an opinion about a rule you disagree with

B. Select one of the topic sentences you wrote for **Practice A**. Write several sentences that give facts or reasons to support your opinion. Then write the last sentence, in which you should again state your opinion. State it in a different way than you did the first time.

Apply ◆ Think and Write

Opinions and Reasons ◆ Have an argument with yourself. (You can't lose!) Choose something you feel very strongly about. Draw a line down the center of a piece of paper. On the left side, write *My Opinion*. On the right side, write *The Other Side*. List as many reasons as you can for both sides of the argument.

> ✎ **Remember**
> to give facts
> and reasons
> to support your
> opinion.

Focus on Persuasive Words

Words have great power. They can move us. They can persuade us. They can make us laugh or cry. They can stir us to action. They can soothe us to sleep. How is it that words can do all this?

John Adams knew the answer. You will recall his talk with Samuel Adams earlier in this unit. He persuaded Sam to ride a horse. John Adams did not use force. He did not offer Sam a reward. No, he used something made out of thin air. Words!

JOHN ADAMS'S WORDS: good, proud, new, great, statesmen, heroes

Samuel Adams wanted *honor* for the new nation. He did not want to put a *stain* on American history.

Words create feelings. That is what makes them so powerful. Some of these feelings are good—as with the word *honor*. Some are bad—as with the word *stain*.

Here are three more examples. In them, each pair of words means about the same thing. But the first word gives a good feeling. It is marked with a plus (+). The second word gives a bad feeling. It is marked with a minus (−).

(+)	(−)	(+)	(−)	(+)	(−)
slender,	skinny	young,	childish	amusing,	silly

The Writer's Voice ♦ Some words call forth feelings. These feelings may be good or bad. Such words are powerful. Suggest at least five more words that John Adams might have used to persuade Samuel. Choose words that give good feelings. The words should also fit the subject well.

Working Together

Writers choose powerful words when they are trying to persuade their readers. Work with your group on activities **A** and **B**.

A. Discuss each pair of words. Put a minus (−) above the word in each pair that gives bad feelings.

1. horse, nag
2. shack, house
3. fragrance, odor
4. beg, ask
5. animal, beast

6. daring, reckless
7. racket, sound
8. unusual, weird
9. gossip, talk
10. carefree, careless

In Your Group

- Encourage others to share ideas.
- Keep the group on the subject.
- Agree or disagree in a pleasant way.
- Record the group's ideas.

B. Each underlined word in the following paragraph gives bad feelings. Suggest a more favorable word to replace each one. Use a dictionary if necessary.

My friend Tom owns a black-and-white mutt named Shadow. This pint-size pet is as nosy as a kitten. He often has to be bawled out. Once while Tom and I were gabbing on the phone, Shadow chewed up a pair of ancient sneakers. Another time he met a skunk behind Tom's hovel. The odor from that showdown lasted for weeks. Life with Shadow is hair-raising.

THESAURUS CORNER • Word Choice

Look up the following nouns in the Thesaurus. For each noun, choose a synonym that gives good feelings. Then choose another synonym that gives less favorable feelings. Use each synonym in an original sentence that shows these feelings.

answer   **group**   **road**

Writing a Persuasive Argument

Writers often try to persuade readers to agree with them. Sometimes the writer has to change a reader's mind. The writer gives facts and reasons. These details help support the writer's opinion.

In *Why Don't You Get a Horse, Sam Adams?*, John Adams thinks that Samuel should ride a horse. He says that riding is healthful, sociable, convenient, and fast. Finally, he explains why it will be good for the new America. This last reason persuades Samuel to try riding a horse.

Know Your Purpose and Audience

MY PURPOSE

In this lesson you will write a persuasive argument. Your purpose will be to persuade someone to try something.

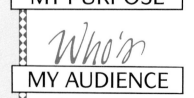

MY AUDIENCE

Your audience will be a partner from your class. Later you can make tape recordings or a "Try This!" book.

1 Prewriting

First decide what you want to persuade your partner to try. Next gather convincing facts and reasons.

Choose Your Topic ♦ Think of foods, television shows, sports, and games that you enjoy. Make a list of those things. Then circle your topic choice.

Think About It

Explore all possible topics. Go over your list carefully. Which one would be more fun to persuade your partner to try? Which one do you enjoy most? Maybe you could choose one that is easy to learn. Maybe your partner needs a challenge.

Talk About It

Choose classmates who know you well. Ask them to help you remember all the things you enjoy doing. Often your friends remember things that you have overlooked.

Topic Ideas

raise goldfish
(play checkers)
watch quiz shows
cook Italian food
play piano
read mysteries
collect stamps
plant flowers

Choose Your Strategy ◆ Here are two strategies to help you gather facts and reasons to persuade your partner. Read both strategies. Then decide which idea you will use.

PREWRITING IDEAS

CHOICE ONE

Nonstop Writing

Write your opinion at the top of a piece of paper. Then write every persuasive argument you can think of. Write for five minutes without stopping. You don't need to write complete sentences. If you can't think of anything for a moment, write *word, word, word*.

Model

You should try playing checkers.
easy to learn... play at all ages... word, word, word, word, word, word... portable... cheap... like a puzzle... exciting with good players... can find secondhand

CHOICE TWO

A Thought Balloon

Discuss your topic with your partner. Try to persuade your partner that he or she should try your activity. Then record your partner's responses in a thought balloon. It can help you decide what reasons to use when you write your persuasive argument.

Model

I don't know how to play checkers. It's too hard.

Dawn

2 Writing

Review your nonstop writing notes or your thought balloon. Then begin your persuasive argument by stating your opinion. Write as if you are talking to your partner. Here are three ways a topic sentence could begin.

- ♦ I think you would really enjoy ____.
- ♦ David, some day you should try ____.
- ♦ Have you ever thought about ____?

As you write, include facts and reasons that support your topic sentence. You might arrange your facts or reasons from least important to most important. End your persuasive argument with a strong conclusion.

Sample First Draft ♦

Dawn, my idea is that you would enjoy playing Checkers. I know you would be good at it. It is so much fun. You can play checkers with people of all ages and abilities.

First of all, the game is really quite easy. It is also inexpensive. new games cost only a few dolars, and used ones cost even less.

When you play with experts, it is hard but exiting.

3 Revising

When you revise, you have a chance to improve your writing. This idea may help.

REVISING IDEA

FIRST   Read to Yourself

Review your purpose. Did you persuade your partner to try something? Did you give facts or reasons to support your opinion? Do you believe your facts or reasons will persuade your partner?

Focus: Have you used the most persuasive words you can think of?

THEN   Share with a Partner

Read your persuasive argument aloud to your partner. Note your partner's responses. Below are some helpful guidelines.

The Writer

Guidelines: Read your argument with feeling. Note your partner's responses.

Sample questions:
- What reasons persuaded you the most?
- **Focus question:** What is a more persuasive word for _____?

The Writer's Partner

Guidelines: Listen carefully to the writer's reasons.

Sample responses:
- I was persuaded when you said _____.
- A more persuasive word might be _____.

Revising Model ♦ Look at this argument that is being revised. The revising marks show the writer's changes.

Opinion is a
more exact noun
than *idea*.

These reasons were
moved to make
a stronger
conclusion.

The writer added
a persuasive
detail.

Challenging is a
more persuasive
word than *hard*.

> *opinion*
> Dawn, my ~~idea~~ is that you
> would enjoy playing Checkers. I
> know you would be good at it.
> It is so much fun. You can play
> checkers with people of all ages and
> abilities.
> First of all, the game is really quite
> You can learn the basic rules in less than an hour.
> easy. ∧ It is also inexpensive. new
> games cost only a few dolars, and
> used ones cost even less.
> ⟶ When you play with experts, it
> *challenging*
> is ~~hard~~ but exiting.

Read the revised argument above as the writer has decided
it *should* be. Then revise your own persuasive argument.

Grammar Check ♦ Exact nouns make your writing clearer.

Word Choice ♦ Do you want to find a better word for a
word like *idea*? A thesaurus can help you find words.

Revising Checklist

☐ **My purpose:** Did I
write a persuasive
argument? Did I try
to persuade
someone to try
something?

☐ **My audience:** Will
my audience be
persuaded?

☐ **Focus:** Did I use
persuasive words?

4 Proofreading

Be courteous to your readers. Proofread your writing to make sure it is neat and correct.

Proofreading Model ♦ Here is the sample argument.
Notice that red proofreading marks have been added.

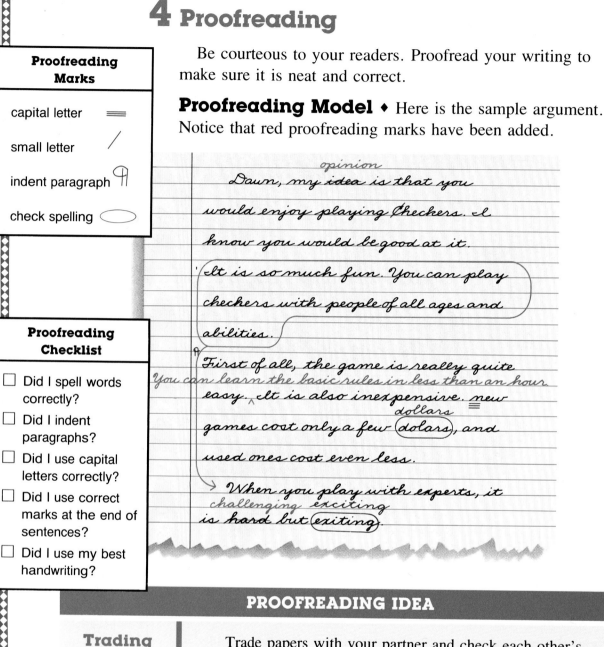

opinion
Dawn, my idea is that you would enjoy playing Checkers. I know you would be good at it.
It is so much fun. You can play checkers with people of all ages and abilities.
First of all, the game is really quite easy. It is also inexpensive. new
You can learn the basic rules in less than an hour
dollars
games cost only a few (dolars), and used ones cost even less.
When you play with experts, it
challenging   exciting
is hard but (exiting).

PROOFREADING IDEA

Trading with a Partner

Trade papers with your partner and check each other's work. It is sometimes easier to find someone else's mistakes. If you find a mistake, put a check next to it or circle it. Point out to your partner the mistakes you found. Help each other fix the mistakes.

After proofreading your persuasive argument, give it a title. Then make a neat copy.

5 Publishing

Below are two ways you can share your persuasive arguments with a wider audience.

Why Not Play Checkers?

Dawn, my opinion is that you would enjoy playing checkers. I know you would be good at it.

First of all, the game is really quite easy. You can learn the basic rules in less than an hour. It is also inexpensive. New games cost only a few dollars, and used ones cost even less.

It is so much fun. You can play checkers with people of all ages and abilities. When you play with experts, it is challenging but exciting. Let me teach you how to play!

PUBLISHING IDEAS

Share Aloud

Make a tape recording of your persuasive argument. Make it sound as if you are actually talking to your partner. Have your partner listen carefully. Record your partner's responses. Your partner should tell if she or he was persuaded, and why.

Share in Writing

Collect all the persuasive arguments into an illustrated book called ''Try This!'' Leave a blank page after each argument. You and your classmates can read each argument. On the blank page, tell whether you will try the activity, or add other comments.

CURRICULUM
•CONNECTION•

Writing Across the Curriculum
Social Studies

In this unit you drew thought balloons. You used them to help you imagine other people's points of view. For example, you made a thought balloon for Samuel Adams. You imagined his feelings about riding a horse. Imagining what people long ago thought and felt can be important. It can help you to understand and enjoy history.

Writing to Learn

Think and Imagine ◆ Look at this painting. What can you tell about the soldiers from the way they are dressed? Look carefully at the drummer boy. What might he be thinking? Write a thought balloon for the drummer boy.

Thought Balloon

THE LOST DRUMMER BOY *painting by Edward Percy Moran*
Courtesy Petersen Galleries, Beverly Hills

Write ◆ Write about the drummer boy. Tell how he might feel about where he is.

Writing in Your Journal

In the Writer's Warm-up you wrote about life in colonial America. Would you like to have lived then? What would be the best or the worst things about living at that time? Write your opinions in your journal.

BOOKS TO ENJOY

 ## Read More About It

What's the Big Idea, Ben Franklin?
by Jean Fritz
This is another entertaining book by Jean Fritz. This time she tells about the many interests of Benjamin Franklin.

A New Look at the Pilgrims: Why They Came to America *by Beatrice Siegel*
Learn more about the story behind the famous trip in the *Mayflower*. You will find out why the Pilgrims left England, and what they hoped to find when they arrived in the New World.

Book Report Idea Town Crier Report

In colonial times, a town crier delivered news. He would ring a bell, then call out his message. Spread the news about a good book you enjoy.

Make a Scroll ♦ Use a large sheet of paper. Roll the ends so it looks like a scroll. Write the important details of the book. Call for attention by saying, ''Hear ye! Hear ye!'' Tell enough about your book to persuade others to read it.

UNIT REVIEW

Unit 2

Nouns   *pages 52–59*

A. Write the noun in each group of words.

1. swayed, camel, about
2. dune, thirsty, yelled
3. endless, rode, footprint
4. bright, sunshine, above
5. night, cool, darken

B. Write the plural of each singular noun.

6. glass
7. lake
8. box
9. moose
10. woman
11. donkey
12. family
13. lunch

C. Write each sentence. Draw one line under each common noun. Draw two lines under each proper noun.

14. The group crossed the Rocky Mountains.
15. The seven men reached the Grand Canyon.
16. The explorers met people from California.
17. Finally the travelers reached Mexico.

Capital Letters and Periods
pages 60–61

D. Write the underlined proper nouns correctly. Use capital letters and periods where they are needed.

18. dr powers and her children went to philadelphia.
19. Many people were in the city for the fourth of july celebration.
20. The family toured independence hall on friday.
21. lisa enjoyed watching the sailboat parade on the delaware river.
22. The family met mr and mrs r pell.
23. market street was very crowded.
24. The group would see the fireworks at john f kennedy stadium.

Apostrophes   *pages 62–65*

E. Write the possessive form of each noun.

25. woman
26. citizens
27. Dr. Watts
28. baby
29. horse
30. Eskimos
31. telescope
32. island

Compounds   *pages 66–67*

F. Write the two words that form each compound word.

33. afternoon
34. wildlife
35. sunflower
36. nighttime
37. grandparent
38. schoolhouse
39. whalebone
40. underground

Fact and Opinion   *pages 80–81*

G. Write *fact* or *opinion* for each sentence.

41. Deep-sea diving is exciting.

42. People tried it more than two thousand years ago.

43. Some divers breathed through reeds.

44. Anyone can get rich from diving.

45. Modern diving suits are waterproof.

46. The suits are not very comfortable.

Main Idea and Details
pages 82–83

H. Read the paragraph. Then choose the correct answer to each question.

Blue whales are the largest animals in the world. Many adults are one hundred feet long and weigh about one hundred tons. They feed on tiny shrimplike animals. Baby blue whales gain about 200 pounds a day.

47. Write the main idea of the paragraph.

  a. Baby blue whales gain about 200 pounds a day.

  b. Blue whales are the largest animals in the world.

  c. Many adults are one hundred feet long and weigh about one hundred tons.

48. Which detail best supports the topic sentence?

  a. They feed on tiny animals.

  b. Baby blue whales grow fast.

  c. They are one hundred feet long.

Topic Sentence and Details
pages 84–85

I. Read the paragraph. Then choose the correct answer to each question.

A glacier is a slow-moving river of ice. When new snow falls on a mountain it pushes down on the old snow. Finally the snow packs down until it is ice. When it is very thick and heavy, the icy snow slides down the mountain. As the glacier slides along, it is like a river.

49. Write the topic sentence of the paragraph.

  a. A glacier is a slow-moving river of ice.

  b. Finally the snow packs down until it is ice.

  c. As the glacier slides along, it is like a river.

50. Which detail best supports the topic sentence?

  a. Old snow is under new snow.

  b. Snow can get very heavy.

  c. Icy snow slides down the mountain.

CUMULATIVE REVIEW

Unit 1: Sentences   *pages 6–11*

A. Write each sentence. Then write *declarative, interrogative, imperative,* or *exclamatory* to show what kind of sentence each one is.

1. Please direct me to the bus station.
2. I hope we are not late.
3. Is this the right way?
4. I believe it is.
5. What trouble this is!
6. What's the matter?
7. See for yourself.
8. Walk faster if you can.
9. Hurray, we made it!

B. Write *subject* if the subject is underlined. Write *predicate* if the predicate is underlined.

10. <u>We</u> are learning about the value of insects.
11. <u>Busy insects</u> carry pollen from one plant to another.
12. Bees <u>provide honey and wax</u>.
13. <u>Children</u> had pull toys in ancient Egypt.
14. <u>Greek and Roman children</u> played with boats.
15. The people of Asia <u>developed tops</u>.

Unit 2: Nouns   *pages 52–59*

C. Write the noun in each group of words.

16. road, many, smooth
17. crunchy, salty, pretzel
18. roared, automobile, loudly
19. zoo, swept, crowded
20. played, phonograph, sing
21. spaceship, delayed, gigantic
22. clock, loud, passed
23. cheered, exciting, baseball
24. pulled, friendly, dentist
25. skateboard, new, speedy
26. steel, icy, crossed
27. connecting, pipes, reaches
28. pencil, wrote, sharp
29. flashed, small, camera
30. hang, poster, long
31. puppy, adopted, cute
32. tossed, healthy, salad
33. arrived, holiday, happy

D. Write the plural of each singular noun.

34. child
35. tree
36. dress
37. banana
38. deer
39. bush
40. weaver
41. walrus
42. costume
43. goose
44. factory
45. bench
46. foot
47. branch
48. picnic
49. lady
50. man
51. watch
52. key
53. penny
54. tooth
55. dish

E. Write each sentence below. Draw one line under each common noun. Draw two lines under each proper noun.

56. Dr. Murphy lives next to J.P. Smith.
57. My aunt flew to San Antonio.
58. Mrs. Oppenheimer met the family.
59. Their friends stayed for Labor Day.
60. The Ames River overflowed its banks.
61. Students crossed Anderson Bridge.
62. Flashlights flickered on Pond Road.
63. The lights went off in City Hall.
64. Mayor Vellucci helped the citizens.

Unit 2: Capital Letters and Periods
pages 60–61

F. Write each proper noun correctly. Use capital letters and periods where they are needed.

65. ms anita j santiago
66. january
67. north carolina
68. a a milne
69. dr david travis
70. thanksgiving day
71. new orleans
72. yellowstone park
73. north sea

Unit 2: Apostrophes   *pages 62–65*

G. Write each sentence. Use the possessive form of each noun in parentheses ( ).

74. Do you know _____ new address? (Joe)
75. I can see the _____ tracks. (rabbits)
76. This _____ work is fine. (artist)
77. My _____ birthday is Sunday. (uncle)
78. The party is at _____ house. (Chris)
79. The _____ big event is the gift. (party)
80. He received tickets to the _____ game. (school)
81. The _____ star player is hurt. (team)
82. He is _____ favorite player. (everyone)
83. We visited the _____ zoo. (city)
84. My _____ brother works at the zoo. (friend)
85. _____ jobs are very important. (People)
86. A _____ menu is posted. (day)
87. The _____ food is prepared. (animals)
88. The grizzlies smell the _____ aroma. (food)
89. The _____ entrance is open. (zookeeper)
90. We peek inside the _____ den. (bears)
91. The little _____ noses wiggle. (cubs)

LANGUAGE PUZZLERS

Unit 2 Challenge

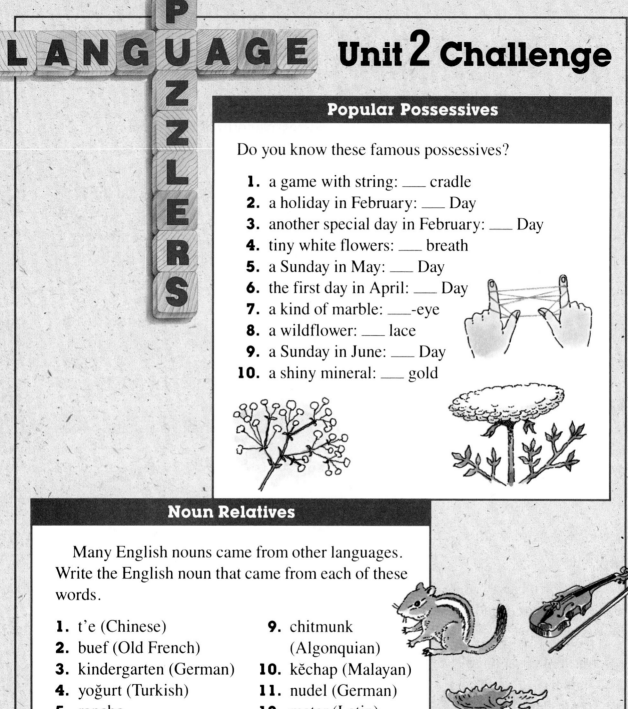

Popular Possessives

Do you know these famous possessives?

1. a game with string: ___ cradle
2. a holiday in February: ___ Day
3. another special day in February: ___ Day
4. tiny white flowers: ___ breath
5. a Sunday in May: ___ Day
6. the first day in April: ___ Day
7. a kind of marble: ___-eye
8. a wildflower: ___ lace
9. a Sunday in June: ___ Day
10. a shiny mineral: ___ gold

Noun Relatives

Many English nouns came from other languages. Write the English noun that came from each of these words.

1. t'e (Chinese)
2. buef (Old French)
3. kindergarten (German)
4. yoğurt (Turkish)
5. rancho (Mexican Spanish)
6. violino (Italian)
7. moos (Algonquian)
8. wafel (Dutch)
9. chitmunk (Algonquian)
10. kĕchap (Malayan)
11. nudel (German)
12. mater (Latin)
13. familia (Latin)
14. scholē (Greek)
15. seamrōg (Irish)
16. koekje (Dutch)

Unit 2 Extra Practice

1 Writing with Nouns

p. 52

A. Each sentence below contains three nouns. Write each sentence. Underline every noun.

1. Show the dinosaur to a friend in school.
2. Tell children in class about the model.
3. Each student brought a hobby to class.
4. One girl carried her fish in a little bowl.
5. A boy set up a show of ships.
6. One student made a train of wood.
7. The teacher set up tables in the lunchroom.
8. My friend brought a parrot with beautiful feathers.
9. Another student brought stamps in an album.
10. Two girls hung a plant from the ceiling.
11. The painting was a picture of a kitten.
12. A folder of old coins lay open on the shelf.
13. Hamsters and gerbils exercised in cages.
14. Only one child brought a model of an airplane.
15. The class had sent invitations to each home.

B. Write each sentence. Underline every noun.

16. The room was finally ready for the show.
17. A line formed in the hallway.
18. A person at the door took each ticket.
19. In the kitchen the teacher was pouring juice.
20. Two brothers brought muffins from home.
21. A small girl carried a large picture.
22. Children had decorated the walls with art.
23. The guests thought every hobby was interesting.
24. The prize was in a box by the window.
25. The judge would soon announce the winner.
26. My favorite model was the little town with the tiny automobiles.

2 Singular Nouns and Plural Nouns

p. 54

A. Write each underlined noun. After each noun write *singular* or *plural*.

1. My parents often take us to the orchard.
2. We pick fresh peaches in the summer.
3. We usually bring our own basket.
4. Sometimes we borrow small boxes.
5. We pick apples in the fall.
6. Long poles will reach the high branches.
7. We weigh the fruits on a scale.
8. My mother often makes a pie.
9. She fills it with berries.
10. This warm dessert is a special treat.

B. Write each sentence below. Use the plural of each word in parentheses ( ).

11. Sometimes we buy (jug) of cider.
12. The (apple) can be made into cider.
13. The (worker) dump apples into huge (press).
14. Then they turn the (handle).
15. The juice pours out into the (tub).
16. The cider house is filled with wonderful (aroma).

3 Spelling Plural Nouns

p. 56

A. Write each singular noun below. Then write the plural form of each.

1. foot	7. baby	13. moose
2. penny	8. mouse	14. kitty
3. goose	9. woman	15. pony
4. grandchild	10. sheep	16. reindeer
5. ox	11. child	17. factory
6. lady	12. library	18. elk

B. Each sentence below has two plural nouns. One plural noun is not correct. Write each sentence correctly.

19. Some animal babys are called cubs.
20. Teams of oxes pulled the cart.
21. Butterflys and dragonflies are pretty.
22. Do mouses have teeth?
23. Three childs fed the geese.
24. Two mans rode horses.
25. The mooses wandered by the reindeer.
26. Birds like to eat berrys.
27. Many families watched the bunnys.
28. The elephant had long sharp tooths called tusks.

4 Common Nouns and Proper Nouns
p. 58

A. Write each underlined noun. Then write *common* or *proper* after each.

1. Georgia is a beautiful state.
2. Its geography includes mountains, hills, and plains.
3. The Appalachian Trail begins here and ends in Maine.
4. Stone Mountain has a huge sculpture of three heroes.
5. Thirty people can sit on the shoulder of Robert E. Lee.

B. Write each sentence below. Draw one line under each common noun. Draw two lines under each proper noun.

6. The nickname of Georgia is the Peach State.
7. Peanuts are a major crop here.
8. Georgia is also known for its pecans.
9. This state has many famous people.
10. Juliette Low began a group for girls.
11. Franklin D. Roosevelt lived in the Little White House in Warm Springs.
12. Jimmy Carter grew peanuts in Plains.
13. Martin Luther King, Jr., was born in Atlanta.

5 Using Capitals with Proper Nouns

p. 60

A. Write the following nouns. Use capital letters for each proper noun.

1.	month	**6.**	sumner lake	**11.**	yuma desert
2.	mexico	**7.**	rigby pond	**12.**	oregon
3.	country	**8.**	wilson street	**13.**	rio grande
4.	texas	**9.**	city	**14.**	ocean
5.	lake	**10.**	october	**15.**	isle of palms

B. Write each sentence. Capitalize the proper nouns.

16. We traveled across the united states.

17. Our favorite lake was lake huron.

18. In minnesota we liked the forests.

19. I found colorful rocks in the mojave desert.

20. We followed a river called the gila river.

21. We enjoyed visiting yosemite national park.

22. Have you ever swum in the pacific ocean?

23. That was in early august.

24. Next year we will plan a trip to canada.

6 Singular Possessive Nouns

p. 62

A. Write each sentence below. Use the possessive form of each noun in parentheses ( ).

1. The wild ____ food is leaves and roots. (gerbil)

2. This ____ active time can be day or night. (pet)

3. Twelve young can be in the ____ litter. (female)

4. A hopping gerbil could be a ____ cousin. (kangaroo)

5. Its birthplace is ____ high plains. (Asia)

6. The ____ walls might be made of glass. (cage)

7. The ____ wheel makes a whirring sound. (animal)

8. The gerbil is the ____ favorite animal. (class)

9. Ms. ____ favorite is named Fuzzy. (Barnes)

B. Write the possessive form of each singular noun.

10.	insect	**15.**	Rita	**20.**	snake
11.	woman	**16.**	family	**21.**	Dr. Rooker
12.	mouse	**17.**	Jim	**22.**	spider
13.	Cindy	**18.**	book	**23.**	Ramón
14.	room	**19.**	fur	**24.**	Mrs. Hayes

7 Plural Possessive Nouns   *p. 64*

A. Write the possessive form of each plural noun.

1.	ladies	**6.**	geese	**11.**	classes
2.	citizens	**7.**	nieces	**12.**	babies
3.	scouts	**8.**	men	**13.**	foxes
4.	deer	**9.**	soldiers	**14.**	mice
5.	pirates	**10.**	drivers	**15.**	sheep

B. Write the sentences below. Use the possessive form of each plural noun in parentheses ( ).

16. Ancient (Greeks) tunics were loose coverings.

17. Greek (actors) masks were happy or sad faces.

18. The (Romans) togas were like draped sheets.

19. In the Middle Ages, (peasants) clothing was simple.

20. Some (men) hats were worn both indoors and out.

21. These fancy hats showed the (lords) importance.

22. (Rulers) crowns were once symbols of power.

23. (Monks) cloaks had great, full hoods.

24. Iron mesh was used for (knights) armor.

25. (Jesters) caps were trimmed with bells.

26. (Women) working dresses were called gray gowns.

27. The (warriors) shields protected their bodies.

28. (Children) clothes were just like those of adults.

29. (Gentlemen) wigs were large and costly.

30. Hoops under skirts were made of (whales) bones, wire, or wood.

UNIT THREE

USING LANGUAGE TO CREATE

=== **PART ONE** ===

Unit Theme *Nature*

Language Awareness Pronouns

=== **PART TWO** ===

Literature *Poetry*

A Reason for Writing Creating

Writing
IN YOUR JOURNAL

WRITER'S WARM-UP ◆ When you think of nature, what comes to mind? Is it animals? Do you imagine mountains, woods, or forests? Maybe you picture a bright orange sunset or an angry storm cloud. Close your eyes for a minute. Think about the word *nature*. Write in your journal. Tell about the pictures that come to your mind when you think about nature.

◆ GETTING ◆
STARTED

Change each underlined word to a noun in this sentence: *They saw it yesterday.* Can you think of nouns that make the sentence scary? Funny? Sad? Happy?

1 Writing with Pronouns

You know that a noun names a person, place, or thing. A pronoun is a word that takes the place of a noun or nouns. Use pronouns in your writing to avoid repeating the same nouns.

Read the sentences below. What noun does each underlined pronoun replace?

1. Poets write about many topics. They often choose nature.
2. Linda writes poems. She enjoys writing them.

In **1** the pronoun *they* takes the place of the noun *poets*. In **2** the pronoun *she* stands for *Linda*, and *them* stands for *poems*.

Pronouns can be singular or plural.

Singular Pronouns	Plural Pronouns
I, you, she, he, it me, her, him	we, you, they us, them

Summary ◆ A **pronoun** takes the place of a noun or nouns. When you write, use pronouns to avoid repeating the same nouns.

Guided Practice

Name the pronouns in the sentences below.

1. Ramón reads a poem he has written about the sea.
2. Sara enjoys poetry because she likes the beauty of words.
3. They are working on a book of poems together.
4. Ms. Wong asked them to finish it by next week.

Practice

A. Find and write the twelve pronouns in these sentences.

5. Poets can help us look at the world in new ways.
6. They often write about the beauty of nature.
7. I enjoy poems about the changing seasons.
8. Alvin showed me a poem about the first day of spring.
9. He says that animals make good subjects for poems.
10. Do you agree with him?
11. We often borrow poetry books from Mrs. Watie.
12. She has written some delightful poems about trees.
13. Alvin convinced her to read them at the town picnic.
14. It was a special day for the town of Oakwood.

B. Rewrite each sentence. Use the correct pronoun to replace the underlined noun or nouns.

15. Susan and Jennifer wrote a poem about a horse.
16. Susan read the poem to Roger.
17. Roger enjoyed the poem.
18. Roger said that the poem made Roger smile.
19. Susan asked Megan if Roger would read the poem.

C. These sentences tell about a young poet named Ben. Write each sentence. Use pronouns to complete the sentences.

20. Last night Ben saw a falling star. ____ wrote a poem about ____ .
21. Ben showed the poem to some friends. ____ liked ____ .
22. Ben's friends told ____ that ____ liked the poem.
23. Ben replied, "All of ____ have said kind words."
24. Ben said to ____ , "May ____ always be great friends!"

Apply ◆ Think and Write

From Your Writing ◆ List the pronouns that you used in the Writer's Warm-up. Write the noun or nouns that each pronoun replaced.

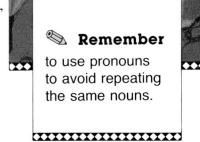

> ✎ **Remember**
> to use pronouns
> to avoid repeating
> the same nouns.

You and your friends are having a picnic. Tell what everyone is eating. Do not mention anyone by name. Use pronouns instead.

2 Subject Pronouns

You have learned that pronouns take the place of nouns. In the sentences below, the underlined words are pronouns.

1. **Wendy is learning about famous American poets. She has read some poems by Robert Frost.**
2. **Robert Frost had been a teacher and a farmer. He wrote many poems about nature.**
3. **The poems were written many years ago. They are still read today by people of all ages.**

In **1** the pronoun *she* replaces the noun *Wendy*. In **2** the pronoun *he* replaces the noun *Robert Frost*. In each case the pronoun replaces the noun that is the subject of the sentence. What pronoun in **3** replaces the noun *poems*?

Remember the following subject pronouns: *I*, *you*, *she*, *he*, *it*, *we*, and *they*. The pronoun *I* is always capitalized.

> **Summary** ♦ These pronouns are used in the subject of a sentence: *I*, *you*, *she*, *he*, *it*, *we*, and *they*. Use these pronouns to replace nouns that are the subjects of your sentences.

Guided Practice

Name the pronoun in each sentence.

1. We all enjoy the poems of Robert Frost.
2. He often wrote poems about the outdoors.
3. They describe many animals and plants.
4. Yesterday I visited Aunt Clara.
5. She owns several books of poems by Frost.

Practice

A. These sentences tell more about the poet Robert Frost. Write the sentences. Underline the pronoun in each sentence.

   6. We are studying the poetry of Robert Frost.
   7. He was one of the great American poets.
   8. You may have read some of Frost's poems.
   9. They have earned many awards.
 10. Yesterday I read a poem called ''The Pasture.''
 11. It was the first poem ever published by Frost.
 12. He describes a visit to a field in autumn.
 13. I borrowed a book of Frost's poems from Aunt Clara.
 14. She is president of the town poetry club.
 15. Next week we will learn about another great poet.

B. Write each sentence. Use a pronoun in place of the underlined word or words.

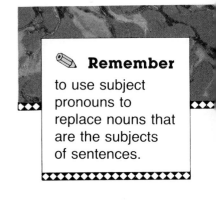

 16. Nature poets often write about the seasons.
 17. My sister has written poems about cold winter nights.
 18. My brother and I enjoy reading her poems.
 19. Jared prefers to write poems about spring.
 20. This poem is about a rainy April afternoon.
 21. Stacy's poems tell about beautiful sunsets in summer.
 22. Jared and Stacy like writing poetry.
 23. Mrs. Mason wants to present a display of poems.
 24. The exhibit will be placed in the school cafeteria.
 25. On Friday Mr. Romano will set up the display.
 26. Jared, Stacy, and I have offered to help.

Apply ♦ Think and Write

Creative Writing ♦ Pretend that you have just met a famous poet. Write sentences about the experience. Use a subject pronoun in some of your sentences.

> ✎ **Remember**
> to use subject pronouns to replace nouns that are the subjects of sentences.

◆ GETTING ◆ STARTED

Play "Whom Do You Know?" Make up sentences that follow this pattern: *I know her. She knows us. We know ____ .* Keep going until you run out of sentences.

3 Object Pronouns

You know that some pronouns are used in the subject of a sentence. You can use these pronouns to replace nouns in the predicate of a sentence: *me, you, him, her, it, us,* and *them.*

Read the sentences below. Notice the underlined words.

1. **a.** Mr. Gómez read <u>poems</u> to <u>Jill</u>.
   b. Mr. Gómez read <u>them</u> to <u>her</u>.
2. **a.** Diane asked <u>Ken</u> to read <u>a poem</u>.
   b. Diane asked <u>him</u> to read <u>it</u>.

In **1** the pronoun *them* replaces the noun *poems*. Also, the pronoun *her* takes the place of the noun *Jill*. Each of these pronouns replaces a noun in the predicate of a sentence. In **2** what pronoun replaces the noun *poem*? What noun does the pronoun *him* replace?

> **Summary** ◆ These pronouns are often used in the predicate of a sentence: *me, you, him, her, it, us,* and *them.*

Guided Practice

Name the pronoun in each sentence below.

1. Paul entertained us with some funny poems.
2. Paul read them out loud to the class.
3. The poem about penguins delighted me most.
4. Paul wrote it during a trip to the zoo.
5. The class thanked him for sharing the poems.
6. Did Paul tell you about the class trip?

Practice

A. Write each sentence. Underline the pronoun in the sentence.

7. The teacher asked us to write about an animal.
8. Snakes have always fascinated me.
9. Gary does not like them.
10. Mice and hamsters interest him.
11. Gary showed us a hamster named Hazel.
12. Gary wrote a delightful poem about her.
13. The class enjoyed it very much.
14. The next day Gary brought us a mouse.
15. Janet let it out of the cage.
16. Does a tiny mouse frighten you?

B. Write the sentences. Use a pronoun in place of the underlined word or words.

17. Penguins are unusual birds. Land and water are both comfortable places for penguins.
18. Penguins cannot fly. This information surprised Tony.
19. A penguin is an excellent swimmer. Flippers help the penguin swim in the water.
20. The teacher asked Maria to write a poem about penguins.
21. Maria will read the poem to David and me.

C. Write each sentence. Use pronouns to complete the sentences.

22. Grandpa gave ____ a pet gorilla.
23. Mom took ____ to the zoo.
24. The zookeeper handed ____ some bananas.
25. A friend wrote a poem about ____ .
26. Then the gorilla followed ____ home!

Apply ◆ Think and Write

Reacting to Animals ◆ Write sentences about a small animal that some people find frightening. Use a pronoun in the predicate of some of your sentences.

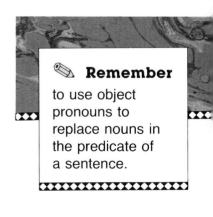

✎ **Remember**
to use object pronouns to replace nouns in the predicate of a sentence.

GETTING STARTED

Take turns asking questions like ''Whose books are these?'' or ''Whose house is that?'' Use a pronoun in each answer. (''These are her books.'' ''That is our house.'')

4 Possessive Pronouns

Read the sentences below. Notice the words in the boxes and the underlined words.

1. a. Mark's book contains some fantastic poetry.
   b. His cousin is reading some poems by Aileen Fisher.
2. a. Aileen Fisher's home is in the mountains.
   b. Her poems usually involve nature.

The words in the boxes are possessive nouns. They show that someone owns or has something. In sentence **1a** Mark has a book. In sentence **2a** Aileen Fisher has a home.

The underlined words are possessive pronouns. They stand for possessive nouns. Possessive pronouns also show ownership. In sentence **1b** the pronoun *his* shows that Mark has a cousin. What does the pronoun *her* in sentence **2b** show?

Remember the following possessive pronouns: *my, your, his, her, its, our,* and *their.*

> **Summary** ◆ A **possessive pronoun** shows ownership. Possessive pronouns can replace possessive nouns.

Guided Practice

Name the possessive pronoun in each sentence.

1. Where is my book of nature poems?
2. Its cover is green and brown.
3. Has your cousin seen the book?
4. The book was written by our favorite poet.
5. Her name is Aileen Fisher.

Practice

A. These sentences tell more about the poet Aileen Fisher. Find and write the possessive pronoun in each sentence.

6. Our class is studying the work of Aileen Fisher.
7. Many of her poems are written especially for children.
8. Fisher shares their sense of wonder about nature.
9. Her country house is the perfect setting for a poet.
10. Its windows provide a view of miles and miles of trees.
11. "Barefoot" is one of my favorite poems by Aileen Fisher.
12. In the poem, her yard is covered with soft clover and dandelions.
13. Friends are invited to kick off their shoes and play.
14. Imagine that your yard is filled with flowers!
15. Michael pictures bright yellow dandelions in his yard.

B. Write the sentences. Use possessive pronouns in place of the underlined words.

16. Two friends sat under a tree in <u>Pam's</u> yard.
17. <u>Pam and Joe's</u> bicycles were parked near the tree.
18. The friends saw a nest in <u>the tree's</u> branches.
19. <u>Tiny birds'</u> heads popped out of the nest.
20. <u>One bird's</u> wings flapped up and down.
21. Suddenly a smile appeared on <u>Joe's</u> face.
22. Joe said to Pam, "<u>Pam's</u> tree deserves a poem."
23. Pam said, "<u>Pam's</u> tree would like that very much."
24. Joe read <u>Joe's</u> poem about the tree.
25. Joe began, "This tree is <u>Pam and Joe's</u> friend."

Apply ♦ Think and Write

Dictionary of Knowledge ♦ Look up *dandelion* in the Dictionary of Knowledge. What does this yellow flower look like to you? Write some sentences describing dandelions. Use possessive pronouns in your sentences.

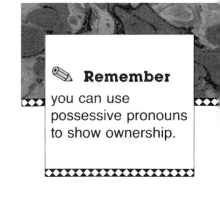

✎ **Remember**
you can use possessive pronouns to show ownership.

Pretend you are looking into a mirror. The person in the mirror is looking back at you. Make up sentences that tell what the two of you are doing. Use these pronouns: *I*, *me*, *we*, and *us*.

5 Using *I* and *me*, *we* and *us*

Read the sentences below.

1. Frank and I are writing some poems for school.
2. We wrote a poem about the stars.
3. The other students are helping Frank and me.
4. Ms. Thompson has given us much encouragement.

The subjects are underlined in sentences **1** and **2**. Notice the pronouns *I* and *we*. In sentences **3** and **4** the predicates are underlined. Notice the pronouns *me* and *us*.

To name yourself, use the pronoun *I* or *me*. When you name yourself along with someone else, always name yourself last.

Sometimes *we* or *us* is used before a noun. Read each sentence without the noun. Decide whether *we* or *us* is correct.

We boys worked on the poems together.
The teacher discussed the poems with us students.

> **Summary** ◆ Use *I* in the subject of a sentence and *me* in the predicate. Use *we* in the subject of a sentence and *us* in the predicate. Remember to use pronouns correctly when you speak and write.

Guided Practice

Name the correct word or words to complete each sentence.

1. My friend and (I, me) are writing a book of poems.
2. Mr. Reed helped (we girls, us girls) plan the book.
3. He talked with (Beth and I, Beth and me) yesterday.

Practice

A. Write each sentence. Use the correct word or words in parentheses ( ).

4. (Tina and I, Me and Tina) are fascinated by the stars.
5. (We, Us) girls used a telescope last night.
6. Mom helped (Tina and I, Tina and me) set it up in the backyard.
7. (Mom and I, Me and Mom) had waited for a clear night.
8. Dad explained to (we children, us children) that the stars are millions of miles away.
9. Mom showed (Tina and me, me and Tina) the Big Dipper.
10. (My family and I, Me and my family) will visit a planetarium soon.
11. The trip excites (Tina and I, Tina and me).
12. Dad told (we, us) that the stars have often inspired poets.
13. Later (me and my sister Tina, my sister Tina and I) wrote a poem about a star.
14. (We two girls, Us two girls) saved the poem.

B. Use *I* or *me* to complete each sentence. Write the sentence.

15. Tina and _____ visited a planetarium.
16. The guide showed _____ a model of the solar system.
17. He told Tina and _____ that the sun is actually a star.
18. Tina and _____ tried to imagine the sun shining at night.
19. Then _____ wrote a poem called ''Sunny Night.''
20. Tina asked _____ if she could read the poem.

Apply ♦ Think and Write

Pronoun Sentences ♦ Write some sentences about yourself and your best friend. Use the pronouns *I*, *me*, *we*, and *us*.

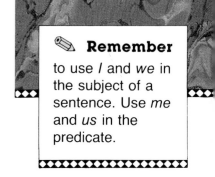

✎ **Remember**
to use *I* and *we* in the subject of a sentence. Use *me* and *us* in the predicate.

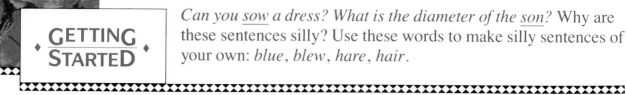

Can you <u>sow</u> a dress? What is the diameter of the <u>son</u>? Why are these sentences silly? Use these words to make silly sentences of your own: *blue*, *blew*, *hare*, *hair*.

VOCABULARY ♦
Homophones

Read the paragraph below. Notice the underlined words.

A <u>deer</u> took a bus to the <u>fair</u>. "Ten dollars," said the driver. "<u>Dear</u> me!" said the <u>deer</u>. "What a high <u>fare</u>!"

The underlined words are **homophones**. They sound alike, but they have different meanings. They are also spelled differently. The word *deer* names a four-legged forest animal. *Dear* is a word that expresses surprise or trouble. What is the difference in the meaning of *fair* and *fare*?

Be sure to spell homophones correctly when you write, or you may confuse readers.

Building Your Vocabulary

Name the homophones in the sentences below.

1. The wind blew clouds across the blue sky.
2. Do you use the right homophones when you write?
3. Which one of the runners won the race?
4. Would you count how much wood the woodchuck chucked?
5. Hal thought he heard a herd of reindeer on the roof.
6. Ned thought he knew when the zoo's new gnu would arrive.

Choose the correct homophone to complete each sentence below.

1. Snow White said, "Someday my (prints, prince) will come."
2. Bill's (bear, bare) legs were sunburned.
3. The seamstress said her work was just (sew-sew, so-so).

Think of some more homophones. What does each homophone you think of mean?

Practice

A. Make a list of all the pairs of homophones you find in this story.

The Tale of the Missing Hair

"Oh dear," said the deer to her friend, the hare. "You have two spots of hair missing from your tail. That bear over there also has some bare spots in his fur. In fact, he has eight bare spots. I asked him what they're due to. He replied, 'I don't know. Do you?' I told him that no, I didn't. But I thought it might have been something he ate."

A horse overheard this tale and said in a hoarse voice, "The main part of my mane is missing. I've also felt weak all week. I asked my mother if the weather might be the cause. She looked me in the eye and said, 'Son, it could be the sun, I suppose.' "

The wise old owl knew, of course. "Listen carefully," he said. "Your missing fur is caused by sap that drips from the tall yew tree. You stand under it for shade. When autumn comes in four weeks, new hair will grow back shortly." But the horse was sad because he wanted his mane to grow back longly!

B. Write pairs of homophones for the clues below.

ocean; to look at
before two; did not lose
to run away; tiny insect

LANGUAGE CORNER ◆ Word Histories

Here is a picture of an animal that is tall like a camel and spotted like a leopard. This animal was once called a *camelopard*. What is it called now?

How to Revise Sentences with Pronouns

You know that you can use pronouns instead of nouns in sentences. You can use pronouns instead of repeating the same noun too often. For example, read the sentences below.

1. Billy asked Billy's sister to plant flowers with Billy in Billy's and Billy's sister's yard.
2. Billy asked his sister to plant flowers with him in their yard.

The noun *Billy* is used five times in sentence **1**. Do you know anyone who talks or writes like that? Sentence **2** uses pronouns rather than repeating the noun *Billy* over and over. The pronouns make sentence **2** much easier to read and understand.

Pronouns can help make your writing easier to understand. Use pronouns to improve your writing.

The Grammar Game ◆ Replace each underlined word or group of words with a pronoun from the Pronoun Pool.

<u>Betsy and Laura</u> wrote
to <u>my classmates and me</u>
a gift for <u>Dad</u>
<u>my neighbor and I</u> laughed
borrowed <u>the book</u>
<u>Meg's</u> friend
<u>the boys' basketball team</u>
when <u>Abraham</u> leaves

PRONOUN POOL		
him	our	they
their	he	his
me	them	us
she	it	we
you	her	I

Working Together

Do activities **A** and **B** as a group. Use pronouns to help make your writing easier to read and understand.

A. Complete each sentence with names of two group members. Then rewrite the sentences using pronouns in place of the words in ( ).

1. ____ and ____ think that (____ and ____) look alike.
2. ____ and ____ will go to (____ 's) house.
3. Has anyone seen (____'s and ____'s) jackets?
4. (____ and I) can meet ____ this afternoon at the library.
5. ____ says (____) left the keys in (____'s) locker.

In Your Group

- Keep everyone on the subject.
- Take turns sharing ideas.
- Pay attention to each person's ideas.
- Agree or disagree in a pleasant way.

B. Rewrite the paragraph below, using pronouns instead of repeating the same nouns too often. Your group must agree that the new paragraph makes sense.

Mark still could not solve the mystery. Mark called Pam to see if Pam could help. Together Mark and Pam made a list of clues. The list was a short list. ''Mark and I need more help,'' Pam said. ''I think we should call the others right away. Tell the others to think hard or Pam, Mark, and the others won't finish on time!''

WRITERS' CORNER ◆ Fuzzy Sentences

Be careful not to replace too many nouns with pronouns in your writing. Sometimes replacing a noun with a pronoun can make sentences fuzzy, or unclear. In the fuzzy sentences below, can you tell who got on the bus?

FUZZY: Ken waved to Dan. Then he boarded the bus.
IMPROVED: Ken waved to Dan. Then Ken boarded the bus.

Read what you wrote for the Writer's Warm-up. Did you write any fuzzy sentences? If so, can you improve them?

LANDSCAPE WITH RAINBOW
painting by Robert Scott Duncanson
National Museum of American Art, Smithsonian Institution, Gift of Loernard Granoff.

USING LANGUAGE
TO
CREATE

=== **PART TWO** ===

Literature *Poetry*

A Reason for Writing Creating

CREATIVE
Writing

FINE ARTS ◆ Look at the painting at the left. Do you see the two people? What do you suppose they are doing there? Do you think one person is selling the land to the other? Do you think they are planning to build a house and barn? What do you think they are talking about? Write the conversation the two are having. Give them each a name, so they can speak to each other.

CREATIVE THINKING ♦
A Strategy for Creating

A CLUSTER MAP

Creating is making up or expressing something new. Poetry is one kind of creative writing. Poets often see things in new, fresh ways.

A comparison is a fresh way of seeing something. After this lesson you will read poems that make comparisons. Later you will write poems that make comparisons.

What is a comparison? A comparison is telling how one thing is like another thing. For example, you can make comparisons about dark gray clouds. What can you say they are like? How many things can you think of? Here is what a poet from India thought.

> The dark gray clouds,
> the great gray clouds,
> the black rolling clouds are elephants
> going down to the sea for water. . . .

Did you enjoy the poet's fresh idea about the clouds? How do you think the poet thought up this idea? How did you think up your ideas about clouds?

 ## Learning the Strategy

It can be fun to think up many ideas about one topic. For example, imagine that it's a rainy day and you are bored. You have one piece of paper. What can you do with it? Imagine that you just hit your first home run. Your big brother wants to hear all about it. How many details can you remember to let him know what it was like?

A cluster map can help you think up ideas. Here is a cluster map about things to do with a piece of paper. The topic is in the center circle. Ideas about the topic are in circles attached to the topic circle. When you think up ideas about a topic, you are *elaborating* on it. Can you elaborate on this topic? What ideas can you add?

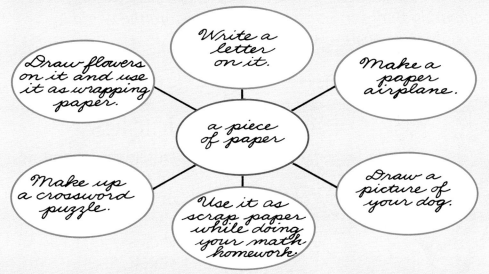

Using the Strategy

A. Imagine that you want to write a song about feeling happy. What things make you feel good? Elaborate on that topic. Make a cluster map to get ideas for your song.

B. Later you will read some poems. One is about an icicle. Others are about sparrow tracks, a moonlit hill, a tortoise, and a horse. Make a cluster map about one of these topics. Write everything that the topic reminds you of. Then read to find out what ideas the poet had.

Applying the Strategy

- How did your cluster map help you think up ideas about feeling happy?
- What is one time when you had to think up many ideas about something?

CREATIVE THINKING: Elaborating

LITERATURE

A poet once saw some hills and imagined they were sleeping dragons. Another once said the full moon looked like a big, round cheese. Poets are always surprising us with their fresh, new ways of seeing and comparing things in our world. Try to picture the world in a new way through these poets' eyes.

OAK TREE FROM THE AHWAHNEE TERRACE, YOSEMITE NATIONAL PARK, C. 1936
photograph by Ansel Adams

Icicles

Outside my window,
on the edge
of the roof,
icy-fingered
icicles
clutch
a row
of frozen
white fairy
stockings
hanging out
to dry.

—*J. S. Baird*

A lonely sparrow
Hops upon the snow and prints
Sets of maple leaves.

—*Kazue Mizumura*

Under a small, cold
winter moon, fields and hills gleam
bald and white as eggs.

—*Ransetsu*

THE STARK TREE, 1956
photograph by Wynn Bullock

The dark gray clouds,
the great gray clouds,
the black rolling clouds are elephants
going down to the sea for water.
They draw up the water in their trunks.
They march back again across the sky.
They spray the earth with the water,
and men say it is raining.

—*from India*

Although he never moves house,
the tortoise, like a removal van,
lurches down the road.

—*José Juan Tablada*

HORSE
photogravure by Frank Eugene

horse

In the stall's gloom,
His back, curved
Like a high sofa,
Turns on unseen
Legs, looms closer,
Until his long
Head forms above
The door, his face
Of thin silk over
Bone: to be stroked
Carefully, like
Fine upholstery
On a hard chair.

—*Valerie Worth*

Reader's Response

If you were going to learn one of these poems, which one
would you choose? Why?

Poetry

Responding to Literature

1. Kazue Mizumura compares a sparrow's footprints to maple leaves. What do a bird's footprints remind you of?

2. Choose the poem that paints a clear picture in your mind. Draw the picture that the poem suggests. Copy the poem and attach it to your picture. Show your picture and read the poem aloud to your classmates.

3. The poem from India says that clouds are elephants that make rain by spraying water from their trunks. Think about what else could cause rain. Make up a story about it.

Writing to Learn

Think and Elaborate ♦ One of the poets looked at a horse and saw other things. Choose another animal. Make a cluster map like this one. What does the animal remind you of?

Cluster Map

Write ♦ Write about your animal. You might want to write a short poem about it.

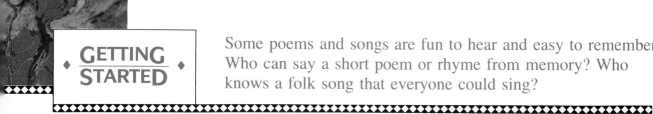

Some poems and songs are fun to hear and easy to remember. Who can say a short poem or rhyme from memory? Who knows a folk song that everyone could sing?

SPEAKING and LISTENING ◆
Reading Poetry Aloud

In many ways, poetry is like music. It has sounds and rhythms for us to hear.

Reading poetry aloud is the best way to hear and enjoy a poem's images and music. A reader's voice makes the poet's words come alive. To read poetry well, though, takes imagination and practice. Here are some helpful guidelines for becoming good readers and listeners.

Reading a Poem Aloud	1. Choose a poem that you enjoy reading. 2. Practice reading it aloud and following the poem's natural rhythm. As you read, look for complete thoughts. Pause briefly for commas and at the end of each verse. 3. Think about how your voice can add meaning to the poem. Ask yourself, Is this poem meant to be read quickly or slowly? Should I raise my voice here, or lower it there? 4. Picture the poem's images as you are speaking. 5. Speak in a clear, natural voice so your listeners can understand you.
Being an Active Listener	1. Imagine your own pictures for the poem. 2. Listen for the sounds and repeated words that help you remember the poem. 3. Picture yourself saying the poem, too.

Summary ◆ Be sure to choose a poem you like for reading aloud. Practice reading it for its rhythm, complete thoughts, and punctuation. Speak clearly, using your voice to add meaning to the words.

Guided Practice

Say each sentence twice. First say the words quickly. Then say them slowly. Which way fits the meaning of the words?

1. The quick brown fox leaped over the fence.
2. The huge old elephant walked proudly in the parade.
3. In a flash the storm flooded the streets.

Practice

A. Work with a partner. One person reads this poem quickly. The other reads it slowly and steadily. Which way fits its meaning better? Why?

> Although he never moves house,
> the tortoise, like a removal van,
> lurches down the road.
>
> — *José Juan Tablada*

B. You read the poem below on page 131. With your class, prepare a choral reading of it. Begin by talking about the word pictures in the poem. Look for complete thoughts. How can your voices add to the poem's meaning? How will you show its rhythm? Will you add music?

Group 1: The dark gray clouds,
Group 2: the great gray clouds,
Group 3: the black rolling clouds are elephants
   All: going down to the sea for water.
Group 1: They draw up the water in their trunks.
Group 2: They march back again across the sky.
Group 3: They spray the earth with water,
   All: and men say it is raining.

Apply ◆ Think and Write

Dictionary of Knowledge ◆ Read the article about choral reading in the Dictionary of Knowledge. How would you plan a choral reading of the poem in the article? Make some notes. Then tell others about your plan.

> ✎ **Remember**
> to use your voice to add meaning to the poems you read aloud.

◆ GETTING STARTED ◆

Do you remember the verse "Roses are red, Violets are blue"? Do you know the next two lines of this verse?

WRITING ◆
Quatrains

Poets often write poems in groups of four lines. A group of four lines of poetry is called a quatrain. Many quatrains have a pattern of rhyming sounds. Listen for the rhyming sounds in this poem.

Trip: San Francisco

I went to San Francisco. **A**

I saw the bridges high **B**

Spun across the water **C**

Like cobwebs in the sky. **B**

— Langston Hughes

There is a special way to show the rhyming patterns in poems. Each sound at the end of a line is given a letter name. The poem "Trip: San Francisco" has a rhyming pattern. In this quatrain the first line ends with *Francisco;* this end sound is called A. The next end sound, *high,* does not rhyme with *Francisco,* so it is called B. The third line ends with another word that does not rhyme, *water,* so it is called C. The fourth line ends with *sky,* which rhymes with *high*—sound B—so it is also called B. The pattern, then, is ABCB. This is the rhyming pattern most often used in a quatrain.

Other patterns are shown in the poems on page 137. Each poem has two quatrains, but they have very different rhyming patterns.

Notice the letter names at the end of each line of "Night Song." The poet has used the same word, *window,* to end the first line of each quatrain. In both quatrains the second and fourth lines end with rhyming words.

Use the letters A, B, C, and D to figure out the rhyming pattern of "Running Moon."

Night Song

Out of the **window** [A]
A yellow **balloon** [B]
Is caught in the **treetop** [C]
And looks like a **moon.** [B]

Into the **window** [A]
It smiles at **me** [D]
And asks me to lift **it** [E]
From out of the **tree.** [D]

— *Myra Cohn Livingston*

Running Moon

Sometimes when we drive out at **night**
I see a half moon, thin and **white.**
It runs beside us like a **hound,**
It's there whenever I turn **round.**

I say, "Good moon, come on, good **moon**!
It won't be long, we'll be home **soon,**"
And when we stop, there in the **sky**
The moon stands still, as still as **I.**

— *Elizabeth Coatsworth*

> **Summary** ♦ A **quatrain** is a group of four lines of poetry that may rhyme in different ways.

Responding to Poetry

1. When Langston Hughes visited San Francisco, he saw bridges spun like cobwebs. Tell about something you saw somewhere that reminded you of something else.

2. Two poets saw the moon in different ways—as a yellow balloon and as a running hound. Make a list of things that the moon looks like to you. Compare lists with a partner.

Apply ♦ Think and Write

Creative Writing ♦ Look at your list of different ways to see the moon. Choose your favorite idea. Then write the first line of a quatrain about it. Finish your poem if you wish.

> ✎ **Remember**
> that you can use different rhyming patterns when you write quatrains.

Focus on Similes and Metaphors

The poet Valerie Worth describes the back of a horse as "curved/*Like* a high sofa." The Japanese poet Ransetsu shows us fields and hills that "gleam/bald and white *as* eggs." Both poets are using a kind of comparison called a **simile**. A simile compares two unlike things by using the word *like* or *as*.

> **SIMILE:** The brook sparkled *like* a thousand diamonds.
> **SIMILE:** His reply was as cheery *as* morning sunshine.

Another kind of comparison is called a **metaphor**. A metaphor says that one thing *is* another. The poet J. S. Baird is using a metaphor when he says that icicles are icy fingers. Metaphors are much like similes, but without the *like* or *as*.

> **METAPHOR:** The trees were ghosts sighing in the darkness.

To what are black clouds compared in the metaphor on page 131? What are the sparrow's prints in the snow called on page 130?

The Writer's Voice ◆ Similes and metaphors are not just used in poetry. You will often see both used in fiction, too. Identify the similes and metaphors in these sentences.

1. His voice boomed like thunder.
2. At daybreak the fog was a gray blanket.
3. My sister is as restless as a caged leopard.
4. The highway below us was like a corkscrew.
5. Mayor Wiggins is a whirlwind of activity.

Working Together

Similes and metaphors are common in poetry. You will use them in other kinds of writing, too. Do activities **A** and **B** as a group.

A. Pretend that your group is a tiny insect—an ant, a fly, or a beetle, for instance. Decide what insect your group will be. Then discuss where you are—for example, on a leaf in the garden, on a window of a house. Take turns sharing what you imagine you are seeing from that spot. Keep a list of these ideas. Have each person choose something on the list to write a sentence about. The sentence should contain a simile or a metaphor.

B. Have one person read aloud the poem about clouds on page 131. Then, as a group, suggest other things that are like clouds. Keep a list. Each person then chooses one idea from the list and makes a drawing. This drawing illustrates the metaphor. Print at the top of the drawing "Clouds Are . . ."

In Your Group

- Encourage everyone to share ideas.
- Be sure people understand what to do.
- Record ideas on a list.
- Show appreciation for others' ideas.

THESAURUS CORNER ♦ Word Choice

Write the following sentences on paper. Look up the underlined words in the Thesaurus. Replace each underlined word with a synonym that fits the meaning of the sentence. Then use your imagination to complete each simile.

1. The road was as narrow as _____ .
2. The tree was as strong as _____ .
3. The sun walks across the sky like _____ .

Writing a Poem

What is a snowflake like? Ask three people this question. You will probably get three different answers. Every person has a unique vision, a different way of seeing things.

Poets often use comparisons to express their special visions. The poet Ransetsu says moonlit winter hills are as bald and white as eggs. To a poet from India, dark gray clouds are elephants. Similes and metaphors like these help us view things in fresh, new ways.

Know Your Purpose and Audience

MY PURPOSE

In this lesson you will write a poem. Your purpose will be to express your special vision of something. How? With comparisons—similes or metaphors.

MY AUDIENCE

Your audience will be an older friend or relative. Later, you can send your poem to that special person. You can also share your poems with classmates at a poetry fair.

1 Prewriting

First choose a topic for your poem. Then gather ideas.

Choose Your Topic ◆ With your classmates, play a game of similes and metaphors. Begin by completing the items below under "Topic Ideas."

Think About It

As you play the game, make your own list of comparisons that you might like to use in a poem. Which do you like best? Which seems like the freshest idea? Circle that one as your choice.

Talk About It

Play the game of similes and metaphors with your classmates. Try to think of as many different endings as you can for the starters below. Then offer new starters for other players to end. See how many you can list.

Topic Ideas

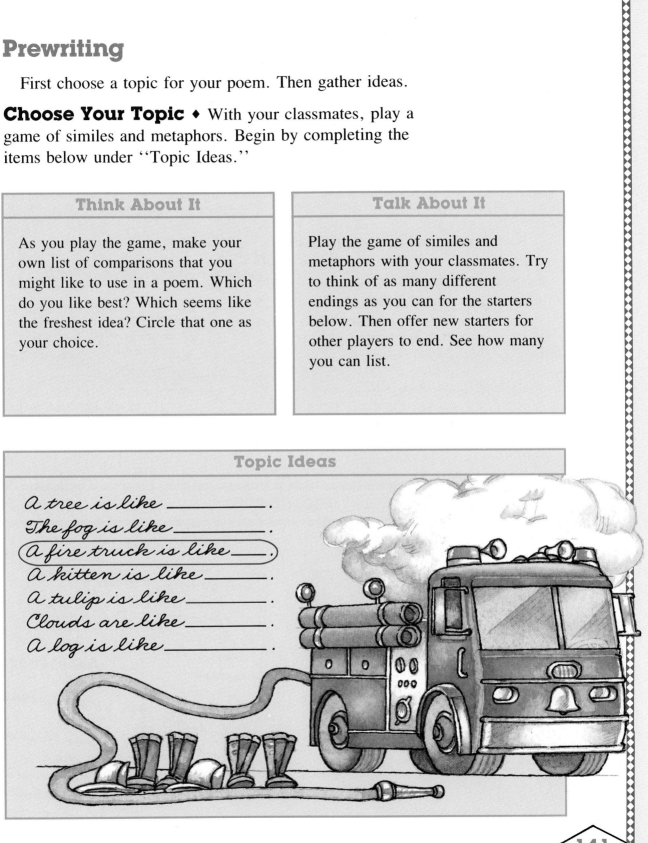

A tree is like _____ .
The fog is like _____ .
⟨A fire truck is like _____ .⟩
A kitten is like _____ .
A tulip is like _____ .
Clouds are like _____ .
A log is like _____ .

Choose Your Strategy ◆ Here are two strategies for gathering ideas for your poem. Read both. Then try the one you think will help you more.

PREWRITING IDEAS

CHOICE ONE

A Cluster Map

A cluster map can help you think of many comparisons. Write your topic in the center circle. What does your topic remind you of? Think of as many comparisons as you can. Write them in circles around the topic circle.

Model

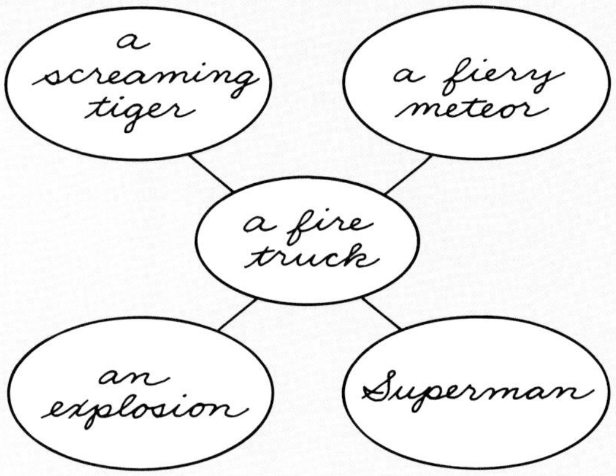

a screaming tiger

a fiery meteor

a fire truck

an explosion

Superman

CHOICE TWO

A Comparison Chart

A comparison chart can help you think of many ideas about one comparison. First decide what two things to compare. Then list details about how they are alike. Do they look alike? Sound alike? Smell alike? Taste alike? Feel alike? Do they act alike?

Model

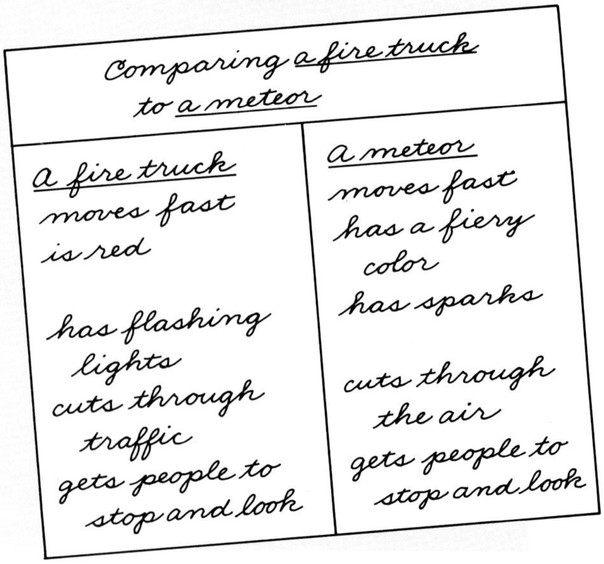

Comparing a fire truck to a meteor

a fire truck	a meteor
moves fast	moves fast
is red	has a fiery color
has flashing lights	has sparks
cuts through traffic	cuts through the air
gets people to stop and look	gets people to stop and look

2 **Writing**

How do you write a poem? Look back at the poems in this unit for ideas. Notice that a poem does not have to rhyme.

Your cluster map or comparison chart can help you write your poem. Look at the ideas you wrote down. Include similes or metaphors based on those ideas. Here are two sample beginnings:

◆ A fire truck is like a meteor.
◆ Look at that fire truck!

Sample First Draft ◆

A fire truck is a Meteor.
It pushes through trafick
like a Meteor through the air.
people stop to stare
at the fiery red streak.
The truck's lights are like sparks.

3 Revising

This idea may help you revise your poem.

REVISING IDEA

FIRST Read to Yourself

Think about your purpose. Did you write a poem that expresses your special vision of something? Think of your audience. Will an older friend or relative enjoy reading your poem? Which part do *you* like best—and why?

Focus: In your poem, did you compare one thing to another? Did you include similes or metaphors?

THEN Share with a Partner

Ask a partner to read your poem aloud. Listen carefully. These guidelines may help you.

The Writer

Guidelines: Listen to your poem. Do you like it the way it is? Do you want to make changes?

Sample questions:
- Can you tell what two things I am comparing?
- **Focus question:** Can you find a simile or a metaphor in my poem?

The Writer's Partner

Guidelines: Read the poem slowly and clearly. Give the writer helpful ideas.

Sample responses:
- The part I liked best was _____.
- Another way _____ and _____ are alike is _____.

Revising Model ◆ Here is a poem that is being revised. The marks show changes the writer wants to make.

The writer changed this metaphor to a simile.

Thrusts is a more vivid word than *pushes*.

The writer's partner said this would be a better ending.

The writer decided a possessive pronoun sounded better.

> ~~like~~
> A fire truck is ∧ a Meteor.
> ~~thrusts~~
> ~~It~~ pushes through trafick
>
> like a Meteor through the air.
>
> ⟨people stop to stare
>
> at the fiery red streak.⟩
> Its
> ~~The~~ truck's lights are like sparks.

Read the above poem with the writer's changes. Then revise your own poem.

Grammar Check ◆ Replacing some nouns with pronouns adds variety to your writing.

Word Choice ◆ Do you want to replace a word like *push* with a more vivid word? A thesaurus can help you find one.

Revising Checklist

☐ **My Purpose:** Did I write a poem? Did I express my special vision of something?

☐ **My Audience:** Will my older friend or relative enjoy reading my poem?

☐ **Focus:** Did I compare one thing to another? Did I include similes or metaphors?

4 Proofreading

Look for and fix mistakes in your poem. Your reader will appreciate your efforts.

Proofreading Model ◆ Here is the poem about a fire truck. Notice the proofreading changes in red.

Proofreading Marks

capital letter	═
small letter	/
check spelling	⬭

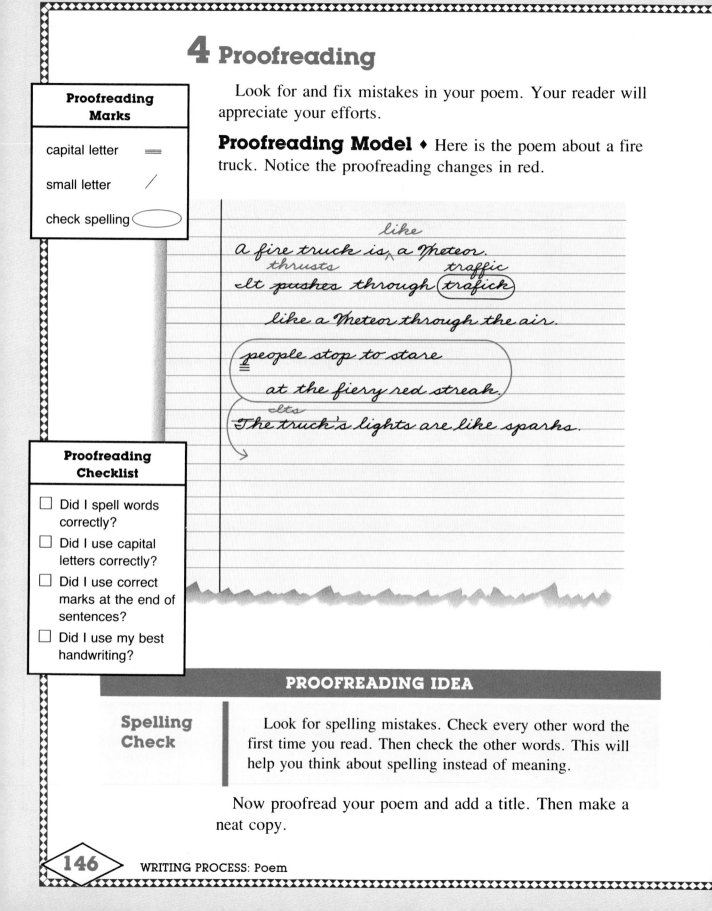

Proofreading Checklist

- ☐ Did I spell words correctly?
- ☐ Did I use capital letters correctly?
- ☐ Did I use correct marks at the end of sentences?
- ☐ Did I use my best handwriting?

PROOFREADING IDEA

Spelling Check

Look for spelling mistakes. Check every other word the first time you read. Then check the other words. This will help you think about spelling instead of meaning.

Now proofread your poem and add a title. Then make a neat copy.

5 Publishing

Here are some ideas for sharing your poem with others.

Red Streak

A fire truck is like a meteor.
It thrusts through traffic
like a meteor through the air.
Its lights are like sparks.
People stop to stare
at the fiery red streak.

PUBLISHING IDEAS

Share Aloud

Have a poetry fair with your classmates. Take turns reciting your poems for each other. Ask your audience to listen for similes and metaphors.

Share in Writing

Illustrate your poem. Write a friendly letter to your friend or relative. Explain that you wrote the poem in school. Send or give your letter and poem to that friend or relative. Perhaps this special person will let you know how he or she liked your poem.

CURRICULUM
◆CONNECTION◆

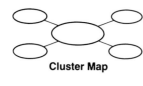

Writing Across the Curriculum   Music

Some people say that a song is "poetry set to music." In this unit you made a cluster map to get ideas for a poem. In the same way, you can get ideas for a song.

Writing to Learn

Think and Discover ◆ What could you write a song about? The photograph below may give you some ideas. Choose a topic for a song. Then make a cluster map of ideas about your topic. Let each idea suggest another and another.

Cluster Map

Write ◆ Use ideas from your cluster map to compose the words for a song. Add a title. You may want to make up a tune or use a familiar tune so you can sing your song.

Writing in Your Journal

In the Writer's Warm-up you expressed your feelings about nature. During the unit you read poems about nature. Look back at the poems in the unit. What new ideas about nature come to mind? In your journal write a few lines for a new poem about nature.

BOOKS TO ENJOY

◆ Read More About It

Words with Wrinkled Knees: Animal Poems *by Barbara Juster Esbensen*

From hummingbird to hippopotamus, a poet takes a look at animals. She has found fresh ways to describe a variety of familiar creatures.

My Song Is a Piece of Jade

by Toni de Gerez

The poems in this collection originally came from the ancient Toltecs of Mexico. You can read them in Spanish as well as English.

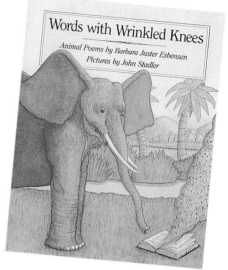

Words with Wrinkled Knees
Animal Poems by Barbara Juster Esbensen
Pictures by John Stadler

◆ Book Report Idea Word Painting

Explore the world of words to create a new kind of book report your classmates will enjoy.

Create a Word Painting

Think about the book you want to share. Make a list of words to describe what you like about it. Choose a nature topic, such as flowers, a rainbow, or a starry sky. Sprinkle your words throughout a nature scene, as though they are part of it. Don't forget to give the title and author.

tempting taste

stubborn stems

rosy

chorus of crunch

Flavors of Summer by Walter Leonard

shining

speckled skin

Unit 3

Pronouns   *pages 112–121*

A. Write each sentence. Use a subject pronoun in place of the underlined word or words.

1. Jessica and Barbara play the piano.
2. Sometimes Jim and I play duets.
3. Miranda often sings solos.
4. Emilio and Armand bought a set of drums.
5. Ken plays the violin.
6. The violin takes a lot of practice.

B. Write each sentence. Use an object pronoun in place of the underlined word or words.

7. Last summer Bonnie took Max on a trip.
8. Bonnie remembered the festival all year.
9. Some friends saw Max and Frank.
10. They walked over to see Susan.
11. Susan's mom put a blanket on the grass.
12. They shared lunch with Bonnie and me.
13. We listened to Susan and Max sing.

C. Write each sentence. Use a possessive pronoun in place of the underlined word or words.

14. Jack, may I borrow Jack's clippers?
15. I want to clip Tasha's and my dog.
16. Duchess's fur is getting very long.
17. Duchess ate Duke's lunch.
18. Did she eat Baron's and Fifi's lunch, too?
19. Duchess was frightened away by Baron's growl.
20. Duke, get Duke's leash.
21. Let's go to John's and my house.
22. Sue will bring Sue and Nick's dog.

D. Use the correct form of the pronoun in parentheses ( ). Write each sentence.

23. Betty and (I, me) went skating.
24. Carl brought skates for Betty and (I, me).
25. (We, Us) put on our skates.
26. I watched Betty and (he, him).
27. Then (she, her) and I raced.
28. (We, Us) girls skated very fast.
29. I showed Carl and (she, her) a trick.
30. Carl and (she, her) tried it.
31. Betty and (he, him) practiced for a long time.
32. Mom fixed lunch for (we, us) kids.
33. My friends and (I, me) were hungry.

Homophones   *pages 122–123*

E. Write each sentence. Use the correct homophone in parentheses ( ).

34. You can put the piano (here, hear).
35. The cats licked (their, there) paws.
36. Charlene (one, won) the foot race.
37. I felt too (week, weak) to get up.
38. We painted the (stares, stairs).
39. How much is the bus (fair, fare)?
40. How long did the king (rain, reign)?
41. Do you (know, no) our town's history?
42. I think I'll (write, right) a book of poems.
43. My great-grandmother (new, knew) a lot.

Poetry   *pages 138–139*

F. Write *simile* or *metaphor* for each description.

44. Her smile was a ray of hope.
45. The game was as slow as molasses.
46. The telephone ring sounds like a buzzer.
47. The rabbit stood like a statue.
48. The fox was a villain.
49. The breeze was like a soft mist.
50. The puddle was as deep as a wading pool.
51. The fog was a blanket of gray.
52. The cat tiptoed like a ballerina.
53. The boat's sails are soaring kites.

G. Choose a kind of transportation you know about. Complete each comparison. Ask your classmates to guess what you are.

54. I am as fast as ____.
55. I am bigger than a ____.
56. I am smaller than a ____.
57. My lights shine like ____.
58. My wheels are as large as ____.
59. I make a noise like a ____.

H. Write metaphors to complete these lines.

60. A summer day is ____.
61. The swimming hole is ____.
62. My dog is ____.
63. My wet hair is ____.
64. The log in the water is ____.

Proofreading

I. Proofread each sentence. Then write each sentence correctly.

65. Our schools library is full of books.
66. I've been talking to a Librarian.
67. She knows printing was invented by the Egyptian's.
68. The chinese were first to print paper.
69. They carved pictures on wood blocks
70. Next they put ingk on the surface.
71. then they pressed paper on top.
72. Pam and me did some carving.
73. I carved a scene showing two deers.

LANGUAGE PUZZLERS

Unit 3 Challenge

Hidden Pronouns

Find the eighteen different pronouns hidden in this puzzle. (Hint: Some pronouns may share letters with other pronouns.)

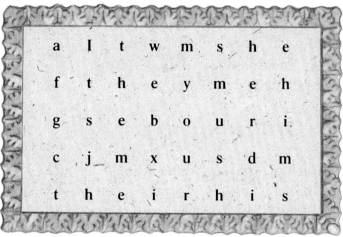

a	I	t	w	m	s	h	e
f	t	h	e	y	m	e	h
g	s	e	b	o	u	r	i
c	j	m	x	u	s	d	m
t	h	e	i	r	h	i	s

Which pronoun is hidden in five places? Which pronouns are hidden twice?

Tongue Twisters

Write a tongue twister for each item below.

EXAMPLE: (Ivan and I)

Ivan and I ice-skated idly in Iona, Idaho.

1. Mimi and me
2. we weavers
3. us umpires
4. Ida and I
5. Miguel, Michelle, and me
6. us unlucky uncles
7. we Wisconsin winners
8. Irene Ives and I
9. Mirabella Miller and me
10. my miniature mule and me

Ask a classmate to read your tongue twisters aloud quickly.

Unit 3 Extra Practice

1 Writing with Pronouns p. 112

A. Write each sentence. Underline each pronoun.

1. Shirley writes about puppet shows she has given.
2. Jonathan draws cartoons because he likes art.
3. They are working on a story together.
4. Mrs. Sanders told them to finish it this week.
5. We will print it in the next copy of *Wilton News*.
6. Jamie asked the principal if he could talk to her.
7. The principal told us that the children study hard.
8. I told her that Wilton School is tops with me.
9. She mentioned that students use the media center a great deal.
10. We will write a story about the media center next.
11. It has more films and tapes than most schools.
12. Films are interesting because they contain valuable information in an exciting form.
13. Of course, we learn from books, too.
14. You should come to visit the schools.

B. Write the pronoun in the second sentence. Then write the noun or nouns it replaces.

EXAMPLE: Mrs. Sanders is a writer. She writes well.
ANSWER: She, Mrs. Sanders

15. Mrs. Sanders teaches students about news stories. She started the paper.
16. *Wilton News* is six years old. It is a fine paper.
17. Writers try out every year. They write articles.
18. Jenny and I handle games. We write about all the games—from chess to field hockey.
19. Ning wrote most of the next paper. Ask him for details.
20. Mother reads the paper every week. She enjoys the news.

Practice ◆ Practice ◆ Practice ◆ Practice ◆ Practice ◆ Practice ◆ Practice

2 Subject Pronouns

p. 114

A. Write each sentence. Underline the pronoun.

1. We know all the people working at the hospital.
2. Often you can find Mr. Gurney in the kitchen.
3. Sometimes he helps fix the meals for the patients.
4. On Tuesday I met Alice Kelly in the waiting room.
5. She fills out the forms for new patients.
6. Last week I heard from my cousin Carol in Cleveland.
7. She has found a new job.
8. It is with the Safety and Health Department.
9. They need a person to inspect factories.
10. You can work in many different places.
11. We spoke to Carol's brother last night.
12. He was glad that Carol is working.
13. Once a month she tests the air in each factory.
14. It is a challenging job.
15. I know Carol can do the job well.

B. Write each sentence. Use a subject pronoun in place of the underlined word or words.

16. Bob repairs typewriters.
17. One daughter works with him.
18. These people have been doing this for years.
19. On Saturdays Stewart and I like to watch them work.
20. Often the job takes a great deal of skill.
21. Mona works in a restaurant.
22. The restaurant is owned by Mr. Nick Pappas.
23. Lynn and Mike wash the pots and dishes.
24. Manuel takes the orders.
25. Once in a while my mother and I like to go there.
26. Marge and Herb have chores to do every week.
27. Every night Herb takes out the garbage.
28. Marge has to weed the vegetable garden.
29. Marge cannot believe how fast the weeds grow!
30. The weeds are sometimes taller than the vegetables.

3 Object Pronouns

p. 116

A. Write each sentence. Underline the pronoun in the sentence.

1. Mrs. Pritsky asked us to introduce Carla.
2. The new student told us about winter in Alaska.
3. Carla showed us some photographs.
4. The pictures of polar bears interested me most.
5. Carla took them from a safe distance.
6. The whole class thanked her for the talk.
7. Erica gave me a book about arctic animals.
8. Nature helps them live in a very cold place.
9. A wolf's thick coat protects it from cold and wind.
10. An arctic fox can fool us.
11. The white fur hides it in the snow.
12. Pictures of a male musk-ox made us laugh.
13. Long hair covers him completely.
14. Arctic hares surprise me, too.
15. Pads on the hares' feet keep them warm.
16. Erica may lend you the book next.

B. Write each sentence. Use a pronoun in place of the underlined word or words.

17. Snow can bury people.
18. Skiers must watch out for a snowslide.
19. Janice told Ken and me about rescue work.
20. Mr. Cruz had given Janice lessons.
21. Specially trained dogs can save skiers.
22. Janice covers a doll with snow, just for practice.
23. The dog sniffs the snow to find the doll.
24. Then Janice helps the dog to dig faster.
25. The two workers pull the rag doll out.
26. This story amazed Edith.
27. Another story really surprised Edith and me.
28. Rescue workers found three people after a snowstorm.
29. A snow cave had protected the three from the cold.
30. The rescue workers brought first aid.

4 Possessive Pronouns

p. 118

A. Write each sentence. Underline the possessive pronoun.

1. Our breakfast is usually cereal.
2. Fill my cup with milk.
3. My shoes are tied.
4. The children will find their coats.
5. When will his father come?
6. Her parents will be here at noon.
7. Our office closes soon.
8. Her coat is green.
9. Which is your hat?
10. My Saturday afternoon is spent with Mrs. Day.
11. Mrs. Day needs help with her shopping.
12. Our friends walk dogs for sick people.
13. Everyone is grateful for their help.
14. One Saturday a puppy slipped out of its collar.
15. No one heard my call.
16. Cars beeped their horns at the runaway pup.
17. Is that your dog?
18. Martha is his dogwalker.
19. Your job is not an easy one.

B. Write the sentences below. Use possessive pronouns in place of the underlined words.

20. On Sunday the Young Helpers met at Jane's apartment.
21. The members' meeting lasted an hour.
22. Jake's brother had a suggestion to make.
23. He said that we can cook people's breakfasts.
24. We stored the food at David's apartment.
25. Mary and Jerry's parents drove us across town.
26. Mrs. Santini's dog barked wildly at the door.
27. The dog's bark didn't mean anything.
28. Jake put down Jake's shopping bag.
29. Mrs. Santini really enjoyed Mrs. Santini's hot meal.
30. Jane was pleased with Jane's work.

5 Using *I* and *me, we* and *us*   *p. 120*

A. Write each sentence. Use the correct form of the pronoun in parentheses ( ).

1. Our teacher is taking (we, us) to the museum.
2. The bus came early for (we, us) students.
3. Sally and (I, me) got on the bus.
4. Miss Turner told Sally and (I, me) to sit together.
5. (We, Us) singers began to sing.
6. Bob asked (we, us) whistlers to join in.
7. (My friends and I, I and my friends) were excited.
8. (Julia and I, Julia and me) like dinosaurs.
9. (We, Us) students went to the Hall of Dinosaurs.
10. The guide told (Jenny and I, Jenny and me) to think about life 65 to 225 million years ago.
11. (I and Marcus, Marcus and I) saw a film about the Age of Reptiles—the Mesozoic Era.
12. (We, Us) children learned that some dinosaurs are really closer to birds than to reptiles.
13. Marcus told (we, us) boys that the smallest dinosaur was the size of a chicken.
14. (My class and I, Me and my class) stood close enough to see the patches used for missing bones.
15. The huge frame of bone and metal towered over (the teacher and me, me and the teacher).
16. Scientists tell (we, us) students they are not sure why the dinosaurs died out.
17. (Nan and I, Nan and me) saw the fierce tyrannosaur.

B. Write each sentence. Use *I* or *me* to complete the sentence.

18. Tom and ____ saw a calendar made of fig-tree bark.
19. The guide told ____ about these calendars.
20. She showed Maria and ____ the Aztec Stone Calendar.
21. Sue and ____ said it was like a huge carved wheel.
22. Then ____ saw a small bone calendar of the moon.

Praying Mantis

UNIT FOUR

USING LANGUAGE TO
INFORM

════════════════ **PART ONE** ════════════════

Unit Theme   *Artists at Work*

Language Awareness   Verbs

════════════════ **PART TWO** ════════════════

Literature   *Are Those Animals Real? How Museums Prepare Wildlife Exhibits*
by Judy Cutchins and Ginny Johnston

A Reason for Writing   Informing

Writing
IN YOUR JOURNAL

WRITER'S WARM-UP ◆ What do you already know about the work artists do? Perhaps you have watched a painter or a jewelry maker. Don't forget that architects, dancers, photographers, and writers are artists, too. Artists work on different kinds of projects and use many materials. Maybe you have worked on some kinds of art projects yourself. Write in your journal about the work of artists.

Take turns acting out different kinds of artists at work. List all the actions that are guessed correctly.

1 Writing with Action Verbs

You have learned that every sentence has a subject and a predicate. The subject tells who or what the sentence is about. The predicate tells what the subject is or does. The predicate of each sentence below is in green.

Art **decorates our homes and our schools.**

A famous statue **stands on our town green.**

The art teacher **greeted the students.**

The students **painted beautiful pictures.**

Look at the underlined word in each predicate. This word is an action verb. It tells what action the subject does.

The verbs *decorates*, *stands*, *greeted*, and *painted* tell about actions we can see. Other action verbs tell about actions we can't see. Read the following examples.

■ Nina <u>enjoys</u> art class.   Joey <u>wanted</u> a new paintbrush.

Summary ◆ An **action verb** shows action. Action verbs tell what the subjects of your sentences do.

Guided Practice

Name the action verb in each sentence.

1. Henry weaves baskets for the craft show.
2. Our class painted a mural on the playground wall.
3. The chef decorated the cake with flowers.
4. The actress learned her lines for the play.
5. Marie sketches landmarks in the city.

Practice

A. Write the action verb in each sentence.

6. Artists practice their craft for years.
7. Photographers experiment with different light.
8. Some artists draw in pen and ink.
9. Actors attend skill-building classes.
10. Many dancers study ballet from childhood.
11. Writers improve their work through revision.

B. Write the sentences. Choose one of the action verbs below to complete each one. Use each verb only once.

used	enjoyed	amazed	displayed
stitched	lived	painted	showed

12. Grandma Moses greatly ____ painting.
13. As a child she ____ berries for color.
14. For many years she ____ pictures with yarn.
15. She ____ pictures of country scenes.
16. Some pictures ____ people collecting maple syrup.
17. Her wonderful paintings ____ an art collector.
18. Famous museums ____ her paintings.
19. Mrs. Moses ____ until the age of 101.

C. What steps do you follow when you paint a picture? Complete each sentence with an action verb.

20. I ____ about my painting.
21. I ____ my supplies.
22. Then I ____ to paint.
23. Next I ____ details.
24. Finally I ____ my painting.

b. Rendering of Grandma Moses from a photograph, Copyright © 1952 (renewed 1980), Grandma Moses Properties Co., New York.

Apply ◆ Think and Write

From Your Writing ◆ Read what you wrote for the Writer's Warm-up. List five action verbs that you used. Exchange lists with a partner. Use your partner's words in new sentences.

✎ **Remember**
that action verbs describe
what happens
to your subject.

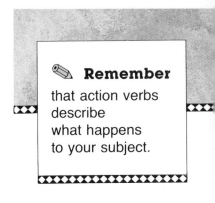

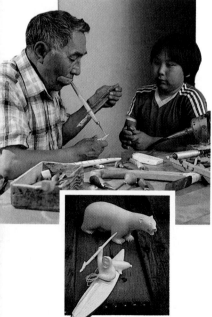

Look around your classroom. Describe how your classmates might be feeling by looking at their facial expressions.
For example:

Sara is happy.   *Tom is excited.*   *Luke and Bob are glad.*

2 Linking Verbs

You have learned about verbs that show action.

> **Grandma Moses** <u>painted</u> **country scenes.**
> **She** <u>used</u> **wood instead of canvas.**
> **The President** <u>congratulated</u> **her on her 100th birthday.**

Some verbs do not show action. Instead, they tell what the subject is or was. They are called linking verbs. In the sentences below the linking verbs are underlined.

> **Martha and William Noah** <u>are</u> **Eskimo artists.**
> **Their picture of a bison** <u>is</u> **beautiful.**
> **The bison** <u>was</u> **a rich chocolate-brown color.**

The forms of the verb *be* are shown below. These are often used as linking verbs.

am   is   are   was   were

> **Summary** ♦ A **linking verb** shows being. It tells what the subject is or was.

Guided Practice

The verb is underlined in each sentence below. Tell if it is an action verb or a linking verb.

1. Some Eskimo artists <u>use</u> stencils.
2. Bone and stones <u>are</u> good tools, too.
3. Soapstone sculpture <u>is</u> important to Canadian Eskimos.
4. The artists <u>carve</u> the stone into interesting shapes.
5. Ivory buttons <u>are</u> popular decorations on clothing.
6. Many Eskimos <u>make</u> ivory toys for children.

Practice

A. Write *action verb* or *linking verb* for the underlined word in each sentence.

7. Early artists <u>used</u> natural things to color their art.
8. Berries, ground leaves, and soil <u>were</u> common.
9. Today many kinds of paint <u>are</u> available.
10. Painting tools <u>are</u> different now, too.
11. Painters <u>work</u> with brushes and painting knives.
12. Watercolor painting <u>is</u> a popular art.
13. A good art store <u>carries</u> the necessary supplies.
14. A soft brush <u>is</u> best for watercolor painting.
15. Watercolor artists usually <u>paint</u> on paper.
16. Watercolors <u>dry</u> faster than other paints.

B. Write each sentence. Underline the verb. Write *action verb* or *linking verb* after each sentence.

17. A jeweler is another kind of artist.
18. Peter Fabergé was a jeweler and a goldsmith.
19. His jewels made him famous.
20. Fabergé created jeweled eggs.
21. His eggs were gifts for Russian royalty.
22. People collect these beautiful eggs today.
23. Rings, bracelets, and necklaces are all jewelry.
24. Jewelers design much gold jewelry.
25. Many women wear gold earrings.
26. Precious stones and gems are also popular.

PETER THE GREAT
Fabergé Egg, 1903
Virginia Museum of Fine Arts, Richmond

C. Write sentences of your own. Use these linking verbs.

27. were   **28.** am   **29.** is   **30.** was   **31.** are

Apply ♦ Think and Write

Information About Art ♦ Describe your favorite work of art. It can be a painting, sculpture, song, or piece of jewelry. Underline any linking verbs you use in your description.

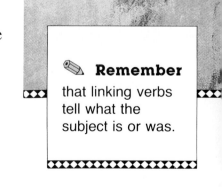

✎ **Remember**
that linking verbs tell what the subject is or was.

Pretend that you are looking at a piece of art, but you don't know what it is. Think of nice things to say to the artist. Use a linking verb in each sentence. You might start with, ''These lines are wonderfully crooked.''

3 Using Linking Verbs

Look at the underlined words in the sentences below. They are forms of the linking verb *be*. The form of *be* that is used depends on the subject of the sentence. The subject may be a singular noun, a plural noun, or a pronoun.

A sculptor is an artist.   His statues were marble.
Rodin was a sculptor.   The statues are impressive.

When the correct subject and verb are used together, we say they agree. Study the chart below.

Using the Forms of *be*		
Use *am* and *was*	with *I*	I am
Use *is* and *was*	with *she*, *he*, *it*, and singular nouns	He is The artist was
Use *are* and *were*	with *we*, *you*, *they*, and plural nouns	They are The statues were

NEWSPAPER READER
lifesize bronze sculpture by J. Seward Johnson

Summary ◆ When you speak and write, make sure that the form of *be* agrees with the sentence subject.

Guided Practice

Tell which form of the verb *be* agrees with the subject of each sentence. The subject is underlined.

1. Many Greek statues (was, were) stone.
2. Seward Johnson (is, am) an American sculptor.
3. This sculpture (are, is) bronze.
4. Those bowls (am, are) clay.

Practice

A. Write each sentence. Use the correct form of *be* in parentheses ( ).

5. I (am, is) interested in artists' tools.
6. Paintbrushes (was, were) pig hair at one time.
7. The sable brush (is, are) very soft.
8. One artist's tool (was, were) very valuable.
9. The diamond-edged drill (are, is) sharp.
10. An airbrush (is, am) useful for painting.
11. Some designers' tools (was, are) pencils and rulers.
12. Sharp stones (was, were) the tools of early artists.

B. Write each sentence. Use *is* or *are* to complete each one.

13. The palace ____ full of works of art.
14. This antique clock ____ charming.
15. The dining-room chairs ____ magnificent.
16. The table ____ fine wood.
17. The kitchen tiles ____ handpainted.
18. The design in the rug ____ unique.
19. The windows ____ stained glass.

C. Complete each sentence. Use a form of the linking verb *be* in each one.

20. That new building ____ .
21. Many school and office buildings ____ .
22. Solar homes ____ .
23. City Hall ____ .
24. A famous architect ____ .
25. The statues of the Presidents ____ .
26. The monument in the park ____ .

Apply ◆ Think and Write

Describing Your Art ◆ Write sentences describing a piece of your own artwork. Use a form of *be* in each sentence.

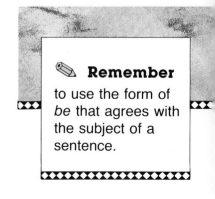

✎ **Remember**
to use the form of *be* that agrees with the subject of a sentence.

The secret design for a new cartoon character has been stolen!
Tell what you and other people were doing at the time of
Chipper Chipmunk's disappearance.
EXAMPLES: *The twins were napping. Meg was painting a picture.*

4 Main Verbs and Helping Verbs

Sometimes a verb is more than one word.

> Walt Disney <u>was trying</u> to become a filmmaker.
> He <u>had worked</u> hard to succeed.
> For many years people <u>have enjoyed</u> his films.

In each sentence above there is a main verb and a helping verb.
Trying, *worked*, and *enjoyed* are the main verbs. The **main
verb** is the most important verb. *Was*, *had*, and *have* are
helping verbs. A **helping verb** works with the main verb.

Using Helping Verbs	
When the helping verb is *am*, *is*, *are*, *was*, or *were*, the main verb ends in *-ing*.	The movie <u>is playing</u>. I <u>am walking</u> to the theater. My friends <u>are coming</u> too.
When the helping verb is *has*, *have*, or *had*, the main verb often ends in *-ed*.	The cartoonist <u>has finished</u>. The printers <u>have hurried</u>. They <u>had finished</u> the movie.

> **Summary** ◆ A **helping verb** works with the main verb.
> Forms of *be* and *have* are often used as helping verbs.

Guided Practice

The verbs are underlined in the sentences below. Tell whether
each word is a main verb or a helping verb.

1. Artists <u>are hired</u> in the film industry.
2. The filmmaker <u>is thinking</u> about a new cartoon character.
3. Experts <u>have selected</u> a horse to be the film's star.

Practice

A. Write each sentence. Draw one line under the main verb. Draw two lines under the helping verb.

4. The photographer was taking pictures.
5. He had watched all day for the right light.
6. The shadows were dancing on the leaves.
7. A small animal was crouching in the brush.
8. A tiny movement had attracted the photographer.
9. Bright eyes were glittering through the shadows.
10. The photographer has focused the camera.
11. Everything is standing still.
12. The animal has moved carefully into the open.
13. *Click!* He had waited weeks for this shot.

B. Write each sentence. Use the helping verb *is*, *are*, or *has* to complete each one.

14. The photographer ____ organizing the exhibit.
15. She ____ selected photographs from around the world.
16. Now she ____ arranging them in a display.
17. Visitors ____ coming to the museum.
18. Darryl ____ walked through the exhibit twice.

C. Complete each sentence. Use a main verb and a helping verb in each one.

19. This new camera ____ .
20. These photographs of the game ____ .
21. Sometimes the team ____ .
22. The action shots ____ .
23. The sports section of the paper ____ .

Apply ◆ Think and Write

Photos in Action ◆ Write some sentences telling about photographs of you in action. Use a main verb and a helping verb in each sentence.

✎ **Remember**
to use the correct helping verb with the main verb.

GETTING STARTED

Play "Simon Does, Did, Will Do."
EXAMPLE: *Simon buys brushes.*
Simon carried them home.
Simon will paint with watercolors.

5 Tenses of Verbs

The form of a verb shows when the action takes place.

■ 1. Greg <u>paints</u>.   2. Rosie <u>sketched</u>.   3. Irma <u>will carve</u>.

These sentences show action in different times, or tenses. In sentence **1** the verb *paints* is in the **present tense**. It shows action that happens now. In sentence **2** the verb *sketched* is in the **past tense**. It shows action that already happened. In sentence **3** the verb *will carve* is in the **future tense**. It shows action that will happen.

The past tense usually ends in *-ed*. The future tense is formed with the helping verb *will*. Study the chart.

Present Tense	Past Tense	Future Tense
Eli <u>shapes</u> tiles.	Nina <u>shaped</u> one.	Sam <u>will shape</u> one.
Ned <u>washes</u> brushes.	Kate <u>washed</u> pots.	Jo <u>will wash</u> a cup.
Nate <u>fires</u> tiles.	Lee <u>fired</u> a vase.	Ann <u>will fire</u> a pot.

Summary ◆ The **tense** of a verb shows the time of the action. When you write a paragraph or story, the verbs should usually be in the same tense.

Guided Practice

Tell the tense of each underlined verb below.

1. Our clay tiles <u>look</u> colorful.
2. We <u>arranged</u> them in a pattern.
3. Next we <u>will make</u> a mural.
4. Jack <u>spreads</u> cement.
5. Em <u>placed</u> the tiles.
6. We <u>will watch</u>.

Practice

A. Write each verb. Then write *present*, *past*, or *future* after each one.

7. We learn about colors in art class.

8. We mixed the primary colors together last week.

9. The mixture created three different colors.

10. We will experiment with other combinations next week.

11. Perhaps we will discover a brand-new color.

B. Choose the future-tense verb from the parentheses ( ) to complete each sentence. Write the sentences.

12. Next week we ____ how to make stained glass. (will learn, learned)

13. We ____ with colored paper. (practice, will practice)

14. Then the art teacher ____ us how to cut glass. (shows, will show)

15. We ____ foil around the edges of the glass. (will wrap, wrapped)

16. The sunlight ____ through the glass. (will shine, shines)

C. Rewrite the paragraph below. Use the past-tense form of each verb in parentheses ( ).

Our class (**17.** learns) about Chinese customs. We (**18.** celebrate) the Chinese New Year. We (**19.** design) costumes for the parade. Some students (**20.** use) colored paper for a dragon costume. It (**21.** looks) very fierce. Our parents (**22.** watch) the parade. They (**23.** cheer) when the dragon (**24.** passes) them. Firecrackers (**25.** boom.) Everyone (**26.** enjoys) the celebration.

Apply ✦ Think and Write

Costume Information ✦ Describe a costume you might design for a parade. Write a paragraph about it. Use the same tense for all of the verbs in your paragraph.

✎ **Remember**
that you can use forms of verbs to show when things happened.

If you went on a camera safari, what are some of the things you would try to do or see? In your answers, use verbs that end in *y*. For example: *carry, try, hurry, dry*.

6 Spelling Verbs Correctly

Mark helped set up a display at the Museum of Natural History. He wrote about it in his journal. Notice how he spelled the underlined words.

We <u>studied</u> films of kangaroos. We <u>tried</u> to remember how they looked. Some <u>hopped</u> in great leaps. Young ones <u>crammed</u> themselves into the mother's pouch. The display <u>copies</u> the natural setting of kangaroos.

Some verbs end in a consonant and *y*. Change the *y* to *i* before adding *-es* or *-ed*.

stud<u>y</u>	stud<u>ies</u>	stud<u>ied</u>
tr<u>y</u>	tr<u>ies</u>	tr<u>ied</u>

Some verbs end in one vowel and one consonant. Double the final consonant before adding *-ed*.

■ ho<u>p</u> ho<u>pped</u> cra<u>m</u> cra<u>mmed</u>

> **Summary** ◆ The spelling of some verbs changes when *-es* or *-ed* is added. Remember these spelling changes when you write.

Guided Practice

Read each sentence. Spell the past-tense form of the verb in parentheses ( ).

1. We (plan) the kangaroo display.
2. I (copy) the plan.
3. We (hurry) to finish our drawings.
4. I (hum) as I painted the background scene.

Practice

A. Write the past-tense form of each verb.

    5. apply   **10.** trap

    6. grab   **11.** bury

    7. rely   **12.** tug

    8. chop   **13.** satisfy

    9. marry   **14.** stir

B. Write the *-es* present-tense form of each verb.

    15. steady   **20.** vary

    16. fry   **21.** worry

    17. hurry   **22.** rally

    18. copy   **23.** multiply

    19. reply   **24.** pity

C. Use the past-tense form of the verbs below to complete the sentences.

    cry   **throb**   **slip**   **study**   **scurry**

    25. The wildlife artist ____ through the jungle.

    26. Her heart ____ with tension.

    27. A monkey ____ a warning to other animals.

    28. Many animals ____ through the brush.

    29. The artist ____ the scene around her.

D. Write sentences of your own. Use the past-tense form of the verbs below.

    30. carry   **31.** empty   **32.** rap   **33.** wrap

Apply ♦ Think and Write

Dictionary of Knowledge ♦ Read about Rachel Carson in the Dictionary of Knowledge. Pretend that you have set up a display based upon her work. Write some sentences telling about your display. Use past-tense verbs in your sentences.

✎ **Remember**

to check your spelling of forms of verbs.

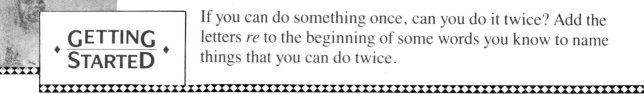

If you can do something once, can you do it twice? Add the letters *re* to the beginning of some words you know to name things that you can do twice.

VOCABULARY ♦
Prefixes

Read these "addition problems."

■ re + build = rebuild   dis + agree = disagree
                   un + likely = unlikely

The words *build*, *agree*, and *likely* are base words. A **base word** is the simplest form of a word. The word parts *re-*, *dis-*, and *un-* are prefixes. A **prefix** is a letter or letters added to the beginning of a word. A prefix changes the meaning of a word.

Study the prefixes in the chart below.

Prefix	Meaning	Example
dis-	not, opposite of	displease
un-	not, opposite of	uneven
re-	again, back	refill

Building Your Vocabulary

Change the sentences below by adding prefixes to *happy* and *kind*. Form words that can replace the underlined words.

Hal was happy, but Sarah was sad.
Cora was kind, but Casey was cruel.

Change the sentences below. Add *dis-* to the underlined words. Notice how the meanings change.

That was a very honest report.
Remember to connect the TV set.
The magician suddenly appeared.

Practice

A. Make good safety sense. Add the prefix *un-* or *dis-* to the underlined word to change the meaning of each sentence.

1. Never <u>obey</u> traffic lights.
2. It's <u>safe</u> to ride a bike at night.
3. It's <u>wise</u> to cross in the middle of a busy street.
4. It's <u>sound</u> advice to ride two on a bike.
5. We <u>approve</u> of people who break traffic rules.

B. Write the meaning that completes each sentence.

6. If *place* means "to put down," <u>replace</u> means _____.
7. If *afraid* means "frightened," <u>unafraid</u> means _____.
8. If *fuel* means "to put fuel in," <u>refuel</u> means _____.
9. If *load* means to "to fill," <u>unload</u> means _____.
10. If *like* means "to feel good about," <u>dislike</u> means _____.
11. If *cover* means "to hide," <u>discover</u> means _____.
12. If *equal* means "the same," <u>unequal</u> means _____.

C. 13–18. Form six new words by adding *re-* and *un-* to *pack*, *fold*, and *used*. Write a sentence for each word you form.

LANGUAGE CORNER • Borrowed Words

Did you know that you can speak many languages? The word *judo* comes from Japanese. *Potato* comes from Spanish. *Pizza* comes from Italian. Find out where the words below came from:

kindergarten
(Hint: *Sauerkraut* comes from this country.)

shampoo
(Hint: New Delhi is the capital of this country.)

How to Revise Sentences with Verbs

You have been working with verbs and learning how to use them in sentences. Verbs are important to your writing. Choosing exact verbs can give specific information to your readers. Read the sentences below. How does replacing the verb change the information in these sentences?

1. Josh broke the glass pitcher.
2. Josh smashed the glass pitcher.
3. Josh chipped the glass pitcher.

Notice that using a different verb in each sentence gives a very different picture of what happened. Which sentence might make you think that Josh was angry? Which sentence gives the idea that perhaps the pitcher can be fixed?

Use exact verbs in your writing to give readers the information they need. Exact verbs will also make your writing more interesting to read.

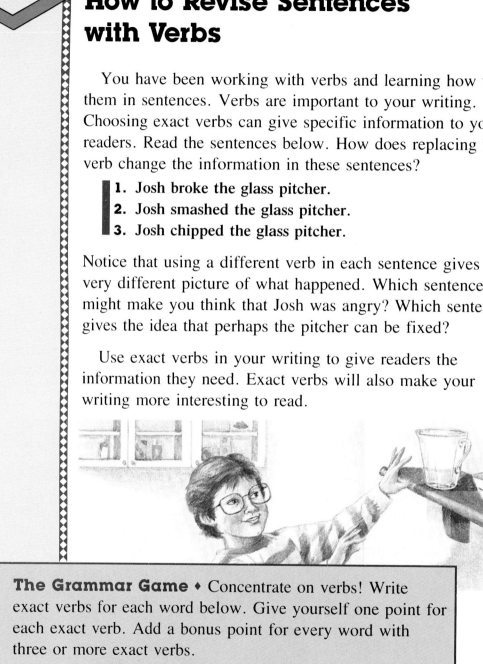

The Grammar Game ♦ Concentrate on verbs! Write exact verbs for each word below. Give yourself one point for each exact verb. Add a bonus point for every word with three or more exact verbs.

take   clean   ride   tell   sleep

Working Together

See how exact verbs can give specific information. Work with your group on activities **A** and **B**.

A. Everyone has different talents. Complete the sentences below with names of group members or classmates. Then rewrite the sentences, using exact verbs to replace each underlined word.

    1. ___ <u>makes</u> beautiful paper flowers.
    2. Our teacher <u>laughs</u> at ___'s funny jokes.
    3. Our class always <u>likes</u> poems written by ___ .
    4. We clapped when ___ <u>threw</u> the first ball.
    5. Everyone <u>eats</u> ___'s baked treats with pleasure.

B. Add a verb to complete each familiar sign. Then create new ones by using different verbs of the group's choice. How many different signs can you make?

    6. Please do not ___ the animals.
    7. Wet Paint! Do not ___ .
    8. ___ off the grass!
    9. Fragile! ___ with care.
    10. Slippery when wet. ___ with caution.

In Your Group

- Let everyone share ideas.
- Look at others when they are speaking.
- Use people's names during discussion.
- Record everyone's ideas.

WRITERS' CORNER ◆ Overused Verbs

Only you can prevent boring sentences. You can prevent them by not overusing, or repeating, the same verbs too often.

OVERUSED: Gina goes to soccer practice on her bicycle. She goes to the warm-up before going to the field.

IMPROVED: Gina rides to soccer practice on her bicycle. She attends the warm-up before arriving at the field.

Read what you wrote for the Writer's Warm-up. Did you use any verbs too often? Can you replace some with more exact verbs?

DEADLINE
*painting by Norman Rockwell
printed by permission of the Estate of Norman Rockwell
copyright 1938 Estate of Norman Rockwell
Photograph courtesy Saturday Evening Post Society.*

UNIT FOUR

USING LANGUAGE TO
INFORM

=== PART TWO ===

Literature *Are Those Animals Real? How Museums Prepare Wildlife Exhibits*
by Judy Cutchins and Ginny Johnston

A Reason for Writing Informing

CREATIVE *Writing*

FINE ARTS ◆ Norman Rockwell painted pictures for the covers of *The Saturday Evening Post* for many years. This painting shows a self-portrait of Mr. Rockwell doing what he does best. What do you do best? Do you draw or cook or play a sport? Write a letter to Norman Rockwell. Tell him what you do best. You might want to include a drawing of yourself doing what you do best.

CRITICAL THINKING ◆
A Strategy for Informing

AN OBSERVATION CHART

One reason for writing is to give information. After this lesson you will read part of *Are Those Animals Real?* It is an informative article. It tells how an artist builds giant insects for a museum. Later you will write an informative article to explain how to do something.

Here is part of *Are Those Animals Real?* Notice how the writers give details to help us "see" how the artist worked.

> Before the artist began to make the model he studied the praying mantis carefully. He took photographs and made sketches. . . . The artist decided to make the head of soft clay. A layer of liquid rubber was painted over the soft clay head. After it dried, the stretchy rubber mold was cut and peeled from the clay head. Liquid plastic was poured into the rubber mold to make the clear plastic head. . . .

Observing, or noticing, details can be important. To make his model, the artist had to observe the praying mantis. To write the book, the writers had to observe the artist.

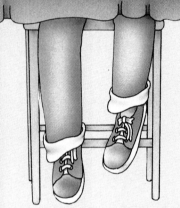

Learning the Strategy

You may often need to observe details. Suppose you want to give a friend directions to your house. What details might help your friend find the way? Suppose you are writing to a pen pal. What details might you describe about your school?

An observation chart can help you keep track of details you want to remember. For example, think about writing a letter to a pen pal describing your gym class. To help you write the letter, you might prepare a chart like this.

Gym Class	
What I See	floor mats, balls, volleyball net, ropes, balance beams
What I Hear	music, shouting, laughing, balls bouncing, whistles
What I Feel	smooth volleyball, rough climbing ropes, hands stinging, sweat tickling my back

Using the Strategy

A. Pretend a creature from another planet visits your class. The creature picks up your pencil. The creature observes the pencil and asks many questions about it. Write an observation chart for the creature. The topic will be "A Pencil." Some of the subtopics might be "What It Looks Like" and "What Humans Do with It." Write as many details as you can.

B. You are going to read about an artist who makes insect models. Before you read, observe a real insect or a picture of one. Then make an observation chart. Some of your subtopics might be "Color," "Size," and "Legs." As you read *Are Those Animals Real?*, notice what kinds of details the artist observes.

Applying the Strategy

+ What additional subtopics might you add to your chart about an insect? How would you decide?
+ When might you want or need to observe details?

from

Are Those Animals REAL?

How Museums Prepare Wildlife Exhibits

by Judy Cutchins and Ginny Johnston

Outside his workshop window, an artist had been watching a fascinating insect—a praying mantis. It lived in a little bush and spent most of the day sitting quietly with its sharply hooked front feet raised and folded.

The artist thought that the praying mantis would make a wonderful exhibit for the museum. But it would be hard for visitors to see because the real insect was just too small for an exhibit. The praying mantis was only three inches long. The artist wanted to make a giant praying mantis many times larger than life. It would be 25 times larger than the real insect. The model would be six feet long!

Before the artist began to make the model he studied the praying mantis carefully. He took photographs and made sketches from different angles. Then, in the workshop, the hard part of the job began. What could be used to build such a creature? The artist decided to make the head of soft clay. A layer of liquid rubber was painted over the soft clay head. After it dried, the stretchy rubber mold was cut and peeled from the clay head. Liquid plastic was poured into the rubber mold to make the clear plastic head that would be used in the exhibit.

Next, the body and legs were carved from a lightweight foam material. Thin metal rods were pushed into each leg to make the giant mantis strong. The rods also allowed the artist to bend the legs a little for the final shape.

The wings were the biggest challenge of all. After cutting the shape from clear plastic sheeting, the artist built up each vein by squeezing tile cement out of a catsup dispenser. This took over four hours.

Finally, the body was put together and coated all over with a special liquid that hardens and dries clear. Then the artist painted the model with oil paints to match the colors of the real praying mantis.

After weeks of work, the giant insect was finished and ready to display.

Museums all over the world exhibit larger-than-life animals—from grasshoppers to spiders to microscopic pond life.

Like the museum artist, you can make an interesting creature for a classroom exhibit. Just use your imagination and follow these simple directions.

How to Make a Leaf Creature

You will need
pencil * paper * white glue   eight-inch by ten-inch posterboard   objects from nature, such as leaves, twigs, berries, nuts, and seeds.   (A variety of objects with different colors and textures will help make your creature more interesting.)

The first step in making a leaf creature is to decide how you want your creature to look. Make a sketch. Be creative! There are many possible ways to combine the objects you have gathered.

Next, arrange the leaves, twigs, and other objects on the posterboard to form your creature. When everything is in place, glue the objects down. It takes only a little bit of glue, so be careful not to use too much. Be sure to let the glue dry thoroughly.

Last, label your new creature. Then hang it up for others to see.

Library Link ♦ *Books that tell how to make other fascinating creatures are available at your local library.*

Reader's Response

What insect would you choose for a larger-than-life museum exhibit? Why?

Are Those Animals REAL?

Responding to Literature

1. Make a drawing of an imaginary insect. Then show your new creature to your classmates. Tell them one surprising thing that it is able to do.

2. What are the advantages and disadvantages of studying insects by using larger-than-life models?

3. What do insects do? List as many words as you can to tell what insects do. You might start with the word *buzz*.

Writing to Learn

Think and Observe ◆ The artist observed the insect before he made the model. What do you know that you can observe? Copy the chart below. Then observe an animal, a busy street, or something you find interesting. Fill your chart with details.

(name your subject here)	
What I See	
What I Hear	
What I Feel	

Observation Chart

Write ◆ Write about what you observed. Include the details from your chart.

Choose an "Art Director" to draw a funny face. This person then tells the class how to draw the face without showing his or her drawing. When everyone has finished, compare drawings.

SPEAKING and LISTENING ◆
Directions

Often you need to tell others how to do something. Perhaps you play soccer and your friend wants to learn the game. Perhaps you grow flowers and your neighbor wants to learn how to grow them, too. Remember that you are the expert. Your listener is learning. Do not be shy about telling every little detail. Your listener will be glad you did.

Knowing how to give and how to follow directions are skills you use often. It takes skill to give directions that are easy to follow. In the same way, it takes skill to understand, remember, and follow directions you hear. These skills can be practiced. They can be improved.

How to Give Clear Directions	1. Look at your listeners and speak clearly. 2. Keep directions simple, and give all the steps in order. Use words like *first, second, next,* and *last* to show the correct order. 3. Are any materials needed? If so, tell what they are. 4. Explain any special terms you use. 5. Ask if there are any questions.
How to Listen to Directions	1. Listen to remember the directions in order. 2. Picture each step in your mind. 3. Repeat the directions to yourself. 4. Ask questions if you are not sure of something.

Summary ◆ When you give directions, explain completely and give the steps in order. When you listen to directions, picture the steps and repeat them to yourself.

Guided Practice

Below are directions for making a colorful sketch. Say them in order. Tell what words helped you figure out the order of the directions.

1. Then take a dark crayon. Black is best. Crayon heavily over the other colors.
2. First, get crayons, drawing paper, and something to use to scratch a design, such as a comb or fork.
3. Last, scratch a design. Your scratch lines will be in beautiful colors.
4. Second, color all over the paper with bright colors.

Practice

A. Read the directions in the **Guided Practice** to a partner. Read the directions in order, and ask your partner to pretend to follow them.

B. With a partner, take turns giving and following directions. For example, you could explain how to draw an ostrich, how to find a certain word in a dictionary, or how to make a poster. Ask your partner to follow your directions exactly, doing <u>only</u> what you say. This way, you will find out if your directions are clear and complete.

Apply ◆ Think and Write

Writing Directions ◆ Follow the directions in the **Guided Practice** and color over a piece of paper. Instead of scratching a design, though, scratch words. You could write a message to yourself, a rhyme, a riddle, a slogan, or a joke—whatever you like. (Be careful not to tear the paper when you scratch.)

✎ **Remember**
to give all the steps in order when you give directions.

◆ GETTING ◆
STARTED

Take turns giving directions for doing something simple, such as making a sandwich. Leave out one step. For example, do not say, "Put the second slice of bread on top of the filling."

WRITING ◆
Details That Give Information

In Unit 2 you learned that a paragraph is a group of sentences that tell about one main idea. You know that the topic sentence of a paragraph states the main idea. The other sentences in the paragraph give details that tell more about the topic sentence.

The sentences below are part of a paragraph from *Are Those Animals Real?* Notice the details the writer used to tell about the materials that were needed to build a giant praying mantis.

> The artist decided to make the head of soft clay. A layer of liquid rubber was painted over the soft clay head. After it dried, the stretchy rubber mold was cut and peeled from the clay head.

Details are small things, but they make a big difference. They are not only useful, but necessary. They bring your writing into focus. With each detail the picture becomes clearer. Details help your reader picture the action.

When you are writing directions or instructions, you need to give your reader complete information. Important details, even small ones, cannot be left out. Imagine directions for making egg salad that did not include this detail: *You must hard-boil the eggs!*

> **Summary** ◆ Writers use details to help the reader picture exactly what they are explaining. When you write to give information, be sure to include all the important details.

Guided Practice

Read these directions. Tell the details you would add to make the directions clear and complete. Which detail is not needed?

<u>How to Ride a Bicycle</u>

Sit on the bicycle seat. Make the wheels go around. Hum or whistle a tune to yourself. Ride down the street.

Practice

A. Read the paragraph that explains how to set an alarm clock. Then write <u>only</u> the directions that are clear and complete.

To set an alarm clock, first be sure the clock is giving the correct time. Wipe off any fingerprints or smudges you find on it. Then find the stem on the back of the clock that is used to set the alarm. Decide if you like the color of the stem. Pull out the stem, and look at the alarm hand on the front of the clock as you turn the stem. Stop turning when the alarm hand reaches the time you want. Wish that you didn't have to get up so early. Leave the stem out so the alarm will ring at the set time.

B. Write this paragraph that gives information about a school assembly. Complete it by adding detail sentences that answer the questions in parentheses.

Come to the assembly on Wednesday, the sixth of January. (What time will it begin?) (Where will it be held?) This should be an exciting assembly. We will see a demonstration of origami, the Japanese art of paper sculpture. (Who will the speaker be?)

Apply ◆ Think and Write

Dictionary of Knowledge ◆ Read the article about origami. Write a paragraph that gives information about this Japanese art. Use details to paint a clear word picture.

Courtesy of Wheaton Village, Millville, New Jersey

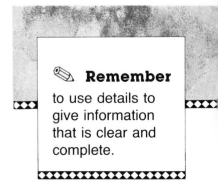

✎ **Remember**
to use details to give information that is clear and complete.

◆ GETTING ◆
STARTED

Think of a secret person, place, or thing. Others try guessing
your secret by asking questions that can be answered *yes* or *no*.
Max's question: *Is it an animal, Lucia?*
Lucia's answer: *No, it is not an animal, Max.*

WRITING ◆
Using Commas

A comma (,) is a signal that tells a reader to pause. Notice
the commas in the sentences below.

Isaac, did you see the Eskimo art at the library?
Yes, I especially liked the tiny seals.
Well, my favorites were the bears made of silver.
No, I don't think there were any silver pieces.
You might be right, Isaac.

In the sentences below, commas are used to separate words
in a series. A series is made up of three or more items. No
comma is used after the last word in the series. The last
comma goes before the word *and*.

The artists carve, smooth, and polish their work.
Students, teachers, parents, and friends see the display.

Summary ◆ Use a **comma** after *yes, no,* or *well* at the
beginning of a sentence. Use a comma to set off the
name of a person spoken to. Use a comma to separate
words in a series.

Guided Practice

Tell where commas belong in each sentence below.

1. Helen did Eskimo artists work all year long?
2. No they did most of the art work in winter Polly.
3. Storms ice and wind kept them inside.
4. They worked on tools ornaments and weapons.
5. We have looked listened and learned a lot today!

Practice

A. Write each sentence below. Add commas where they are needed.

6. Mr. Quinn where did Eskimo artists get supplies?
7. Well they used what they had around them.
8. They might use bone leather ivory stone and wood.
9. Most art works were quite small Steven.
10. Buttons combs and handles were art projects.
11. Many artists chose a certain animal for luck Maria.
12. It might be a bear bird fox or walrus.
13. Yes I saw many pieces with those animals on them.
14. Did the artists sell trade or give away their works?
15. Steven they sometimes used them for trading.

B. Write each sentence. Use a comma *only* if the first word is the name of a person spoken to.

16. Kevin tell me if that is a deer.
17. Mrs. Gray thinks it is a moose.
18. Martha let's check the encyclopedia.
19. Kevin I found out it is definitely a moose.
20. Mrs. Gray knew by the shape of the antlers.

C. Complete each sentence by adding words to form series. Remember your commas!

21. ____ ____ and ____ are on the shopping list.
22. Let's ____ ____ and ____ today.

Apply ◆ Think and Write

Questioning for Information ◆ Write three questions you might ask an Eskimo artist. Then write answers the artist might give that begin with *yes* or *no*. Try to use lists of things. Here is an idea: *Do you work with wood? No, I use sealskin, fur, and leather.*

> ✎ **Remember**
> to use commas to show your readers where to pause.

Focus on Directions

Before you started this unit, did you know how artists make larger-than-life models of insects? Probably not. Few of us have ever seen museum artists at work. Yet now you know something about the process. You learned it by reading a set of directions.

Good directions have certain qualities:

◆ *They are clear*. You cannot ask questions of a set of directions. Directions must be carefully planned. They must be clearly written.

◆ *They are complete*. If even a small step is left out, the directions may not be usable.

◆ *They are in the correct order*. Most processes have one best order. Good directions follow this logical, step-by-step order.

◆ *They contain time-order words*. Such words as *first, next, after,* and *last* help to show the correct order of the directions. Order words are handy signposts for the reader.

The Writer's Voice ◆ Directions should follow the four rules listed. Look back at the directions for preparing a giant praying mantis. Review the steps for making the praying mantis's head. Do the authors' directions follow the four rules? Explain.

Working Together

Directions must be clear and complete. They must be written in the correct order, usually with time-order words. As a group, work on activities **A** and **B**.

A. Put the following mixed-up sentences in order. The time-order words will help. To check on your answer, look back at the selection from *Are Those Animals Real?*

Then he made the wings from clear plastic sheeting. The giant insect was finished. After completing the head, he made the body and legs from a foam material. The artist decided to make a giant model of a praying mantis. The head required a rubber mold. Finally, he put the body together and painted it. First, he made the plastic head for the praying mantis.

B. Everyone knows how to make something. It may be a paper airplane. It may be French toast. As a group, decide on something that a group member does well. Prepare a set of step-by-step directions for doing it. Finally, have one person in the group present the directions to the rest of the class.

THESAURUS CORNER ◆ Word Choice

Copy the sentences below. Use the Thesaurus and Thesaurus Index to replace each verb in dark type with a better synonym. Underline each time-order word.

Let me **educate** you to fry an egg. **Witness** closely. First, put a little butter in the pan. Then **smash** the eggshell on the edge of the pan or counter. Next, drop the egg gently in the pan; don't **pitch** it, or the yolk will break. Cook the egg over a low heat. In about a minute, you can **gobble** your fried egg.

WRITING PROCESS
INFORMING

Writing a How-to Article

Are Those Animals Real? informed us of how one artist makes insect models. A similar kind of writing is a how-to article. In a how-to article, the writer tells the reader exactly how to do something.

If you wanted to make pizza, you wouldn't read an article about pizza parlors. You would read a pizza recipe. A recipe is a tiny how-to article. It lists materials and steps. It gives directions you can follow.

Know Your Purpose and Audience

What's MY PURPOSE

Now it is your turn to write a how-to article. Your purpose will be to teach your readers exactly how to do something.

Who's MY AUDIENCE

Your audience will be younger students. Later, you might visit a younger class and give a demonstration. You might also create a display of how-to articles.

1 Prewriting

Before you begin to write, choose your topic. Then gather details about your topic for your article.

Choose Your Topic ◆ Make a list of the things you can do. Then circle your topic choice.

Think About It	Talk About It
First make your list of things you can do. Then go over your list again. Cross out those things that a younger child would not be able to do. Then choose from what is left. Which do you like best? Which would be the most fun for a child to do?	Work with a partner. Tell each other what you know how to do well. Maybe your partner can make a paper airplane or a beaded necklace. Maybe you know how to set a table or make a crayon rubbing. Keep going until you have used up all possible topics.

Topic Ideas

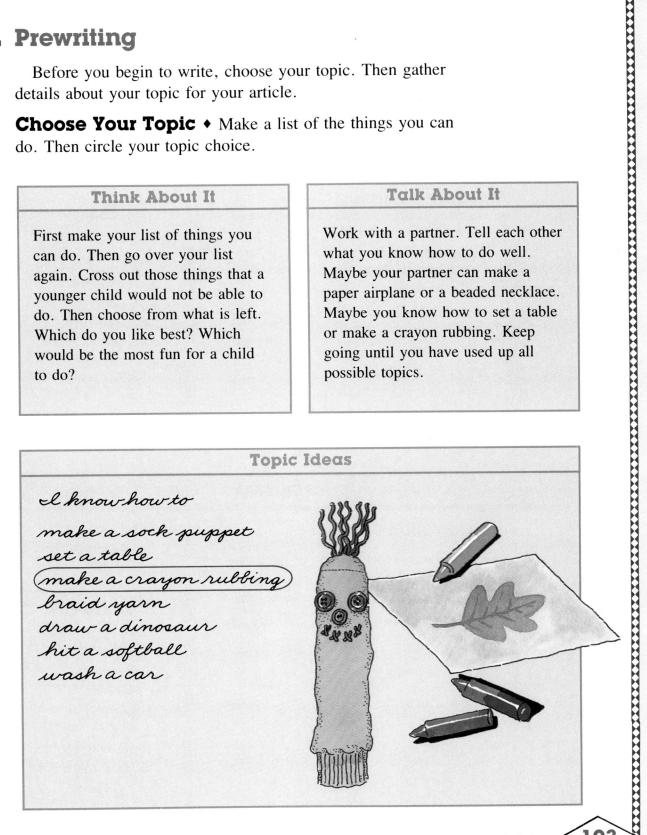

I know how to
make a sock puppet
set a table
(make a crayon rubbing)
braid yarn
draw a dinosaur
hit a softball
wash a car

Choose Your Strategy ◆ Here are two ways to gather details for your article. Read both strategies. Then decide which idea you will use.

PREWRITING IDEAS

CHOICE ONE

Teaching a Partner

Teach a partner how to do your activity. Explain the materials you need. Explain the steps. Then ask your partner these questions and take notes: Which steps were clear? Which steps were hard to follow? Are there any steps I should add?

Model

How to Make a Crayon Rubbing

Materials: My partner wanted to know what kind of paper to use.

Steps: My partner didn't understand how to hold the crayon.

CHOICE TWO

An Observation Chart

Make an observation chart. Close your eyes. Picture yourself doing your activity. Write the details you observe. List the materials and the steps on your chart.

Model

How to Make a Crayon Rubbing

Materials	crayons, paper, an item such as a leaf, coin, or key
Steps	1. Put item under paper. 2. Hold crayon sideways. 3. Rub crayon over paper.

2 Writing

Use your prewriting notes to help you write your article. First write an introductory paragraph. Tell what you will teach and try to catch your reader's interest. Here are some ways to begin.

- ♦ You can make ____ all by yourself. It is fun and easy!
- ♦ Do you know how to ____? Here is how to do it.

Next write a paragraph listing the materials and steps. Use words like *first*, *next*, and *last* to make the order clear. Add a closing paragraph suggesting ways to display or use the finished item.

Sample First Draft ♦

Do you know how to make crayon rubbings? these directions will show you how.

Get some Drawing Paper and crayons. Then collect flat things to rub. Leaves, keys, and coins is good. Then hold a crayon on its side. Next place the things under a sheet of paper. Push the crayon against it in a gentle but firm way. Now rub. What you rubed will make an interesting design. Try rubbing other things

| **Introduction** |
| 1. Name project. |
| 2. Grab interest. |

| **Body** |
| 1. List materials. |
| 2. Explain steps. |

| **Conclusion** |
| Suggest ways to display or use. |

3 Revising

Are your directions clear and complete? Now is the time to make improvements. This idea may help.

REVISING IDEA

FIRST Read to Yourself

Think about your purpose. Did you explain how to do something? Think about your audience. Will younger children be able to follow the steps?

Focus: Did you give clear, step-by-step directions? Put a wavy line ～～ under any parts that are unclear.

THEN Share with a Partner

Ask your partner to read along silently as you read aloud. Then ask your partner to explain the steps without looking at your article. Did your partner understand?

The Writer

Guidelines: Read slowly. Listen carefully as your partner explains the steps back to you.

Sample questions:
- Were there any parts that were not clear?
- **Focus question:** Did I give all the steps in the right order?

The Writer's Partner

Guidelines: As the writer reads, try to picture the steps in your mind. Give helpful ideas.

Sample responses:
- I wasn't sure how to ____.
- Maybe you need an extra step to tell about ____.

Revising Model ♦ The article below is being revised. The marks show changes the writer wants to make.

The writer's partner noticed the incorrect linking verb.

This step was in the wrong order.

Press is a more exact word than *push*.

The word *it* was confusing. *The paper* is a better detail.

> Do you know how to make
> crayon rubbings? these directions
> will show you how.
>   Get some Drawing Paper and
> crayons. Then collect flat things to
>   are
> rub. Leaves, keys, and coins is good.
> (Then hold a crayon on its side.) Next
> place the things under a sheet of paper.
> Press   the paper
> Push the crayon against it in a gentle
> but firm way. Now rub. What you
> rubed will make an interesting
> design. Try rubbing other things that

Read the revised article above. Read it the way the writer thinks it *should* be. Then revise your own article.

Grammar Check ♦ Sentences need subjects and verbs that agree.

Word Choice ♦ Is there a more exact word for a word like *push*? A thesaurus can help you find exact words.

Revising Checklist

☐ **My Purpose:** Did I explain how to do something?

☐ **My Audience:** Will younger children be able to follow the steps?

☐ **Focus:** Did I give all the steps in the right order?

4 Proofreading

Now is the time to fix errors in spelling, punctuation, capitals, and handwriting.

Proofreading Model ♦ Here is the how-to article about making crayon rubbings. Notice that red proofreading marks have been added.

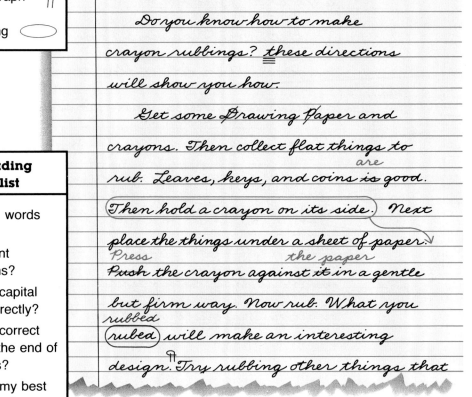

PROOFREADING IDEA

Handwriting Check

Check the space between words. Are any words too crowded? Then make sure your letters are spaced nicely. For example, if the letters *cl* are crowded, they may look like *d*.

Now proofread your how-to article and add a title. Then make a neat copy.

5 Publishing

Now that you have written your how-to article, it's time to share it. Here are two ways to do it.

How to Make Crayon Rubbings

Do you know how to make crayon rubbings? These directions will show you how.

Get some drawing paper and crayons. Then collect flat things to rub. Leaves, keys, and coins are good. Next place the things under a sheet of paper. Then hold a crayon on its side. Press the crayon against the paper in a gentle but firm way. Now rub. What you rubbed will make an interesting design.

Try rubbing other things that you find. Hang your finished rubbings on the wall or make an art book.

PUBLISHING IDEAS

Share Aloud

Arrange to visit a younger class. Choose one of the younger children to be your partner. Together show the steps in your activity. Then let the other children try the activity or tell if they would like to try it.

Share in Writing

Create a how-to board. Display your how-to article. Add a sample of the finished product or a picture of yourself doing the activity. Add some blank sheets of paper. Encourage classmates to try the projects and write comments.

CURRICULUM
•CONNECTION•

Writing Across the Curriculum Art

In this unit you wrote a how-to article for younger children. Before you could tell them how to do something, you had to learn to do it yourself. You probably learned by observing. Observing can also help you enjoy works of art.

Writing to Learn

Think and Observe ◆ Look at this picture. Make an observation chart. Name or describe the details that you see in this painting. Take your time. Look carefully. List as many details as you can.

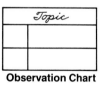

Observation Chart

THE TABLE
painting by Georges Braque

Write ◆ Look at your observation chart. What details did you see right away? What details did you notice after you had looked at the painting awhile? Describe one thing that you did not see at first.

Writing in Your Journal

In the Writer's Warm-up you wrote about how artists worked. Throughout this unit you learned that artists create many different kinds of art. In your journal write some things you have recently learned about art.

BOOKS
TO ENJOY

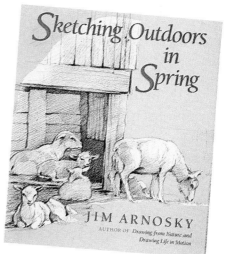

◆ Read More About It

Sketching Outdoors in Spring
by Jim Arnosky
This book combines an artist's sketchbook and diary. The author tells a little about each picture he drew from actual observation.

Castle *by David Macaulay*
David Macaulay can help you think about artists of another kind. Hundreds of artists and craftspeople worked together to build the great medieval castles. This book creates a story of the building of a castle in 13th century Wales.

◆ Book Report Idea Mini-Books

Making books is an ancient art. For your next book report, why not share your opinions in a handmade mini-book?

Create a Mini-book
Make a cover of paper or fabric-covered cardboard. Sew or staple pages inside. Use your most artistic writing for the title and author. Write a sentence or two on each page. Tell your readers why you liked the book. Remember to use interesting details. Display your mini-books.

UNIT REVIEW

Unit 4

Verbs   *pages 160–171*

A. Write each sentence. Underline the verb. Write *action verb* or *linking verb* after each sentence.

1. My family entered a sand sculpture contest.
2. Everyone contributed to our success.
3. My older sister is an architect.
4. She designed a modern home.
5. The judges are very strict about the rules.
6. We were the second-prize winners.

B. Write each sentence. Use the correct form of *be* in parentheses ( ).

7. The teachers and students (is, are) busy.
8. The Snow Festival (is, are) an important event.
9. I (was, were) a guide last year.
10. Our principal (is, are) always helpful.
11. The fourth graders (was, were) noisy yesterday.
12. The class float (was, were) difficult to make.

C. Write each sentence. Draw one line under the main verb. Draw two lines under the helping verb.

13. Alexander Fleming was studying bacteria.
14. He was growing bacteria in dishes.
15. One day he had found some mold.
16. Something had surprised him.
17. No bacteria were growing near the mold.
18. We had learned about penicillin.
19. Doctors have used this medicine.
20. I have read about Fleming.
21. His discovery is stirring interest.
22. Penicillin has saved many lives.

D. Write the verb in each sentence. Then write *present, past,* or *future* to show the tense.

23. Nearly everyone likes football.
24. We watched the game at the stadium.
25. The team will play away next week.
26. We will go to see them.
27. We played in the schoolyard.
28. Our teacher is the referee.
29. Schools organized football teams.
30. Many teams practice during the summer.
31. Rules for the game developed slowly.
32. One change allows the forward pass.

E. Write the past-tense form of each verb.

33. worry	**41.** huddle
34. spy	**42.** snap
35. examine	**43.** type
36. collect	**44.** wobble
37. marry	**45.** study
38. prefer	**46.** seem
39. scurry	**47.** hurry
40. spot	**48.** permit

F. Write the *-es* present-tense form of each verb.

49. hurry	**57.** pry
50. carry	**58.** worry
51. cry	**59.** rely
52. satisfy	**60.** scurry
53. fry	**61.** terrify
54. pity	**62.** dignify
55. dry	**63.** try
56. marry	**64.** supply

Prefixes   *pages 172–173*

G. Write each word. Draw a line under the prefix. Then write the meaning of each word.

65. review	**73.** disappear
66. unable	**74.** unwise
67. discover	**75.** rename
68. uncomfortable	**76.** recover
69. disloyal	**77.** disown
70. reopen	**78.** unlocked
71. reheat	**79.** unknown
72. uneven	**80.** displease

Directions   *pages 184–187*

H. The message below is written in code. Study the message and decide what the code is.

dl0 dlanoDcaM saw a remraf. eH dah lla sdnik fo slamina. yehT edam a tol fo esion.

81. Now study the directions that explain how to use the code. Write these directions in the correct order.

   a. Then write the next word backwards.

   b. Second, decide on a code.

   c. After all the words are written backwards, let a friend read the message.

   d. Write the first word backwards.

   e. Write the message in the code.

   f. First think of a message to write.

Commas   *pages 188–189*

I. Write each sentence with commas where they are needed.

82. Tracy have you ever been to a fair?

83. Yes I went to a country fair once.

84. Fairs were good places to buy things Marty.

85. Farmers could buy a horse a cow or some cloth.

86. Well trade fairs were held long ago.

87. China India and Mexico had them.

CUMULATIVE REVIEW

Unit 1: Sentences   *pages 6–11*

A. Write each sentence. Begin with a capital letter. Use periods and question marks correctly.

1. what time will your train arrive
2. it will be nice to see you
3. my family has planned a picnic
4. will you be able to go with us
5. we are going to the beach
6. do you like to swim
7. my sister has a new raft
8. would you like to use it
9. we will have a wonderful time
10. i will meet you at the station
11. are you as excited as I am

B. Write each sentence. Begin with a capital letter. Use periods and exclamation marks correctly.

12. the new town museum is open
13. how interesting it will be
14. our town was founded in 1774
15. what a long time ago that was
16. the museum will have ten displays
17. the displays will be on three floors
18. one display has old photos
19. oh, I'm excited about our tour
20. our class is going there on Friday
21. the bus will leave at ten o'clock
22. i can hardly wait

C. Write *subject* if the subject is underlined. Write predicate if the *predicate* is underlined.

23. A turtle's shell has two layers.
24. Bony plates make up the inner layer.
25. The outer layer has a hard structure.
26. Turtles do not have teeth.
27. Some turtles live for one hundred years or longer.
28. Sea turtles swim very quickly.
29. Turtles hatch from eggs.
30. A few types feed on almost nothing but plants.
31. Three kinds of tortoises live in the United States.
32. Most tortoises move very slowly.
33. These reptiles measure up to four feet long.

Unit 2: Nouns   *pages 54–59*

D. Write the plural of each singular noun.

34. foot
35. glass
36. watch
37. test
38. tooth
39. radish
40. berry
41. boot
42. tax
43. branch
44. ox
45. box
46. mouse
47. bus
48. library
49. fox
50. deer
51. store
52. business
53. holiday
54. baby
55. inch

E. Write each underlined noun. Then write *common* or *proper* after each one.

56. The ancient Chinese played soccer.
57. The Romans took the sport to England.
58. John F. Kennedy played football.
59. My cousin Rita plays volleyball.
60. William G. Morgan invented the game in Massachusetts.
61. Tennis was first played in France.
62. Mary E. Outerbridge introduced tennis in America.
63. Terry Jackson plays softball for the Central Cougars.

Unit 2: Capital Letters and Periods
pages 60–61

F. Write the proper nouns correctly. Use capital letters and periods where they are needed.

64. barbara j simpson
65. reno, nevada
66. rover
67. grand rapids, michigan
68. vice president dawes
69. edison illuminating company
70. nile river
71. senator thompson
72. harry g barnes, jr
73. dr ann walker
74. independence day
75. hudson river
76. hollywood boulevard

Unit 2: Apostrophes *pages 62–65*

G. Write the possessive form of each noun.

77. house
78. tomatoes
79. fairs
80. professor
81. founders
82. Mrs. Ross
83. companies
84. nation
85. photographs
86. government
87. boots
88. fountain
89. individuals
90. bus
91. science
92. program
93. Carlos
94. businesses
95. mice
96. citizens
97. stories
98. autumn

Unit 3: Pronouns *pages 112–121*

H. Write each sentence. Underline each pronoun.

99. I went to France last year.
100. It is a large country.
101. Mom and Dad went with me.
102. Uncle Claude met us at the airport.
103. We did a lot of sightseeing.
104. Claude took me to work with him.
105. He is a sculptor.
106. You should see the statue he did.
107. Aunt Marie likes it.
108. She says the statue is of her.
109. I went to the Alps with Mom and Dad.
110. They want to go back in the winter.
111. Claude and Marie will join them.

I. Write each sentence. Use a pronoun in place of the underlined word or words.

112. Liz and Clay read about Benjamin Franklin.
113. Benjamin Franklin signed four documents.
114. Trudy and I know he invented things.
115. Ed told Trudy and me about it.
116. Franklin invented bifocal glasses.
117. I asked Ellen what else he invented.
118. Another invention was lightning rods.
119. We learned much about Franklin.

J. Write each sentence. Use a possessive pronoun in place of the underlined word or words.

120. This museum's main hall is huge.
121. George Washington's picture is there.
122. Martha Washington's picture is too.
123. This is the Washingtons' home.
124. John's and my family also has a picture.
125. The picture's colors are dark.
126. The people's faces are hard to see.
127. They are my father's ancestors.

K. Write each sentence. Use the correct form of the pronoun in parentheses ( ).

128. Our British cousins visited (Tom and me, me and Tom).
129. (Tom and I, I and Tom) met them.
130. (We, Us) four went to Lexington.
131. Tom took a picture of (Heather and I, Heather and me).
132. (Me and Heather, Heather and I) stood by the Minuteman statue.
133. Pat read the inscription to (Tom and me, Tom and I).
134. Heather asked (we, us) Americans about the Revolution.
135. (Me and Tom, Tom and I) took them to Concord.

UNIT 4: Verbs *pages 160–171*

L. Write *action verb* or *linking verb* for each underlined word.

136. This is the story of Paul Revere.
137. It was the night of April 18, 1775.
138. Paul Revere waited for a signal.
139. The signal was in the church tower.
140. Paul crossed the river in a rowboat.
141. Then he rode away on horseback.
142. The colonists were ready for the British.

M. Write each sentence. Use the correct form of *be* in parentheses ( ).

143. Duane (is, are) my friend.
144. Yesterday we (was, were) on a walk.
145. The roads (am, are) interesting.
146. Duane (is, are) interested in bugs.
147. I (am, are) interested in plants.
148. Our walk (was, were) about two miles.
149. There (was, were) two goats.
150. One (was, were) light brown.

N. Write each sentence. Use the helping verb *are* or *have* to complete each sentence.

151. We _____ going to Tony's farm.
152. I _____ watched Tony feed the animals.
153. We _____ talked about his sheep.
154. They _____ grazing in the field.
155. Men _____ sheared the sheep.
156. Bags of wool _____ waiting by a truck.
157. Tony's parents _____ sold wool for many years.
158. They _____ keeping some this year.

O. Write the *-es* present-tense form of each verb.

159. scurry
160. pity
161. horrify
162. ferry
163. envy
164. classify

P. Write the past-tense form of each verb.

165. hurry
166. plan
167. fry
168. chop
169. rely
170. marry
171. flip
172. copy
173. skim
174. chat

UNIT 4: Commas   *pages 188–189*

Q. Write each sentence. Use commas where they are needed.

175. Cecil are you going to the meeting?
176. Yes we are getting our picture taken.
177. What is the picture for Judy?
178. Well it's going to be in our album.
179. Marvin have you had yours taken?

R. Write each sentence. Use commas where they are needed.

180. The caterpillar was long green and hairless.
181. Duffy watched sniffed and licked it.
182. Sounds of birds sheep and goats reached our ears.
183. Duffy ran jumped and swam in the pond.
184. I saw wild grapes milkweed and cattails in the marsh.
185. Walking with Duffy is fun in spring summer winter and fall.

LANGUAGE PUZZLERS

Unit 4 Challenge

A Verb Crossword

Copy the crossword graph. Then solve the puzzle.
(Hint: Each answer is the past-tense form of a verb.)

Across
2. mixed with a spoon
4. attempted
5. fastened
7. burst
8. drank (dog-fashion)
9. watched secretly
10. no longer wet

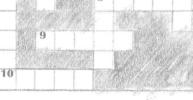

Down
1. depended on
2. slid on a wet floor
3. snarled or tangled
4. spoke in court
6. sent an application for a job

What Am I?

Use the verbs below to complete the sentences. Then try to guess what each thing is.

swim   discovered   will grow   dropped
live   will fly   travel   will sit

1. Last autumn I ___ from an oak tree.
   Soon I ___ ___ to be an oak tree too.
   What am I?

2. I ___ in a cocoon now.
   Next spring I ___ ___ with my colorful wings.
   What am I?

3. I ___ through wires to light your lamp.
   Benjamin Franklin ___ me in lightning.
   What am I?

4. Now I ___ like a fish.
   As a frog I ___ ___ on lily pads.
   What am I?

Unit 4 Extra Practice

1 Writing with Action Verbs

p. 160

A. Write each sentence. Underline the action verb.

1. The marchers listened to the bugle.
2. They started down Pennsylvania Avenue.
3. The Navy band played ''Stars and Stripes Forever.''
4. Every state decorates a float.
5. Every four years our country elects a President.
6. We call January 20 Inauguration Day.
7. The President waits on the steps of the Capitol.
8. He lifts his right hand.
9. The President repeats the oath of office.
10. Then he delivers a speech.
11. He promises his best effort to the people.
12. Finally the parade starts.
13. The President waves to the people.

B. Write the sentences. Use an action verb to complete each sentence.

EXAMPLE: We ____ about our trip to Washington.

ANSWER: We talked about our trip to Washington.

14. Our band ____ money for the trip.
15. The students ____ in straight rows.
16. Those from New York ____ bright flags.
17. Drum majors ____ their batons.
18. Navajo Indians from Arizona ____ native music.
19. People from Georgia ____ peanuts to the crowd.
20. Alaskan huskies ____ a special sled.
21. A thousand balloons ____ in the sky.
22. The governor of our state ____ from her car.
23. The crowd ____ excitedly.
24. Everyone ____ the parade.

2 Linking Verbs
p. 162

A. Write each sentence. Then write *action verb* or *linking verb* for each underlined word.

1. Many old inventions <u>are</u> strange to us today.
2. Mustaches <u>were</u> popular in the 1800s.
3. Men <u>used</u> special clips on their mustaches.
4. The clips <u>kept</u> the mustache clean during meals.
5. The drawings in this book <u>are</u> interesting.
6. They <u>show</u> different kinds of bathtubs.
7. People <u>carried</u> one kind of tub like a suitcase.
8. The tub <u>is</u> useful in more than one way.
9. The case <u>holds</u> either clothes or water.

B. Write each sentence. Underline the verb. Write *action verb* or *linking verb* after each sentence.

10. This bicycle is an early one.
11. The back wheel was larger than the front one.
12. The rider pushed the pedals on the back wheel.
13. A giant single-wheeled cycle was a surprise.
14. The seat was low.
15. The big outer wheel rolled forward.
16. A short handle steered the wheel.
17. Bicycle designs are simpler now.
18. Today people ride trim, light models.

3 Using Linking Verbs
p. 164

A. Write each sentence. Use the correct form of *be* in parentheses ( ).

1. Women (was, were) rulers in many countries.
2. Cleopatra (was, were) one of the most famous.
3. She (is, are) a legend even today.
4. We (is, are) curious about Eleanor of Aquitaine.
5. She (was, were) a queen in the twelfth century.

B. Write each sentence. Use *was* or *were* to complete each one. Look at the chart on page 164.

6. Mary Tudor ____ a daughter of Henry VIII.
7. She and Elizabeth ____ half sisters.
8. Their lives ____ very interesting.
9. Mary ____ queen of England from 1553 to 1558.
10. Her actions ____ often harsh.
11. The next queen ____ Elizabeth.
12. Her reign ____ a welcome change.
13. Elizabeth ____ ''Good Queen Bess'' to her subjects.
14. She ____ a strong and clever ruler.
15. Both of these women ____ important queens.

4 Main Verbs and Helping Verbs

p. 166

A. Write each sentence. Draw one line under the main verb. Draw two lines under the helping verb.

1. Many scientists are studying animals today.
2. Some have examined bears in winter.
3. Bears' sleep is controlled by a brain chemical.
4. Those snakes are cooling themselves.
5. The penguins have huddled together for warmth.
6. The animals are adjusting their temperatures.
7. I have wondered how animals sleep in winter.
8. More than one scientist is hoping to find out.
9. The young woodchucks were waiting for winter.
10. A fine snow was falling in the forest.
11. The woodchuck had gathered food all fall.
12. Its weight has increased from all the food.
13. Last spring it was scampering in the woods.
14. Two winters ago a fox had lived in this hole.
15. Some bears are resting in a den nearby.
16. Their brains are making special chemicals.
17. Their long winter sleep has started.

B. Write each sentence. Use the helping verb *are* or *have* to complete each sentence.

18. Sunny March days ____ warmed every living thing.
19. Bees ____ cooled their tongues with nectar.
20. The sea gulls ____ turned away from the sun.
21. Four snakes ____ warming themselves on a rock.
22. The dogs ____ letting their tongues hang out.
23. Some birds ____ splashed water on their feathers.
24. In the swamp the alligators ____ opened their jaws.
25. At the zoo polar bears ____ swimming in the pool.

5 Tenses of Verbs
p. 168

A. Write each verb. Then write *present*, *past*, or *future*.

1. Wanda talked about the Kingdom of Merwood.
2. A dragon threatened the kingdom.
3. A fiery cloud pours from its throat.
4. King Zoti will ask for help.
5. Soldiers from Dal attack the monster.
6. The dragon forces them back with its flame.
7. Todd the Dragon Fighter created a dragon bait.
8. Kirsten smears the bait with butter.
9. The dragon will swallow the bait.
10. The villagers will thank Kirsten and Todd.

B. Write each sentence below and underline the verb. Write *present*, *past*, or *future* to show the tense.

11. Wanda talks to us about storytelling.
12. First you pick one of your favorite tales.
13. You will read it aloud a few times.
14. Your voice sets the mood of the story.
15. You will think about the people in the story.
16. Nate and Lenore practiced storytelling.
17. They will tell their stories to the first-graders.

6 Spelling Verbs Correctly   *p. 170*

A. Read each sentence. Write the past-tense form of the verb in parentheses ( ).

1. Martha (empty) the old trunk.
2. Who (knot) the string around these letters?
3. In one letter her grandfather (beg) for an answer.
4. Martha's grandmother (reply) quickly.
5. Martha (carry) the letters to her room.

B. Write the past-tense form of each verb.

6.	drop	11.	supply
7.	pin	12.	stir
8.	throb	13.	worry
9.	dry	14.	tug
10.	wrap	15.	hum

C. Write the *-es* present-tense form of each verb.

16.	bury	21.	fly
17.	pity	22.	pry
18.	rely	23.	bully
19.	carry	24.	fry
20.	ferry	25.	scurry

D. Write each sentence. Use the past tense of the verb in ( ).

26. Joey (study) his family's history.
27. Charles Smith (try) to strike it rich.
28. He's the one who (marry) Mary Stone.
29. They (plan) to find gold in California.
30. Charles and Mary (hurry) out West.
31. In the mountains heavy snow almost (trap) them.
32. Finally they (pan) for gold in the Sacramento River valley.
33. Joey (copy) this story for his album.
34. Then he (map) their journey.

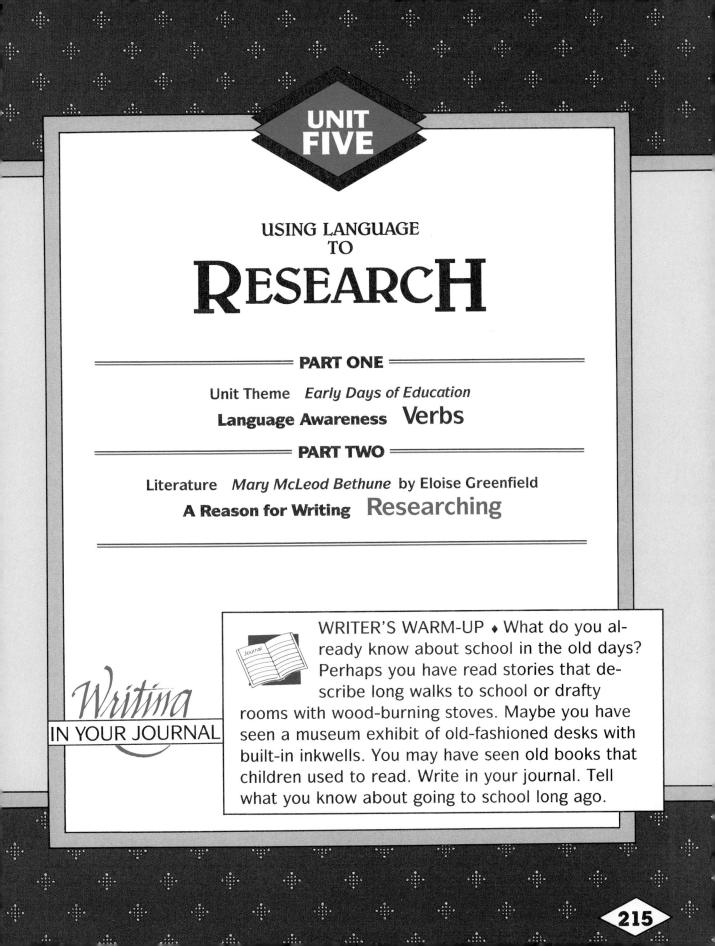

UNIT FIVE

USING LANGUAGE TO

RESEARCH

PART ONE

Unit Theme   *Early Days of Education*

Language Awareness   Verbs

PART TWO

Literature   *Mary McLeod Bethune* by Eloise Greenfield

A Reason for Writing   Researching

Writing
IN YOUR JOURNAL

WRITER'S WARM-UP ♦ What do you already know about school in the old days? Perhaps you have read stories that describe long walks to school or drafty rooms with wood-burning stoves. Maybe you have seen a museum exhibit of old-fashioned desks with built-in inkwells. You may have seen old books that children used to read. Write in your journal. Tell what you know about going to school long ago.

1 Using Subjects and Verbs That Agree

When you use verbs in the present tense, make sure each verb agrees with its subject. With certain subjects this means adding *-s* or *-es* to the verb.

With *he*, *she*, *it*, or a singular noun, add *-s* or *-es*.

| The student learns. | My cousin teaches. |
| He works hard. | She misses school. |

With *I*, *you*, *we*, *they*, or a plural noun, do not add *-s* or *-es*.

| The students learn. | My cousins teach. |
| They work hard. | They miss school. |

If a verb ends in *ch*, *sh*, *s*, *ss*, *x*, or *z*, you add *-es*. Notice the words *teaches* and *misses* above.

> **Summary** ◆ A verb in the present tense must agree with the subject of the sentence.

Guided Practice

Name the verb in parentheses ( ) that agrees with the subject.

1. The students (remember, remembers) their fourth grade teacher, Kathleen Ames.
2. They (find, finds) her diary in the town library.
3. The diary (tell, tells) about Kathleen's life.
4. A young Kathleen (live, lives) on North Haven Island.
5. She (wish, wishes) that she could become a teacher.

Practice

A. These sentences tell more about Kathleen Ames, a teacher during the 1800s. Write each sentence. Choose the verb in parentheses ( ) that agrees with each subject.

6. Each morning Kathleen (cross, crosses) the fields to the school.
7. Some children (ride, rides) to school on horseback.
8. Orilla (hitch, hitches) her pony to a fence.
9. Kathleen's students (push, pushes) the door open.
10. All the students (sit, sits) in the same room.
11. One teacher (teach, teaches) every subject.
12. She (build, builds) the fire in the stove.
13. It (warm, warms) the drafty schoolroom.
14. The windows (rattle, rattles) in the wind.
15. At recess Elmer (fix, fixes) the porch railing.

B. Write each sentence. You may need to add *-s* or *-es* to make the verb agree with the subject.

16. Irene _____ in water from the well. (bring)
17. Each student _____ with one bucket of water. (wash)
18. Another bucket _____ drinking water. (hold)
19. You _____ this happened a long time ago. (know)
20. We _____ learning about earlier times in America. (like)
21. Ron _____ he could visit the 1800s for a day. (wish)

C. Write six sentences using the verbs below.

22. talks	**24.** answers	**26.** discuss
23. listen	**25.** watches	**27.** rushes

Apply ♦ Think and Write

From Your Writing ♦ Choose five action verbs you used in the Writer's Warm-up. Write a new sentence for each verb you choose.

> ✎ **Remember**
> to use verbs that agree with the subjects of your sentences.

Go back to the 1800s in a time machine. Tell a round-robin story about what you did in those days. Use these words: *began, did, flew, went, grew, rode, saw, threw, wrote.*

2 Using Irregular Verbs

The past tense of most verbs is formed by adding *-ed*. Verbs that do not follow this rule are called irregular verbs.

Study this chart of common irregular verbs. You will use these words often as you speak and write.

Verb	Past	Past with *have*, *has*, or *had*
begin	began	begun
do	did	done
fly	flew	flown
go	went	gone
grow	grew	grown
ride	rode	ridden
see	saw	seen
throw	threw	thrown
write	wrote	written

Summary ♦ The past tenses of **irregular verbs** are not formed by adding *-ed*. When you speak and write, use the correct forms of irregular verbs.

Guided Practice

Name the verb that correctly completes each sentence.

1. Kathleen Ames (wrote, written) often in her diary.
2. In this entry she has (went, gone) across the island.
3. Winter had (began, begun) earlier than usual.
4. Kathleen (rode, ridden) to school on a sleigh.
5. Her students had (saw, seen) the sleigh coming.

Practice

A. Write each sentence about Kathleen Ames and her students. Choose the correct past form of the verb in parentheses ( ).

6. Many students (wrote, written) their lessons on slates.
7. I have (saw, seen) some of their schoolbooks.
8. A student has (wrote, written) her name in this one.
9. All of Kathleen's students have (grew, grown) up now.
10. Most have (went, gone) to the mainland to live.
11. Many (saw, seen) Kathleen on visits home.
12. They (flew, flown) or took the ferry back to the island.
13. Her students (threw, thrown) a party for her one hundredth birthday.
14. They remembered what she had (did, done) for them.
15. They had (threw, thrown) the party to thank her.

B. Write each sentence. Use the correct past form of the verb in parentheses ( ).

16. After years of teaching, Kathleen ____ to college. (go)
17. Her trip ____ with a boat ride to the mainland. (begin)
18. Then she ____ on a train to northern Maine. (ride)
19. Kathleen ____ up on a tiny island. (grow)
20. She had never ____ a train before. (ride)
21. Her sisters ____ to her with news from home. (write)
22. They had ____ many changes in their town. (see)
23. The years had ____ by quickly. (flew)
24. After college Kathleen ____ some serious thinking. (do)
25. She had ____ to think about teaching again. (begin)

Apply ◆ Think and Write

A Friendly Letter ◆ What might you see if you left an island home for a job on the mainland? Describe your trip in a letter to someone back home. Use at least five verbs from the chart in this lesson.

> ✎ **Remember**
> to use the correct past forms of irregular verbs.

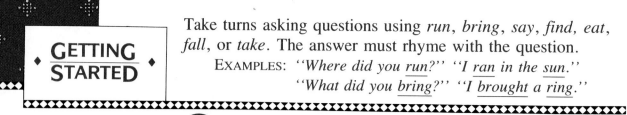

GETTING STARTED

Take turns asking questions using *run*, *bring*, *say*, *find*, *eat*, *fall*, or *take*. The answer must rhyme with the question.

EXAMPLES: *"Where did you run?" "I ran in the sun."*
"What did you bring?" "I brought a ring."

3 Using Irregular Verbs

Some irregular verb forms follow a pattern. Look at the verbs *run* and *come* in the chart below. Notice that the verb and the past form with *have*, *has*, or *had* are the same.

Which forms of the verbs *bring*, *say*, and *find* are the same? What verbs in the chart have three different forms?

Verb	Past	Past with *have, has,* or *had*
		same form
run	ran	run
come	came	come
	same form	
bring	brought	brought
say	said	said
find	found	found
	adds -en to present	
eat	ate	eaten
fall	fell	fallen
give	gave	given
take	took	taken

Summary ◆ Some **irregular verbs** follow a pattern in the way they are formed.

Guided Practice

Name the past-tense form of each verb below. Then name the form of each verb when it is used with *have*, *has*, or *had*.

1. give **2.** come **3.** say **4.** take **5.** eat

Practice

A. These sentences tell about homes of the 1800s. Write each sentence. Choose the correct past form of the verb.

6. Early settlers had (bring, brought) many ideas to America.
7. They (bring, brought) ideas for building homes.
8. Often they had (find, found) the right materials.
9. Swedish settlers had (came, come) from a country with forests.
10. They (find, found) trees here for building log cabins.
11. My grandmother has (gave, given) me an old book.
12. It had (fell, fallen) behind a trunk in the attic.
13. One picture (gave, given) me an idea of a typical old home.
14. Grandma (say, said) that wood houses were common.
15. Styles for Early American homes (came, come) from many different countries.

B. For each sentence, use the correct past form of the verb.

16. The settlers soon ____ time to build schools. (find)
17. The teacher had ____ a large box of books. (bring)
18. On nice days the students ____ lunch outdoors. (eat)
19. It had ____ a long time to learn their lessons. (take)
20. Everyone ____ their multiplication tables aloud. (say)

C. Write five sentences using the irregular verbs below. Use a past form of each verb.

21. run **22.** fall **23.** take **24.** eat **25.** say

Apply ♦ Think and Write

Dictionary of Knowledge ♦ Read about *McGuffey's Readers*. Imagine that you are a fourth grader in the year 1850. Write about your day at school. Tell about your schoolbooks and your classroom. Use some words from the chart in this lesson.

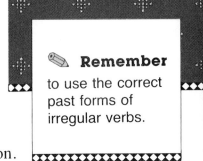

✎ **Remember** to use the correct past forms of irregular verbs.

Have you ever said, "I'm sorry"? *I'm* is a short way of saying *I am*. Here are two more sayings: "It's about time!" and "You're out!" Can you think of others? Say each phrase the long way.

4 Contractions with Verbs

When you speak or write, you can often join two words to form one shorter word. These new words are contractions. Some contractions are formed by joining a pronoun and a verb. Notice the spelling of the underlined contraction below.

■ **Our new neighbors asked if we'd ever milked a cow.**

Which word in the sentence below is a contraction?

■ **I've never been in a dairy shed before.**

Study the chart. When you write a contraction, put an **apostrophe** (') where one or more letters have been left out.

Pronoun	+ Verb	= Contraction
pronoun	+ am	= I'm
pronoun	+ are	= we're, you're, they're
pronoun	+ is or has	= he's, she's, it's
pronoun	+ have	= I've, we've, you've, they've
pronoun	+ had or would	= I'd, he'd, she'd, we'd, you'd, they'd
pronoun	+ shall or will	= I'll, we'll
pronoun	+ will	= he'll, she'll, you'll, they'll

Summary ◆ A **contraction** is a shortened form of two words. Some contractions join a pronoun and a verb.

Guided Practice

Name the contractions you can form with these words.

1. I am **2.** they have **3.** he will **4.** you are **5.** we had

Practice

A. Write each sentence. Choose the correct contraction.

6. After the children came home from school, (they'd, they're) help with chores.
7. (They're, They'll) gathering firewood today.
8. Tomorrow (we've, we'll) help our neighbor raise his new barn.
9. (He's, He'll) helped us many times in the past.
10. In the spring (I'm, I'll) plant crops.
11. In a pioneer family (you'll, you've) got to work hard.
12. Even a small child knows (she's, she'll) needed.
13. (She's, She'd) collect eggs and berries.
14. (We've, We're) not used to doing so many chores today.
15. At least, I know (I'm, I've) not!

B. Find the two words in each sentence that can form a contraction. Write each sentence using a contraction.

16. We have read about Tom Sawyer's school.
17. He would study the words in his spelling book.
18. If you come to the museum, you will see his speller.
19. I have heard that it was written by Noah Webster.
20. I would like to see a *McGuffey's Reader*, too.
21. It is printed in black and white, not color.
22. You would enjoy looking at the pictures in the *Reader*.
23. We are awaiting a special treat from our teacher.
24. Soon she will bring in some antique schoolbooks.
25. Of course, they will have to be handled very carefully.

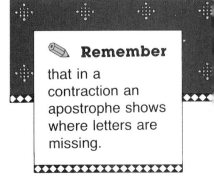

Apply ♦ Think and Write

Using Contractions ♦ Write five sentences about things that happen at school. Use a contraction in each sentence. Exchange your work with a partner. Find the contractions in each other's work. Tell what two words make up each contraction.

> ✏️ **Remember**
> that in a contraction an apostrophe shows where letters are missing.

Pretend to be an animal. Have a partner ask questions to guess the animal. Use a contraction with each ''no'' answer.
EXAMPLES: *''Do you have whiskers?'' ''No, I don't have whiskers.''*
''Can you fly?'' ''No, I can't fly.''

5 Contractions with *not*

When you write, contractions can help you capture the way people talk. Which sentence below sounds better to you?

Edgar: "I cannot play because I did not bring my banjo."
Emily: "I can't believe that you didn't bring it!"

Some contractions are formed from a verb and the word *not*. The chart shows how to form these contractions. You write an apostrophe where the letter *o* in *not* has been left out.

Verb + *not* = Contraction			
is + not = isn't	did + not = didn't
are + not = aren't	have + not = haven't
was + not = wasn't	has + not = hasn't
were + not = weren't	had + not = hadn't
do + not = don't	could + not = couldn't
does + not = doesn't	should + not = shouldn't
would + not = wouldn't	

Two other contractions are formed differently. *Won't* stands for *will not*. *Won't* comes from the Middle English words *wol not*. The contraction *can't* is short for one word, *cannot*.

> **Summary** ◆ Some contractions are formed from a verb and *not*. Contractions help you write the way people talk.

Guided Practice

Name the contractions you can form with these words.

1. is not　　**2.** will not　　**3.** have not　　**4.** could not

Practice

A. Write contractions for the words below.

5. were not	**10.** does not	**15.** will not
6. could not	**11.** is not	**16.** are not
7. had not	**12.** did not	**17.** cannot
8. do not	**13.** should not	**18.** have not
9. was not	**14.** would not	**19.** has not

B. You have learned about school and work in the 1800s. The sentences below tell what people did for fun. Write them. Use a contraction to replace the underlined words.

20. Television had not been invented in 1800.

21. Families did not have VCRs either.

22. You could go to operas or plays, but there were not any movies.

23. Families that could not go to the opera sang together at home.

24. Since there was not always a book to read, people told many stories.

25. It does not take long to learn a dance, so they had barn dances.

26. People would not come without their fiddles and banjos.

27. It is not hard to make simple toys, like dolls or hoops.

28. Do not you think it would be fun to make your own toys?

29. Should not the library have a book on games from Early America?

Apply ♦ Think and Write

Using Contractions ♦ Write some sentences telling about games and toys that had not yet been invented in the 1800s. In each sentence, use a contraction formed from a verb and *not*. Share your sentences with a partner.

> ✎ **Remember**
> that you can use contractions to capture the way people talk.

The equine galloped across the field with a saddle on its back. What do you think equine means? How can you tell?

VOCABULARY ◆
Context Clues

Sometimes you hear or read words that are new to you. Often the other words used with a new word give a clue to its meaning. Such clues are called context clues. **Context clues** help you understand the meaning of a new word.

Four kinds of context clues are described in the chart.

Kind of Clue	Example
A *synonym*, or a word that has almost the same meaning	I am interested in cartography, or *mapmaking*.
An *antonym*, or a word with an opposite meaning	Reading maps is fascinating, never *boring*, to me.
A *definition* of the new word	An atlas is *a book of maps*, and I found this one in the attic.
Further information about the new word's meaning	Perhaps Great-aunt Lillie is its proprietor. *It might belong to her.*

Building Your Vocabulary

What do the underlined words mean in the sentences below?

1. Some children in early schools wrote on slates rather than paper. The slates were made from a kind of thin rock.
2. Scholars, or students, in early schools had few books.
3. Young scholars in early schools learned to cipher. Today students learn to solve problems in mathematics.
4. Students also had to memorize, or learn by heart, poems and speeches.

Practice

A. Write the meaning for each underlined word. Choose the meaning from the words in parentheses ( ).

1. The <u>tattered</u> schoolbook, with its torn cover and pages, was printed in 1928. (low-cost, ragged)
2. It brought back happy <u>recollections</u> for Grandmother of when she was a child in school. (memories, bad dreams)
3. The <u>schoolmarm</u>, Mrs. Spartan, began class every day at 7:00 A.M. (teacher, mother)
4. The class was <u>disciplined</u>, not badly behaved. (orderly, short)
5. The children <u>toiled</u> at their studies, learning to read, spell, and write. (took their time, worked hard)
6. Grandmother later studied at a <u>normal school</u> to become a teacher herself. (teacher-training school, high school)

B. Use context clues to find the meaning of each underlined word. Write the word and its meaning.

7. My grandfather likes to <u>relate</u> stories of his childhood. I listen to them at night.
8. "When I was a boy," he said, "life was no <u>bed of roses</u>. We worked from early morning till late in the evening."
9. "We <u>journeyed</u> twelve miles to school and back."
10. "We had to feed the chickens, milk the cows, and stack hay in the <u>loft</u> just under the roof of the barn."
11. "We always <u>turned in</u> and were fast asleep by eight!"

LANGUAGE CORNER ◆ Echo Words

Some words sound like the thing they name. Think about the words below. They name sounds, and they copy, or *echo*, the sounds they name.

plunk   zoom   crash

Make a list of other words that name sounds.

How to Revise Sentences with Verbs

You know that verbs can tell about the past time or the present time. It is important to keep verbs in the same time in a piece of writing. Do you know why this is important? Read what Jan wrote about school days in 1776.

> Samuel woke at dawn. After he gets dressed, he hurried to the kitchen. The fire crackles in the stove, and wonderful smells filled the air. For breakfast he eats johnnycake, mush, and fresh milk. After Samuel finished his chores, he leaves for school.

Some of the verbs are in the past time and some are in the present time. Mixing times makes the paragraph hard to read and understand. Jan revised her paragraph, using only past-time verbs. Does her paragraph sound better now?

> Samuel woke at dawn. After he got dressed, he hurried to the kitchen. The fire crackled in the stove, and wonderful smells filled the air. For breakfast he ate johnnycake, mush, and fresh milk. After Samuel finished his chores, he left for school.

The Grammar Game ♦ Try to make a verb times table! Write all the present-time verbs on one list. Make a second list of all the past-time verbs.

washes	bring	arranged	glare	dug
made	fell	scream	cried	glare
type	copied	tripped	grin	forget

How quickly can you write every verb in the present time?

Working Together

Do activities **A** and **B** as a group. You will see how using verbs in the same time makes your writing easier to read.

A. Write each sentence and underline the verbs. Then make the verbs in each sentence tell about the same time. Use the directions in parentheses ( ).

1. Gail loved animals and wants to be a veterinarian. (present time)
2. George attended cooking school and prepares a French meal for his friends. (past time)
3. Lou and Jo play trumpets and marched in the parade. (present time)
4. We sing a song and clapped our hands. (past time)

B. Complete the paragraph with present-time verbs. Then copy the paragraph again using the same verbs in the past time.

School ____ on September 7. Everyone ____ on the first day at 8:15 A.M. We ____ our health forms to the office. Then we ____ to our classrooms. Later the principal ____ to all the students. We ____ our day at 3:30 P.M.

WRITERS' CORNER • Choppy Sentences

Choppy writing uses too many short sentences. Choppy sentences can make your writing dull and boring.

CHOPPY: My aunt has a ranch. She raises horses. She raises cattle. Cowhands work on the ranch. They work hard. They work hard every day.

IMPROVED: My aunt has a ranch. She raises horses and cattle. Cowhands work hard on the ranch every day.

Read what you wrote for the Writer's Warm-up. Did you use too many short sentences? Can you improve them?

COUNTRY SCHOOL
painting by E. L. Henry
Yale University Art Gallery, Mabel Brady Garvan Collection.

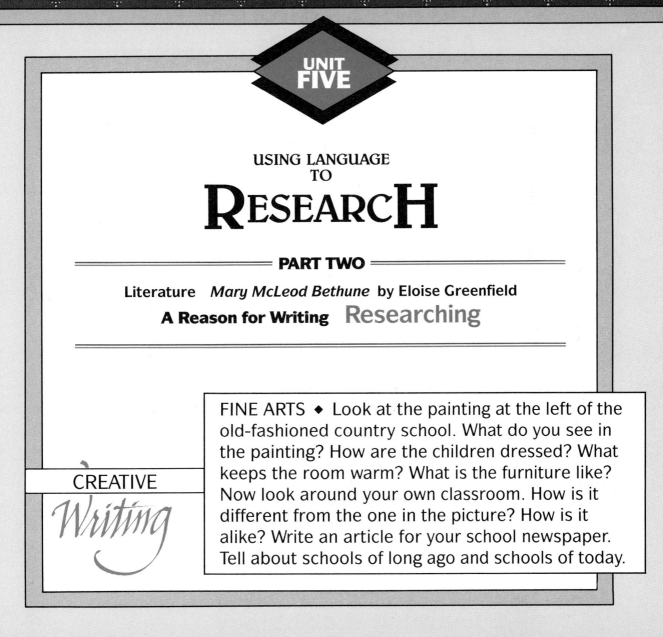

USING LANGUAGE
TO
RESEARCH

PART TWO

Literature   *Mary McLeod Bethune* by Eloise Greenfield
A Reason for Writing   Researching

CREATIVE
Writing

FINE ARTS ◆ Look at the painting at the left of the old-fashioned country school. What do you see in the painting? How are the children dressed? What keeps the room warm? What is the furniture like? Now look around your own classroom. How is it different from the one in the picture? How is it alike? Write an article for your school newspaper. Tell about schools of long ago and schools of today.

CREATIVE THINKING ♦
A Strategy for Researching

A THOUGHT BALLOON

Researching is gathering information. Sometimes a writer does research and writes about a person's life. This writing is called a biography. A **biography** is a true story about a real person.

After this lesson you will read part of a biography. It is about Mary McLeod Bethune, who was a famous teacher. Later you will write a biography based on your own research.

How can a writer make a person seem real? One way is to describe the person's thoughts and feelings. This passage tells how Mary felt about learning to read.

> After dinner, the children gathered around their mother as she sat in her favorite chair and told them true stories. . . . Listening to the stories, Mary wanted even more to be able to read. She talked about reading all the time. She told everybody in her family over and over that she didn't know how but someday she would learn to read. . . .

Have you ever wanted something as much as Mary did? If you have, you can put yourself in her place. You can imagine how she felt. Thinking about your own experiences helps you understand another person's point of view.

 ## Learning the Strategy

It is often helpful to see things from someone else's point of view. For example, suppose you plan to take your little sister to a movie. How might knowing her point of view help you choose one she would like? Suppose a cat followed you home from school. How could you write a story about the cat? You could write it from your own point of view. You could also pretend it was the cat telling the story. You could even write it as if your parents were telling the story.

How can you imagine someone else's point of view? Put yourself in that person's place. For example, pretend you are your mother. The door opens, and in comes your child with a cat. What goes through your mind? Making a thought balloon is one way to help imagine someone's thoughts.

Oh, no! A cat! I'm too busy to take care of a cat! It does look hungry and cold, though. The children will have to take care of it.

my mother

Using the Strategy

A. Think about your desk. How many years has it been in this school? How many children have used it? What has happened to it? If your desk could think, what would its thoughts be? Make a thought balloon for your desk.

B. You have read a little about Mary McLeod Bethune. Later you will read about the first time she went to school. Try to imagine how she probably felt on that first day. Make a thought balloon for her. Then, as you read, see if Mary felt the way you thought she would.

Applying the Strategy

♦ How did you figure out how Mary would feel?
♦ When might understanding another person's point of view be important to you?

AWARD
WINNING
AUTHOR

from

Mary McLeod Bethune

by Eloise Greenfield

Many years ago a teacher named Mary McLeod
Bethune had a dream. She dreamed that every
black child in America could get an education.
In 1904, Mrs. Bethune started her own school
for black children in Florida. Years later the

school became a college, and Mrs. Bethune became its president. Mary McLeod Bethune then found other ways to work for the education of black children. She gave speeches all over the United States. When she died in 1955, Mrs. Bethune's work had changed many lives.

Mary McLeod Bethune's love for learning began when she was a child in South Carolina. This is a true story of Mary's childhood.

Mary was born in the log cabin on July 10, 1875. She was the fifteenth child and two others were born later. Mary loved the farm. When she was very small, her father let her ride on the back of Old Bush, the mule with the bushy tail, as he pulled the plow. When she was a little older, she weeded the vegetables and picked cotton. In the house, she swept the floor and washed and shined the kerosene lamps and helped take care of the younger children.

Every morning and evening the family stood in front of the fireplace and said prayers and sang hymns together. After dinner, the children gathered around their mother as she sat in her favorite chair and told them true stories about Africa and talked about the Bible.

Listening to the stories, Mary wanted even more to be able to read. She talked about reading all the time. She told everybody in her family over and over that she didn't know how but someday she would learn to read.

One day when Mary was eleven years old, Miss Emma Wilson, a black teacher, came with the answer. She told Mary's parents that the Presbyterian Church had sent her to Mayesville to start a one-room school for black children.

Mr. and Mrs. McLeod wanted all of their children to go to school, but there was too much work to be done on the farm. Only one could go. That one, they decided, would be Mary.

On the first day of school, Mary left home early, carrying her lunch in a tin bucket. The school was five miles away, but she was happy to walk each mile. Every step was taking her closer to something that she had wanted for a long, long time.

Miss Wilson was a good teacher and Mary was a good student. She studied hard every day, and soon she could read short words and work arithmetic problems. In the evening, she taught her family what she had learned in school. Sometimes neighbors would ask her to read their mail for them or figure out the money they should get for selling their cotton.

A few years later, Mary was graduated from Miss Wilson's school. Her parents sat with the others who had come to hear their children recite and sing on their last day there. Mary received a scholarship to Scotia Seminary, a school for black girls in Concord, North Carolina. The scholarship meant that she would not have to pay.

Mary was nervous about leaving her family for the first time and taking her first train ride. But she was excited, too. Her mother made a dress for her out of a piece of cloth that was pretty, although it wasn't new. Neighbors knitted stockings and crocheted collars as gifts. They made some of their dresses over to fit Mary.

On going-away day, her family and friends went to the train station to see her off. There was a lot of talking and laughing and kissing. They were sorry to see Mary leave, but their happiness was greater than their sadness. Mary was going off to get an education.

Library Link ♦ *For the rest of her life, Mary would use her education to help others learn. Read more about her contributions in* Mary McLeod Bethune *by Eloise Greenfield.*

◆ Reader's Response

Why was Mary able to do so many things that others couldn't do?

Mary McLeod Bethune

Responding to Literature

1. Mary had many hopes and dreams. What do you think Mary dreamed of when she was your age? Tell about one possible dream.

2. Make a character collage for Mary. Draw a picture of Mary. Surround her with pictures of objects that were important to her. You may want to draw the objects or cut out pictures from magazines. Share your collage and tell how the items you chose represent Mary.

3. If you were able to speak with Mary, what questions would you ask her? Write three questions. Then trade questions with a partner. Try to answer each other's questions as Mary would.

Writing to Learn

Think and Imagine ♦ Mary took her first train ride alone when she was still young. What might she have been thinking as the train sped along? Write Mary's thoughts in a thought balloon.

Thought Balloon

Write ♦ Use your thought balloon to write a page in Mary's journal. Write what Mary might have written. Tell how she might have felt about leaving home and going away to school.

If it were possible to meet Mary McLeod Bethune, what would you ask her? Ask a question that could *not* be answered by just a "yes" or a "no."

SPEAKING and LISTENING ◆
Interviews

If you ever watch the news on TV, you have seen interviews. An interview is a question-and-answer discussion between two people. The interviewer is a reporter who wants to get the facts. The person being interviewed may be in the news, or that person may know a lot about a topic that is in the news. The interviewer asks questions to get the facts.

Interviews are a fine way to get the facts firsthand. When you want to know the facts about something, why not ask a person who knows? Why not interview that person? Here are some guidelines to help you conduct an interview, either in person or over the telephone.

Asking Interview Questions	1. Always prepare a list of questions <u>before</u> the interview. Try not to ask questions that can be answered with a simple *yes* or *no*. 2. Ask questions that begin with *who*, *what*, *when*, *where*, *why*, and *how*. 3. Be polite. Thank the person for helping you get the facts.
Being an Active Listener	1. Use your question list to help you stay on the topic. 2. Let the other person talk. That is what you want. 3. Listen carefully to the person's answers. You may need to ask other questions based on the answers you get.

Summary ◆ An **interview** is a question-and-answer discussion. Prepare questions for an interview ahead of time. Use questions that begin with *who, what, when, where, why,* and *how.*

Guided Practice

Tell which questions below could be answered *yes* or *no*. Tell which questions would be answered with interesting facts.

1. Why did you decide to start a school, Mrs. Bethune?
2. How did you get the money you needed to start a school?
3. Did you miss your family when you went away to school?
4. Did you study science in school?
5. What problems did you have when the school first opened?

Practice

A. You are interviewing different people about their jobs. Write two questions you might ask each person listed below.

6. a police officer
7. a bus driver
8. an actor
9. a scientist

B. With a partner, take turns pretending to be each of the people in **Practice A.** Read each question you wrote. Have your partner answer it. If your partner can answer the question with *yes* or *no*, you need to ask the question in a different way.

SAMPLE QUESTION:	Is being a police officer a difficult job?
ANSWER:	Yes.
BETTER QUESTION:	What is the most difficult thing about being a police officer?

Apply ◆ Think and Write

Interview Questions ◆ What famous person would you like to interview? Write that person's name. Under the name write six questions you would ask. Use each of these words to begin one question: *who, what, when, where, why, how.*

✎ **Remember**
that an interview is a good way to get firsthand information.

An author is writing a new book called *Growing Up in America*. What subjects that would interest you might be included? How many different subjects can you and your classmates name?

STUDY SKILLS ◆
Using the Library

Libraries have books on almost any subject you can imagine.

Fiction books contain made-up stories. Fiction books are grouped in alphabetical order by the author's last name.

Nonfiction books give facts. *Biographies* are books about people's lives. Nonfiction books are grouped by subject. Books on the same subject have the same **call number** printed on their spines and are filed alphabetically by the author's last name.

Reference books give facts on many subjects. *Dictionaries*, *atlases* (books of maps), and *encyclopedias* are reference books.

A **card catalog** or computer listing can help you find books in a library. The card catalog usually has three cards for each book: a **title card**, an **author card**, and a **subject card**.

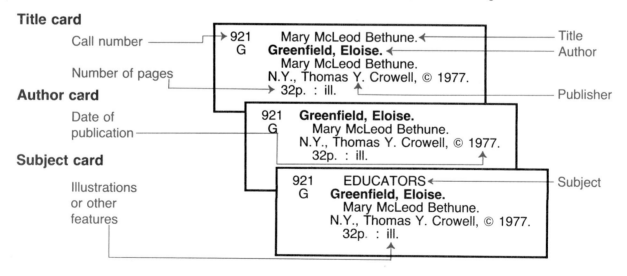

Title card
Call number
Number of pages

Author card
Date of publication

Subject card
Illustrations or other features

Title
Author
Publisher
Subject

921 G   Mary McLeod Bethune.
Greenfield, Eloise.
Mary McLeod Bethune.
N.Y., Thomas Y. Crowell, © 1977.
32p. : ill.

921 G   **Greenfield, Eloise.**
Mary McLeod Bethune.
N.Y., Thomas Y. Crowell, © 1977.
32p. : ill.

921 G   EDUCATORS
Greenfield, Eloise.
Mary McLeod Bethune.
N.Y., Thomas Y. Crowell, © 1977.
32p. : ill.

Summary ◆ Books in a library are listed by title, author, and subject in a card catalog or computer listing.

Guided Practice

Identify each book below as *fiction*, *nonfiction*, or *reference*.

1. a book about Harriet Tubman   **3.** a book of maps

2. a book about an imaginary boy   **4.** a book about penguins

Practice

A. What kind of book would tell about each item below? Write *biography*, *atlas*, *dictionary*, or *encyclopedia*.

     5. how to say *heir*   **7.** a map of the state of Georgia

     6. facts about glass   **8.** the full life story of Marie Curie

B. Use the cards in this lesson to answer these questions.

     9. What is the title of the book?

   10. Who is Eloise Greenfield?

   11. What subject includes Mary McLeod Bethune?

   12. What happened in 1977?

C. Write *title*, *author*, or *subject* to tell which card to use in a library card catalog.

   13. space   **14.** *Tales of Africa*   **15.** a book by Thomas Fall

D. For each item below, write the word or words you would look up in the card catalog or computer listing.

   16. the author of the book *Log Cabin Life*

   17. information about Daytona Beach, Florida

   18. other books by Eloise Greenfield

Apply ♦ Think and Write

The Card Catalog ♦ Write the name of a subject that interests you. In the library, look through the card catalog or computer listing. Write the titles, authors, and call numbers for three books on that subject. Which do you want to read?

✎ **Remember**
that you can find books in a card catalog by author, title, or subject.

Play ''The Name Chain.'' One player says a first name: *Louis*. Each player adds a name, then repeats all the names in alphabetical order: *Trish—Louis, Trish*. How long a chain of names can you make?

STUDY SKILLS ♦
Using an Encyclopedia

Suppose you are doing research for a report on Mary McLeod Bethune. Your friend, meanwhile, is writing a report on tree frogs. Whatever your topic, the encyclopedia is often a helpful source of information. An **encyclopedia** is a set of reference books with articles about people, places, and things.

Using an encyclopedia is easy. Each book is called a **volume**. Volumes are arranged in alphabetical order, and may also be numbered. The last volume is an **index** that lists every topic the encyclopedia contains. The index tells the volume and page number to help you find an article easily.

Articles in each volume of an encyclopedia are arranged by topics in alphabetical order. You must know what key word of a topic to look for to find information. The **key word** is usually the most important word. Here are some topics with their key words underlined:

how the **dictionary** was created   uses of **chalk** today
natural resources of **Maine**   building **railroad** tracks

Articles about people appear in alphabetical order by their last names. Suppose you want to learn about Emma Willard. Why would you look in Volume 21?

> **Summary** ♦ Articles in an encyclopedia are arranged by topics in alphabetical order.

Guided Practice

Use the encyclopedia in this lesson to answer each question.

1. How many volumes are in the encyclopedia set?
2. What is special about the last volume?
3. What articles will you find in Volume 12?
4. What key word would help you find out how to tune a piano?

Practice

A. Which volume of the encyclopedia in this lesson would have an article about each topic below? Write the volume number.

5. Helen Keller	**9.** Bethune-Cookman College
6. horses	**10.** Horace Mann
7. the White House	**11.** potato fields
8. the Civil War	**12.** South Carolina

B. Write the key word for each topic below. Then write the volume number for finding the article in the encyclopedia on the opposite page.

13. important farm products of Florida
14. when the calculator was invented
15. how eyeglasses work
16. how Louis Braille helped blind people learn to read

C. Just for fun, think of articles you could find in Volume 19 of this lesson's encyclopedia. For each item below, write a topic that begins with *t*.

EXAMPLE: food   **ANSWER:** tomato

17. animal   **18.** place   **19.** sport   **20.** famous person

Apply ◆ Think and Write

Key Words ◆ Write the key word for a topic that interests you. Then write three questions related to your topic.

✎ **Remember**
that you need a key word to look up something in an encyclopedia.

You are going to the store to pick up something for dinner. You want to leave a note saying where you are going, what you are buying, and when you will return. The catch: Your note must be five words or less. What might the note say?

WRITING ◆
Taking Notes in Your Own Words

How can you keep track of important facts when you gather information for a report? Taking notes is a big help. When you take notes, you do not have to write in full sentences. You can use your own short phrases, or groups of words.

Hallie read the article below. She took notes in her own words to help her remember important facts.

BETHUNE, MARY McLEOD (1875–1955), educator and President's adviser. Born in South Carolina, Mary was raised with sixteen brothers and sisters. Her parents had been slaves. Mary worked hard to get an education. After college she became a teacher. Mary decided to begin her own school for black children in Daytona Beach, Florida.

Money was a problem. Most of Mary's students were poor. Mary convinced some wealthy people to donate money. The school slowly grew. In 1923 it joined with Cookman Institute as Bethune-Cookman College. Mary became its president. She worked hard for equal rights. Mary was picked by President Franklin D. Roosevelt to be one of his advisers.

Here are Hallie's notes on the first paragraph of the article.

> *Mary McLeod Bethune was an educator.*
> *— born 1875, South Carolina; died 1955*
> *— worked hard in school, became teacher*
> *— started own school in Florida*

Summary ◆ Use your own words when taking notes on what you read.

Guided Practice

Say the main idea of each sentence below in your own words.

1. Mary McLeod had a strong wish to learn.
2. Mary began her education at Scotia Seminary in North Carolina.
3. At Moody Bible Institute she was the only black student.
4. Her first teaching job was in the town where she was born.
5. She left for Florida with a lot of hope but only $1.50.

Practice

A. Take notes on each sentence. Use your own words.

> **EXAMPLE:** Mary's first school opened in the fall of 1904.
> **NOTES:** own school began in autumn 1904

6. Her students were eager to learn but very poor.
7. Mary had to raise money to keep her school going.
8. Mary organized a choir to sing for rich audiences.
9. Mary's school survived and grew larger.
10. In 1923 the school joined with Cookman Institute to form Bethune-Cookman College.
11. During World War II Mary went to Washington, D.C.
12. She was an adviser for the Women's Army Corps.
13. Mary was a friend of President and Mrs. Roosevelt.
14. Mary helped to organize the new United Nations.
15. In 1960 a stone statue was built to honor Mary.

B. Read the second paragraph of the article about Mary McLeod Bethune. Take notes on the important facts. Use your own words. You don't have to use full sentences.

Apply ♦ Think and Write

Dictionary of Knowledge ♦ Find the entry for Horace Mann. Read the facts and details about his career in education. Take notes in your own words.

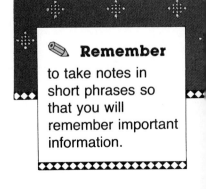

✎ **Remember**
to take notes in short phrases so that you will remember important information.

Mr. Amato stated this idea: *Students should have free time for reading every day*. Take turns giving details that support Mr. Amato's idea. Then state another idea about school. Take turns giving details that support that idea.

WRITING ◆
An Outline

An outline is a written plan for a research report. In an outline, you can clearly see how main ideas and supporting details fit together. Main ideas are listed in the order that they happened or in another useful order. Each supporting detail is listed under the main idea it tells more about.

Start by giving your outline a title. It can be the title of your report.	**Emma Willard, Education Pioneer**
Write Roman numeral **I**, followed by a period. Write the first main idea here. Indent the next line. Write the capital letters **A.**, **B.**, **C.**, and so on. Next to each letter, list facts to support the main idea you wrote next to Roman numeral **I**.	I. Early years of her life A. Born in Connecticut, 1787 B. Went to public school C. Taught herself at home
The next main idea follows Roman numeral **II**. Indented capital letters, each with a fact to support the second main idea, follow.	II. Notices problems in women's education A. Women not taught math B. No science or history C. Kept out of some schools
Here is the third main idea, with four supporting facts. Notice that the first word on each line begins with a capital letter.	III. New ideas for her own school A. Better school needed B. Should have a library C. Should have science labs D. Should display good art

Summary ◆ An **outline** organizes information. Each main idea is followed by supporting details.

Guided Practice

Use the outline on page 248 to answer the questions.

1. What is the title of the outline?
2. How many main ideas does the outline have?
3. How many details support the first main idea?

Practice

A. Use the outline on page 248 to answer the questions.

4. The first main idea is "Early years of her life." What is the second main idea?
5. How many details support the second main idea?

B. Copy the outline below. Next to each line write *title*, *main idea*, or *supporting detail*.

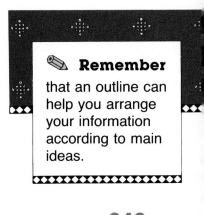

A Special Kind of School

I. George Vanderbilt bought land
  A. Woods and forests in North Carolina
  B. Vanderbilt wanted private forest
  C. Had to improve land

II. Carl Schenck had better ideas
  A. Nature should be cared for
  B. Taught others how to protect land
  C. Started Biltmore Forest School

C. Write the items below in order. Give your outline a title.

I. Apples
II. Oranges
A. Grown in groves
A. Grown in orchards
B. Peeled with fingers
B. Peeled with paring knife
C. Boiled for sauce
C. Squeezed for juice

Apply ◆ Think and Write

A Report Paragraph ◆ Each Roman numeral section of an outline is the basis for a paragraph. Use the information on page 248 to write a paragraph about Emma Willard.

> ✎ **Remember**
> that an outline can help you arrange your information according to main ideas.

Focus on Facts

A **fact** is something that you can prove to be true. Facts form the backbone of reports you write for school—and for much of your other writing. Everyone wants to know the facts. But be careful when you choose them in your writing. Not all facts are equal. Some facts are more important than others and can be used in different ways.

As a writer, you will deal with two kinds of facts: important facts and interesting facts. An important fact is one that must be included in what you write. Suppose you write a biography of George Washington. Is it important to state that he was our first President? (Yes. The fact is important.) Is it important to state that he liked to eat cream of peanut soup? (No, but it is interesting.)

Here are the two kinds of facts from the book *Mary McLeod Bethune*.

> **IMPORTANT:** In 1904, Mary McLeod Bethune started a school for black girls in Daytona Beach, Florida.
>
> **INTERESTING:** Mary McLeod Bethune and her students mashed berries and used the juice as ink.

When you write nonfiction, be sure to include the important facts. Then choose facts to interest your readers.

The Writer's Voice ◆ Do you remember important facts? Interesting facts? Write down the first three facts you think of when you recall the biography of Mary McLeod Bethune. What kinds of facts are they? Why did the author include them?

Working Together

What makes a fact important? Rely on your common sense to give you the answer as you do activities **A** and **B** with your group.

In Your Group

- Encourage everyone to share ideas.
- Choose someone to report the group's ideas.
- Agree or disagree in a pleasant way.
- Help the group reach agreement.

A. Go over the facts below with your group. Decide which ones are important and which are just interesting. Choose someone to record the important facts in one list and the interesting facts in another.

1. Mary McLeod Bethune was an excellent singer.
2. She helped write the United Nations charter.
3. She founded the National Council of Negro Women.
4. Mrs. Bethune paid $21 a month rent for her school.
5. She loved to square dance.
6. She served as president of Bethune-Cookman College.
7. Mrs. Bethune was the first black woman to head a federal agency.
8. She had wanted to become a missionary in Africa.
9. Her school started with only five little girls enrolled.

B. As a group, work on a paragraph about Mary McLeod Bethune. Use the facts on the previous page and this page. Include all the important facts and any interesting facts that you wish. When you are finished, compare the paragraphs of the different groups.

THESAURUS CORNER • Word Choice

Look up the word *find* in the Thesaurus. Write five sentences about searching for and finding facts. Use a different synonym for *find* in each sentence. Be sure that each synonym fits the meaning of the sentence.

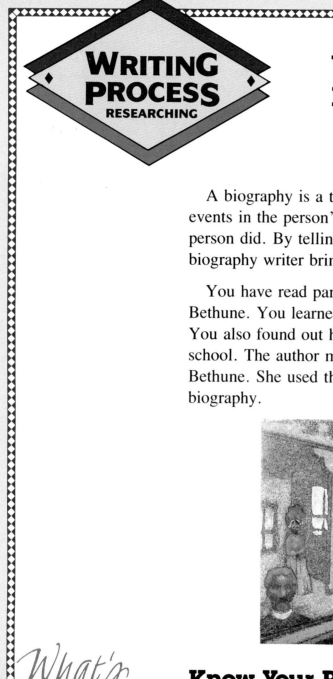

WRITING PROCESS
RESEARCHING

Writing a Biography

A biography is a true story about a real person. It describes events in the person's life and explains important things the person did. By telling the person's words and feelings, a biography writer brings the person to life.

You have read part of a biography of Mary McLeod Bethune. You learned about her childhood and education. You also found out how she felt when she left for a faraway school. The author must have read a lot about Mary McLeod Bethune. She used the information to write an interesting biography.

Know Your Purpose and Audience

Now it is your turn to introduce readers to a person you admire. Your purpose will be to write a biography about a real person.

Your audience will be your classmates. Later you might be interviewed by your classmates about your person. You might also create a display of biographies.

What's
MY PURPOSE

Who's
MY AUDIENCE

1 Prewriting

First choose a topic—a person you want to write about. Then gather information about that person.

Choose Your Topic ◆ Make a list of real people to write about. Then circle your topic choice.

Think About It

Whom do you admire? You might choose a person from history or one who is alive today. List all the people who interest you. Which one would you like to learn more about? Circle that person as your topic choice.

Talk About It

Discuss with your classmates all the people you have learned about in school. You might choose an explorer or an author. Ask others what sports or movie stars they admire. You might use library books for ideas.

Topic Ideas

Real People to Write About

1. *Rita Moreno*
2. *John F. Kennedy*
3. *(Wilma Rudolph)*
4. *E. B. White*
5. *Abraham Lincoln*
6. *Mahalia Jackson*

Choose Your Strategy ◆ These strategies may help you gather information. Read both. Then decide which idea you will use.

PREWRITING IDEAS

CHOICE ONE

Taking Notes

Do research and take notes about your person. On cards, write notes in your own words. Include the title and author of each book, or source. Then put your cards in the order you want to use in your biography. Use your notes to help make an outline.

Model

> Topic: Wilma Rudolph
> — at 4 very sick, left leg paralyzed
> — learned to walk again, then run
>
> Source: Great Sports Stars by Kim Wong

CHOICE TWO

A Thought Balloon

Think of an important event in your person's life. Put yourself in that person's place. Have you read how that person felt about it? Can you imagine? Make a thought balloon. Tell how the person might have felt about that event.

Model

> My leg is paralyzed, but I promise myself I'll walk someday.

Wilma Rudolph

2 Writing

Put your prewriting notes in front of you. Use them to help you as you write. Begin with a strong sentence to tell who your person is. Here are three ways you could begin.

- ◆ Wilma Rudolph is a famous black athlete.
- ◆ Wilma Rudolph had to work hard to become a runner.
- ◆ Wilma Rudolph is a person I admire.

Next write a paragraph for each main fact you gathered. Try to explain the person's point of view. At the end, sum up the facts. Then tell why you admire the person.

Sample First Draft ◆

Wilma Rudolph is a famous black athleet who became a champion. She is also a brave person. When she was Four, Wilma was sick. The illness paralyzed her left leg.
In time, she started running. She was fast. She worked hard to be even faster. It was high school. In 1960 Wilma ran in the olympic games. She had become so fast that she winned three gold medals! Wilma Rudolph proved that problems don't have to hold you back. I admire her courage and spirit to win.

3 Revising

Now you have written your biography. Would you like to improve it? Here is one idea that may help.

REVISING IDEA

FIRST Read to Yourself

As you read, think about your purpose. Did you write a biography? Did you write a true story about a real person? Think about your audience. Will your classmates enjoy it?

Focus: Have you included facts your readers would like to know? Circle any facts you want to make clearer.

THEN Share with a Partner

Ask your partner to read your biography silently. Then discuss it. These guidelines may help you.

The Writer

Guidelines: Listen to your partner's suggestions. Then make only the changes you feel are important.

Sample questions:
- Do you understand why I admire this person?
- **Focus question:** Did I include enough facts?

The Writer's Partner

Guidelines: Read your partner's biography carefully. Make suggestions politely.

Sample responses:
- I believe you admire this person because _____.
- The part that is not clear to me is _____.

Revising Model

Revising Model ♦ This biography is being revised. Changes the writer wants to make are shown in blue.

The word *courageous* is more exact than *brave*.

The writer explained Wilma's point of view.

The writer's partner suggested moving this fact.

The past tense of the irregular verb *win* was fixed.

Wilma Rudolph is a famous black athleet who became a champion. courageous
She is also a brave person.

When she was Four, Wilma was sick. The illness paralyzed her Wilma, however, was determined she left leg. would walk again.

In time, she started running. She was fast. She worked hard to be even faster. It was high school.

In 1960 Wilma ran in the Olympic games. She had become so fast that she won winned three gold medals! Wilma Rudolph proved that problems don't have to hold you back. I admire her courage and spirit to win.

Read the above biography the way the writer wants it to be. Then revise your own biography.

Grammar Check ♦ Be careful when you form the past tense of irregular verbs. Don't let them trick you!

Word Choice ♦ Do you want a more exact word for a word like *brave*? A thesaurus is a good source of exact words.

Revising Checklist

☐ **My purpose:** Is my biography about a real person?

☐ **My audience:** Will my classmates enjoy the biography?

☐ **Focus:** Did I include interesting facts?

4 Proofreading

Now it is time to check your biography to fix mistakes. A neat correct copy is a courtesy to your readers.

Proofreading Model ♦ Here is the biography about Wilma Rudolph. Notice the proofreading changes in red.

Proofreading Marks

capital letter	≡
small letter	/
indent paragraph	¶
check spelling	⬭

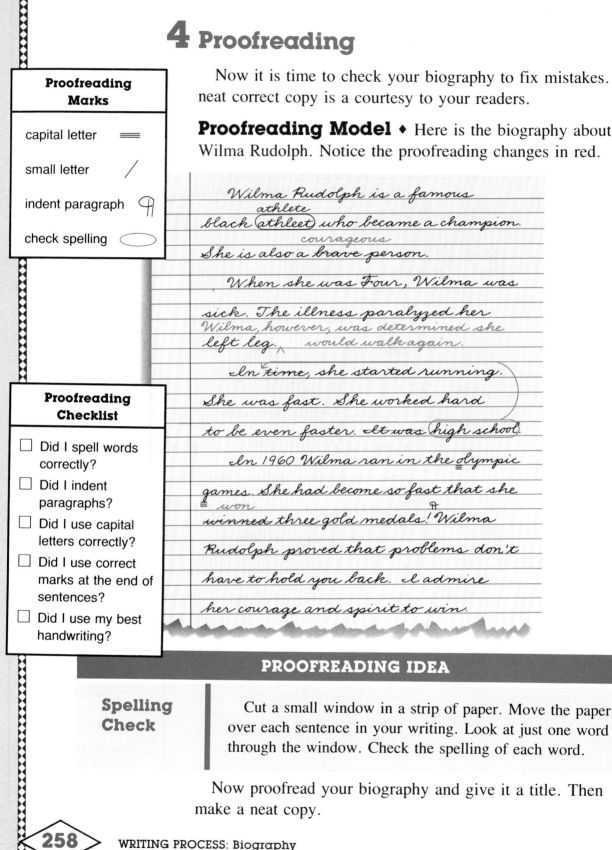

Wilma Rudolph is a famous
black (athleet) who became a champion.
athlete
She is also a brave person.
courageous

When she was Four, Wilma was

sick. The illness paralyzed her

left leg. *Wilma, however, was determined she would walk again.*

In time, she started running.

She was fast. She worked hard

to be even faster. It was (high school).

In 1960 Wilma ran in the Olympic

games. She had become so fast that she

winned three gold medals! Wilma
won

Rudolph proved that problems don't

have to hold you back. I admire

her courage and spirit to win.

Proofreading Checklist

- ☐ Did I spell words correctly?
- ☐ Did I indent paragraphs?
- ☐ Did I use capital letters correctly?
- ☐ Did I use correct marks at the end of sentences?
- ☐ Did I use my best handwriting?

PROOFREADING IDEA

Spelling Check

Cut a small window in a strip of paper. Move the paper over each sentence in your writing. Look at just one word through the window. Check the spelling of each word.

Now proofread your biography and give it a title. Then make a neat copy.

5 Publishing

On a piece of paper, write *Books I Read*. Then look at your note cards. List the books in alphabetical order. For an encyclopedia article, list the title of the article first.

Below are two ways to share your work with classmates.

Wilma Rudolph

Wilma Rudolph is a famous black athlete who became a champion. She is also a courageous person.

When she was four, Wilma was sick. The illness paralyzed her left leg. Wilma, however, was determined she would walk again.

In high school, she started running. She was fast. She worked hard to be even faster.

In 1960 Wilma ran in the Olympic Games. She had become so fast that she won three gold medals!

Wilma Rudolph proved that problems don't have to hold you back. I admire her courage and spirit to win.

PUBLISHING IDEAS

Share Aloud

Pretend you are the person you wrote about. Talk about your life and feelings. Ask your classmates to jot down questions as they listen. Then let them interview you.

Share in Writing

Choose a partner. Make an award badge for the person in your partner's biography. Let the badge tell something special about that person. Make a display of biographies. Title it ''People We Admire.'' Pin the badge to your partner's biography.

CURRICULUM
CONNECTION

Writing Across the Curriculum Math

In this unit you drew thought balloons. You used them to help you imagine other people's points of view. This strategy helped you write a biography of someone. Taking a different point of view can also help you learn math.

Writing to Learn

Think and Imagine ◆ Read the problem below. Put yourself in your teacher's place. Could you teach the class how to do this problem?

> **Dune's Rentals had 36 surfboards rented out.**
>
> **Rounded to the nearest ten, about how many surfboards were rented?**

Write ◆ Pretend you are the teacher of your class. You are planning how to teach the math lesson. Draw a big thought balloon. Inside the balloon, explain how to do the above problem.

Writing in Your Journal

In the Writer's Warm-up you wrote about schools in your great-grandparents' day. Throughout the unit you learned more about schools of long ago. In your journal explain how schools today are different from schools a hundred years ago.

BOOKS TO ENJOY

Read More About It

Mary McLeod Bethune: Voice of Black Hope *by Milton Meltzer*

You have read a little about Mary's early life. If you are interested in knowing more, you may enjoy reading this biography by another author.

Going to School in 1876 *by John J. Loeper*

Did students then have homework? How did a classroom look? What kinds of lessons did students have? This collection of old pictures and personal accounts tells about the past.

Book Report Idea Newspaper Headline

Newspapers use clever headlines to catch attention. For your next book report, grab attention with a newspaper article about your book.

Make Up a Headline

Think of a catchy sentence for a headline. Write it in bold letters at the top of your paper. Then write an article about your book. Just like a real newspaper reporter would do, answer the 5 W questions: *who, what, where, when,* and *why.* Write about the most important points in your book.

BOOK REPORT NEWS

Robert Writes Report With Charcoal

Robert Davis writes his school lessons with a small piece of charcoal. This is the best thing he has to write with.

Robert Davis

UNIT REVIEW

Unit 5

Verbs *pages 216–221*

A. Write each sentence. Use the correct present-tense form of the verb in parentheses ( ).

1. A European bison (run, runs) easily.
2. These animals (roam, roams) the forests of Europe.
3. Dying forests (threaten, threatens) the survival of the bison.
4. A breeding program (help, helps) the animals.
5. Everyone (celebrate, celebrates) the bison's survival.
6. We (want, wants) to preserve this animal.

B. Write each sentence. Use the correct past-tense form of the verb in parentheses ( ).

7. American interest in pandas (begin) in the twentieth century.
8. The Roosevelts had (go) to China.
9. They (bring) home a giant panda.
10. It (eat) for twelve hours a day.
11. The panda had (grow) very large.
12. Scientists (write) about this giant panda.

Contractions *pages 222–225*

C. Write a contraction for each pair of words.

13. we are
14. he is
15. she will
16. you would
17. I am
18. you are
19. they have
20. she has
21. he had
22. it is
23. I would
24. they are

D. Write contractions for the words below.

25. is not
26. are not
27. was not
28. do not
29. did not
30. will not
31. have not
32. has not
33. had not
34. could not
35. should not
36. would not

E. Write each sentence. Use a contraction in place of the underlined words.

37. I have read about Jefferson.
38. We are often reminded of his many talents.
39. Jefferson could not have had a wider variety of interests.
40. We have learned that he loved to study.
41. He would read in many languages.
42. Jefferson did not speak well publicly.
43. He is remembered for his writing.

Context Clues   *pages 226–227*

F. Write the word or words that give you a clue to the meaning of each underlined word.

44. Tina took a <u>morsel</u>, or small bite, of pie.

45. The movie was <u>dull</u>, not interesting.

46. Two female geese, but no <u>ganders</u>, are in the pond.

47. This is a <u>quiver</u>, a case for arrows.

48. The <u>current</u>, or most recent, newspaper is here.

49. We saw a <u>faint</u> or dim light.

50. The wild animal returned home to the <u>den</u>.

51. A finger or toe is called a <u>digit</u>.

52. Mark is <u>generous</u>, or always ready to share.

G. Use the context clue to find the meaning of each underlined word. Write the word and its meaning.

53. A <u>cuttlefish</u> is one of the strangest water creatures.

54. It moves by <u>jetting</u>, or squirting a stream of water with force.

55. <u>Cuttlefish</u> are ten-armed mollusks.

56. A <u>cyclone</u> is a windstorm that forms a whirling pattern.

57. In our hemisphere, cyclones move <u>counterclockwise</u>, not clockwise.

58. A <u>hurricane</u>, a form of cyclone, often occurs with heavy rain.

Using the Library   *pages 242–243*

H. Write *fiction* or *nonfiction* for each title.

59. *A History of San Francisco*

60. *Robots on the Bridge*

61. *The Mystery of the Missing Mouse*

62. *Six Reasons for Conserving Bison*

63. *Once Upon a Rainbow*

64. *Photographing Rare Birds*

65. *Understanding Jet Engines*

66. *Tales My Uncle Told Me*

67. *The True Story of a Pioneer Family*

68. *Exploration of the Coral Seas*

69. *The Monster of Mission Lake*

70. *Folktales of Iceland*

71. *The Man in the Moon*

72. *The First Landing on the Moon*

73. *The Princess and the Porcupine*

I. Write *biography* or *reference* for each title.

74. *Beverly Sills, Opera Star*

75. *A Man of Courage*

76. *Book of Butterflies*

77. *Campsites in the National Parks of North America*

78. *The Life and Work of Eleanor Roosevelt*

79. *The Fifty States*

80. *Florence Nightingale, Nurse*

81. *The Student Dictionary*

82. *The Pocket Thesaurus*

83. *Benjamin Franklin*

84. *A Guide to Identifying Rocks*

LANGUAGE PUZZLERS

Unit 5 Challenge

State Facts

Play this game about states in the United States. Match each item in **Column A** with a fact in **Column B**. (Hint: The form of the verb must agree with the subject of the sentence.)

Column A	Column B
1. Hawaii	visit Colorado's mountains.
2. Arizona	was an Illinoisan.
3. Abraham Lincoln	call their state the Heart of Dixie.
4. Alabamians	is the Grand Canyon State.
5. Massachusetts	is found in Pennsylvania.
6. Many Americans	joined the Union in 1959.
7. The Liberty Bell	was an original colony.

Animal Activities

The clue to this wildlife puzzle is a chain of letters. The last two letters of each subject are the first two letters of the verb in the next sentence. The last two letters of the subject in the last sentence are the first two letters of the verb in the first sentence.

1. A giraffe _ _ _ _ _ _ _ into trees for leaves.
2. A brown hare _ _ _ _ _ on wild grasses.
3. The wildebeest _ _ _ _ _ _ _ under a tree.
4. An ostrich _ _ _ _ _ _ _ _ _ its long neck.
5. Two oxen _ _ _ _ _ a lion away.
6. A tortoise _ _ _ _ _ _ a swampy pond.
7. A piranha _ _ _ _ an alligator.
8. A mosquito _ _ _ _ _ _ _ from a tiny egg.
9. Susan Terasawa _ _ _ _ _ _ _ a baby zebra.
10. The wild mare _ _ _ _ _ _ _ its colt.

Unit 5 Extra Practice

1 Using Subjects and Verbs That Agree

p. 216

A. Write each sentence. Use the correct form of the verb in parentheses ( ).

1. The students (want, wants) to bake bread.
2. The cooking teacher (explain, explains) the recipe.
3. It (call, calls) for three cups of flour.
4. They (collect, collects) the parts of the mixture.
5. Karen (wash, washes) her hands.
6. Dan (pour, pours) some water into a bowl.
7. We (measure, measures) the flour.
8. The yeast (fizz, fizzes) in the warm water.
9. I (add, adds) two teaspoons of salt.
10. The students (stir, stirs) in some butter.
11. Then they (check, checks) the next step.
12. I (reach, reaches) for a fresh bowl.
13. She (rub, rubs) some flour onto her hands.
14. You (turn, turns) the dough out onto the board.
15. We (knead, kneads) the dough until it is smooth.

B. Write each sentence. Use the correct present-tense form of the verb in parentheses ( ).

16. The warm dough ____ up. (puff)
17. The teacher ____ us what to do now. (show)
18. He ____ the dough in the center. (punch)
19. The air ____ out all at once. (rush)
20. Then you ____ the dough over like this. (fold)
21. Jean ____ on the oven. (turn)
22. The students ____ the dough into the pan. (press)
23. The bread ____ for nearly an hour. (bake)
24. I ____ a piece while it is still warm. (taste)

2 Using Irregular Verbs *p. 218*

A. Write each sentence. Use the correct past form of the verb in parentheses ( ).

1. We have (flew, flown) to southwestern Indiana.
2. Abraham Lincoln (grew, grown) up here.
3. He had (began, begun) his life in Kentucky.
4. His family (went, gone) to Indiana in 1816.
5. We had (went, gone) to see Lincoln's log cabin.
6. He (wrote, written) his lessons on a slate.
7. Lincoln (went, gone) to school no more than a year.
8. After he had (did, done) his chores, he studied.
9. By 1828 Lincoln had (grew, grown) very tall.
10. His feet (flew, flown) when he ran.
11. While wrestling he had (threw, thrown) strong men.
12. But he had (saw, seen) nothing of the world.
13. That spring he (rode, ridden) down the Mississippi River on a flatboat.
14. A new life had (began, begun) for him.

B. Write each sentence. Use the correct past form of the verb in parentheses ( ).

15. Lincoln ____ to Illinois to live in 1830. (go)
16. He ____ a number of different jobs. (do)
17. On his own he ____ to study law. (begin)
18. Time had ____ by quickly. (fly)
19. Lincoln ____ popular in Illinois. (grow)
20. He had ____ many miles meeting people. (ride)
21. He ____ that he could win an election. (see)
22. He had ____ some exciting speeches. (write)
23. Lincoln ____ his clothes and books into a bag. (throw)
24. In 1837 the prairie lawyer ____ into Springfield. (ride)
25. His reputation as ''Honest Abe'' had ____(begin)
26. In 1846 he ____ to Washington as congressman. (go)
27. His next stay in Washington ____ him as President. (see)

3 Using Irregular Verbs

p. 220

A. Write the past-tense form of each verb below. Then write the form of each verb that is used with the helping verb *have, has,* or *had*.

1. take   **2.** say   **3.** bring   **4.** fall   **5.** come

B. Write each sentence. Use the correct past form of the verb in parentheses ( ).

6. In 1925 sled-dog drivers (run, ran) a race against death in Alaska.
7. They (bring, brought) medicine to prevent the spread of a serious disease in Nome.
8. The long journey from Seward (took, taken) many days.
9. Since 1973, people have (came, come) to race here.
10. Sometimes the race has (took, taken) over four weeks.
11. Many teams have (find, found) it very rough.
12. Susan Butcher (come, came) to Alaska in 1975.
13. She (say, said) she wanted to win the race.
14. Susan (gave, given) her dogs lots of care.
15. The dogs (ate, eaten) meat or fish every day.

C. Write each sentence. Use the correct past form of the verb in parentheses ( ).

16. During training they had (run) sixty miles a day.
17. Drivers had (bring) booties for the dogs' paws.
18. Susan's lead dog Tekla (fall) right at the start.
19. When they hit the snow-covered tree, Susan had (fall).
20. These setbacks (take) their toll.
21. Her team (find) its second wind anyway.
22. They (run) a good race.
23. The dogs had (eat) all the supplies.
24. The team had (give) its best.
25. Susan (come) in second.
26. She has (say) that next year she will win!

4 Contractions with Verbs   *p. 222*

A. Write the contractions you can form with these words.

1. you are	**4.** he will	**7.** we had
2. they have	**5.** I would	**8.** it is
3. I am	**6.** they had	**9.** you will

B. Write each sentence. Use a contraction in place of the underlined words.

10. We have been reading a new history book.
11. It is about black people in America.
12. Perhaps you will read about Benjamin Banneker.
13. He had educated himself in mathematics.
14. He is known for helping to plan Washington, D.C.
15. Now I can say I have heard of Mary McLeod Bethune.
16. She is remembered for the college she began.
17. She had also worked with President Roosevelt.
18. You would also enjoy hearing about Charlotte Forten.
19. She is still famous today as a teacher.

C. Find the two words in each sentence that can form a contraction. Write each sentence, using a contraction.

20. We will read about the explorer Matt Henson.
21. He had been with Robert Peary at the North Pole.
22. You say you have never read his adventures?
23. Well, they are described in the book Henson wrote.
24. Thurgood Marshall is a name I had often heard.
25. He has served our most important court since 1967.
26. We are reading Sojourner Truth's famous words.
27. I know I shall always remember them.
28. She is known for speaking for women's rights.
29. I have also enjoyed Countee Cullen's poems.
30. Next we will read about the scientist Charles Drew.
31. We have learned how Jesse Owens made sports history.
32. Now we will learn how others have contributed.

5 Contractions with *not*

p. 224

A. Write a contraction for each of these word pairs.

1. has not		**8.**	is not
2. did not		**9.**	do not
3. will not		**10.**	should not
4. are not		**11.**	would not
5. had not		**12.**	does not
6. have not		**13.**	was not
7. were not		**14.**	could not

B. Write the sentences. Use a contraction in place of the underlined words in each sentence.

EXAMPLE: Mom and Dad <u>had not</u> been away many days.
ANSWER: Mom and Dad hadn't been away many days.

15. We <u>did not</u> leave enough time.
16. You <u>should not</u> have waited so long.
17. Why <u>does not</u> Peter finish the dishes?
18. I <u>do not</u> know how much soap to use.
19. Salvador <u>has not</u> started the wash yet.
20. There <u>was not</u> enough hot water left.
21. Claudia <u>cannot</u> do all the cleaning herself!
22. We were afraid we <u>would not</u> finish, but we did.
23. <u>Will not</u> Mom and Dad be surprised?
24. They <u>could not</u> be more pleased with us!

C. Write the answer to each question. Use a contraction with -*n't*.

25. Does he believe in flying saucers? No, he _____ .
26. Did she see one last night? No, she _____ .
27. Could you take a picture of it? No, I _____ .
28. Are they sure it was a flying saucer? No, they _____ .
29. Will you watch for it again tonight? No, I _____ .
30. Was there a news report about it? No, there _____ .

USING LANGUAGE
TO
DESCRIBE

=== PART ONE ===

Unit Theme *Seasons at the Pond*

Language Awareness Adjectives

=== PART TWO ===

Literature *The Trumpet of the Swan* by E. B. White

A Reason for Writing Describing

Writing
IN YOUR JOURNAL

WRITER'S WARM-UP ◆ What do you know about pond life? Maybe a pond in your town attracts birds and other small animals. During the winter a pond that freezes solid can make a perfect ice hockey rink. Yet, even below the frozen surface, some water creatures are alive and well. In summer you can visit a pond and see all the busy creatures. Write about a pond in your journal. Tell what you like best about ponds.

GETTING STARTED

Think of words that describe, such as *awesome*, *blue*, and *charming*. See how many you can name in an alphabetical chain.

1 Writing with Adjectives

Read the paragraph below. It describes the animals you might find at a pond. Notice the underlined words.

The pond is a busy place. Many squirrels scamper in the tall trees nearby. One squirrel with a bushy tail nibbles a hard acorn. Several chipmunks run through the wet grass, chasing a brown rabbit.

Each underlined word above describes the noun that follows it. Words that describe nouns are adjectives. An adjective tells something more about the noun. The words *busy*, *tall*, *bushy*, *hard*, *wet*, and *brown* answer the question "What kind?" The words *many*, *one*, and *several* answer the question "How many?"

You can add interesting details to your writing by using adjectives to describe people, places, and things. Adjectives can help to create clear word pictures.

> **Summary** ◆ An **adjective** describes a noun or a pronoun. Use adjectives to add details to your writing.

Guided Practice

Find the adjective that tells *how many* or *what kind* in each sentence.

1. We went to the pond on a sunny day.
2. We saw several animals there.
3. A snake was sleeping on a flat rock.
4. A swan was making a new nest.
5. One raccoon was catching a fish.

Practice

A. Describe each noun with two adjectives. The picture shows *how many*. Choose the adjective below that tells *what kind*.

hungry   slender   noisy   purple   busy   speckled

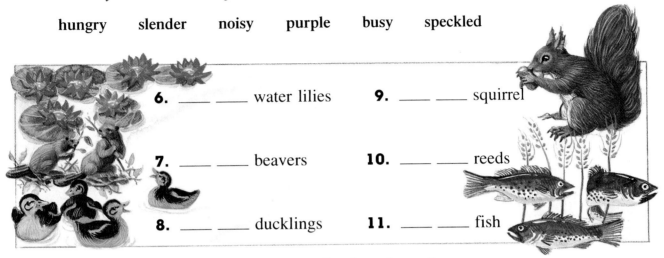

6. ___ ___ water lilies

7. ___ ___ beavers

8. ___ ___ ducklings

9. ___ ___ squirrel

10. ___ ___ reeds

11. ___ ___ fish

B. Write these sentences. Underline the adjectives that tell *what kind* and *how many*.

12. Colorful changes take place at the pond in spring.
13. Warm breezes replace the cold winds of winter.
14. Many buds appear on bare trees.
15. Tall reeds grow from the muddy bottom of the pond.
16. Some birds return from warm climates.

C. Write each sentence below. Add your own interesting adjectives to create vivid word pictures.

17. The ___ heron wades in the ___ water.
18. ___ birds stalk along the ___ shore.
19. ___ heron catches fish with its ___ bill.
20. ___ baby herons fly to their ___ nest.

Apply ◆ Think and Write

From Your Writing ◆ Read what you wrote for the Writer's Warm-up. Try to improve your paragraph by adding more adjectives.

✎ **Remember**
to use adjectives to create vivid word pictures.

Name some things that you would take on a trip. Use these examples to get started.

I would take an orange but not a pear.
I would take an ____ but not a ____.

2 Using *a*, *an*, and *the*

The proper use of *a*, *an*, and *the* will help focus your writing. These words are special adjectives called articles.

> **The** pond is full of activity in summer.
> **The** animals are very busy.
> You would have **a** good time watching them.
> Let's spend **an** afternoon there soon.

The article *the* is used with both singular and plural nouns.

■ the pond   the animals

The articles *a* and *an* are used only with singular nouns. *A* is used before a word that begins with a consonant sound. *An* is used before a word that begins with a vowel sound.

> **a** beaver   **an** eager beaver
> **a** pleasant afternoon   **an** afternoon

Some words that start with *h* begin with a consonant sound. Others begin with a vowel sound. Compare the words *hummingbird* and *honor*. Which is used with *an*?

> **Summary** ◆ The words *a*, *an*, and *the* are a special kind of adjective. They are called **articles**.

Guided Practice

Tell whether *a* or *an* correctly completes each sentence.

1. Summer is ____ enjoyable time of year at the pond.
2. You might see ____ duckling circle the pond.
3. There may be ____ salamander asleep on a rock.

Practice

A. Read the sentences about a pond. Choose the correct article to complete each sentence.

4. (An, The) heat of summer promotes plant growth.
5. Bright flowers shoot up from (a, an) water lily.
6. Leaves grow larger on all (a, the) trees.
7. (A, An) underwater plant spreads its leaves.
8. (A, An) clump of reeds grows along the shore.

B. Write each sentence, using *a* or *an*.

9. We watch ____ sunfish swimming near the bank.
10. Nearby ____ crayfish searches for food.
11. ____ alert frog catches flies.
12. Overhead ____ osprey soars above the pond.
13. Suddenly ____ enormous cloud passes by.
14. Raindrops make ____ splashing sound.
15. ____ patch of dry grass begins to look greener.
16. Then the sun appears from behind ____ cloud.
17. ____ hornet begins to buzz around its nest.
18. It is ____ excellent place to daydream.

C. Describe a visit to a pond.
Complete each sentence.

19. I would like to see a ____ .
20. I think that an ____ .
21. One day last week a ____ .
22. Did you know that an ____ ?
23. I hope that the ____ .

> ✎ **Remember**
> to use the articles
> *a* and *an*
> carefully.

Apply ◆ Think and Write

Animal Nouns ◆ List as many nouns that name animals as you can in two minutes. Write *a* or *an* before each noun.

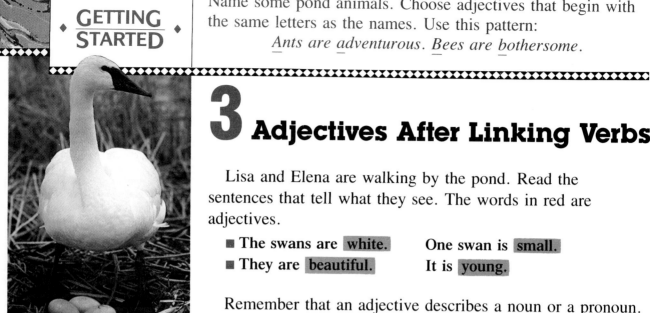

Name some pond animals. Choose adjectives that begin with the same letters as the names. Use this pattern:
Ants are adventurous. Bees are bothersome.

3 Adjectives After Linking Verbs

Lisa and Elena are walking by the pond. Read the sentences that tell what they see. The words in red are adjectives.

- The swans are white.   One swan is small.
- They are beautiful.   It is young.

Remember that an adjective describes a noun or a pronoun. Sometimes an adjective comes before the word it describes.

- The **beautiful** swans return to the pond.

Sometimes an adjective comes after a linking verb, such as *is*, *are*, *was*, or *were*.

- The weather <u>is</u> <u>warm</u>.   It <u>is</u> <u>warm</u>.

A linking verb tells what the subject is or was. It connects the adjective to the subject of a sentence.

Summary ♦ An adjective that follows a linking verb describes the subject of the sentence. Use adjectives after linking verbs to give your reader more information about the subject.

Guided Practice

Name the adjective that follows the linking verb in each sentence. What noun or pronoun does it describe?

1. A swan's nest is large.
2. It is round.
3. The eggs are white.
4. The swan is quiet on her nest.
5. The eggs are warm underneath the swan.

Practice

A. The sentences below tell more about swans' eggs. Write each sentence. Underline the adjective that follows the linking verb. Then draw an arrow to the subject.

> **EXAMPLE:** Each swan's egg is perfect.
> **ANSWER:** Each swan's egg is perfect.

6. In a month the babies are ready.
7. They are active inside their shells.
8. Their bills are sharp.
9. Their necks are powerful.
10. Soon each egg is open.
11. The babies are free at last.
12. They are different from their parents.
13. Their bodies are gray.
14. Their feet are yellow.
15. Now those youngsters are eager for dinner.
16. Until they eat, the babies are hungry.
17. The babies are sleepy after dinner.

B. Write the sentences below. Use an adjective to complete each sentence.

18. This pond is ____.
19. The pebbles are ____.
20. That rock is ____.
21. This tree is ____.
22. The shade is ____.
23. That snake is ____.
24. The turtles are ____.
25. Those frogs are ____.
26. The dragonflies are ____.
27. The chipmunks are ____.

Apply ◆ Think and Write

Describing Pictures ◆ The pictures on this page show materials birds use to build nests. Describe these materials. Use adjectives after linking verbs to create word pictures.

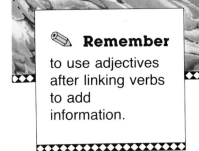

> ✎ **Remember**
> to use adjectives after linking verbs to add information.

Pick an object in your classroom, but don't tell what it is.
Other students will guess by asking you questions such as *Is it
bigger than my foot? Is it heavier than a book? Is it darker
than my sweater?*

4 Adjectives That Compare

When you are writing a description, do you ever compare
one thing with another? Adjectives have two different forms
that are useful in making comparisons.

> A duck is smaller than a blue heron.
> The sandpiper is the smallest of all.

Notice that *-er* is added to the adjective *small* when two
things are compared. Notice that *-est* is added to the adjective
when three or more things are compared.

Sometimes you have to change the spelling of an adjective
when you write the *-er* or *-est* form of the word.

Drop final *e*	fine	finer	finest
Change final *y* to *i*	easy	easier	easiest
Double final consonant	big	bigger	biggest

Summary ◆ Use the *-er* form of an adjective to
compare two persons, places, or things. Use the *-est* form
of an adjective to compare three or more persons, places,
or things. Writers use these forms to tell how things are
alike or different.

Guided Practice

Name the *-er* and *-est* form of each adjective.

1. hot   **2.** lovely   **3.** safe   **4.** clear   **5.** sunny

Practice

A. Write the *-er* and *-est* form of each adjective.

   6. light   **8.** cool   **10.** muddy

   7. flat   **9.** deep   **11.** dense

B. The adjectives in the sentences below compare things at the pond. Write each sentence. Use the correct form of the adjective in parentheses ( ).

   12. A pond is (small, smaller) than an ocean.

   13. Reeds grow (higher, highest) than grass.

   14. Trees are the (taller, tallest) plants of all.

   15. Frogs have (smoother, smoothest) skin than toads.

   16. The bullfrog is the (bigger, biggest) American frog.

   17. Snails are the (slower, slowest) pond creatures.

   18. A ladybug is (tinier, tiniest) than a bee.

   19. A green heron is (shorter, shortest) than a blue heron.

   20. The blue heron is (prettier, prettiest) than the green heron.

C. Write each sentence. Use the *-er* or the *-est* form of the adjective in parentheses ( ).

   21. Most ponds are (shallow) than lakes.

   22. Ducks are the (funny) birds at the pond.

   23. A water snake is (long) than a garter snake.

   24. A trumpeter swan is (noisy) than a mute swan.

   25. Of all the swans at the pond, the black swan is the (rare).

Apply ◆ Think and Write

Dictionary of Knowledge ◆ Read about John Audubon, a naturalist who loved birds. Think of two interesting birds that are very different. Write some comparisons about them.

> ✎ **Remember**
> to use the *-er* and *-est* forms of adjectives to make clear comparisons.

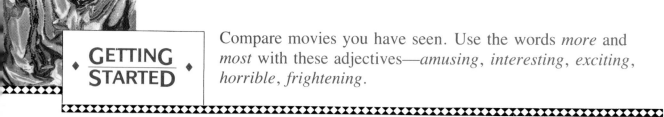

GETTING STARTED

Compare movies you have seen. Use the words *more* and *most* with these adjectives—*amusing, interesting, exciting, horrible, frightening*.

5 Using *more* and *most* with Adjectives

Many adjectives of two or more syllables use *more* and *most* to make comparisons.

Use *more* to compare two persons, places, or things.

■ A swan boat is <u>more</u> elegant than a tugboat.

Use *most* to compare three or more persons, places, or things.

■ We had the <u>most</u> enjoyable time at the pond.

Summary ✦ The words *more* and *most* are often used with adjectives of two or more syllables to make comparisons. Use comparisons in your writing to add interest.

Guided Practice

Tell whether to use *more* or *most* to complete each sentence.

1. The ducks were ____ comical than usual.
2. Rick was even ____ entertaining than the ducks.
3. He made the ____ natural duck calls I've ever heard.
4. The ducks followed him around in the ____ trusting way.
5. Rick seemed even ____ surprised than I was.

Practice

A. Use *more* or *most* to complete each sentence. Write each sentence.

  6. Our pond is the _____ beautiful one I have ever seen.
  7. It becomes _____ popular every year.
  8. It is the _____ important bird refuge in the state.
  9. We are _____ protective of animals now than we were.
  10. We are also _____ aware now of their needs.
  11. The Canada goose is the _____ common bird here.
  12. Even the insects are _____ valuable than you realize.
  13. Balance in nature is the _____ important factor of all.
  14. Discovering the baby swans was the _____ exciting moment of the summer.
  15. The baby swans are now _____ active than the ducklings.

B. Write each sentence. Use *more* or *most* with the adjective in parentheses ( ).

  16. This pond is the (protected) area in the state.
  17. It should be (familiar) to people than it is now.
  18. Informing the public becomes (necessary) each year.
  19. This is a (difficult) job than you may realize.
  20. The newsletter is our (important) project of all.
  21. Our volunteer reporters are (active) than ever.
  22. You are the (skillful) writer that I know.
  23. You could be (helpful) than anyone on the staff.
  24. You would be the (welcome) volunteer of all.
  25. Join us, and do the (meaningful) work of your life.

Apply ◆ Think and Write

Descriptive Comparisons ◆ Think of several wild animals. Write sentences that compare them. Use *more* and *most* with adjectives in your sentences.

> ✎ **Remember**
> to use *more* and *most* to make interesting comparisons.

♦ GETTING ♦
STARTED

Apples are good, bananas are better, but cantaloupe is best of all. Dates are good. . . . Make an alphabet chain about three foods in one food group. Use *good*, *better*, and *best* in each sentence.

6 Adjectives with Irregular Comparisons

Read the sentences below.

The **good** weather yesterday was fine for bird watching.
The clear weather today is even **better**.
The warmer weather tomorrow may be the **best** of all.

The underlined words above are adjectives. Notice that *good* changes its form when it is used to compare.

The adjectives *good*, *bad*, *much*, and *little* have special forms for comparing places, people, and things.

good weather	better weather	best weather
bad storm	worse storm	worst storm
much snow	more snow	most snow
little fog	less fog	least fog

Summary ♦ Some adjectives show comparison in a special way. When you speak and write, use the correct forms of *good*, *bad*, *much*, and *little*.

Guided Practice

Tell which adjective in parentheses ( ) completes each sentence.

1. The pond has (more, most) water than usual this autumn.
2. The leaves have the (better, best) color I have ever seen.
3. Last year we had (less, least) rain than this year.
4. It caused the (worse, worst) drought ever.

Practice

A. Complete each sentence with the correct word in ( ).

5. For animals, autumn brings (more, most) problems than summer.
6. There is (less, least) food available.
7. Soon the cold will be even (worse, worst) than it is now.
8. Then there will be even (less, least) food.
9. Autumn is the (better, best) time for birds to leave the pond.
10. They fly south to a (better, best) climate.
11. Then they will miss the (worse, worst) storms.
12. Frogs have the (less, least) distance of all to go.
13. The (better, best) place for them to sleep is in the mud of the pond.
14. Mud gives the (more, most) protection from the cold.

B. Complete each sentence. Use the correct form of *good*, *bad*, *much*, or *little* to show comparison.

15. A cold winter is the (bad) time of all for animals.
16. They have the (much) trouble finding food then.
17. Spring will bring (good) opportunities.
18. Ice skaters have the (much) fun of all in winter.
19. Swimmers, of course, have the (little) fun.
20. Winter is (bad) than summer for them.
21. Soon we will have (much) heat from the sun.
22. Spring will arrive in (little) time than you think.
23. It will bring (much) rain and flowers.
24. What do you think is the (good) season of all?

Apply ◆ Think and Write

Descriptive Comparisons ◆ Which two seasons of the year do you like best? Why? As you write about them, use *better* and *best* to make comparisons.

> ✎ **Remember**
> to check the forms of any irregular adjectives you used.

Think of more words that could describe Fulton and Lester.
Fulton was hopeful and (?)ful.
Lester was tireless and (?)less.

VOCABULARY ♦
Suffixes

Read these sentences that describe a day in the fall.

Colorful leaves fall from the trees.	color + ful
The ground is *leafy* and wet.	leaf + y
The *cloudless* sky is deep blue.	cloud + less

Each underlined word above has a suffix. A **suffix** is a letter or letters added to the end of a word. The word to which a suffix is added is called the base word. A **base word** is the simplest form of a word. A suffix changes the meaning of a base word to which it is added.

Study the chart below. Notice that the spelling of the base word sometimes changes when a suffix is added.

Suffix	Meaning	Example
-y	having, being like	storm + y = stormy noise + y = noisy mud + y = muddy
-ful	full of	care + ful = careful beauty + ful = beautiful
-less	without	care + less = careless penny + less = penniless

Building Your Vocabulary

Add *-y*, *-ful*, or *-less* to each word in parentheses ( ).

1. The pond is starting to become (ice).
2. Soon (joy) children will skate happily across it.
3. They will have (end) fun.

Practice

A. Write each sentence. Add the suffix *-y*, *-ful*, or *-less* to the word in parentheses ( ).

   1. The (trick) fox snooped around the pond.
   2. He was looking for a (help) little mouse.
   3. A (grace) swan swam in the middle of the pond.
   4. "That (use) fox will never get me here," she thought.
   5. A squirrel with a (bush) tail scurried up a tree.
   6. Suddenly a (fear) bear trudged down to take a drink.
   7. All the animals looked at him and felt (shake).
   8. After his drink the bear ate some berries and felt (sleep).
   9. He stretched out his (power) body and took a nap.

B. Many adjectives that describe weather are formed with *-y*. Add the suffix *-y* to each of the words below. Then write a sentence for each word. Watch out for spelling changes!

   10. sun   **12.** cloud   **14.** fog   **16.** storm
   11. ice   **13.** wind   **15.** rain   **17.** breeze

C. More than one suffix can be used with base words. Add both *-ful* and *-less* to each word below. Then use each word you form in a sentence.

   18. help   **19.** thought   **20.** harm   **21.** use

LANGUAGE CORNER ◆ Imitative Words

Some words imitate sounds made by animals. Dogs *bark*, *howl*, *yelp*, and *snarl*. Cats *mew* and *purr*. Horses *neigh*. Jays *chatter*.

What creatures make these noises?

gobble   coo   hoot   croak
squeal   moan   hiss   buzz

Bark

Growl

Howl

How to Expand Sentences with Adjectives

You know that adjectives are describing words. Adjectives add interesting details to sentences. The adjectives you choose can help readers create clear pictures in their minds. Read the sentences below. Which sentence gives you a clearer picture of the trail?

> **1.** We followed a trail to the river.
> **2.** We followed a narrow, shady trail to the river.

The adjectives *narrow* and *shady* in sentence **2** make it easier to picture what the trail was like. Different adjectives could give a different picture. How do the sentences below change the picture of the trail?

> **3.** We followed a wide, sunny trail to the river.
> **4.** We followed a short, hilly trail to the river.

The Grammar Game ♦ Take some adjective action! Write at least two adjectives for each word below. Choose adjectives that describe each word in different ways.

pickle	banana	garage	rose	package
caterpillar	swan	swamp	motorcycle	storm
dream	holiday	balloon	dinner	library
magazine	elephant	town	concert	syrup

Working Together

As you do activities **A** and **B**, use adjectives to add interesting details to your group's writing.

A. Choose adjectives to describe each underlined noun in the sentences below. Let the group decide whether to add one or two adjectives.

1. The <u>swimmers</u> laughed and ran in and out of the <u>water</u>.
2. The rest of us stretched out on the <u>sand</u> in the <u>sun</u>.
3. The sky was filled with <u>clouds</u>.
4. A <u>dog</u> poked here and there along the <u>bushes</u>.
5. Children were busy building <u>castles</u> and digging <u>holes</u>.

B. Advertisements use lots of adjectives. Complete this ad with adjectives of the group's choice. Then write the ad again, using different adjectives.

Find ____ savings at WHEELS-4-U! Buy a ____ bicycle with ____ baskets and ____ saddlebags. Check the ____ price of our ____ values: ____ skateboards in ____ condition and ____ wagons with ____ stripes. And don't forget our ____ baby carriages. We also stock ____ wheels for everything we sell. Remember, if it rolls, we sell it!

WRITERS' CORNER ◆ Overused Adjectives

Try not to use common adjectives, such as *good* or *bad,* too often. Overusing these adjectives can make your writing boring to read. Use more descriptive words instead.

OVERUSED: The bad snowstorm caused bad road damage.
IMPROVED: The terrible snowstorm caused serious road damage.

Read what you wrote for the Writer's Warm-up. Did you overuse some adjectives? Can you replace them to add more detail to your writing?

CENTRAL PARK, WINTER—SKATING POND
lithograph by Currier and Ives
The Museum of the City of New York.

USING LANGUAGE
TO
DESCRIBE

PART TWO

Literature *The Trumpet of the Swan* by E. B. White

A Reason for Writing Describing

CREATIVE

FINE ARTS ♦ The painting at the left shows people of many years ago skating on a frozen pond. Look at all the people. Pick ten people who interest you. Give each one a name. As you list each name, write the words that each person is saying. You can make up a story about the people if you wish. Tell their story through the words they say.

CREATIVE THINKING ◆
A Strategy for Describing

A CLUSTER MAP

Describing is using details to paint word pictures. After this lesson you will read part of *The Trumpet of the Swan* by E. B. White. In it the author describes a pond and the animals that live there. Later you will write your own description of a place.

Have you ever visited a pond in early spring? This is how E. B. White describes it.

But one day a change came over the woods and the pond. Warm air, soft and kind, blew through the trees. The ice . . . began to melt. Patches of open water appeared. All the creatures . . . heard and felt the breath of spring. . . .

The author does not just say that it was the beginning of spring. He elaborates, or adds details. Which details help you see the pond? Which help you smell the air?

◆ Learning the Strategy

Adding details can make an idea more complete. For example, what are the rules for a fire drill? You might think of "Leave the building quietly." How would you complete the list of fire drill rules? Sometimes details can help you persuade. For example, suppose your friend wants to roller skate. You say, "I'd rather ride bikes." Is that enough to change her mind? How might adding details or reasons help persuade her?

Adding details can also make an idea more interesting. For example, pretend that your favorite color is green. Here is a cluster map about the color green. The topic, green, is in the center circle. Details are in circles attached to the topic circle. How might this cluster map help you write a poem about the color green?

a tall, cool glass of limeade

my favorite sweater

my cat's eyes

green

a four-leaf clover

a grasshopper in the backyard

the smell of freshly mown grass

ripe, juicy grapes

Using the Strategy

A. What does the word *picnic* bring to mind? Make a cluster map. Write *picnic* in the center topic circle. What details does *picnic* make you think of? Write them in detail circles around the topic circle. If you like, use your cluster map to help plan a real family or class picnic.

B. Think about a pond in early spring. What do you see? What do you hear and smell? Make a cluster map. In the topic circle write "pond in early spring." Add as many detail circles as you can. Then read *The Trumpet of the Swan* to "see" more of the pond.

Applying the Strategy

♦ How did you think of all the details about the pond?
♦ When might you want to write down and remember details?

AWARD WINNING AUTHOR

LITERATURE

from

The Trumpet of the Swan

by E. B. White

Every spring, Sam Beaver and his father took a trip to their wilderness camp in Canada. Sam's father liked to fish there, and Sam enjoyed exploring. It was while he was exploring, early one morning, that Sam made a wonderful discovery. He found a small, still pond where two great trumpeter swans had built their nest.

The pond Sam had discovered on that spring morning was seldom visited by any human being. All winter, snow had covered the ice; the pond lay cold and still under its white blanket. Most of the time there wasn't a sound to be heard. The frog was asleep. The chipmunk was asleep. Occasionally a jay would cry out. And sometimes at night the fox would bark—a high, rasping bark. Winter seemed to last forever.

But one day a change came over the woods and the pond. Warm air, soft and kind, blew through the trees. The ice, which had softened during the night, began to melt. Patches of open water appeared. All the creatures that lived in the pond and in the woods were glad to feel the warmth. They heard and felt the breath of spring, and they stirred with new life and hope. There was a good, new smell in the air, a smell of earth waking after its long sleep. The frog, buried in the mud at the bottom of the pond, knew that spring was here. The chickadee knew and was delighted (almost everything delights a chickadee). The vixen, dozing in her den, knew she would soon have kits. Every creature knew that a better, easier time was at hand—warmer days, pleasanter nights. Trees were putting out green buds; the buds were swelling. Birds began arriving from the south. A pair of ducks flew in. The Red-winged Blackbird arrived and scouted the pond for nesting sites. A small sparrow with a white throat arrived and sang, "Oh, sweet Canada, Canada, Canada!"

And if you had been sitting by the pond on that first warm day of spring, suddenly, toward the end of the afternoon, you would have heard a stirring sound high above you in the air—a sound like the sound of trumpets.

"Ko-hoh, ko-hoh!"

And if you had looked up, you would have seen, high overhead, two great white birds. They flew swiftly, their legs stretched out straight behind, their long white necks stretched out ahead, their powerful wings beating steady and strong. "Ko-hoh, ko-hoh, ko-hoh!" A thrilling noise in the sky, the trumpeting of swans.

293

When the birds spotted the pond, they began circling, looking the place over from the air. Then they glided down and came to rest in the water, folding their long wings neatly along their sides and turning their heads this way and that to study their new surroundings. They were Trumpeter Swans, pure white birds with black bills. They had liked the looks of the swampy pond and had decided to make it their home for a while and raise a family.

The two swans were tired from the long flight. They were glad to be down out of the sky. They paddled slowly about and then began feeding, thrusting their necks into the shallow water and pulling roots and plants from the bottom. Everything about the swans was white except their bills and their feet; these were black. They carried their heads high. The pond seemed a different place because of their arrival.

For the next few days, the swans rested. When they were hungry, they ate. When they were thirsty—which was a great deal of the time—they drank. On the tenth day, the female began looking around to find a place to build her nest.

Library Link ◆ *Join in the adventures of an unusual swan named Louis in* The Trumpet of the Swan *by E. B. White.*

Reader's Response

How do you feel when you see or hear the first birds of spring?

LITERATURE: Story

The Trumpet of the Swan

Responding to Literature

1. The coming of spring is a special time. When spring comes to where you live, what changes? What do you do then that you do not do at any other time of the year?

2. If the Trumpeter Swan could speak, what would it say? Picture the swan resting on the pond after a long journey. Tell one thing the swan might say.

3. Sentences can paint word pictures in your mind. Find one sentence in the story that creates a word picture in your mind. Copy it and draw a frame around it. Draw the picture it paints. Display your picture for all to see.

Writing to Learn

Think and Elaborate ♦ What is your favorite season? Is it summer? Or winter? Make a cluster map like the one below. In the center, name your favorite season. Then add other words.

(your favorite season)

Cluster Map

Write ♦ Describe your favorite season. Tell why you like it and what you do when it comes.

Where would you like to be right now? Describe that place without naming it. See if anyone can guess the place from your description of it.

SPEAKING and LISTENING ◆
An Oral Description

Have you ever listened to someone describe a place and wished you were there? Could you picture it in your mind? Hear its sounds? Feel its breezes? Smell its aromas? If so, the speaker knew how to use description. You can learn how to do this, too.

With practice, you can use words to paint pictures. You can use words to create sounds, feelings, smells, and tastes. Here are guidelines to help you.

Describing a Place	1. Does the place have a mood? Is it quiet? Cheerful? Friendly? Lonely? Mysterious? Choose a word that captures its mood. 2. Use your five senses to give details about the place and the mood. Here are some examples for a *cheerful* place. *See* — bright sunshine, golden buttercups, sparkling lake, cloudless sky *Hear* — birds happily chirping, children laughing, someone whistling *Feel* — warm sun, gentle breeze, silky grass *Smell* — wild clover, honeysuckle *Taste* — sweet watermelon, juicy apple
Being an Active Listener	1. Let the speaker's words paint pictures for you. 2. Think of similar places you have visited. 3. Listen for details that describe.

Summary ◆ Use details that describe to tell about a place. Listen to picture and enjoy what is being described.

Guided Practice

Which details tell about a crowded supermarket? Which detail does not belong? What other details could you add?

1. Shoppers bump elbows while sniffing fresh melons.
2. The dark aisles are full of silent shadows.
3. Shopping carts race in every direction.
4. Checkers bustle to the tune of "Have a great day!"

Practice

A. Write *only* the details below that tell about a lonely house. Do *not* write the details that do not belong.

5. Only my footsteps broke the silence.
6. Two friendly cats sat on the cozy sofa.
7. A film of gray dust covered the unused bookshelf.
8. Bright yellow curtains swayed in the summer breeze.

Now add two sentences of your own. Give details about how the lonely house looks, smells, or sounds.

B. Work with a partner. Pretend that he or she has never seen your classroom. Tell your partner four details that describe the room. Give details that appeal to the senses of sight, hearing, touch, smell, and taste. As the listener, suggest details that could be added.

C. Tell a partner five details that describe a busy street corner. Give details that help your partner see or hear what you describe. As the listener, ask questions to find out more about the place.

Apply ◆ Think and Write

Labels That Describe ◆ Draw a picture of a place. It could be a place you know or one you would like to know. Around your picture, write words that describe your place.

✎ **Remember**
that details can help your listeners picture what you describe.

GETTING STARTED

Look in front of you. What is the closest thing you see? What is farthest away? What is on your left? What is on your right?

WRITING ◆
Space Order in Descriptions

Read this paragraph from *The Trumpet of the Swan*. How does the author help us picture the scene?

> Louis liked Boston the minute he saw it from the sky. Far beneath him was a river. Near the river was a park. In the park was a lake. In the lake was an island. On the shore was a dock. Tied to the dock was a boat shaped like a swan. The place looked ideal. There was even a very fine hotel nearby.

E. B. White used space order to help you see where everything was. *Space order* means "the way things are arranged in space." The words that are underlined show space order. They show where the river, park, lake, island, dock, boat, and hotel are located. Do you see how the description matches the picture?

> **Summary** ◆ **Space order** is one way to arrange details in a paragraph. Space order often works well when you are describing a place.

Guided Practice

Tell in what order you would arrange details that describe each item below. Choose *top to bottom*, *bottom to top*, *left to right*, or *front to back*.

1. coins in a stack

2. words in a sentence

3. rows on an airplane

4. a baseball batting order

Practice

A. In what order you would arrange details that describe each item below? Write *top to bottom*, *bottom to top*, *left to right*, *near to far*, or *front to back* to show the order.

5. chapters in a book

6. books on a shelf

7. a totem pole

8. players sitting on a bench

9. a highway disappearing into the distance

B. Write a paragraph. Begin with the topic sentence below. Then write the three details in correct space order.

TOPIC SENTENCE: **Four boats were heading toward the dock.**

10. A swan boat was behind the sailboat.

11. A rowboat was in front of all the other boats.

12. A motorboat was between the rowboat and a sailboat.

C. If Louis landed at your playground, what would he see? Draw a picture of it. Then write a paragraph to describe it. Use space order to organize the details. For example, describe the scene from left to right or from near to far.

Apply ◆ Think and Write

Describing Your Space ◆ Write a paragraph that describes where you sit in your classroom. Are the desks in rows? If so, how many rows? How many desks are in each row? Which row are you in? Which desk? Who sits in front of you? Behind you? On your left? On your right?

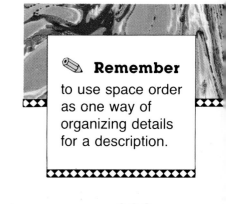

✏️ **Remember**
to use space order as one way of organizing details for a description.

Take turns describing your school cafeteria. Tell about the people and things you see, and the sounds and smells in the room.

WRITING ♦
A Descriptive Paragraph

You know a lot about description. You have used words to help your reader see and hear what you describe. You may even have had your reader touch, smell, or taste along with you! You have given an oral description. You have used space order to organize details. Now you will use all the skills you have learned as you write a descriptive paragraph.

What is a paragraph? You know the answer. It is a group of sentences about one main idea. That main idea is stated in a topic sentence. The other sentences give details about the topic. A paragraph brings information into focus, for both the writer and the reader. See how E. B. White does this in a descriptive paragraph from *The Trumpet of the Swan.*

Topic Sentence

Details

Months went by. Winter came to the Red Rock Lakes. The nights were long and dark and cold. The days were short and bright and cold. Sometimes the wind blew. But the swans and geese and ducks were safe and happy. The warm springs that fed the lakes kept the ice from covering them—there were always open places. There was plenty of food. Sometimes a man would arrive with a bag of grain and spread the grain where the birds could get it.

Summary ♦ A **descriptive paragraph** paints a word picture for your reader.

Guided Practice

Tell one main thing about each place.

1. an amusement park   **3.** a shopping mall   **5.** an attic
2. a dentist's office   **4.** a bus stop   **6.** a beach

Practice

A. Write *a or b* to show which main thing you would tell about each place below. (Hint: The choice is up to you. There are no "wrong" answers.)

7. I would tell about a football field's
   a. size and shape   **b.** sights and sounds

8. I would tell about a barn's
   a. noisy animals   **b.** soft piles of hay

9. I would tell about a library's
   a. musty, dusty smell   **b.** rows and rows of books

B. Study the photographs of the Great Salt Lake. Pretend you are there. Then make a chart like this one. List details in each row. Use your imagination!

At the Great Salt Lake
10. I see
11. I hear
12. I feel
13. I smell
14. I taste

C. Suppose you have a pen pal in another country. Your pen pal asks, "What is an American zoo like?" How would you answer? Think about the main thing you would say to describe it. Then make up a topic sentence for your description.

Apply ♦ Think and Write

Dictionary of Knowledge ♦ Read the entry about the Great Salt Lake. Then write a paragraph describing the lake. Can you use any of the details you wrote for **Practice B**?

✏️ **Remember**
to include descriptive paragraphs in your stories and reports.

Focus on Sensory Words

Earlier in this unit, you read a selection from *The Trumpet of the Swan*. While you were reading, did you *see* the pond? Did you believe it was real? Did you picture the fox in her den? The frog asleep in the mud? Did you feel the drama as the two great white birds glided down to the pond? Probably you did, for the author, E. B. White, is a master of description.

Skilled writers make their descriptions spring to life on the page. They create vivid word pictures. They do this with **sensory words**—words that appeal to the five senses:

■ seeing   hearing   touching   smelling   tasting

Look back to see how E. B. White makes his descriptions vivid. Here are some of the sensory words he uses:

SEEING: The trees have *green* buds; the swans are all *white* except for their *black* bills and feet.

HEARING: The swans make a *stirring sound* . . . like *trumpets;* they make the thrilling noise, *"Ko-hoh, ko-hoh!"*

TOUCHING: The winter pond had been *cold;* the air blowing through the trees is *warm* and *soft.*

SMELLING: The air has a *good, new smell;* there is the *smell of earth.*

The Writer's Voice ◆ Sensory words help a reader see, hear, feel, smell, or taste what is being described. The only sense for which E. B. White did not use sensory words is taste. What are some sensory words that describe taste? What are some of the tastes of spring?

COOPERATIVE LEARNING: Writer's Craft

Working Together

See how good description makes use of sensory words as your group does activities **A** and **B**.

A. Decide which sense or senses each of the following sentences involves. Identify the sensory words.

  1. I recall the howling of the wind, the rattling of the old weather vane, and the crashing of thunder.
  2. Deep-scented lilies sprang from the plain, while from the slopes came the fragrance of mountain laurel.
  3. The morning sky, a pale violet, painted the nearby hills with a bluish hue.
  4. My favorite treats that summer were juicy smoked ham and apple cobbler spiced with cinnamon.
  5. He grasped the rough fibers of the rope, clung, slipped, and fought desperately with burning hands to stay aloft.

B. Make up five original sentences similar to those in activity **A**. Each sentence should focus on a different sense. As a group, present your sentences to the class. Have your classmates identify the sensory words.

THESAURUS CORNER ♦ Word Choice

The description of a mysterious place needs sensory words. Write a description of a mysterious place you know. Use at least three adjectives—or synonyms for them—from the Thesaurus list below. Underline the sensory words in your description.

cold (touching)
dark (seeing)
old (seeing)
strong (tasting or smelling)
calm (hearing)

WRITING PROCESS
DESCRIBING

Writing a Description

In *The Trumpet of the Swan*, E. B. White describes a pond in early spring. He uses details to help you see the pond. He helps you hear sparrows and the swans. You can imagine how the plants smell and how the breeze feels.

Know Your Purpose and Audience

MY PURPOSE

Now it is your turn. In this lesson, you will write a description. Your purpose is to describe an outdoor place.

MY AUDIENCE

Your audience will be younger children. You will try to help them feel that they have visited this special place. Later you and your classmates can read your descriptions to your young audience. You can also create a travel book for the library.

1 Prewriting

First you must choose a topic—a place to write about.
Then you need a way to gather ideas about your topic.

Choose Your Topic ♦ E. B. White wrote about a pond
he knew. Make a list of outdoor places that you know. Then
circle the one you like the best.

Think About It

What outdoor places do you know
well? There may be a place that
only you know about. Look at the
list you make. Picture yourself in
each place. Which place makes you
feel the best? Which is your
favorite? Circle that place as your
choice.

Talk About It

With your classmates, make a list of
outdoor places. Maybe you know a
park, a basketball court, a river, a
field, or a garden. Remember all the
places you have visited with your
family or friends.

Topic Ideas

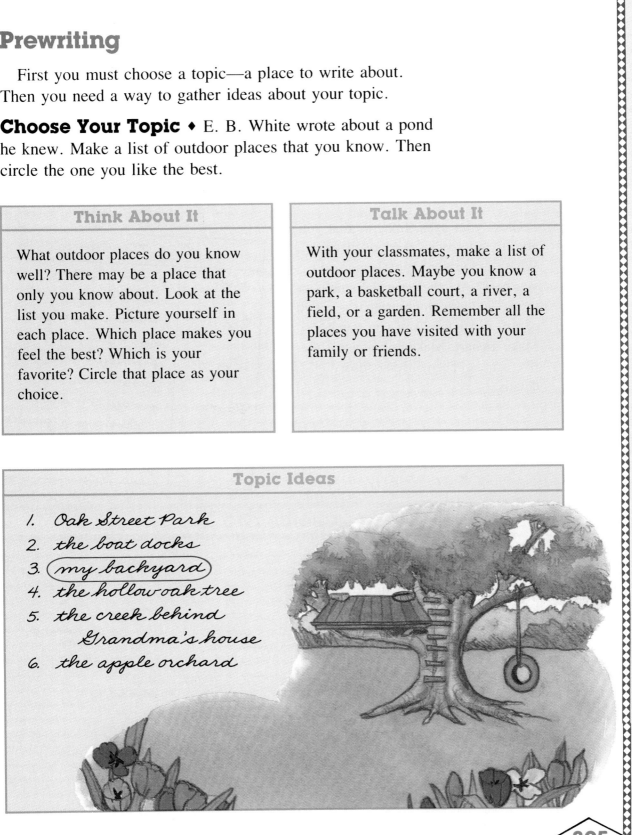

1. Oak Street Park
2. the boat docks
3. (my backyard)
4. the hollow oak tree
5. the creek behind
   Grandma's house
6. the apple orchard

Choose Your Strategy ♦ Here are two ways to gather ideas about your outdoor place. Read both of them. Then use the one you think will help you more.

PREWRITING IDEAS

CHOICE ONE

A Five-Senses Chart

Close your eyes. Imagine that you are in your special outdoor place. What do you see? What sounds do you hear? Are there special smells or tastes? Is there anything that is rough or soft or sticky when you touch it? Make a chart. Make columns for the five senses. Then fill in sensory details.

Model

My Backyard	
See	green bushes red flowers
Hear	birds singing brook gurgling
Smell	freshly cut grass pine sap
Taste	juicy tomatoes from our garden
Touch	soft moss sticky pine bark

CHOICE TWO

A Cluster Map

Make a cluster map about your outdoor place. Name your place in the center topic circle. Think of as many details as you can about your place. Write them in circles around the topic circle.

Model

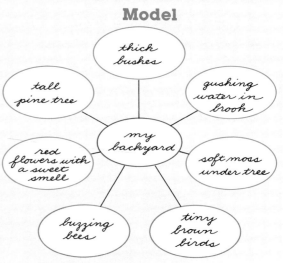

WRITING PROCESS: Description

2 Writing

Use your prewriting notes to help you write down your ideas in sentences. Here are two ways you might begin.

- ◆ My outdoor place is special because ____.
- ◆ Would you like to visit my outdoor place?

After you start, you might use space order to describe your special place. You might start with the farthest detail and end with the closest. You might start at the top and end at the bottom. Use an order that makes sense for your place.

Sample First Draft ◆

My backyard is special. Next to the house are bushes. I made a fort under them. No one can see me there!
    In the middle of my yard is a garden. It has pretty red roses that smell as sweet as my sister's perfume. It has tart, juicie tomatoes that make my mouth pucker. from my fort, I can hear the bees.
    The water gushes and splashes against the rocks. Tiny brown birds come to the Pine tree beside the brook and sing. Behind the garden is a brook.

3 Revising

Now you have finished writing. Did you say what you meant to say? This idea may help you.

REVISING IDEA

FIRST Read to Yourself

Think about your purpose. Did you describe an outdoor place? Consider your audience. Will younger children enjoy your description?

Focus: Did you include sensory details? Did you tell what you see, hear, smell, taste, and touch in your special place? Put a caret (ˆ) where you may want to add a detail.

THEN Share with a Partner

Ask a partner to read your description aloud. Listen as if you were a younger child. Decide which parts to make clearer. Here are some guidelines.

The Writer

Guidelines: Listen as your partner reads. Ask for your partner's suggestions.

Sample questions:
- Will younger children understand my writing?
- **Focus question:** What sensory details might I add?

The Writer's Partner

Guidelines: Read the writer's description aloud. Then give helpful ideas.

Sample responses:
- I could really see ____.
- Maybe you could add a detail about ____.

WRITING PROCESS: Description

Revising Model ♦ This description is being revised.

Thick and *green* help the reader picture the bushes.

Striking is a stronger adjective than *pretty*.

The writer's partner suggested a sound detail.

The writer wanted to make the space order clearer.

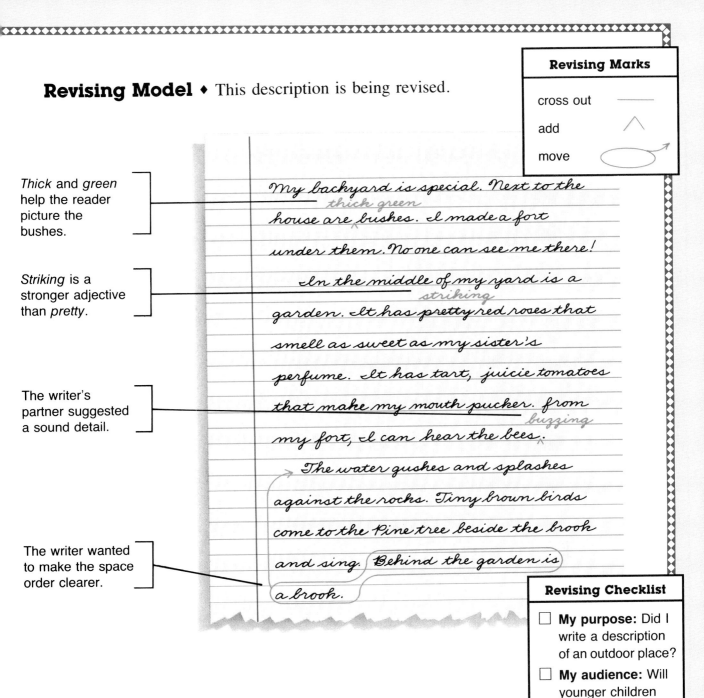

My backyard is special. Next to the
house are ~~thick green~~ bushes. I made a fort
under them. No one can see me there!
In the middle of my yard is a
~~striking~~
garden. It has ~~pretty~~ red roses that
smell as sweet as my sister's
perfume. It has tart, juicie tomatoes
that make my mouth pucker. From
my fort, I can hear the ~~buzzing~~ bees.
The water gushes and splashes
against the rocks. Tiny brown birds
come to the Pine tree beside the brook
and sing. (Behind the garden is)
(a brook.)

Read the description above with the writer's changes. Then revise your own description.

Revising Checklist

☐ **My purpose:** Did I write a description of an outdoor place?

☐ **My audience:** Will younger children understand my description?

☐ **Focus:** Did I tell what I see, hear, smell, taste, and touch in my outdoor place?

Grammar Check ♦ Adjectives help to add sensory details.

Word Choice ♦ Do you want a stronger word for a word like *pretty*? A thesaurus can help you find one.

4 Proofreading

Look back over your description. Fix any mistakes.

Proofreading Model ♦ Here is the description of a backyard. Proofreading changes have been added in red.

Proofreading Marks	
capital letter	≡
small letter	/
indent paragraph	¶
check spelling	⬭

¶ My backyard is special. Next to the
        thick green
house are ᵡbushes. I made a fort
under them. No one can see me there!

   In the middle of my yard is a
                striking
garden. It has pretty red roses that
smell as sweet as my sister's
                          juicy
perfume. It has tart, ⟨juicie⟩ tomatoes
that make my mouth pucker. from
                            buzzing
my fort, I can hear the bees ᵡ.

   The water gushes and splashes
against the rocks. Tiny brown birds
come to the P̷ine tree beside the brook
and sing. ⟨Behind the garden is
a brook.⟩

Proofreading Checklist

- ☐ Did I spell words correctly?
- ☐ Did I indent paragraphs?
- ☐ Did I use capital letters correctly?
- ☐ Did I use correct marks at the end of sentences?
- ☐ Did I use my best handwriting?

PROOFREADING IDEA

One Thing at a Time

Read your description once for spelling mistakes. Read it again for capitals and punctuation marks. Check indenting.

Now proofread your description, and add a title. Then make a neat copy.

5 Publishing

Here are two ways you can share your description.

In My Backyard

My backyard is special. Next to the house are thick green bushes. I made a fort under them. No one can see me there!

In the middle of my yard is a garden. It has striking red roses that smell as sweet as my sister's perfume. It has tart, juicy tomatoes that make my mouth pucker. From my fort, I can hear the bees buzzing.

Behind the garden is a brook. The water gushes and splashes against the rocks. Tiny brown birds come to the pine tree beside the brook and sing. Sometimes I sit on the soft green moss under the tree. Then I close my eyes and listen to the birds.

PUBLISHING IDEAS

Share Aloud	Share in Writing
Read your description aloud to your classmates or to a class of younger children. Ask your listeners to draw a detail from your description.	Make a class travel book. Illustrate your descriptions. Place the illustrations and descriptions in a photo album. Lend your book to the school library. Include some blank pages where readers can write their comments.

CURRICULUM •CONNECTION•

Writing Across the Curriculum   Science

In this unit you wrote a description of an outdoor place. You tried to make your description come alive for your audience by elaborating on, or giving details about, your place. Making a cluster map helps you collect details. A cluster map can also help in science class when you are asked to observe and describe nature.

Writing to Learn

Think and Observe ♦ Choose a place close to home or school such as a field, a lawn, or a city park. Make a cluster map for this area. On your map write details about the land, the buildings, and the animals and birds that live there.

Cluster Map

Write ♦ Use the information from your cluster map to write about the place. Tell why it is a special place for you.

Writing in Your Journal

In the Writer's Warm-up you wrote about how a pond might look at different times of the year. Later you read about Sam, who found a pond that few people had visited. If you could visit a quiet place of your own, where would you go? At what time of year would you go? Describe in your journal what you would see.

312   Curriculum Connection

BOOKS TO ENJOY

Read More About It

Ko-Hoh: The Call of the Trumpeter Swan *by Jay Featherly*

The title of this nonfiction book comes from the way E. B. White described the trumpeter swan's call. Read about trumpeter swans from a scientific point of view.

The Wild Swans *by Hans Christian Andersen*

Travel with swans through a world of fantasy. An evil spell turns Princess Elise's brothers into wild swans. Will Elise be able to rescue them?

Book Report Idea   Story Board

Nature goes through cycles of change. So does a book. The next time you share a book, describe how it changes. Think of its beginning, its middle, and its end.

Create Scenes of Change

Divide a large piece of paper into three sections. In each, describe or sketch a different part of your book. Show one scene from the beginning, one from the middle, and one from the end. Give the title and author. Finally, explain how the scenes go together.

At the beginning | In the middle | Finally

The Fledgling A fantasy novel by Jane Langton

UNIT REVIEW

Unit 6

Adjectives   *pages 272–283*

A. Write each sentence. Then underline the adjective that tells *how many* or *what kind*.

1. A flamingo has long legs.
2. It stands about four feet tall.
3. The birds build muddy nests in swamps.
4. I saw a flamingo with pink feathers.
5. It had a curved neck.
6. The flamingo was about ten years old.
7. It was a graceful bird.
8. Three species live in South America.

B. Write the two adjectives in each group of words.

9. bicycle, first, special
10. show, funny, clever
11. seven, sticky, stamps
12. loyal, happy, friend
13. pen, blue, short
14. twenty, balloons, colorful
15. table, shiny, wide
16. shallow, deeper, temperature
17. weather, cold, damp

C. Choose the correct article in parentheses ( ) to complete each phrase. Then write each phrase.

18. (a, the) Olympic Games
19. (a, an) exciting event
20. (an, the) high jump
21. (the, a) rows of spectators
22. (an, a) gold medal
23. (the, an) flag of a nation
24. (a, an) ice-skating contest
25. (an, the) winning athlete
26. (a, an) close race
27. (a, an) Olympic medalist
28. (an, a) national anthem
29. (an, a) proud nation
30. (an, the) victory parade
31. (a, an) year of training

D. Write the adjective that follows the linking verb in each sentence. Then write the noun or pronoun it describes.

32. A drum is hollow.
33. The drumhead is thin.
34. Kettledrums are different.
35. The vibrations are loud.
36. Bats are interesting.
37. A bat is blind.
38. The creature is furry.
39. Its squeaks are helpful.
40. The echoes are important.
41. The bat's flight is purposeful.
42. It is hungry.
43. Insects are plentiful.
44. The bat is happy.
45. The mice are frightened.

E. Write the *-er* and *-est* form of each adjective.

46. calm
47. strange
48. warm
49. simple
50. hard
51. shiny
52. gentle
53. lovely
54. dim
55. tough
56. fine
57. thin
58. slim
59. fresh
60. dull
61. large
62. rude
63. weird
64. snowy
65. gloomy
66. grand
67. mild

F. Write each sentence. Use the correct form of the adjective in parentheses ( ).

68. A ship is (bigger, biggest) than a boat.
69. Ancient ships were (smaller, smallest) than modern ones.
70. The Phoenicians were the (greater, greatest) experts of all on ships.
71. In the 1500s, ships were built (sturdier, sturdiest) than ever.
72. England specialized in having the (speedier, speediest) ships of all.
73. Americans later developed the (better, best) ships in the world.
74. They were the (faster, fastest) ships that ever sailed.
75. Steel ships were (better, best) than wooden ones in wartime.
76. Steel provided (more, most) protection than wood.

Adjective Suffixes   *pages 284–285*

G. Write each sentence. Add the suffix *-y, -ful,* or *-less* to the word in parentheses ( ).

77. The hikers tried to be (care) on the slippery rocks.
78. Everyone was hungry and (thirst).
79. It had been a long, (event) day.
80. The sky had been (gloom).
81. At times, the rocky trail seemed (end).

Descriptions   *pages 296–301*

H. Write the sensory word in each phrase. Then write *sight, sound, smell, touch,* or *taste* to show which sense the word describes.

82. slimy rocks
83. salty nuts
84. smoky scent
85. glowing gem
86. loud clang
87. fragrant rose
88. smooth fabric
89. peppery soup
90. howling storm
91. bright flash

I. Choose the correct sensory word in parentheses ( ) to complete each sentence.

92. We traveled across the (blistering, slimy) sand.
93. The (foggy, glaring) sun beat down on us.
94. We longed for the shelter of our (misty, shady) tents.
95. At the oasis, (sweet, rare) dates refreshed us.

CUMULATIVE REVIEW

UNIT 1: Sentences   pages 10–11

A. Write each sentence. Draw one line under the subject. Draw two lines under the predicate.

1. Most Arizona Indian tribes live in their ancestors' homelands.
2. These tribes include the Hopis, the Pimas, and the Papagos.
3. Their ancestors lived in Arizona ten thousand years ago.
4. The Navajos and the Apaches arrived about one thousand years ago.
5. The Navajo tribe is the largest in the nation.
6. Navajo legends speak of early days.
7. The Navajos moved south and west.
8. They learned to ride horses.
9. Some Navajos worked with metal.

UNIT 2: Nouns   pages 54–57

B. Write the plural of each singular noun.

10. tribe
11. sheep
12. ranch
13. fox
14. mouse
15. business
16. family
17. bush

UNIT 2: Capital Letters
pages 60–61

C. Write each sentence. Capitalize the proper nouns.

18. I live in the town of algoa.
19. It is near the gulf of mexico.
20. Last friday, our class went on a trip to houston.
21. It is the largest city in the state of texas.
22. We drove on the loop freeway.
23. We ate lunch in sam houston park.
24. Later, we saw the enormous astrodome.
25. On the way home, we visited the johnson space center.
26. It is named for president lyndon baines johnson.

UNIT 3: Pronouns   pages 114–119

D. Write the pronoun in each sentence. Then write whether the pronoun is in the *subject* or the *predicate*.

27. I read an interesting article.
28. It was about a type of snail.
29. People call them periwinkles.
30. Dad gave me one last summer.
31. He found the snail on a rock.
32. The snails help us a great deal.
33. They turn muddy marshes into beaches.
34. The picture shows them at work.
35. You can see the snails eating algae.

E. Write a possessive pronoun for each word or group of words.

36. Martina's
37. the lion's
38. the Navajos'
39. the horse's
40. Diane's
41. the farmers'
42. the farm's
43. Manuel's

Units 4 and 5: Verbs
pages 168–169, 218–221

F. Write the verb in each sentence. Then write *present*, *past*, or *future* to show the tense.

44. My friend travels often.
45. She visited Mexico last month.
46. She learned many interesting customs.
47. Soon I will go to Mexico City.
48. I studied Spanish in school.
49. The language sounds beautiful.
50. My friend and I will talk in Spanish.

G. Write each sentence. Use the correct form of the verb in parentheses ( ).

51. We have (went, gone) to the museum.
52. We (saw, seen) beautiful pottery.
53. Someone (find, found) an ancient jug in Peru.
54. A piece had (break, broken) off.
55. An artist had (fix, fixed) it.
56. A visitor (took, taken) a photo.
57. She has (wrote, written) a story.

Unit 6: Adjectives
pages 272–273, 276–283

H. Write each sentence. Then underline the adjective that tells *how many* or *what kind*.

58. The orange cat is on the desk.
59. He is six years old.
60. Claude has beautiful fur.
61. His muzzle and paws are white.
62. Tonight he is in a bad mood.
63. There are cuts on both ears.
64. This is the third fight that Claude has lost.

I. Write each sentence. Use the correct form of the adjective in parentheses ( ).

65. The (larger, largest) bird on earth is the African ostrich.
66. Many ostriches grow up to be (taller, tallest) than seven feet.
67. (More, Most) other birds are not nearly so large.
68. The (tinier, tiniest) bird of all is the bee hummingbird.
69. Many birds fly to a (warmer, warmest) place for the winter.
70. They seek a place that has (less, least) snow than their old home.
71. The peacock is one of the (more beautiful, most beautiful) birds of all.
72. Ducks seem (more friendly, most friendly) than geese.

Hink-Pink Riddles

The answer to a Hink-Pink riddle is a rhyme made of a one-syllable adjective and a one-syllable noun. A happy father, for example, is a *glad dad*. Guess these Hink-Pinks.

1. What do you call a chubby kitty?
2. What do you call a moonlit evening?
3. What do you call an unusual couple?
4. What do you call a fat dog?
5. What do you call a washed lima?

Make up some Hink-Pink riddles to share with a classmate.

A Canine Chart

Write five sentences that compare two or more breeds of dogs. Include the *-er* and *-est* forms of the adjectives *old*, *heavy*, *light*, *tall*, *short*, and *new*.

Breed of Dog	Beginning of Breed	Average Weight	Shoulder Height
Chihuahua	1500s	1–6 lb.	5 in.
cocker spaniel	1800s	22–28 lb.	14–15 in.
collie	1600s	50–75 lb.	22–26 in.
St. Bernard	1600s	160–200 lb.	25–30 in.
Irish wolfhound	400s	105–140 lb.	30–34 in.

Unit 6 Extra Practice

1 Writing with Adjectives

p. 272

A. Use one of the adjectives below to complete each sentence. Tell if the adjective tells *how many* or *what kind*.

fluffy   red   few   sixty   cold

  1. We saw ____ birds in the field.
  2. The robin had a ____ breast.
  3. A ____ bluebirds were in the tree.
  4. On that warm day I drank ____ juice.
  5. The sky was full of ____ clouds.

B. Write these sentences. Underline the adjectives that tell *what kind* and *how many*.

  6. Did you see the three fuzzy plants?
  7. Fifteen purple blossoms stand out.
  8. We started the pink flowers from tiny seeds.
  9. The forty crocuses grew from small bulbs.
10. One tulip has yellow petals and a red center.
11. Some tall daffodils stand in the deep snow.
12. Many flowers bloom in the narrow windowboxes.
13. The wet snow clings to bare branches.
14. Warm winds and cool showers come with spring.
15. Calm and lazy days will follow.

2 Using *a*, *an*, and *the*

p. 274

A. Write *a* or *an* to complete each sentence correctly.

  1. There is ____ picture on the sign.
  2. It shows ____ animal.
  3. The animal is ____ large gray elephant.
  4. Do you see ____ hand pointing right?
  5. This is ____ easy way to the elephant house.

B. Choose the correct article to complete each sentence. Write each sentence.

6. Can you read (a, the) signs you see here?
7. (A, An) arrow shows direction.
8. What does (a, an) curved arrow mean?
9. Is it a warning for sharp curves in (an, the) road?
10. (A, An) arrow pointing up means one-way traffic.
11. A sign shows a truck on (a, an) wedge.
12. It tells us (a, an) steep hill lies ahead.
13. To find (a, an) airport, follow the airplane signs.
14. That sign means the store closes in (a, an) hour.

C. Use *a* or *an* to complete each sentence. Write each sentence.

15. ____ Native American used signs to tell a story.
16. This was ____ kind of picture writing.
17. Some pictures told about ____ hunting trip.
18. Others show ____ animal being trapped in a cage.
19. The eagle stood for ____ member of a special tribe.
20. Peace was shown by ____ broken spear.
21. A small round building was ____ igloo.
22. What did the symbol for ____ sea lion look like?
23. The picture of ____ foot meant to stand or walk.

3 Adjectives After Linking Verbs *p. 276*

A. Write each sentence. Underline the adjective that follows the linking verb. Draw an arrow to the subject.

EXAMPLE: These experiments are interesting.
ANSWER: These experiments are <u>interesting</u>.

1. These insects are cold-blooded.
2. The air is cool inside the jar.
3. As a result, the insects are quiet.
4. When Frank holds it, the jar is warm from his hands.
5. Now the insects are lively again.

B. Write the sentences below. Use an adjective to complete each sentence.

6. This science project is ____ .
7. In this pile the rocks are ____ .
8. The bowl is ____ .
9. The test is ____ .
10. Be sure that all your answers are ____ .

4 Adjectives That Compare   *p. 278*

A. Write the *-er* and *-est* forms for each adjective.

1. dark   3. cool   5. cloudy
2. wet   4. deep   6. dense

B. Write each sentence. Use the correct form of the adjective in parentheses ( ).

7. The sun is (hot, hotter) than any planet.
8. The (larger, largest) planet of all is Jupiter.
9. Mars is the (redder, reddest) planet in our solar system.
10. Mars is (drier, driest) than Earth.
11. One of Saturn's moons is (bigger, biggest) than Mercury.
12. Earth's moon looks (brighter, brightest) than the stars.
13. Some rocks in space are (wider, widest) than California.
14. Deimos is the (small, smaller) of Mars's two moons.
15. Of all the planets, Saturn has the (greater, greatest) number of moons circling it.

C. Write each sentence. Use the *-er* or the *-est* form of the adjective in parentheses ( ).

16. Venus is the (close) planet to Earth.
17. Pluto takes the (long) time to orbit the sun.
18. Mars is (cold) than Earth.
19. A day on Saturn is (short) than on Earth.
20. The sun is the (near) star.

5 Using *more* and *most* with Adjectives

p. 280

A. Write *more* or *most* to complete each sentence.

  1. This is the ____ exciting assembly ever!
  2. The third-graders had the ____ entertaining skit.
  3. It was even ____ amusing than ours.
  4. Jo Ann was the ____ convincing carrot I've ever seen.
  5. Only the dancing peanut was ____ successful.

B. Use *more* or *most* to complete each sentence. Write each sentence.

  6. A cat is the ____ relaxed animal I know.
  7. Some people find it ____ difficult to relax than others.
  8. Stretching is the ____ pleasant exercise of all.
  9. Lani is ____ interested in fitness than I am.
  10. Exercises that stretch the whole body can be ____ valuable than games.
  11. They will be even ____ useful later in life.
  12. The park is the ____ interesting place to run.
  13. Choosing a variety of foods is the ____ important part of a good diet.
  14. Fruit is ____ healthful than candy.
  15. Some of the ____ familiar foods are good for you.
  16. Pizza contains three of the ____ necessary foods.
  17. Is yogurt ____ delicious than ice cream?
  18. Fish fillets provide ____ protein than milk.

C. Write each sentence. Use *more* or *most* with the adjective in parentheses ( ).

  19. A peanut butter sandwich is (nutritious) without jelly.
  20. Popcorn is the (delicious) snack I eat.
  21. It is also one of the (healthful) of all.
  22. Nuts can be (valuable) than junk food.
  23. Few things are (important) than your health.

6 Adjectives with Irregular Comparisons

p. 282

A. Complete each sentence with the correct word in ( ).

1. Today is even (better, best) than yesterday for a launching.
2. This engine has (more, most) power than that one.
3. Jessica's rocket had the (better, best) flight of all.
4. The second try was (worse, worst) than the first one.
5. Have you heard a (better, best) idea than that?
6. I did the (less, least) work of all on this plane.
7. Richard had the (less, least) success with his flyer.
8. It was (more, most) work than my rocket.
9. His rocket took the (more, most) skill to build.
10. It should have had a (better, best) flight than that.
11. This is the (worse, worst) run you have had.
12. I used (less, least) glue here than on the nose cone.
13. Then I had (worse, worst) luck than before.
14. The rocket body needed (more, most) strength.
15. Jessica made the (better, best) discovery of all.
16. She took (less, least) time to build her rocket.

B. Complete each sentence below. Use the correct form of *good, bad, much,* or *little* to show comparison.

EXAMPLE: Richard spent (much) time on his design.
ANSWER: Richard spent more time on his design.

17. Jessica had the (much) success.
18. She had the (little) trouble with the fins.
19. This is the (good) paint job ever!
20. Do you know a (good) way than this to launch it?
21. The parachute was the (much) trouble of all.
22. This was Gamma rocket's (good) flight ever.
23. It was a (good) launch than yesterday's.
24. There was (much) wind than we expected, though.
25. The landing was the (bad) part of the flight.

Practice ◆ Practice ◆ Practice ◆ Practice ◆ Practice ◆ Practice ◆ Practice

USING LANGUAGE TO

IMAGINE

PART ONE

Unit Theme *Fables*

Language Awareness Adverbs

PART TWO

Literature from *A Chinese Zoo* by Demi
"The Crow and the Pitcher"
retold by Louis Untermeyer

A Reason for Writing Imagining

Writing
IN YOUR JOURNAL

WRITER'S WARM-UP ◆ What do you know about fables? Perhaps you have heard the story of the race between the tortoise and the hare. The hare was confident that he would beat the slow tortoise. Do you know what happened in the end? Where do these fables come from? What can we learn from fables? Write what you know about fables in your journal. Tell why you do or do not like these stories.

Tell how animals move. For example: *Swans glide gracefully*.
Fish swim ____ . *Rabbits run* ____ . *Snails crawl* ____ .
Squirrels scamper ____ .

1 Writing with Adverbs

Read this paragraph about characters in fables.

> **The fox hides <u>slyly</u> behind the bushes. A silly goose talks <u>foolishly</u>, and the hare brags <u>boldly</u>. What does the owl do? You guessed <u>correctly</u>. The owl gives advice <u>wisely</u>.**

Each underlined word above describes an action verb and tells *how*. Words that describe verbs are adverbs. An adverb tells something more about a verb.

Some other adverbs that answer the question "How?" are shown below.

warmly	hungrily	honestly	wildly
loudly	carefully	roughly	softly

Notice that many adverbs end in *-ly*. The underlined adverbs below do not end in *-ly*.

walks <u>fast</u>   speaks <u>well</u>   works <u>hard</u>

> **Summary** ♦ A word that describes a verb is an **adverb**. Some adverbs answer the question "How?" Use adverbs to add details to your writing.

Guided Practice

The sentences below tell about one fable. Name the adverb that describes each underlined verb.

1. A crowd <u>gathered</u> eagerly for the race.
2. The tortoise <u>waited</u> patiently at the starting line.
3. The hare <u>laughed</u> hard at the tortoise.

Practice

A. The sentences below tell about "The Tortoise and the Hare." Find and write the adverb that describes the underlined verb in each sentence.

4. The race <u>began</u> quietly.
5. The tortoise <u>started</u> slowly.
6. The hare <u>moved</u> fast.
7. The hare <u>disappeared</u> quickly from sight.
8. The tortoise <u>continued</u> steadily down the road.
9. Along the path the crowd <u>roared</u> cheerfully.

B. The fable continues. Write each sentence and underline the adverb. Then write the verb it describes.

10. The hare yawned sleepily.
11. He stopped confidently for a nap.
12. Under a shady tree the hare slept well.
13. The tortoise passed the hare safely.
14. The happy turtle waited patiently at the finish line.
15. After the race the runners shook hands politely.

C. Complete each sentence below. Add an adverb that tells how each animal moves.

16. The monkey swings ____ .
17. The kangaroo leaps ____ over the water.
18. The tiger waits ____ .
19. The deer walks ____ across the road.
20. The bird chirps its song ____ .
21. The squirrel nibbles the acorns ____ .

Apply ♦ Think and Write

From Your Writing ♦ Read what you wrote for the Writer's Warm-up. Try to improve your work by adding adverbs to some of your sentences.

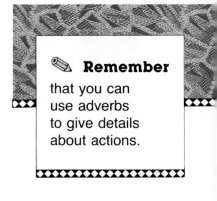

✎ **Remember**
that you can use adverbs to give details about actions.

How would you complete each group of words below?
near and _____   *in and* _____   *now and* _____
here, there, and _____   *yesterday, today, and* _____

2 Adverbs That Tell *Where* and *When*

Remember that adverbs describe verbs. Some adverbs tell *how*. Other adverbs tell *where* or *when*. Read these sentences about a man in ancient Greece.

> Aesop wrote fables <u>here</u>.
> He told his stories <u>everywhere</u>.

Notice that the underlined adverbs *here* and *everywhere* answer the question "Where?"

Now read two sentences about fables.

> A fable <u>always</u> teaches a lesson.
> <u>Often</u> a fable tells about one event.

The adverbs *always* and *often* answer the question "When?"

> **Summary** ◆ Some adverbs answer the question "Where?" Other adverbs answer the question "When?" Use adverbs to give more information about verbs.

Guided Practice

Name the adverb in each sentence below. Which adverbs tell *when*? Which adverbs tell *where*?

1. Get your tickets here for Toby's Time Machine!
2. Shall we go somewhere together?
3. Let's travel to ancient Greece today.
4. There we will meet a clever slave named Aesop.
5. Aesop has written hundreds of fables already.

Practice

A. Write each sentence. Underline the adverb. Then write *when* or *where* to show what question the adverb answers.

6. We bought a book of Aesop's fables yesterday.
7. It has beautiful pictures inside.
8. Children often enjoy the humor of fables.
9. We finally found a book of Indian fables.
10. These fables are known everywhere as the Jatakas.
11. I recently discovered this ancient collection of fables.
12. Tomorrow we will look for some Native American fables.
13. Have you heard of them before?
14. We may find them tucked away in an old bookstore.
15. Have you seen a copy anywhere?

B. Complete each sentence with an adverb that answers the question in parentheses ( ).

EXAMPLE: Put your new book _____. (Where?)
ANSWER: Put your new book there.

16. May I borrow that book _____ . (When?)
17. In fables, mice are _____ brave. (When?)
18. They may not run _____ from danger. (Where?)
19. Foxes in stories are _____ sneaky. (When?)
20. Is a fox hiding _____ ? (Where?)

Apply ◆ Think and Write

Dictionary of Knowledge ◆ Read about fables in the Dictionary of Knowledge. Write some sentences about the actions of the boy who cried ''wolf.'' Use adverbs that tell *where* and *when*. Trade papers with a classmate, and find the adverbs in each other's sentences.

> ✎ **Remember**
> that adverbs give details about the time and the place of events.

GETTING STARTED

Play "Action Compare." Make up sentences like these:
Jesse plays baseball harder than anyone else.
My bike moves the most rapidly of any in town.

3 Adverbs That Compare

You know that you can use adjectives to compare things.

■ The fox is <u>wise</u>. The ant is <u>wiser</u>. The owl is <u>wisest</u>.

In the same way you can use adverbs to compare actions. The *-er* form of an adverb compares two actions. The *-est* form of an adverb compares three or more actions.

The ant worked <u>hard</u>.
The ant worked <u>harder</u> than the cricket.
The ant worked the <u>hardest</u> of all the insects.

Most adverbs that end in *-ly* use *more* and *most* to make comparisons.

The tortoise plodded <u>steadily</u> along.
The tortoise plodded along <u>more steadily</u> than the hare.
The tortoise plodded along the <u>most steadily</u> of all.

> **Summary** ◆ When you use adverbs, use the *-er* form or *more* to compare two actions. Use the *-est* form or *most* to compare three or more actions.

Guided Practice

Choose the correct form of the adverb in parentheses ( ).

1. The goat moved (slowly, more slowly) than the wolf.
2. He stood (nearer, nearest) to the cliff than the wolf.
3. The goat ate the grass (more rapidly, most rapidly) of all.
4. The wolf howled (loud, louder) than the goat.
5. The goat grinned the (more happily, most happily) of all.

Practice

A. Read about a monkey and a crocodile who lived in the jungle. Write each sentence. Use the correct form of the adverb in parentheses ( ).

6. The big monkey jumped (higher, highest) than the small one.

7. It watched (carefully, more carefully) for crocodiles.

8. One monkey swam the (more rapidly, most rapidly) of all.

9. The young crocodile moved (quickly, more quickly) than the old one.

10. The large crocodile stalked the shore (impatiently, more impatiently) than ever before.

B. Write each sentence about Aesop's fables. Add *most* or use the *-est* form of the adverb in parentheses ( ).

11. Aesop's fables were written the (early) of all the fables.

12. His characters behave the (humorously) of all.

13. Animals appear the (frequently) as main characters.

14. We laugh (hard) when we recognize their silly behavior.

15. Of all the animals, we remember the tortoise (fondly).

C. Use the following forms of adverbs in sentences of your own. You might choose to write about the actions of animals.

16. more sharply   **18.** most quietly   **20.** sooner
17. slowest   **19.** most beautifully   **21.** faster

Apply ◆ Think and Write

Comparing Actions ◆ Pretend you are an animal in a story or fable. Write sentences comparing the things you do with the things other animals do. Use adverbs in your comparisons.

> ✎ **Remember**
> to use the correct forms of adverbs to compare actions.

How many different ways can you say this sentence? "I do not know anyone who likes turnips."

EXAMPLE: *Nobody I know likes turnips.*

4 Using Words That Mean "No"

The underlined words in the paragraphs below mean "no." Notice that the adverb *not* comes between a helping verb and a main verb. Remember that contractions ending in *n't* are formed from a verb and *not*.

The mouse did <u>not</u> want to be eaten. "If you let me go, I <u>won't</u> ever forget it," he said to the lion.

Later, caught in a net, the lion could do <u>nothing</u> to get free. <u>Nobody</u> thought the mouse could help a lion. <u>None</u> of the lion's other friends could help him either. The lion had <u>no</u> other way out of the net. He <u>didn't</u> know that the mouse could free him.

Each sentence in the paragraph has only one word that means "no." Two words that mean "no" may not be used in the same sentence.

> **Summary** ◆ The word *not* is an adverb. It means "no." Careful speakers and writers do not use two words that mean "no" in the same sentence.

Guided Practice

Read about "The Fox and the Crow." Name the word that means "no" in each sentence. Find the contractions.

1. The crow never saw anyone around the tree.
2. He didn't expect a fox to walk by.
3. "Nobody sings as sweetly as you," said the fox.
4. "Isn't that a piece of cheese in your beak?" he asked.
5. The fox got the cheese, and the crow had nothing.

Practice

A. Read about "The Miller, His Son, and the Donkey." Write each sentence. Underline the word that means "no."

6. The father and son were not very wise.
7. At first, nobody rode on the donkey.
8. Nothing they did was acceptable.
9. Lots of people gave advice, but none of it helped.
10. The father and son didn't know what to do.
11. They could never please everyone.

B. Read about "The Boy Who Cried Wolf." Write the sentences. Choose the correct word in parentheses ( ).

12. The lonely shepherd boy was (ever, never) happy.
13. He cried "Wolf!" although there (was, wasn't) one.
14. He wasn't lonely when (everyone, no one) came to help.
15. The wolf was (nowhere, anywhere) to be found.
16. When the shepherd cried "Wolf!" again, (anybody, nobody) came.

C. Complete each sentence. Use each of the words below only once. Remember not to use two words that mean "no" in the same sentence.

didn't	not	never	nowhere	won't

17. The traveler ____ .
18. The sun was ____ .
19. The wind ____ .
20. The clouds ____ .
21. This fable is ____ .

Apply ◆ Think and Write

Imaginary Advice ◆ Work with a friend. Write sentences giving wise advice to each other. Use a word that means "no" in each sentence.

✎ **Remember**
to avoid using two "no" words in the same sentence.

Complete this sentence as many times as you can.
We read a really ___ story.
Tell first about an amusing story, then about a sad one.

VOCABULARY ♦
Synonyms and Antonyms

Read the sentences below.

> The big dragon ate a telephone pole.
> The huge dragon ate a tractor trailer.
> The enormous dragon ate a football stadium.

The words *big*, *huge*, and *enormous* are synonyms. **Synonyms** are words that have almost the same meaning. The English language has many synonyms. What are some other synonyms for *big*?

Now read the following sentences.

> The little frog turned into a big prince.
> The huge elephant was saved by a tiny mouse.

The words *little* and *big* and the words *huge* and *tiny* are antonyms. **Antonyms** are words that have opposite meanings.

Using synonyms and antonyms can help make your writing clearer and more interesting.

Building Your Vocabulary

Match each word in **List 1** with its synonym in **List 2**. Then find its antonym in **List 3**.

List 1	List 2	List 3
1. softly	start	slowly
2. sloppy	happiness	loudly
3. find	quietly	lose
4. joy	rapidly	finish
5. begin	discover	sorrow
6. quickly	messy	neat

Practice

A. Write whether the pairs of words are *synonyms* or *antonyms*.

1. old, young
2. dull, interesting
3. strong, weak
4. throw, fling
5. yell, whisper
6. ocean, sea
7. kind, thoughtful
8. old, ancient
9. clean, dirty
10. narrow, wide
11. thin, slender
12. well, badly

B. Complete each "rhyming riddle" below with a synonym or antonym that rhymes with the underlined word.

13. *Up* is to <u>down</u> as *smile* is to _____ .
14. *Dirty* is to <u>clean</u> as *kind* is to _____ .
15. *Begin* is to <u>start</u> as *clever* is to _____ .
16. *Dull* is to <u>bright</u> as *dark* is to _____ .
17. *Cry* is to <u>weep</u> as *rest* is to _____ .
18. *Happy* is to <u>sad</u> as *good* is to _____ .
19. *Young* is to <u>old</u> as *timid* is to _____ .
20. *Loser* is to <u>winner</u> as *thicker* is to _____ .
21. *Powerful* is to <u>strong</u> as *lengthy* is to _____ .
22. *Young* is to <u>youthful</u> as *honest* is to _____ .
23. *Stop* is to <u>go</u> as *fast* is to _____ .
24. *Ill* is to <u>sick</u> as *rapid* is to _____ .

LANGUAGE CORNER ◆ Two-Way Words

You know that many words have more than one meaning. Sometimes a word is its own antonym! What is the difference between

trimming your hat and trimming your hair?

dusting a crop and dusting a table?

seeded rye bread and seeded raisins?

How to Expand Sentences with Adverbs

In this unit you have been learning about how adverbs work in sentences. Verbs don't always give enough information. Adding adverbs can help you give more detail and information to your reader. Read the sentences below. Which one gives you the *least* information?

> **1.** Ana read the news article.
> **2.** Ana read the news article silently.
> **3.** Ana read the news article sadly.

Sentence **1** is a perfectly fine sentence. But adding the adverbs *silently* and *sadly* gives the reader more detail and information. The sentences begin to tell you a story. See how changing the adverbs can give you different stories about Ana.

> **4.** Ana read the news article carefully.
> **5.** Ana read the news article quickly.

Adverbs add important information to your writing. Use adverbs to give your reader a clear word picture.

The Grammar Game ◆ Get the adverb advantage! Think of adverbs to describe each verb below, taking one minute for each. Write as many adverbs as you can.

write	build	watch	cry	study
paint	hold	dance	smile	swim
wait	speak	fall	throw	scream

Working Together

Work with your group on activities **A** and **B**. Use adverbs to add detail and information to your writing.

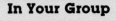
A. Choose adverbs that tell *how* to describe the underlined verbs in the sentences. Then write the sentences again with different adverbs of the group's choice.

1. Everyone <u>worked</u> on this cooking project.
2. Several people <u>searched</u> for a simple recipe.
3. We <u>cleaned</u> the countertops.
4. Two of us <u>peeled</u> potatoes and carrots.
5. We <u>ate</u> our dinner while the music <u>played</u>.
6. The runners <u>raced</u> around the track.

B. Use pronouns or names of group members to complete the sentences below. Then add an adverb that tells *when* or *where* to each sentence.

7. ____ reads mysteries.
8. ____ speaks Spanish.
9. ____ enjoy skating.
10. ____ and ____ run races.
11. ____ stayed home.

12. ____ watches TV.
13. ____ draws and paints.
14. ____ plays the piano.
15. ____ and ____ sleep.
16. ____ looked and saw it.

WRITERS' CORNER ♦ Word Position

Adverbs can take many places in a sentence. Often you can change the position of an adverb without changing the meaning of the sentence.

EXAMPLE: Suddenly the phone rang.
The phone rang suddenly.
The phone suddenly rang.

Read what you wrote for the Writer's Warm-up. Can you move any adverbs without changing the meanings of the sentences?

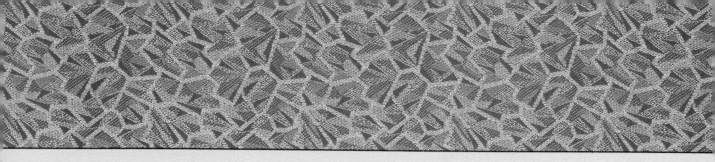

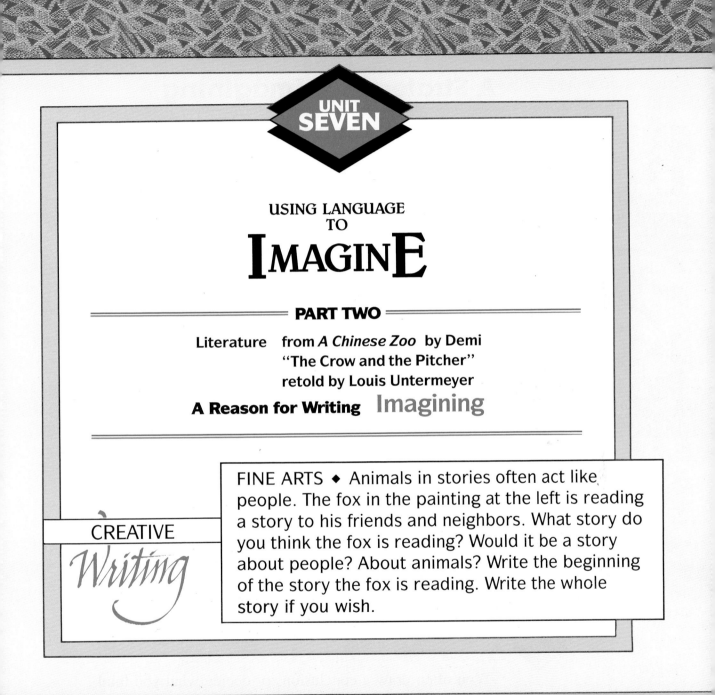

UNIT SEVEN

USING LANGUAGE
TO
IMAGINE

=== **PART TWO** ===

Literature   from *A Chinese Zoo* by Demi
"The Crow and the Pitcher"
retold by Louis Untermeyer

A Reason for Writing   Imagining

CREATIVE
Writing

FINE ARTS ◆ Animals in stories often act like people. The fox in the painting at the left is reading a story to his friends and neighbors. What story do you think the fox is reading? Would it be a story about people? About animals? Write the beginning of the story the fox is reading. Write the whole story if you wish.

CRITICAL THINKING ◆
A Strategy for Imagining

A CONCLUSION SENTENCE

Imagining can be a way of pretending or making believe. One kind of imaginary tale is called a **fable.** In a fable animals often talk and act like people. After this lesson you will read two fables. One is about a dragon king and queen. The other is about a crow. Later you will write a fable.

Here is part of "The Crow and the Pitcher." Is the crow in this fable an imaginary crow? How can you tell?

> Dying of thirst, a Crow suddenly gave a cry of pleasure. "Caw! Caw!" he cried. "A pitcher! A pitcher of water!"
> It was indeed a pitcher, and there was water in it. But it was a large pitcher, and the water left in it was at the very bottom. The Crow could not reach down far enough to get a single sip. . . .

A fable teaches a lesson. The last sentence usually tells what lesson you can conclude from the fable. In "The Tortoise and the Hare," the slow tortoise wins because he does not stop to nap. The conclusion sentence is "Slow and steady wins the race." Would you reach the same conclusion? Can you conclude what lesson the crow might learn in "The Crow and the Pitcher"?

Learning the Strategy

You often draw a conclusion, or decide what you think, from what you observe. For example, you see the end of a ball game on television. However, you miss the final score. From the way the teams behave, can you conclude which one won? Imagine that you live in the city but spend the summer

CRITICAL THINKING: Drawing Conclusions

on a farm. You feel sorry when the summer ends. What would you conclude about your farm experience?

Writing a conclusion sentence can help you decide what you think. Suppose you want to write a story about your summer on the farm. You want to end by telling what you thought, or concluded, about the experience. Tell what happened. Then write a conclusion sentence that begins with the words *I think*.

What happened on the farm:
I fed the animals.
I got to break a wild pony.
I had my own horse.
We picked our own vegetables and had them for dinner.

I think it's great to try a different way of living.

Using the Strategy

A. Remember a time that was very important to you. It could be the day your family moved. It might be the first time you tried to cook something. Write what happened. Then write a conclusion sentence that starts with *I think*.

B. Read the part from "The Crow and the Pitcher" on page 340. Do you think the crow will reach the water? First write what you think will happen. Then write a conclusion sentence to tell what you think the crow will learn. Start your conclusion sentence with *I think the crow will learn (what?)*. Then read to find out if you are right.

Applying the Strategy

- How did you conclude what the crow will learn?
- Have you ever learned a lesson from an experience? Do you think you ever will again? Explain why.

from

A Chinese Zoo

Fables and Proverbs

Adapted by DEMI

There once was a mighty Dragon King who had a beautiful wife. "I really must have her picture painted," he thought to himself. Summoning his best court artist, he instructed him to paint a picture of the Dragon Queen.

The artist slithered up to his mountain studio, high above the clouds, took out his brushes and his silks, and began mixing his paints. He then embarked upon his task. Month after month went by, and the Dragon King heard nothing. Finally, flaming at the mouth, he charged up the mountain to the artist's studio and demanded to see the picture of his wife.

At once the artist unrolled some silk, took out his brushes, and quickly mixed his paints. In a flash a magnificent picture of the Queen emerged on the silk.

"If you can paint such a beautiful picture so quickly," roared the Dragon King, "why did you keep me waiting a whole year?"

Then the artist opened the back door of his studio. A whole mountain of discarded paintings was there: the Dragon Queen sitting, standing, running, rolling, roaring — the Queen pictured in every aspect of life.

"Your Majesty," explained the poor artist, "it took a year to learn how to paint a perfect picture of the Dragon Queen in a flash!"

No great thing is created suddenly.

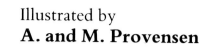

– from *Aesop's Fables*

Selected and Adapted by
Louis Untermeyer   ◆   Illustrated by
A. and M. Provensen

The Crow and the Pitcher

Dying of thirst, a Crow suddenly gave a cry of pleasure.

"Caw! Caw!" he cried. "A pitcher! A pitcher of water!"

It was indeed a pitcher, and there was water in it. But it was a large pitcher, and the water left in it was at the very bottom. The Crow could not reach down far enough to get a single sip.

"Perhaps," he said to himself, "if I push it over, the water would lie on the side and I would have no trouble getting a drink."

But the pitcher was heavy and the Crow was not able to move it at all. He was just about to give up when he thought of something which showed what a clever Crow he was.

He took a pebble from the garden, carried it in his beak, and dropped it in the pitcher. The level of the water rose a little. Then he brought another pebble and dropped that one in, too. The water rose higher. Then he brought another, and the water rose to the top of the pitcher.

With a happy gurgle, he planted his claws firmly on the rim of the pitcher and had one of the best drinks a Crow had ever had in his whole life.

Never give up. There's always a way.

◆ Reader's Response

Why do people tell fables over and over again?

Fables

Responding to Literature

1. Fables usually teach a moral or a lesson. What lessons did you learn from the fables you read?

2. What are fables? What do you know about them? With your classmates, create a definition for *fable*. First write your own definition. Then share ideas and create one definition that everyone likes.

3. In the fable about the Dragon King, the lesson was "No great thing is created suddenly." How else could you say that? Write a new sentence to tell that fable's lesson.

4. How might you have solved the Crow's problem? Draw a picture. Show the Crow using your solution.

Writing to Learn

Think and Decide ♦ Do you like fables as a kind of story? Write a conclusion sentence. First write what you know about fables. Then write one sentence to tell what you think about fables.

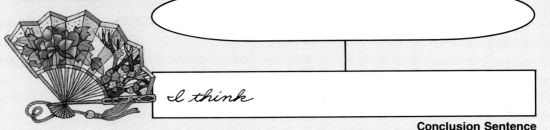

I think

Conclusion Sentence

Write ♦ Write about fables. Tell what you know and what you think.

GETTING
STARTED

You are painting the Dragon Queen's picture. Once again, the Dragon King says it is not perfect! Without speaking, pretend to throw it in the closet with the others.

SPEAKING and LISTENING ♦
Acting Out a Story

Acting is fun, and it helps you learn, too. As you play a story character, you learn to think about and understand the characters you meet in books. When you play a character, begin by asking these questions: *Where am I? What am I doing? Why am I doing it?* Suppose you were playing the crow in "The Crow and the Pitcher."

CROW: I am in a garden, perched on the edge of a large pitcher. I reach my head far down. I stretch my neck. I must get that water! I am so thirsty!

You do not need a written play to act out a part. With a group you can act out a story as you read it aloud. Here are guidelines to follow.

Saying Your Lines	1. If you are the narrator, read everything except what the characters say. 2. If you are a character, say only the words your character says. Do not say, "he said." 3. Act out your role as the narrator reads. Use your body to show how your character feels.
Being an Active Listener	1. If you are in the play, listen for your turn. Be ready to say your lines. 2. If you are in the audience, show appreciation. Laugh and applaud at the right times.

Summary ♦ Acting out a story you have read helps you to understand the story characters.

Guided Practice

Practice reading each of these quotations aloud. Say it with the feeling that is named after the quotation.

1. Caw! Caw! A pitcher! A pitcher of water! (joyful)
2. Perhaps, if I push it over, the water would lie on the side and I would have no trouble getting a drink. (hopeful)
3. I really must have her picture painted. (firm)
4. Why did you keep me waiting a whole year? (angry)
5. It took a year to learn how to paint a perfect picture of the Dragon Queen in a flash! (annoyed)

Practice

A. Act out each situation below. Put yourself in the character's place. Use your face and body to show how you feel. Use words, too. Say what you think that character would say.

6. **CROW:** You try to push the heavy pitcher over.
7. **CROW:** You drop pebbles in the pitcher, one by one.
8. **CROW:** You perch on the pitcher's rim and drink.
9. **DRAGON KING:** You watch the artist paint your wife's picture in a flash.
10. **ARTIST:** You show the Dragon King your studio. It is filled with discarded paintings of the Dragon Queen.

B. Now read the fables on pages 342–344 as plays. Choose people to read the narrator's part and what the different characters say. Other people can silently act out the characters' actions as the fables are read.

Apply ◆ Think and Write

Imaginary Pairs ◆ Imagine two characters from different stories meeting. For example, the crow from ''The Crow and the Pitcher'' could meet Chicken Little. What would they say to each other? Write several sentences about their meeting.

> ✎ **Remember**
> to pay attention to what the other actors say and do when you are acting out a story.

Choose a character from a story everyone knows, such as
"Jack and the Beanstalk." Give three clues about your
character. Ask your listener to guess who you are.

WRITING ◆
The Parts of a Story

No two stories are exactly alike. Some stories are long;
some are short. Some stories are funny; some are serious.
Some tell about things that happen in real life. Others are
make-believe. But every story has these three things:
character, setting, and plot.

The people or animals in a story are the characters. They
may be the kind of people or animals you see every day, or
they may be imaginary.

The setting is when and where a story happens. A story's
setting may be a crowded schoolroom one hundred years ago
or a backyard filled with autumn leaves.

A story must also have a plot. The plot is the series of
events in the story. It tells what happens. Often a character
has a problem. The character may try to find an answer to the
problem. In most stories the problem is solved in the end.

> **Summary** ◆ Three things make up a story: **character,
> setting**, and **plot**.

Guided Practice

Tell whether each of the following is an example of character,
setting, or plot.

1. a house in the mountains	**6.** a big purple cow
2. a policewoman	**7.** the score was tied
3. some campers hear noises	**8.** last summer on the farm
4. winter in the year 2025	**9.** a pumpkin fell from the sky
5. Uncle Ernie	**10.** my twin sister

Practice

A. Write *character, setting,* or *plot* to show which part of a story each item describes.

11. Lucy and Linus
12. just after sunrise
13. a hot, barren desert
14. a wallet is found
15. three wise dolphins

16. a girl rescues a friend
17. days of the dinosaurs
18. the automobile is invented
19. Long John Silver
20. an imaginary country

B. The sentences below are about the fables you read. Write whether each sentence describes a character, the setting, or the plot.

21. The Crow could not tip over the pitcher.
22. The Crow was a clever creature.
23. The garden was filled with pebbles.
24. The Crow picked up a pebble in his beak and dropped it into the pitcher.
25. The artist's studio was on a mountain.
26. The Dragon King had a bad temper.
27. The artist tried and tried to paint a perfect picture.

C. Think of a well-known story, such as "Hansel and Gretel" or "Cinderella." Write the title of the story. Then answer each of these questions about it.

28. Who are the main characters?
29. Where does the story take place?
30. When does the story take place?
31. What is the problem in the story?
32. How is the problem solved?

Apply ◆ Think and Write

Dictionary of Knowledge ◆ Read about the Midas touch. Write about the plot of the story in which King Midas appears. What is the problem in the story?

✎ **Remember**
to include characters, a setting, and a plot in every story you write.

GETTING STARTED

''Tickets, please,'' announced the train conductor.
''Are you ready to order?'' asked the waiter.
''We're number one!'' yelled the football team.
Can you think of other things that people say at their jobs?

WRITING ◆
Quotations

A quotation is the exact words someone speaks. Quotation marks ('' '') show where a speaker's exact words begin and end. Notice the quotation marks in the conversation below.

The Hare asked, "How about a race?"
"Let's do something else," replied the Tortoise.
"Are you afraid you'll lose?" teased the Hare.
"I am not afraid!" snapped the Tortoise.

How to Write Quotations

Use quotation marks before and after a quotation.

Begin the first word in a quotation with a capital letter.

When the quotation comes last, use a comma to separate the speaker from the quotation.

The Hare asked, "How about a race, Tortoise?"

When the quotation comes first, use a comma, a question mark, or an exclamation mark to separate the quotation from the speaker. Remember the period at the end of the sentence.

STATEMENT: "Let's do something else," replied the Tortoise.
QUESTION: "Are you afraid you'll lose?" teased the Hare.
EXCLAMATION: "I am not afraid!" snapped the Tortoise.

Notice how the end mark of a quotation always comes just before the second quotation mark.

One final tip: Try not to use the word *said* too often.

Summary ◆ Use **quotation marks** ('' '') to show the exact words of a speaker.

Guided Practice

Tell where quotation marks are needed.

1. See you later, called the Hare.
2. The Tortoise said, Now I'll catch that Hare.
3. Slow and steady wins the race! said the Judge.

Practice

A. Write each sentence below. Add quotation marks to show the exact words of the speaker.

   4. Help me! cried Mouse.
   5. Lion said, Now I shall eat you up.
   6. I wouldn't be much of a meal for you, said Mouse.
   7. I guess you're right, replied Lion.
   8. Mouse promised, Someday I'll pay back your kindness.
   9. How could a tiny mouse help a king like me? asked Lion.
   10. Lion cried, Untie me from the hunter's rope!
   11. I will save you! called Mouse.
   12. I'm not too small to do big deeds, Mouse said proudly.

B. Write each sentence. Add all the needed punctuation marks.

   13. Those grapes look delicious said Reynaud the Fox
   14. He cried How will I ever reach the grapes
   15. I'm jumping as high as I can Reynaud complained
   16. Those grapes can just rot Reynaud yelled in anger
   17. They would be too sour anyway he grumbled

C. Pretend you are talking with your dog or cat. Write your conversation. Use at least five quotations.

Apply ◆ Think and Write

Quotation Triplets ◆ Using the same idea, write three quotations. Example: *"I love to swim," said Meg. Meg cried, "I adore swimming!" Meg asked, "Isn't swimming fun?"*

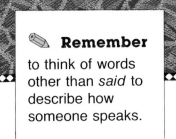

✎ Remember
to think of words other than *said* to describe how someone speaks.

Focus on Fables

A **fable** is a short tale that teaches a moral, or lesson. In "The Crow and the Pitcher," which you read earlier, the lesson is, "Never give up. There's always a way." In most fables, the lesson appears at the end of the story.

The characters in a fable are usually animals that talk and act like people. The animals may do amusing, foolish, or clever things. Their actions show how human beings sometimes behave. Fables can help readers see the difference between wise and foolish, or between good and bad.

Fables have been popular for a very long time. Many people resist being "taught a lesson." But a fable teaches a lesson in an interesting and entertaining way.

♦ You have read two fables—the story of the crow and the pitcher and the story of the artist and the Dragon King. Explain how each one fits the definition of a fable. Which is the more familiar kind of fable? Why?

♦ Is there a lesson at the end of the tale of the artist and the Dragon King? If so, what is it? How does it differ from the lesson at the end of "The Crow and the Pitcher"?

♦ Do you feel that the lesson of the story of the artist and the Dragon King is a useful one? What about the lesson of "The Crow and the Pitcher"? How do you feel about being "taught a lesson" through fables?

The Writer's Voice ♦ What other fables have you read? Tell their lessons, if you can remember them.

COOPERATIVE LEARNING: Writer's Craft

Working Together

Fables are brief and easy to remember. The lesson of a fable applies to human beings everywhere. As a group, work together on activities **A** and **B**.

A. Choose a lesson from a fable. Your group may choose from the five listed below, or it may choose a different one. Discuss the meaning of the lesson. Think of a real-life example that shows the truth of the lesson. Then choose someone to give the explanation of the lesson to the class.

1. Never give up. There's always a way.
2. No great thing is created suddenly.
3. Slow and steady wins the race.
4. Persuasion is stronger than force.
5. We often see only what we want to see.

B. Create another version of a fable. Choose a fable from this unit or another fable that you have read. As a group, discuss ways to change the story. You might choose new characters. You might put the story in today's world. Use your imagination! After listing ideas from the group, write the fable together. Choose someone in the group to record it as you write. Then share your version with the class.

In Your Group

- Contribute ideas to the group.
- Encourage others to share ideas.
- Help the group reach agreement.
- List the group's ideas.

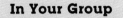

THESAURUS CORNER • Word Choice

Look at the adverb *slowly* in the Thesaurus. Replace it with a synonym in each of these sentences.

1. The mouse chewed slowly but steadily.
2. Slowly, bit by bit, the mouse freed the lion.

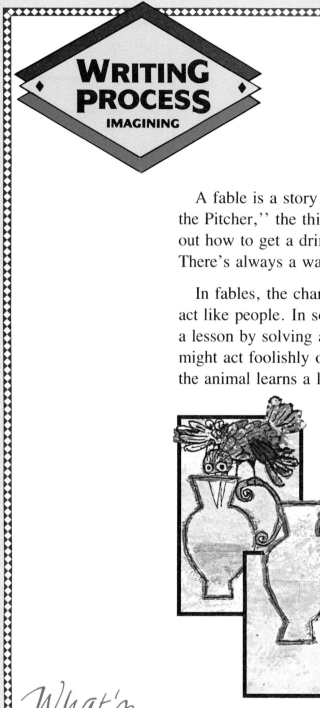

WRITING PROCESS
IMAGING

Writing a Fable

A fable is a story that teaches a lesson. In "The Crow and the Pitcher," the thirsty crow solves a problem. By figuring out how to get a drink, he learns a lesson: "Never give up. There's always a way."

In fables, the characters are usually animals that talk and act like people. In some fables, an animal like the crow learns a lesson by solving a problem. In other fables, the animal might act foolishly or greedily. When things turn out badly, the animal learns a lesson the hard way.

Know Your Purpose and Audience

What's MY PURPOSE

In this lesson your purpose will be to write a fable. It will tell how an animal character learns a lesson.

Who's MY AUDIENCE

Your audience will be your classmates. Later, you and your classmates may tape record or display your fables.

1 Prewriting

Plan your fable. First choose your topic and your animal character. Then gather your ideas.

Choose Your Topic ♦ List your favorite animals. Next list a problem each might have. Choose the pair that you like best.

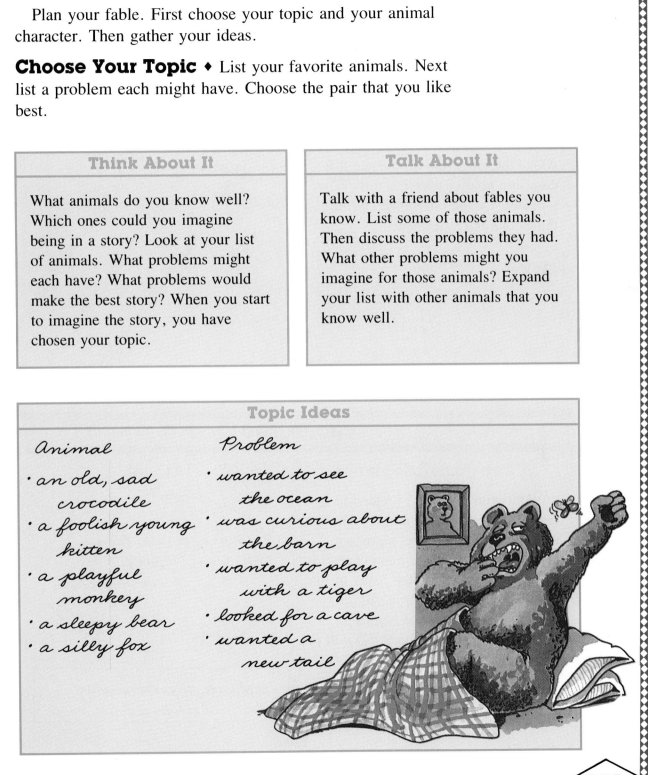

Think About It

What animals do you know well? Which ones could you imagine being in a story? Look at your list of animals. What problems might each have? What problems would make the best story? When you start to imagine the story, you have chosen your topic.

Talk About It

Talk with a friend about fables you know. List some of those animals. Then discuss the problems they had. What other problems might you imagine for those animals? Expand your list with other animals that you know well.

Topic Ideas

Animal
- an old, sad crocodile
- a foolish young kitten
- a playful monkey
- a sleepy bear
- a silly fox

Problem
- wanted to see the ocean
- was curious about the barn
- wanted to play with a tiger
- looked for a cave
- wanted a new tail

Choose Your Strategy ♦ Read the two strategies below.
Choose one to help you gather ideas for your fable.

PREWRITING IDEAS

CHOICE ONE

A Plot Line

Make a plot line like this one.
Along the top, write a sentence that
describes your character and its
problem. On the other lines, write
things that might happen.

Model

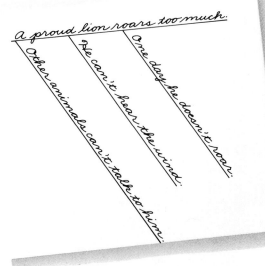

a proud lion roars too much.

One day he doesn't roar.

He can't hear the wind.

Other animals can't talk to him.

CHOICE TWO

A Conclusion Sentence

Work with a partner. Pretend to be
two characters in your fable. Talk
about the main character's problem.
Decide what lesson the main character
will learn. Then write the name of the
character and the problem. Add a
conclusion sentence that begins "I
think (name for your character) will
learn ____."

Model

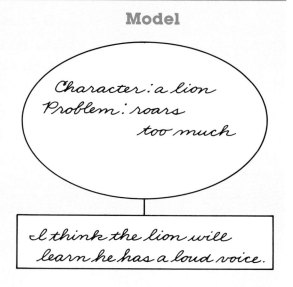

Character: a lion
Problem: roars
            too much

I think the lion will
learn he has a loud voice.

2 Writing

How can you begin your fable? You might make a statement about your character. You might prefer to have the character speak. Here are two examples for the lion fable.

- Statement: Once there was a proud lion who ____.
- Quotation: ''Roar! I love to make noise!'' said the lion.

Use your plot line or your conclusion sentence notes to help you continue. Make sure that your fable has a beginning, a middle, and an end. Write quotations to show what your characters say. At the end of the fable, write the lesson the character learns. Keep writing until you are finished. Don't worry about mistakes. You can correct them later.

Sample First Draft ◆

Once a lion roared all the time.

His friends were unhappy.

The bee said, "you can't hear me buzz."

The bird said she was trying to sing.

The wind blue. It was a fine sound, but no one could hear it

Finally the tiger became angry.

"Please be quiet!" He said to the lion.

"We can't here anything but you!"

The lion stopped. He heard the wind. He listened to his friends.

it was the best day of his life.

Lesson: The lion has a loud voice.

3 Revising

Think about your fable. Do you want to make changes to make it better? Here is one way to help you revise.

REVISING IDEA

FIRST Read to Yourself

Think about your purpose. Did you write a fable? Think about your audience. Will they enjoy your fable? Decide which part you like best. Can you tell yourself why you like it?

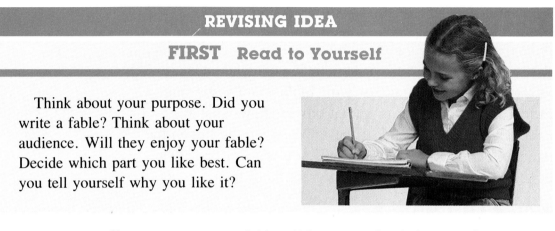

Focus: Does your fable tell how an animal character learns a lesson?

THEN Share with a Partner

Sit beside your partner. Read your fable aloud as your partner reads along silently. Then talk about your fable. These guidelines may help you.

The Writer

Guidelines: Read clearly. Listen to your partner's ideas.

Sample questions:
- Is there any place where I should add a quotation?
- **Focus question:** Did you understand how my character learned a lesson?

The Writer's Partner

Guidelines: Read along silently as the writer reads to you. Give your opinions in a helpful way.

Sample Responses:
- You might add a quotation when _____ speaks.
- Can you explain the lesson _____ learned more clearly?

Revising Model ♦ Here is a sample fable. The revising marks show the changes the writer wants to make.

The writer's partner suggested using a quotation here.

Lovely is a more exact word than *fine*.

The adverb *loudly* helped to tell *how* the tiger spoke.

The writer's partner thought the lesson could be clearer.

> Once a lion roared all the time.
>
> His friends were unhappy.
>
> ~~The bee said, "You can't hear me buzz."~~
> *The bird said, "You can't hear me sing."*
> The bird said ~~she was trying to sing.~~
>   *lovely*
> The wind blue. It was a ~~fine~~
>
> sound, but no one could hear it.
>
> Finally the tiger became angry.
>   *loudly*
> "Please be quiet!" He said ∧ to the lion.
>
> "We can't here anything but you!"
>
> The lion stopped. He heard the
>
> wind. He listened to his friends.
>
> ~~it was the best day of his life.~~
>   *Sometimes the loudest*
> Lesson : ~~The lion has a loud voice.~~
> *voice isn't the best.*

Read the revised sample above. Read it the way the writer has decided it *should* be. Then revise your own fable.

Grammar Check ♦ Adverbs that tell *where*, *when*, or *how* can help to make your meaning clear.

Word Choice ♦ Can you find more exact words for words like *fine*? A thesaurus can help you improve your choice.

4 Proofreading

Making your writing correct and readable is a way of being polite to your readers.

Proofreading Model ◆ Here is the revised sample fable. Notice that the writer has now added red proofreading marks to the blue revising marks.

Proofreading Marks

capital letter	≡
small letter	/
indent paragraph	¶
check spelling	⬭

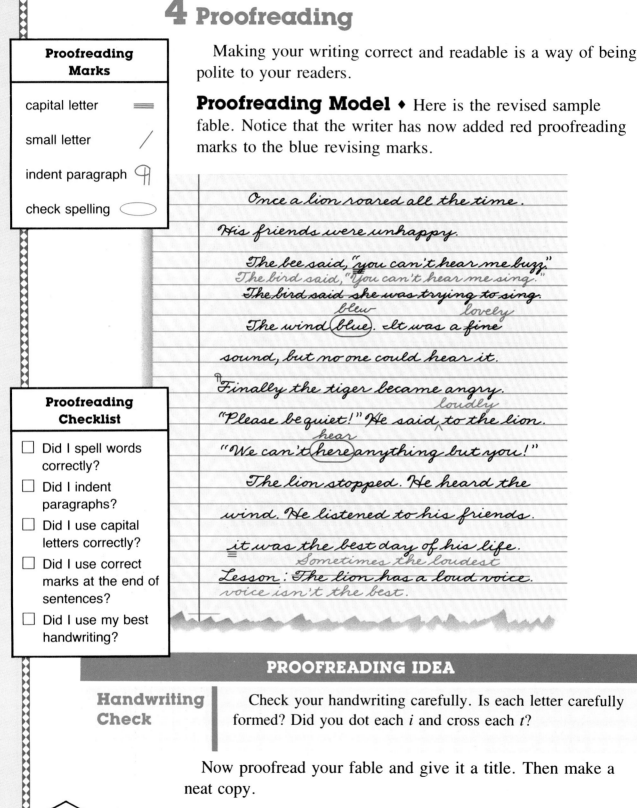

Once a lion roared all the time.

His friends were unhappy.

The bee said, "you can't hear me buzz."
The bird said, "You can't hear me sing."
The bird said she was trying to sing.
The wind (blue). It was a fine
blew   lovely

sound, but no one could hear it.

Finally the tiger became angry.

"Please be quiet!" He said to the lion.
loudly

"We can't (here) anything but you!"
hear

The lion stopped. He heard the

wind. He listened to his friends.

it was the best day of his life.
Sometimes the loudest

Lesson: The lion has a loud voice.
voice isn't the best.

Proofreading Checklist

- ☐ Did I spell words correctly?
- ☐ Did I indent paragraphs?
- ☐ Did I use capital letters correctly?
- ☐ Did I use correct marks at the end of sentences?
- ☐ Did I use my best handwriting?

PROOFREADING IDEA

Handwriting Check

Check your handwriting carefully. Is each letter carefully formed? Did you dot each *i* and cross each *t*?

Now proofread your fable and give it a title. Then make a neat copy.

5 Publishing

Sharing fables is an old custom in our world. Here are two ways to share your fable with others.

The Roaring Lion

Once a lion roared all the time.
His friends were unhappy.
The bee said, "You can't hear me buzz."
The bird said, "You can't hear me sing."
The wind blew. It was a lovely sound, but no one could hear it.
Finally the tiger became angry.
"Please be quiet!" he said loudly to the lion. "We can't hear anything but you!"
The lion stopped. He heard the wind. He listened to his friends. It was the best day of his life.
Lesson: Sometimes the loudest voice isn't the best.

PUBLISHING IDEAS

Share Aloud

Make a tape recording of your fable. Your partner may introduce you on the tape. Play the tape and ask your classmates to guess the lesson your animal character learned.

Share in Writing

Hang your fable on a bulletin board. Cover the fable's lesson with paper. Beside the fable, hang a card that says *Guess the lesson!* Read your classmates' fables and write your guesses on the cards beside those fables.

CURRICULUM
•CONNECTION•

Writing Across the Curriculum
Social Studies

When you wrote a fable for this unit, you ended it with a conclusion sentence. Drawing conclusions is an important skill in social studies, too. You learn many facts about other items and other places. What do the facts mean? Writing conclusion sentences can help you decide.

Writing to Learn

Think and Decide ♦ The way you live may depend on where you live. Look at the photo. What can you conclude about the place? The climate? The work people do there?

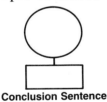

Conclusion Sentence

Write ♦ Write a conclusion sentence or paragraph. Tell what you think it would be like to live in this town.

Writing in Your Journal

In the Writer's Warm-up you wrote what you knew about fables. You learned that a fable is a story that teaches a lesson about life. Think about the fables you learned about in this unit. In your journal write a sentence stating the lesson of a fable you will remember.

Read More About It

Fables *by Arnold Lobel*
Mr. Lobel has written some witty modern fables for this beautiful book. He also did the colorful illustrations. Read these fables, then try to make up some of your own.

Doctor Coyote: A Native American Aesop's Fables *by John Bierhorst*
When explorers came from Europe, they brought Aesop's fables with them. Aztec and American Indians blended those tales with their own folktales. The result is Coyote the Trickster. See how these fables compare with Aesop's fables.

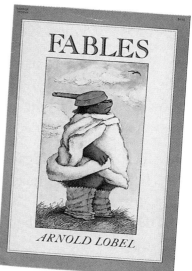

Book Report Idea   Partner Skit

Acting can be fun. With a partner, make up a skit about a book and present it to the class.

Create a Skit ✦ Work with a partner. Use your imagination to make up a skit about the book. You could act out a favorite scene. You could pretend that the author is talking with one of the characters. You could even imagine that a character is paying you a visit. Practice your skit, then perform it for your classmates.

UNIT REVIEW

Unit 7

Adverbs   *pages 326–331*

A. Write the adverb in each sentence. Then write *how, when,* or *where* to show what question the adverb answers.

1. The moth lays eggs everywhere.
2. In April the egg mass is suddenly alive.
3. Dozens of larvae begin to climb up.
4. They hang from threads and climb repeatedly.
5. Once on a plant, they begin eating.
6. They form a hard case and are transformed inside.

B. Write each sentence. Use the correct form of the adverb in parentheses ( ).

7. Of all animals, elephants splash the (more noisily, most noisily).
8. The baby deer runs (faster, fastest) than its mother.
9. The hawk flew (more swiftly, most swiftly) than the dove.
10. The lion roared the (louder, loudest) of all.

Words That Mean "No"
pages 332–333

C. Write each sentence. Use the correct word in parentheses ( ).

11. You don't remember (anything, nothing) about the flood.
12. Nobody (ever, never) saw anything like it.
13. We couldn't find (anyone, nobody) who felt safe.
14. There wasn't (any, no) real warning.
15. Nobody had (ever, never) repaired the dam.
16. Didn't (nobody, anyone) notice the clogged spillway?
17. The water couldn't go (nowhere, anywhere).
18. Not one of us (was, wasn't) ready.
19. There wasn't (anything, nothing) to do but run.

Synonyms and Antonyms
pages 334–335

D. Write each pair of words. Then write *synonym* if the words are synonyms. Write *antonym* if the words are antonyms.

20. hard, easy
21. hurry, rush
22. empty, full
23. feast, eat
24. quick, slow
25. wish, hope
26. crooked, bent
27. soiled, clean
28. nervous, calm
29. odd, strange
30. common, rare
31. prevent, stop

E. Choose a synonym in the parentheses ( ) to replace the underlined word in each sentence.

32. Have you heard about Terri's <u>perilous</u> trip? (safe, dangerous)
33. The animal was <u>enraged</u> by the noise. (angered, pleased)
34. The sudden snowstorm <u>halted</u> traffic. (started, stopped)
35. The quiet lake's waters were <u>tranquil</u>. (rough, calm)
36. How did you <u>smash</u> the glass? (mend, break)
37. Mindy kept her bike <u>spotless</u>. (filthy, immaculate)
38. My teeth chattered in the <u>frigid</u> weather. (hot, freezing)
39. This is an <u>easy</u> assignment. (effortless, difficult)

Stories   *pages 348–349*

F. Write *character, plot,* or *setting* to show which part of a story each item describes.

40. a mysterious stranger
41. an escape from the planet Mars
42. the surface of the moon
43. the lonely hermit
44. a daring rescue is carried out
45. Black Beauty
46. a forgotten island
47. two best friends
48. the team wins the game
49. on a submarine
50. she discovers the truth

Quotations   *pages 350–351*

G. Write each sentence. Use quotation marks to show the exact words of the speaker.

51. Let's go fishing, suggested Tony.
52. That's a good idea, agreed Nancy.
53. Merlin asked, What time should we get up?
54. I think five o'clock, replied Betty.
55. Five o'clock! yelped Rico.
56. Is that too early? laughed Maria.
57. Al grumped, Even birds aren't up.
58. Well, we could go later, said Ken.
59. Janice reminded, We'd have to skip breakfast.
60. I can't survive without breakfast! cried Justin.

H. Write each sentence. Add the commas, quotation marks, and end marks that are needed. Begin each quotation with a capital letter.

61. This is a good place to fish announced Martin
62. Are you sure questioned Gary
63. Val said we caught six trout here
64. How many got away teased Lana
65. Myron said I think I'll row a bit
66. Jerry asked may I go with you
67. I think the boat will hold three stated Rosa
68. Ned replied that seems a bit much
69. Who's going to catch the first fish challenged Pat
70. I am boasted José

Tom Swifties

Tom Swifties are puns that are based on adverbs. Using different adverbs, write more Tom Swifties like the ones below.

1. "This chili is too spicy," said Tom heatedly.
2. "I fixed the air conditioner," said Tom coolly.
3. "These grapes are sour," said Tom bitterly.
4. "Would you like honey on your toast?" asked Tom sweetly.
5. "I sharpened all the pencils," said Tom pointedly.

Adverbs in Code

Ten adverbs are written in code below. Can you figure them out? (Hint: 1 = a and 2 = b.)

1. 6-1-19-20
2. 19-12-15-23-12-25
3. 17-21-9-3-11-12-25
4. 3-1-12-13-12-25
5. 18-1-16-9-4-12-25

6. 12-1-26-9-12-25
7. 8-21-14-7-18-9-12-25
8. 8-1-16-16-9-12-25
9. 23-5-12-12
10. 19-23-5-5-20-12-25

Use the same code to write some adverbs for a classmate to figure out.

Unit 7 Extra Practice

1 Writing with Adverbs

p. 326

A. The verb is underlined in each sentence below. Find the adverb in each sentence and write it.

1. The shortstop threw wildly.
2. The right fielder hit hard.
3. The ball sank rapidly to the ground.
4. A runner moved safely to third base.
5. The crowd cheered loudly.
6. The sun shone brightly.
7. The home team ran eagerly.
8. An umpire shouted loudly.
9. We scored easily.
10. Their manager waved impatiently.
11. A new pitcher strolled lazily to the mound.
12. He tipped his cap politely.
13. Our base runner moved carelessly off the bag.
14. Their pitcher threw hard to first base.
15. Our manager watched helplessly.

B. Write each sentence. Underline the adverb. Then write the verb it describes.

16. Peter eyed the hot dogs hungrily.
17. He counted his money carefully.
18. He asked quietly for a hot dog.
19. Peter drank some juice thirstily.
20. Our base runner walked slowly off the field.
21. The crowd roared loudly.
22. Our team scored more runs quickly.
23. The crowd cheered joyfully.
24. Both teams played well.
25. They greeted each other cheerfully.
26. Our day of baseball ended happily.

C. Write each sentence. Draw one line under the adverb. Draw two lines under the verb it describes.

27. We waited patiently for the solar eclipse.
28. The scientists checked their equipment carefully.
29. We talked happily with the other observers.
30. I looked eagerly at my watch.
31. The day darkened gradually.
32. We waited anxiously for total darkness.
33. I looked cautiously through the special glass.
34. Everyone stood quietly at the special moment.
35. The moon passed slowly in front of the sun.
36. We cheered wildly when it was over.
37. We talked excitedly about the event for days.

2 Adverbs That Tell *Where* and *When*

p. 328

A. Write each sentence. Underline the adverb. Then write *when* or *where* to show what question the adverb answers.

1. Cheetahs often dwell in game parks.
2. Hyenas drive them away.
3. Cheetahs stay far from visitors.
4. Sometimes these cats are friendly.
5. They come out to see humans.
6. Two scientists arrived in East Africa yesterday.
7. They saw tourists everywhere.
8. Tomorrow they are going to a game park.
9. Cheetahs wander for miles there.
10. Some are frightened away by the tourists.
11. They can run away at top speeds.
12. Others never act afraid.
13. The scientists left their hotel early.
14. As they reached the gate, they looked up.
15. A cheetah sat there in the tree.
16. Finally they saw their first cheetah.

B. Write each sentence. Complete each sentence with an adverb that answers the question in parentheses ( ).

EXAMPLE: Cheetahs ——— compete with lions. (When?)
ANSWER: Cheetahs often compete with lions.

17. The cheetah jumps ——— . (Where?)
18. A scientist drives ——— . (Where?)
19. The animals ——— act friendly. (When?)
20. We can stay ——— at the game park. (When?)
21. Don't leave your camera ——— . (Where?)

C. Complete each sentence with one of the adverbs below. Use each word only once.

away   never   up   today   far   now

22. An Arabian boy is talking to his camel right ——— .
23. "Stand ——— , you lazy animal."
24. "We're leaving the mountains ——— ."
25. "We're going ——— ."
26. "You have to walk ——— this morning."
27. "You ——— listen when I talk to you!"

3 Adverbs That Compare   *p. 330*

A. Write each sentence. Use the correct form of the adverb in parentheses ( ).

1. Scientists examine fossils (closely, more closely) than most people.
2. Large dinosaurs moved (slowly, more slowly) than small ones.
3. The small mammals moved the (faster, fastest) of all.
4. They worked (hard, harder) than others to find food.
5. These creatures adjusted the (more quickly, most quickly) to change.
6. Reptiles felt the cold (sharply, more sharply) than other animals.

B. Write each sentence. Use the correct form of the adverb in parentheses ( ).

   7. The bigger plant-eater swam (faster, fastest).

   8. It watched (carefully, more carefully) for lizards.

   9. Dark waters protected it (completely, more completely) than the open air.

 10. A large meat-eater stalked the shore (impatiently, more impatiently) than ever.

 11. It opened its jaws (wide, wider) than before.

 12. Which of the two dinosaurs worked (harder, hardest)?

 13. Archaeopteryx jumped the (higher, highest) of all.

 14. A triceratops moved (slowly, more slowly) than some other dinosaurs.

 15. One sea reptile dived (faster, fastest) than the others.

 16. Allosaurus bit the (more sharply, most sharply) of all.

C. Write each sentence. Add *most* or use the *-est* form of the adverb in parentheses ( ).

 17. Scientists study fossils the (carefully).

 18. Crocodiles lived (long) of all archosaurs.

 19. That one could have sunk (fast) of all.

 20. This one may have eaten the (quickly).

 21. Of the three, that one spread its wings (rapidly).

D. Write each sentence. Use the correct form of the word in parentheses ( ).

 22. Scientists study dolphins (closely) than whales.

 23. Dolphins hear (sharply) than most other mammals.

 24. They swim (fast) than sharks.

 25. They learn (quickly) than monkeys.

 26. Some porpoises jump (high) than dolphins.

 27. Dolphins breathe (deep) than land mammals.

 28. They can hold their breath (long) than other mammals.

 29. Dolphins learn to do tricks (early) than the others.

 30. The bottle-nosed dolphin learns the (fast) of all.

4 Using Words That Mean "No"   *p. 332*

A.   Write each sentence. Underline the word that means "no."

   1.   We had not decided on a place for our picnic.
   2.   None of us had ever been to Lake Lacy.
   3.   "I never thought of going there," cried Cathy.
   4.   We didn't forget the paper plates.
   5.   We have no napkins, however.
   6.   Aunt Sarah has not forgotten the coleslaw.
   7.   Nobody makes better salads.
   8.   She never uses a recipe, either!
   9.   Sid can't go anywhere with us again!
  10.   He asked none of us about bringing his pets.
  11.   He should never have taken the ant farm.
  12.   Mom says she doesn't understand Sid.
  13.   He won't come without his ants.
  14.   He likes nothing better than watching them.
  15.   He isn't even helping Betty with her fire.
  16.   There is nobody who cooks better than Betty.
  17.   Bob's potato salad hasn't any eggs in it.

B.   Choose the correct word in parentheses ( ) to complete
each sentence. Write the sentences.

   EXAMPLE: He never makes (anything, nothing) with vinegar.
    ANSWER: He never makes anything with vinegar.

  18.   Bob never adds (any, no) pickles, either.
  19.   Nobody can (ever, never) say there's too little food.
  20.   We couldn't find (anybody, nobody) to take the leftovers.
  21.   There (was, wasn't) no place to put it all.
  22.   I hadn't (ever, never) seen so much to eat.
  23.   We were so full we couldn't go (anywhere, nowhere).
  24.   No amount of trying (could, couldn't) get us moving.
  25.   Luckily there (were, weren't) no dishes to do.
  26.   Nothing (is, isn't) easier to clean than paper.
  27.   We won't go on (any, no) more picnics this year.

UNIT EIGHT

USING LANGUAGE TO
CLASSIFY

Writing
IN YOUR JOURNAL

WRITER'S WARM-UP ◆ What do you already know about the ocean? Perhaps you live near an ocean or have taken a trip to the seashore. Maybe you have combed the beach, looking for shells or driftwood. Have you dug for clams? Have you played in the ocean waves? What kinds of sea life do you find in and around the ocean? Write about the ocean in your journal. Tell what you would do at the ocean and what sea life you could find there.

You found the sentence below in a bottle. Put real words in place of the nonsense words.

The gliff oogled the bram tilly for um.

1 Reviewing the Parts of Speech

You have studied five parts of speech: nouns, pronouns, verbs, adjectives, and adverbs.

	Definition	Example
Noun	A **noun** names a person, place, or thing.	The Atlantic is an ocean.
Pronoun	A **pronoun** takes the place of a noun or nouns.	Have you seen it?
Verb	An **action verb** shows action.	The waves rolled in.
	A **linking verb** shows being.	The water is salty.
Adjective	An **adjective** describes a noun or a pronoun.	The Pacific is large. It is a deep ocean.
Adverb	An **adverb** describes a verb.	The waves break noisily.

Summary ♦ A **part of speech** tells how a word is used in a sentence.

Guided Practice

Name the part of speech for each underlined word.

1. Water covers over seventy percent of the earth's surface.
2. On calm days, waves lap gently at the shore.
3. You can see where waves have washed sand away.

Practice

A. Write each underlined word. Next to it, write *noun*, *pronoun*, *verb*, *adjective*, or *adverb*.

    4. The Pacific Ocean <u>is</u> deeper than the Atlantic Ocean.
    5. The Mariana Trench is the deepest <u>trench</u> in the world.
    6. Earthquakes occur <u>regularly</u> at the bottom of the ocean.
    7. The Hawaiian Islands were formed by <u>volcanoes</u>.
    8. <u>They</u> rose from the ocean floor.
    9. The Atlantic and Arctic oceans <u>meet</u>.
  10. The <u>Arctic Ocean</u> freezes in the winter.
  11. The ice breaks into <u>huge</u> floes in the summer.
  12. The floes <u>gradually</u> melt and disappear.
  13. <u>Dr. Byrne</u> saw explorers camped on an ice floe.

B. Write each sentence, using the correct word in parentheses ( ). Then write the part of speech for the word you chose.

  14. The ocean is filled with (common, salt).
  15. You can float (easily, sink) in salty water.
  16. (Yours, Salty) water is not good to drink.
  17. We (swim, often) in the ocean every summer.
  18. A day at the (sunny, beach) provides hours of fun.

C. Write each sentence. Use the information in parentheses ( ) to help you complete each one.

  19. The ocean is filled with animals and ____ . (noun)
  20. ____ people protect the sea animals. (adjective)
  21. We ____ down to the shoreline. (verb)
  22. The waves rushed ____ across the sand. (adverb)
  23. One huge wave splashed ____ . (pronoun)

Apply ♦ Think and Write

From Your Writing ♦ List in columns the nouns, verbs, pronouns, adjectives, and adverbs you used in the Writer's Warm-up.

✎ **Remember**
to use the parts of speech carefully to express ideas clearly.

2 Simple Subjects

You know that every sentence has two parts—a subject and a predicate. Remember that the subject names someone or something. The simple subject is the most important word in the subject.

The sentences below are about the oceans of the world. The subject of each sentence is shown in blue. The simple subject is underlined.

> The five biggest <u>oceans</u> are really one huge ocean.
> Our <u>continent</u> is almost completely surrounded by water.
> <u>It</u> is nearly an island.
> Some <u>seas</u> are full of activity.
> <u>Currents</u> move ocean water around the world.

A simple subject can be a noun, such as *oceans*, *continent*, *seas*, or *currents*. It can also be a pronoun, such as *it*.

> **Summary** ◆ The **simple subject** is the main word in the complete subject.

Guided Practice

A line has been drawn between the subject and the predicate of each sentence. Name the simple subject.

1. The shoreline | has changed over the years.
2. Our neighbor's cottage | was close to the water.
3. A storm | blew mighty waves against the cliff.
4. It | washed away tons of sand and rock.
5. High tides | carried off some of our neighbor's yard.

Practice

A. Notice the line between each subject and predicate below. Write each subject. Then underline the simple subject.

6. The shoreline | has many different shapes.
7. Steep cliffs | rise out of the water on some shores.
8. A wide, sandy beach | appeals to sunbathers.
9. The Maine shoreline | is often a mound of rocks.
10. Driftwood | captures the eye of an artist.
11. Marshy lands | provide nesting places for birds.
12. A lonely sandpiper | walks along the sand dunes.

B. Choose the simple subject from the parentheses ( ) to complete each sentence. Write the sentences.

13. (Often, We) went to a beach.
14. My (brothers, sunburned) found a horseshoe crab.
15. A small wading (sandy, bird) ran along the beach.
16. (I, Old) found a shark's tooth in the sand.
17. Some large (seals, diving) were swimming offshore.
18. (Little, Periwinkles) cluster near the tide pool.
19. Marine (animals, salty) feed on the surrounding algae.

C. Use the nouns and pronouns below as simple subjects to complete the paragraph. Write the paragraph.

we   island   evenings   bird-watcher   geese

This (**20.** ___) is a bird sanctuary. (**21.** ___) watch the migrating birds that rest here. Brightly-colored (**22.** ___) nest in the grass. A sharp-eyed (**23.** ___) spotted a snowy egret. The long summer (**24.** ___) are a good time for bird-watching.

Apply ◆ Think and Write

Seashore Subjects ◆ Write five sentences about the seashore. Use a different simple subject in each sentence.

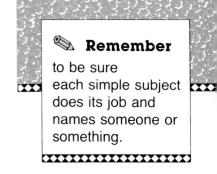
✎ **Remember**
to be sure each simple subject does its job and names someone or something.

Make up tall tales about groups of animals at the beach.
EXAMPLES: *A dog and a turtle danced a jig.*
Some seahorses and starfish jogged along the sand.

3 Compound Subjects

You know that the main word in the complete subject of a sentence is the simple subject.

> <u>Seawater</u> contains a great variety of minerals.
> The most common <u>mineral</u> is salt.

Read the sentences below. These sentences have more than one main word in the subject.

> <u>Shells</u> and <u>seaweed</u> settle along the seashore.
> Spiny <u>crabs</u> and colorful <u>fish</u> scurry along the reef.

Notice that the main words in the examples above are joined by *and*. In each example the two simple subjects share the same predicate.

> **Summary** ◆ A sentence may have more than one simple subject. When you write, you can use the word *and* to join simple subjects.

Guided Practice

The subject of each sentence is underlined. Name the two main words in each subject.

1. <u>Scientists and explorers</u> study the ocean.
2. <u>The currents and waves</u> mix the water of the ocean.
3. <u>Huge blue whales and tiny plankton</u> live in the sea.
4. <u>The sea and the land</u> supply us with minerals and other resources.
5. <u>Giant kelp and other seaweeds</u> grow on the ocean floor.

Practice

A. The subject of each sentence is underlined. Write each subject. Then underline the two simple subjects.

6. Plants and animals live in the ocean.
7. The water and the shore are home to the plants.
8. Sunlight and minerals nourish the plants.
9. The surface water and open sea support animal life.
10. Starfish and lobsters look for food at the bottom of the ocean.

B. Write each sentence. Underline the simple subject or subjects in each sentence.

11. Plankton are tiny, floating plants and animals.
12. Most ocean animals depend on plankton for food.
13. Oysters and other creatures creep along the ocean floor.
14. Their food is carried to them by ocean currents.
15. Snails and geese feed on some ocean plants.

C. Write the paragraph. Complete the sentences with the words below.

boats and rafts   **clams and mussels**   **explorers**
   tools and weapons   **Greeks and Phoenicians**

(**16.** ____) explored the oceans long ago. These early (**17.** ____) discovered many benefits of the sea. (**18.** ____) were made from ocean rocks. Tasty (**19.** ____) were good food. Small (**20.** ____) were developed for fishing near shore.

Apply ◆ Think and Write

A Classified Paragraph ◆ List some things from the sea that we use. Write a paragraph telling how the things are used. Try to use two simple subjects joined by *and* in some of your sentences.

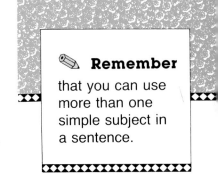

✎ **Remember**
that you can use more than one simple subject in a sentence.

◆ GETTING STARTED ◆

How many ways can a person move in water? Change the underlined word in the sentence below to find out.

I drifted down the river.

4 Simple Predicates

You have just reviewed the subject of a sentence. This lesson reviews the other part of a sentence, the predicate. You know that the predicate includes all the words that tell what the subject is or does. The simple predicate is the most important word in the predicate.

Read each sentence below. The predicate is shown in green. The simple predicate is underlined.

| Ocean waters <u>flow</u> in great streams.
| The water level <u>changes</u> during the day.
| These changes <u>are</u> ocean tides.
| Ocean water always <u>moves</u>.

The simple predicate of a sentence is a verb. It can be an action verb, such as *flow*, *changes*, or *moves*. It can also be a linking verb, such as *are*.

Summary ◆ The **simple predicate** is the main word or words in the complete predicate.

Guided Practice

A line has been drawn between the subject and the predicate of each sentence. Name each simple predicate.

1. Ocean currents | run like large rivers in the ocean.
2. The winds | control the direction of the currents.
3. Currents in the northern hemisphere | flow clockwise.
4. The Gulf Stream | is one of the earth's strongest currents.
5. It | moves along the east coast of North America.

Practice

A. In each sentence below the predicate is underlined. Write each predicate. Then underline the simple predicate.

6. The land <u>affects the currents, too.</u>
7. Sometimes, land <u>is in the way of an ocean current.</u>
8. Then the ocean current <u>curves past the land.</u>
9. This moving water <u>is set off in a new direction.</u>
10. Differences in temperature <u>cause ocean currents.</u>
11. Cold, deep water currents <u>move toward the equator.</u>
12. The warmed water <u>rises near the equator.</u>

B. Choose the simple predicate from the parentheses ( ) to complete each sentence. Write the sentences.

13. We (deep, call) large, moving rivers of water *currents*.
14. The sun (warms, land) ocean water at the equator.
15. Warm water (flows, sand) away from the equator.
16. The strength of the ocean current (cold, changes) with the seasons.
17. The ocean temperature (varies, tides) from year to year.

C. Use the verbs below as simple predicates to complete the paragraph. Write the paragraph.

are   depend   carries   live   move

Ocean currents (**18.** ___) caused mainly by wind. They (**19.** ___) ocean water around the world. The Gulf Stream (**20.** ___) warm water north from the equator. Many fish (**21.** ___) in this warm water area. Some fish (**22.** ___) on the current to bring them food.

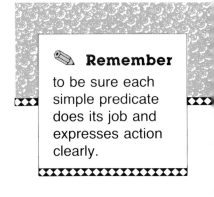

> ✎ **Remember**
> to be sure each simple predicate does its job and expresses action clearly.

Apply ◆ Think and Write

Dictionary of Knowledge ◆ Read the article about red algae. Then write a paragraph about some important uses for red algae. Underline the simple predicates in your sentences.

GETTING STARTED

Think of a word that names an animal. Then tell two things the animal does.

EXAMPLE: *A seal waddles and barks.*

5 Compound Predicates

You know that the main word in the complete predicate of a sentence is the simple predicate. Remember that the simple predicate of a sentence is a verb.

> I <u>know</u> some facts about worms.
> Sea worms <u>move</u> along the ocean floor.

Some sentences have more than one main word in the predicate.

> Some worms <u>live</u> and <u>feed</u> in the ocean.
> Marine worms <u>burrow</u> and <u>poke</u> through the sand.

Notice that the verbs in the examples above are joined by *and*. In each example the two simple predicates share the same subject.

> **Summary** ◆ A sentence may have more than one simple predicate. When you write, you can use the word *and* to join simple predicates.

Guided Practice

Name each verb in the sentences below. Tell which sentences have two verbs. Which sentences have only one verb?

1. Sponges live and grow at the bottom of the ocean.
2. These animals attach themselves to rocks and plants.
3. A sponge sits and pumps water through its body.
4. Water enters and sweeps through the sponge.
5. Warm, tropical seas contain sponges.

Practice

A. Write each sentence. Underline the one or two verbs in each sentence.

    6. Coral animals work and build limestone shelters.

    7. Anemones fool their prey.

    8. Their colors decorate the ocean with brightness.

    9. Their bodies flow and dance gracefully in the water.

    10. The tentacles of an anemone trap and poison fish.

    11. The jellyfish drift through the water.

    12. This animal slides and moves like an umbrella.

    13. Jellyfish squeeze and push water out of their bodies.

    14. Their tentacles wave and gather food.

    15. They swim and float near the coastline.

    16. Shrimp grow and shed their shells.

    17. Gooseneck barnacles hang upside down from the bottom of a ship.

B. Use these verb pairs to complete the sentences. Write each sentence.

feeds, hides   **work, play**   **explore, study**
      builds, provides   **bend, sway**

    18. Scientists ____ and ____ the coral reef.

    19. The coral reef community ____ and ____ many animals.

    20. Tiny animals ____ and ____ along the beautiful reef.

    21. Soft corals ____ and ____ in a heavy current.

    22. The reef ____ and ____ a home for millions of plants and animals.

Apply ✦ Think and Write

Picturing the Ocean ✦ Close your eyes and picture the ocean. Write some sentences about the animals you see. Use two verbs joined by *and* in each sentence.

> ✎ **Remember**
> that you can use more than one verb in a sentence.

Paul and Paula are deep-sea divers exploring a sunken ship. Work with a partner to make up sentences that tell what Paul and Paula found. For example: *Paul found a gold picture frame, and Paula found a silver mug.*

6 Compound Sentences

A simple sentence has one subject and one predicate. It expresses one complete thought.

Many people's jobs depend on the sea.
Oceanographers study the sea.

Study the sentence below. It contains two simple sentences joined by *and*. It is a compound sentence.

A lobster stays in its burrow all day, and it looks for food at night.

Read the compound sentence below. What are the two simple sentences?

■ **The lobsters smell the bait, and they crawl into the traps.**

Summary ◆ A **simple sentence** expresses one complete thought. A **compound sentence** contains two simple sentences joined by the word *and*. Using compound sentences can add variety to your writing.

Guided Practice

Tell whether each sentence below is a simple sentence or a compound sentence.

1. Some fishers wade into the water with nets.
2. Clam diggers always work at low tide, and they wear high rubber boots.
3. Clams squirt jets of water, and they dig down in the sand.
4. Some clams can be eaten, and they taste delicious.
5. Clamshells make attractive craft items.

Practice

A. Read each sentence. Write *simple* or *compound* for each sentence.

6. Sailors have explored the seas for centuries.
7. Columbus explored the Western Hemisphere, and Magellan went around the world.
8. Abel Tasman sailed in the South Pacific.
9. Gerardus Mercator made a science of mapmaking.
10. Marco Polo traveled to Asia in the thirteenth century, and he spent many years in Peking.
11. He brought back information about the Asians.
12. Robert Peary explored the Arctic, and he reached the North Pole first.
13. Peary joined the United States Navy, and he became a rear admiral.
14. Photographers record underwater life, and divers bring up interesting finds.
15. Jacques Cousteau is famous for underwater exploration.

B. Add a simple sentence to each group of words to form a compound sentence. Write the compound sentences.

16. I swam in the Pacific Ocean, and ____ .
17. My brother and I went diving for pearls, and ____ .
18. My aunt has an underwater camera, and ____ .
19. We explored a sunken ship, and ____ .
20. Manuel looked around the ship, and ____ .

Apply ◆ Think and Write

Creative Writing ◆ Imagine that you are a sea captain. Write three simple sentences about your life. Then for each sentence add **, and** and another simple sentence.

> ✎ **Remember**
> that you can use the word *and* to join two simple sentences into a compound sentence.

◆ GETTING STARTED ◆

You have been hired by Water World, Inc., to invent new rides for its amusement park. Use compound sentences to explain the rides you have invented.

7 Commas in Compound Sentences

Read the following simple sentences.

■ **Two merchants left Europe in 1260. They traveled east.**

You can make a compound sentence with those two simple sentences. Notice that a comma is used before the word *and*.

■ **Two merchants left Europe in 1260, and they traveled east.**

Two simple sentences can often be joined to make a compound sentence. What compound sentences can be formed from the pairs of sentences below?

> **Europeans were new visitors to Asia. They were curious about it.**
> **The two merchants crossed central Asia. They reached China.**

Summary ◆ When you write a compound sentence, place a comma before the word *and*.

Guided Practice

Tell where a comma is needed in each sentence.

1. The emperor of China was interested in Europe and he invited the merchants to return.
2. The two men went back to Venice and they soon returned to China with a young man.
3. The boy was Marco Polo and he was seventeen years old.
4. The emperor liked Marco and he sent the lad on trips.
5. Many of Marco's trips were by sea and he saw many lands.

Practice

A. Write each sentence. Add a comma where it is needed.

6. Marco remembered interesting sights and he told the emperor about them.
7. The emperor made him governor and Marco taught the people about life in Europe.
8. The merchants were tired and they wanted to go home.
9. The emperor liked them and he wanted them to stay.
10. Finally he sent them to Persia and their voyage began.
11. They sailed to Persia and ambassadors went with them.
12. The journey to Venice was difficult and it totaled fifteen thousand miles of travel.
13. The sailors had been away twenty-six years and no one knew them.
14. The travelers gave a feast and they displayed their riches from the East.
15. Marco told of his adventures and everyone listened.

B. Write each pair of sentences as a compound sentence.

16. There was a battle at sea. Marco Polo was captured.
17. He told his stories in prison. A man wrote them down.
18. Marco had sailed the China Sea. He had visited Ceylon.
19. Europeans learned much about Asia. They never forgot Marco.
20. We still read Marco's stories. His voyages amaze us.

Apply ♦ Think and Write

Telling About Your Travels ♦ Marco Polo sailed to many lands. If you could sail anyplace in the world, where would you go? What would you do when you got there? Write some compound sentences telling about your travels.

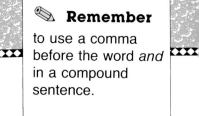

> ✎ **Remember**
> to use a comma before the word *and* in a compound sentence.

Use two words that are spelled alike to complete each sentence.
C___ you open this c___ of paint?
Sl___ this sl___ of paper under the door.

VOCABULARY ♦
Homographs

These students are having trouble understanding their teacher. Why?

Many fish live in schools.

Many words look and sound alike but are not the same words at all. These words are called homographs. **Homographs** are words that are spelled alike but that have different meanings. Some homographs sound alike.

The word *flag*, for example, can mean "pennant or banner." It can also mean "to become tired." *Flag* has a third meaning, too. It names a flower that is like an iris.

Words like these are homographs. *Homograph* comes from two Greek words meaning "written alike."

Building Your Vocabulary

Tell which two words in each sentence are homographs. Then tell the meaning of each homograph.

1. The bird picked up the dollar bill in its long bill.
2. The snake shed its skin near our shed.
3. The mouse bit off a little bit of bread.
4. Push with all your might and the door might open.
5. The man standing by the well said he was doing very well.
6. Linda can crush a tin can in her bare hands.

Practice

A. Use the homographs below to complete the sentences.

ring   hide   duck   like   jam

1. Do you ___ movies ___ the one we saw last night?
2. A truck full of ___ caused a terrible traffic ___.
3. Mel put on his ___ when the phone started to ___.
4. We had to ___ when the ___ flew straight at us.
5. The trapper tried to ___ the deer ___ in a safe place.

B. Use the homograph pairs below to write a sentence in which both homographs are used.

EXAMPLE: a ship's <u>hold</u>   to <u>hold</u> in one's hand
ANSWER: Will you <u>hold</u> my coat while I check the ship's <u>hold</u>?

6. a dog's <u>bark</u>   a tree's <u>bark</u>
7. a <u>fair</u> day   a county <u>fair</u>
8. a <u>lock</u> of hair   a <u>lock</u> and key
9. he turned <u>left</u>   he <u>left</u> the party
10. to <u>loaf</u> around   a <u>loaf</u> of bread
11. to take a <u>rest</u>   the <u>rest</u> of the cake

LANGUAGE CORNER ◆ Idioms

An **idiom** is a combination of words used in an unusual way. The words of an idiom don't have their usual meanings.

Have you ever been *all ears*? Have you ever had a *word on the tip of your tongue*? Have you ever seen it *raining cats and dogs*?

Make up some "Have you ever" questions of your own.

How to Combine Sentences

Two sentences with ideas that go together can be combined. Combining sentences can add variety to your writing. What two facts about Rachel Carson are expressed in example **1**?

> **1.** Rachel Carson loved the sea. Her books warned people about the danger of pollution.
>
> **2.** Rachel Carson loved the sea, and her books warned people about the danger of pollution.

Both sentences in example **1** give us facts about Rachel Carson. Example **2** uses a comma and the word *and* to combine the two sentences into one strong sentence.

A comma and the word *but* can also join sentences with ideas that go together. Since both sentences in example **3** tell about being a scientist, they can be combined.

> **3.** Rachel wanted to be a marine biologist. Few people thought women could be scientists.
>
> **4.** Rachel wanted to be a marine biologist, but few people thought women could be scientists.

Two sentences with related ideas can also be joined with a comma and the word *or*. Different kinds of sentences can be joined, too. What kinds of sentences are combined below?

> **5.** Do you want to be a scientist?
>   Do you want to be a writer?
>
> **6.** Do you want to be a scientist,
>   or do you want to be a writer?

The Grammar Game ◆ Create your own sentence examples! Write at least three pairs of sentences that can be combined with a comma and the word *or, but,* or *and*. Be sure your new sentences join related ideas!

Working Together

See how combining sentences will help you join ideas that go together. Work with your group on activities **A** and **B**.

A. Combine each pair of sentences below by using a comma and the word *or, and,* or *but*. Then make up more sentences about sea creatures and combine them.

1. Beluga whales chirp and click. Some people call them canaries of the sea.
2. Are sea horses tiny horses that swim? Are they just fish that look that way?
3. Sea lions look like seals. Only sea lions have ears that you can see.

B. Can you combine any sentences in this paragraph? Think about how ideas in the sentences could go together. Then write the paragraph with your joined sentences.

We agreed to work with partners for this project. Bill is my partner. He went to the library today. Every book about sharks was checked out. I offered to try again tomorrow. I could go on Saturday.

In Your Group

- Ask questions to get people talking.
- Show appreciation for people's ideas.
- Look at others when they are talking.
- Help the group reach agreement.

WRITERS' CORNER • Stringy Sentences

Be careful not to string together, or combine, too many ideas into one sentence. Stringy sentences are hard to read.

Jacques Cousteau wrote about his voyages on the *Calypso,* and once the divers were lost undersea, but Cousteau's crew was rescued, and I would like to be a deep–sea diver, or I might work as a marine biologist.

Can you improve this sentence by forming several shorter sentences? Read what you wrote for the Writer's Warm-up. Did you write any stringy sentences? If you did, can you improve them, too?

LAST CHANCE
painting by Eugene Garin
Courtesy Simic Galleries, Carmel, California.

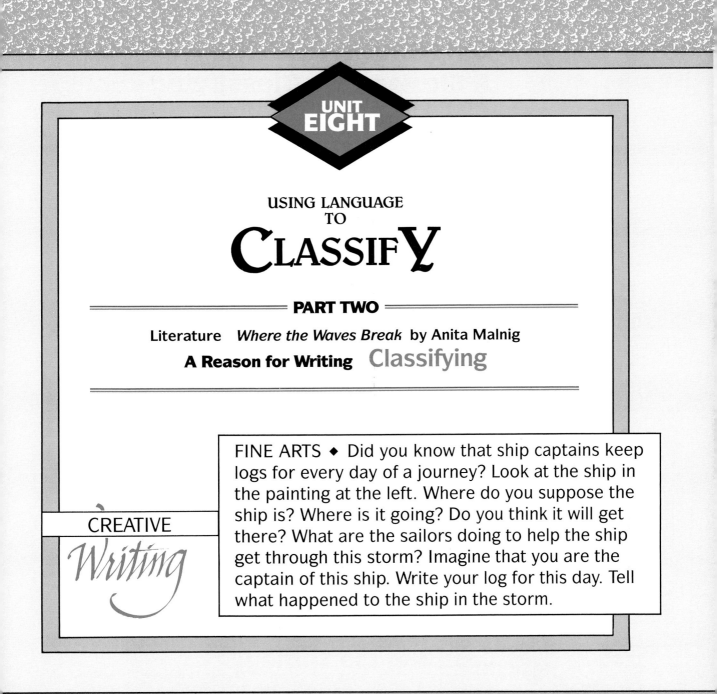

UNIT EIGHT

USING LANGUAGE TO
CLASSIFY

PART TWO

Literature *Where the Waves Break* by Anita Malnig

A Reason for Writing Classifying

CREATIVE *Writing*

FINE ARTS ◆ Did you know that ship captains keep logs for every day of a journey? Look at the ship in the painting at the left. Where do you suppose the ship is? Where is it going? Do you think it will get there? What are the sailors doing to help the ship get through this storm? Imagine that you are the captain of this ship. Write your log for this day. Tell what happened to the ship in the storm.

CRITICAL THINKING ♦
A Strategy for Classifying

AN OBSERVATION CHART

Classifying means sorting things into groups. It means putting together things that belong together. One way to classify is to tell how things are alike or different.

After this lesson you will read part of *Where the Waves Break*. In it the author tells how things at the seashore are alike or different from each other. Later you will write about how two similar things are really different.

To **contrast** is to tell how things are different. This is how *Where the Waves Break* contrasts high tide and low tide.

> If you go to the beach at different times of the day, you will notice that the shore looks different. Sometimes the water comes far up on the shore, covering rocks and beach. This is called high tide. At other times you can walk far out on the beach, over the area that was covered by water during high tide. This is low tide. . . .

How did the author know the differences between high tide and low tide? She went to the beach. She observed the beach at different times of day. She observed high and low tides. She noticed and remembered many details.

Learning the Strategy

Observing details is often important. Suppose you are writing to someone far away. You want to tell about your school. How could observing details from your classroom window make your letter more interesting? Suppose your school has a relay-race team. You wonder if you would like to join. How could observing a relay race help you decide?

An observation chart is a way to record and remember details. Here is a chart about a relay race. Would these details make you want to join the team?

The Relay Race	
What I Saw	two teams of nine runners, clouds of dust, Jimmy fell and skinned his knee, our team won at the last second
What I Heard	sneakers slapping dirt, Jimmy yelling "ouch," cheers
What I Felt	dust in my eyes, hot sun, heart pounding

Using the Strategy

A. Open your reading book. Find a big picture at the beginning of a section. Pretend that you can step into the picture. Make an observation chart. Make up headings such as ''Who Is in the Picture'' and ''What Is Happening.'' Fill in details. Then challenge a partner to find the picture that matches your chart.

B. Pretend you are at the seashore. Make an observation chart. Make up headings like ''What I See,'' ''What I Hear,'' and ''What I Feel.'' Fill in details. Then read *Where the Waves Break*. Did the author use any of your details? Can you find new details for your chart?

Applying the Strategy

• How did you ''observe'' the seashore without really being there?
• What would you like to observe closely? Why?

CRITICAL THINKING: Observing

LITERATURE

from

Where the Waves Break

by Anita Malnig

The edge of the sea is a curious place. Whether the coastline is rocky or sandy, life at the seashore brews and bubbles, but seeing it often takes a sharp eye. Whole neighborhoods of sea creatures may live under the rocks or burrowed in the sand. Some sneak out for food at night, dodging larger animals. Others never leave their damp, dark hiding places. Still other animals are in disguise, looking more like plants than animals. The closer you look, the more you will see.

If you go to the beach at different times of the day, you will notice that the shore looks different. Sometimes the water comes far up on the shore, covering rocks and beach. This is called high tide. At other times you can walk far out on the beach, over the area that was covered by water during high tide. This is low tide. Low tide is a good time to look for shells and rocks or for animals that live in the sand.

LITERATURE: Nonfiction

One of the best places to look for sea animals at low tide is in a tide pool. This is a small pool of ocean water that the tide leaves in a rocky hole on the shore.

If you look into a tide pool, you will find a small community of sea creatures living there. Each tide-pool community is different, of course, depending on where you find it. Yet you're likely to see the same kinds of sea animals in almost every one. Soft sponges and hard-shelled mussels are two kinds of sea creatures you'll find in many tide pools. You'll often see snails sliding along the rocks, searching for food to eat.

Another animal commonly found in tide pools is the starfish. The starfish gets its name because its arms, also called rays, often make it look like a star. Along those arms the starfish has little tube feet tipped with suction cups. These can grasp rocks tightly and are used by the starfish to move around. At the end of each arm is a sensitive eyespot. This eyespot cannot see things, but it can tell light from dark.

Some starfish may throw off parts of their arms if they are disturbed. New arms will grow in about a year.

The starfish's mouth is in the middle of the underside of its body. With its arms it can pull at the shells of bivalves like clams and mussels. When a clam's shells open just the tiniest bit, the starfish pushes its stomach out of its mouth and into the bivalve. Now the stomach is inside out and can begin to digest the clam meat while outside of the starfish's body.

Starfish lay their eggs in water. The eggs have developed inside of the starfish's arms and come out of tiny holes on the upper sides, near the bases of the arms.

You'll find starfish on the rocks or in the water of tide pools or in sandy puddles on the beach just about all over the world.

Brittle stars are similar to their cousins the starfish and get their name from the ease with which they break off arms. As with starfish, brittle star arms grow back. Their arms, however, are usually longer and more flexible than those of starfish, helping them to move faster. Sometimes the brittle star slithers along by stretching an arm forward, fixing the tip of it to a surface, then pulling its body forward by wriggling and bending the stretched-out arm. The brittle star can also crawl about in two other ways. One arm can lead, two can trail behind, and the two in between can move in a rowing or pushing motion. Or four arms can row and the fifth will trail behind.

The tube feet on a brittle star's arms usually don't have suction cups. They are used to breathe, to feel around, and to "sniff" out the small living and dead animals that brittle stars like to eat.

You can find brittle stars in all the oceans of the world. Some live in deep water and some in shallow water, including tide pools. You'll never find brittle stars on the rocks above the water, though. They need to be in water all the time.

Library Link ♦ *You can discover more about the wildlife at the seashore by reading* Where the Waves Break: Life at the Edge of the Sea *by Anita Malnig.*

Reader's Response

If you visited a seashore, what would you look for?

Where the Waves Break

Responding to Literature

1. *Where the Waves Break* told many interesting facts. What fact surprised you the most? Why?

2. Were you more interested in the brittle star or the starfish? Draw a picture of your favorite. Then write one sentence about your picture. Tell what interested you most.

3. What do people like to do at the seashore? Make a class list. Then choose three activities that most interest you. You might want to find out more about them at the library.

Writing to Learn

Think and Observe ♦ Imagine that you could watch a starfish or a brittle star. Copy and finish the observation chart below. Record details of what you would see, hear, and feel.

(name your subject here)	
What I See	
What I Hear	
What I Feel	

Observation Chart

Write ♦ Use your chart to write a paragraph. Tell about the starfish or the brittle star.

Look around you. Find two things that are similar, such as a chalkboard eraser and an eraser on a pencil. Tell how they are alike. Then tell how they are different.

SPEAKING and LISTENING ♦
Comparisons

Joe is comparing whales and dolphins. He is telling how they are alike and how they are different. When you make a comparison of two things, you study them carefully. Scientists, for example, use comparisons to classify animals.

Here are guidelines to help you make comparisons when you speak and when you listen.

Making Comparisons	1. Tell your listeners what you are going to compare. This is like using a topic sentence when you write. **EXAMPLE: Whales and dolphins are both alike and different.** 2. Begin by telling how the things are alike. Then tell how they are different. **EXAMPLE: Whales and dolphins both live in the ocean. Both are mammals. Most whales, however, are much larger than even the largest dolphins. While all dolphins have teeth, not all whales do.** 3. If possible, use pictures or diagrams as you point out likenesses and differences.
Being a Critical Listener	1. Listen for the speaker's "topic sentence." Find out what he or she will tell you. 2. Listen for likenesses. Listen for differences. Picture them in your mind. 3. Make your own comparisons, too, as you listen.

Summary ♦ Use **comparisons** when you speak and when you write. Note how things are alike and how they are different.

Guided Practice

Compare two games of strategy, such as checkers and dominoes. Tell how they are alike and how they are different.

Practice

A. Prepare a comparison to present to a group of classmates.

1. Choose two things to compare. Here are some ideas: two pets, a wild animal and a pet, two foods, two sports or hobbies, two forms of transportation.
2. Write a sentence that tells what you will compare. You may use a question, such as *How do a dog and a cat compare as pets?*
3. Make a list of how the two things are alike.
4. Make a list of how the two things are different.

B. Use the comparison you prepared in **Practice A.** Tell your group how the things you chose are alike and different. Use the guidelines for speaking in this lesson. When it is your turn to listen, use the listening guidelines.

C. Listen as someone reads the following passage from *Where the Waves Break.* Then tell how the beach is different at different times of the day.

    If you go to the beach at different times of the day, you will notice that the shore looks different. Sometimes the water comes far up on the shore, covering rocks and beach. This is called high tide. At other times you can walk far out on the beach, over the area that was covered by water during high tide. This is low tide.

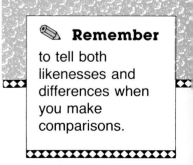

Apply ◆ Think and Write

Written Comparisons ◆ Compare what you are like now with what you were like when you were younger. How are you the same? How have you changed? Write about it.

> ✎ **Remember**
> to tell both likenesses and differences when you make comparisons.

WRITING ◆
A Paragraph That Contrasts

Two starfish, two snails, two seashells, two sponges—the things in each pair are alike, or similar, in many ways. Yet they are different. Such differences are called *contrasts*. Contrasts are important. They are important to scientists and to writers. They are what make each thing unique, or special.

Scientists use contrasts when they classify plants and animals. Writers use contrasts when they describe or explain something. The paragraph below contrasts the two main groups of whales. Notice how the writer has organized it.

Topic Sentence

Details That Give Contrasts

Whales are classified into two groups by contrasting how they eat. One group of whales eat with their teeth. The other group do not have teeth. Instead they have a whalebone strainer in their mouth. They swim with their jaws open and strain tiny plants and creatures out of the ocean for their food.

Summary ◆ A **paragraph that contrasts** one thing with another tells how the things are different. It often begins with a topic sentence that tells what is being contrasted. Writers use contrasts when they describe or explain something.

Guided Practice

Look at the photographs of the finger sponge and the encrusting sponge. Contrast them. Tell ways in which they are different. Consider their shapes, colors, surfaces, and so on.

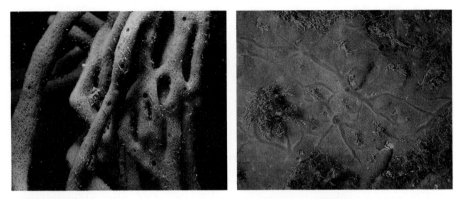

finger sponge   **encrusting sponge**

Practice

A. Each sentence below asks you to contrast two items. For each pair, make a list of three ways in which the items are different.

1. Contrast an ocean with a lake.
2. Contrast a snail with a turtle.
3. Contrast visiting the beach with visiting the mountains.
4. Contrast living in the city with living in the country.
5. Contrast living in a house with living in an apartment.

B. Write a paragraph that contrasts two things. You may contrast a pair of things from **Practice A** if you wish. Remember to begin your paragraph with a topic sentence.

Apply ♦ Think and Write

Dictionary of Knowledge ♦ Look up the entry for dolphins. Contrast the bottle-nosed dolphin with the common porpoise. List the ways in which the two animals are different.

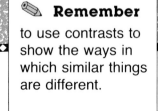

✎ **Remember**
to use contrasts to show the ways in which similar things are different.

Focus on Likenesses and Differences

How can you tell the difference between an African elephant and an Indian elephant? What do football and soccer have in common? Is a boulevard the same as a parkway?

One way to answer these questions is to examine **likenesses** and **differences.** Writers often use this method to compare two people, places, or things. Scientists focus on likenesses and differences when they write about the different classes, or groups, of plants or animals.

Notice how the author of *Where the Waves Break* uses this method to describe two kinds of sea creatures.

LIKENESSES: Brittle stars are similar to their cousins the starfish and get their name from the ease with which they break off arms. As with starfish, brittle star arms grow back.

DIFFERENCES: Their arms, however, are usually longer and more flexible than those of starfish, helping them to move faster.

The Writer's Voice ◆ The sea is full of creatures that can be compared to one another. Among them are whales and dolphins, sand sharks and mako sharks, sea lions and fur seals. Suggest at least three other pairs of ocean dwellers that might be compared for likenesses and differences.

Working Together

Observe closely to note likenesses and differences as you do activities **A** and **B** with your group.

A. The photographs show two creatures of the sea. With your group, make two lists. On one list, tell how the creatures are alike. On the other list, tell how they are different.

bull kelp

brown algae

B. As a group, write a paragraph based on the lists in activity **A**. Begin with a topic sentence. Then tell about the likenesses and differences your group has observed between the two creatures. Edit and improve the paragraph until your group is satisfied with it.

> **In Your Group**
>
> ◆ Contribute ideas to the group.
> ◆ Choose someone to record the group's ideas.
> ◆ Encourage everyone to share.
> ◆ Help the group reach agreement.

THESAURUS CORNER ◆ Word Choice

Look up the word *group* in the Thesaurus. Choose five synonyms for *group*. Write a sentence containing each synonym. In each sentence, tell what item belongs in the group. (For example, "*bunch* of *grapes*" in the Thesaurus.) Do not use the same item as the one in the Thesaurus.

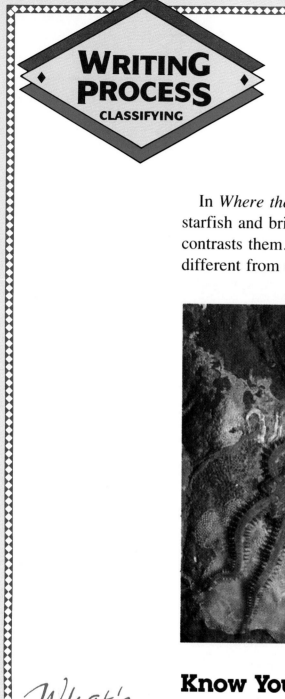

WRITING PROCESS

CLASSIFYING

Writing an Article That Contrasts

In *Where the Waves Break*, Anita Malnig tells about starfish and brittle stars. They are similar, but the author contrasts them. That means that she tells us how they are different from each other. We learn how to tell them apart.

Know Your Purpose and Audience

MY PURPOSE

Like Anita Malnig, you can contrast two similar things. In this lesson you will write an article. Your purpose will be to show how two things are different.

MY AUDIENCE

Your audience will be your classmates. Later you can read your articles aloud to each other. You can also create a magazine.

1 Prewriting

First you must choose your topic. That is, you must decide what two things you will contrast. Then you will need to gather some ideas about your topic.

Choose Your Topic ♦ Look around you. What two things can you see that are somewhat alike but also different? Make a list, then circle your choice.

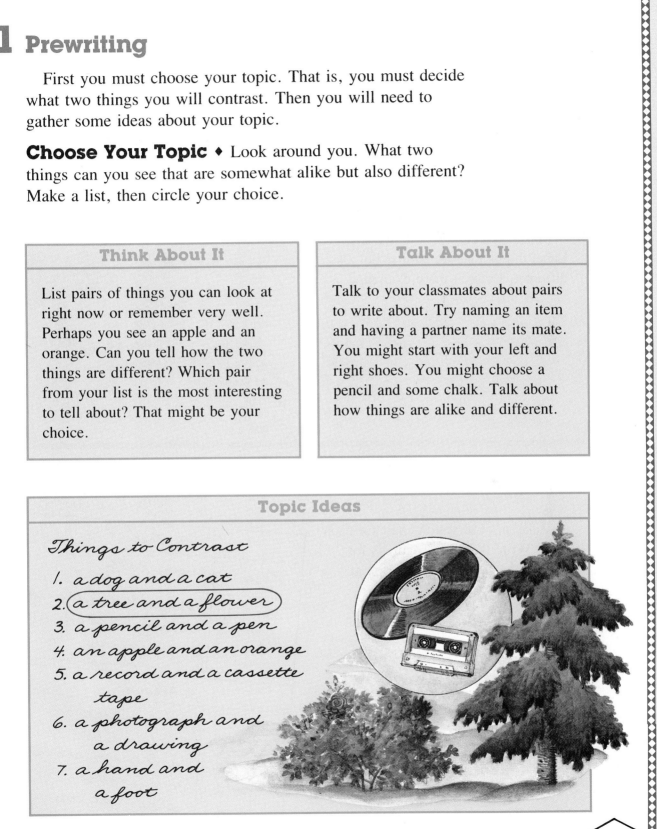

Think About It

List pairs of things you can look at right now or remember very well. Perhaps you see an apple and an orange. Can you tell how the two things are different? Which pair from your list is the most interesting to tell about? That might be your choice.

Talk About It

Talk to your classmates about pairs to write about. Try naming an item and having a partner name its mate. You might start with your left and right shoes. You might choose a pencil and some chalk. Talk about how things are alike and different.

Topic Ideas

Things to Contrast

1. *a dog and a cat*
2. *(a tree and a flower)*
3. *a pencil and a pen*
4. *an apple and an orange*
5. *a record and a cassette tape*
6. *a photograph and a drawing*
7. *a hand and a foot*

Choose Your Strategy ◆ Here are two ways to gather ideas about your topic. Read both. Then use the one you like better.

PREWRITING IDEAS

CHOICE ONE

Sketches

Make sketches of your two items. Label things that are similar but also different. Look at these examples.

Model

soft green stem
very small
four or five leaves
has a flower

hard brown trunk
very tall
thousands of leaves
most trees have no flowers

CHOICE TWO

Observation Charts

Make an observation chart for each item. Write the same headings for both. Then fill in details. Look at these examples.

Model

a Tree	
Size	very tall
Looks	hard brown trunk many leaves no flowers

a Flower	
Size	very short
Looks	soft green stem 4-5 leaves flower at top

2 Writing

To write a four-paragraph article, follow this plan.

Paragraph 1: Name your items. Say they are different.
Paragraph 2: Tell about one item.
Paragraph 3: Tell about the other item.
Paragraph 4: Name your items. Say they are different.
             Say it a different way than in paragraph 1.

Sample First Draft ♦

Trees are plants. Flowers are plants. However, they are different. They are as different as tigers and kittens.

Most trees are very tall. Some have great trunks. The trunks are hard and brown or black. Most trees have no flowers but many leaves. Flowers are much smaller than trees. They have soft green stems. A flower usily grows at the top of each stem. along each stem are four or five leaves.

Trees and flowers are in the same Family. However, they are different.

3 Revising

Here is one way to help you revise.

REVISING IDEA

FIRST   Read to Yourself

Think about your purpose. Is your article about two things? Think about your audience. Will your classmates understand what you wrote? Put a wavy line ∼∼∼ under parts you want to make clearer.

Focus: Did you contrast your two items? Did you tell how they are different?

THEN   Share with a Partner

Ask a partner to be your first audience. Let your partner read your article silently. Then ask your partner for ideas. These guidelines may help.

The Writer

Guidelines: Listen to your partner's ideas. Make the changes *you* want to make.

Sample questions:
- Did I tell enough about both items?
- **Focus question:** Do you understand how the two items are different?

The Writer's Partner

Guidelines: Read carefully. Then give helpful ideas.

Sample responses:
- Maybe you could tell more about _____.
- Another difference I can think of is _____.

Revising Model ♦ This article is being revised.

Revising Marks

cross out ———

add ∧

move ⌢→

Two sentences were combined to make a compound subject.

The writer's partner said this makes a stronger ending.

Massive is a stronger word than *great*.

The writer used a specific number for clearer contrast.

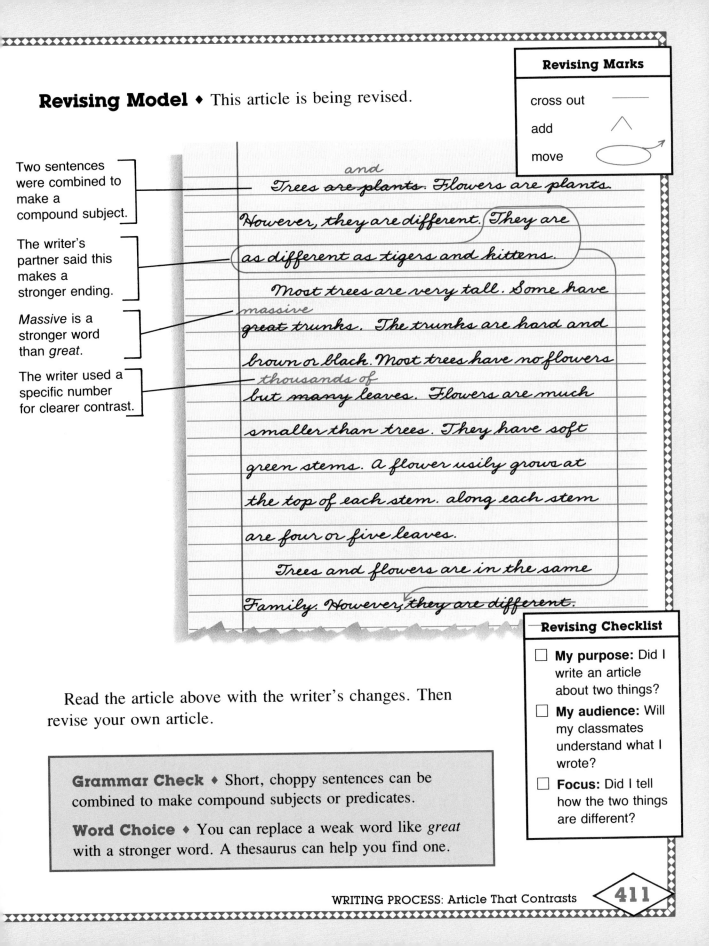

> *and*
> Trees are plants. Flowers are plants.
> However, they are different. ⟨They are
> as different as tigers and kittens.⟩
>   Most trees are very tall. Some have
> *massive*
> ~~great~~ trunks. The trunks are hard and
> brown or black. Most trees have no flowers
>   *thousands of*
> but many leaves. Flowers are much
> smaller than trees. They have soft
> green stems. A flower usily grows at
> the top of each stem. along each stem
> are four or five leaves.
>   Trees and flowers are in the same
> Family. However, they are different.

Read the article above with the writer's changes. Then revise your own article.

Grammar Check ♦ Short, choppy sentences can be combined to make compound subjects or predicates.

Word Choice ♦ You can replace a weak word like *great* with a stronger word. A thesaurus can help you find one.

Revising Checklist

☐ **My purpose:** Did I write an article about two things?

☐ **My audience:** Will my classmates understand what I wrote?

☐ **Focus:** Did I tell how the two things are different?

4 Proofreading

Now look at your article again. Proofread for mistakes in spelling, capital letters, punctuation, and indenting.

Proofreading Model ♦ Here is the article about trees and flowers. Proofreading changes have been added in red.

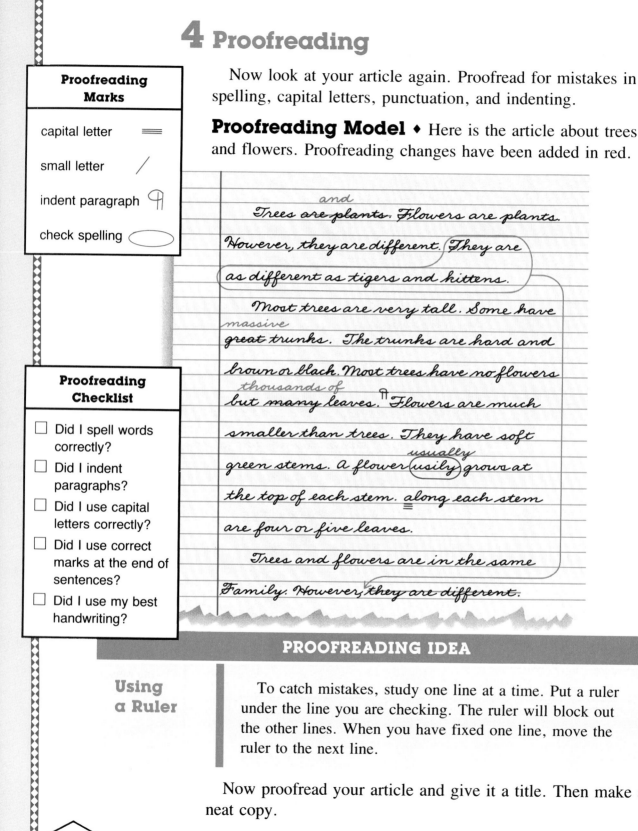

Proofreading Marks

capital letter	≡
small letter	/
indent paragraph	¶
check spelling	◯

Proofreading Checklist

- ☐ Did I spell words correctly?
- ☐ Did I indent paragraphs?
- ☐ Did I use capital letters correctly?
- ☐ Did I use correct marks at the end of sentences?
- ☐ Did I use my best handwriting?

and
Trees are plants. Flowers are plants.
However, they are different. They are
as different as tigers and kittens.
   Most trees are very tall. Some have
massive
great trunks. The trunks are hard and
brown or black. Most trees have no flowers
thousands of
but many leaves. ¶ Flowers are much
smaller than trees. They have soft
usually
green stems. A flower usily grows at
the top of each stem. along each stem
are four or five leaves.
   Trees and flowers are in the same
Family. However, they are different.

PROOFREADING IDEA

Using a Ruler

To catch mistakes, study one line at a time. Put a ruler under the line you are checking. The ruler will block out the other lines. When you have fixed one line, move the ruler to the next line.

Now proofread your article and give it a title. Then make a neat copy.

5 Publishing

Here are two ways to share your article with classmates.

Contrasting Trees and Flowers

Trees and flowers are plants. However, they are different. Most trees are very tall. Some have massive trunks. The trunks are hard and brown or black. Most trees have no flowers but thousands of leaves.

Flowers are much smaller than trees. They have soft green stems. A flower usually grows at the top of each stem. Along each stem are four or five leaves.

Trees and flowers are in the same family. However, they are as different as tigers and kittens.

PUBLISHING IDEAS

Share Aloud

Form a small group. Let the group look at your prewriting sketches or charts. Read your article aloud. Ask who can name one more difference between the two items. Score a point for anyone who does.

Share in Writing

Create a magazine for your class library. You and your classmates can illustrate and bind together your articles. Take turns borrowing the magazine to read. Write notes to tell the writers why you liked their articles.

CURRICULUM •CONNECTION•

◆ **Writing Across the Curriculum** Science

In this unit you read a selection contrasting two kinds of starfish. You also wrote an article contrasting two similar things. Before you wrote, you had to spend time observing your subject. You found that it was helpful to organize your observations in a chart. Observation charts can help you in science class as well.

Writing to Learn

Think and Observe ◆ Make observation charts about two types of weather. Write what you would see, hear, and feel in each kind of weather. Also write how you feel. For example, are you cold, warm, wet? Are you lazy, unhappy, or full of energy?

Topic	

Observation Chart

Write ◆ Use the information from your chart to write about the weather. Be sure to include how each type of weather makes you feel.

◆ Writing in Your Journal

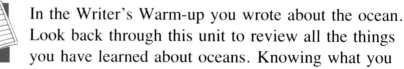

In the Writer's Warm-up you wrote about the ocean. Look back through this unit to review all the things you have learned about oceans. Knowing what you know now, would you like to live on the shore of an ocean? Would you rather be an explorer sailing the high seas? Explain your choice in your journal.

BOOKS TO ENJOY

◆ Read More About It

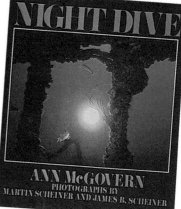

Homes in the Sea: From the Shore to the Deep *by Jean H. Sibbald*

Although the sea is home to thousands of creatures, different ones live in different parts of it. Which creatures make their homes in shallow waters or where the water is cold and dark?

Night Dive *by Ann McGovern*

What must it be like to dive deep into the sea? The author shares the excitement of nighttime scuba diving.

◆ Book Report Idea Pearls in the Oyster

Some oysters contain a precious gem called a pearl. Many books contain a wonderful scene or character that seems like a treasure. Share a pearl from your book for your next report.

Create an Oyster and its Pearl ◆ Make a seashell that can open from construction paper. On the outside of the shell, give the title and author of your book. Inside, write a few comments about the book. Save the best comment for a ''pearl.'' Use a small, separate piece of paper for the pearl.

Island of the Blue Dolphins by Scott O'Dell

This book is about the adventure of an Alaskan girl. She lives all alone for years on an island in the Pacific Ocean.

Unit 8

Sentences   *pages 374–385*

A. Write each underlined word. After the word, write *noun, pronoun, verb, adjective,* or *adverb.*

1. Jack <u>met</u> a friend in town.
2. They ate <u>lunch</u> together.
3. Jack ordered <u>hot</u> soup.
4. <u>He</u> had a sandwich, too.
5. Mia <u>surprisingly</u> ordered that also.
6. <u>Soon</u> it was time for Mia to go.
7. <u>She</u> was going to the library.
8. They have some <u>wonderful</u> tapes.
9. Mia <u>listens</u> to tapes often.
10. She was there on <u>Tuesday</u>.

B. Write the simple subject of each sentence. Then write the simple predicate.

11. Jean's car needs washing.
12. We decided to help her.
13. Jan got a bucket and hose.
14. My brother found some rags.
15. All of us wore old clothes.
16. First we gave it a good wash.
17. Then everyone used the rags.
18. We polished until lunchtime.
19. By then the car was gleaming.
20. Mr. Murphy was very impressed.

C. Write each sentence. Draw one line under the main word or words in the subject. Draw two lines under the verb or verbs in the predicate.

21. Helen's birthday is today.
22. She and her aunt went shopping.
23. They went all the way downtown.
24. Pat rode a bus and met them there.
25. All of them went out to lunch.
26. They talked and laughed together.
27. Helen carried a big shopping bag into the house.
28. The contents of the bag looked heavy.
29. Helen opened the bag and showed us.
30. It was full of clothes.
31. She had spent all her birthday money.

D. Write *simple* or *compound* for each sentence.

32. Henry and I wrote a play.
33. He made costumes, and I painted scenery.
34. Rochelle did the publicity.
35. She posted ads and called the paper.
36. We told our friends and neighbors.
37. Tina brought chairs and benches.
38. Henry learned his lines, and I practiced a scene with him.
39. Everything was ready, and the stage was set.
40. It was a grand event.

Commas   *pages 386–387*

E. Write each sentence. Add a comma where it is needed.

41. Today is a holiday and the weather is good.
42. We're going to the beach and Joe is coming with us.
43. He asked his mother and she said he could go.
44. We grabbed our bathing suits and Dad brought the towels.
45. We got in the car and we were on our way.
46. The sand was hot and the water was cool.
47. We ate lunch and then we rested.
48. We built a huge castle and then Dad took a picture.
49. We raced to the water and we washed off the sand.
50. Dad called us and we ran to him.
51. I carried the picnic basket and Joe helped with the umbrella.
52. Dad piled everything in the car and we drove home.
53. We had supper and then we talked.

Homographs   *pages 388–389*

F. Write two sentences for each homograph. Show two meanings for each word.

54. hold
55. long
56. store
57. well
58. leaves
59. fast
60. hide
61. kind
62. faint

Comparisons   *pages 400–401*

G. Choose the phrase that tells how the items in each pair are different.

63. snow, rain
    a. types of weather
    b. feel wet
    c. fall from the sky
    d. fall in flakes
64. oak trees, pine trees
    a. have roots
    b. have acorns
    c. have branches
    d. have trunks
65. baseball, basketball
    a. played in innings
    b. are sports
    c. played with a ball
    d. played by two teams

H. Choose the word that tells how each pair of items is alike.

66. mice, elephants
    a. kinds of mammals
    b. large in size
    c. chased by cats
    d. have trunks
67. train, car
    a. travel on tracks
    b. carry passengers
    c. pulled by a locomotive
    d. travel on roads
68. cherries, bananas
    a. are fruits
    b. have pits
    c. have a yellow skin
    d. have a round shape

CUMULATIVE REVIEW

Units 1 and 8: Sentences
pages 6–9, 376–383

A. Write each sentence. Then write *declarative, interrogative, imperative,* or *exclamatory* to show what kind of sentence each one is.

1. When is vacation over?
2. Next Monday is the last day.
3. It couldn't be!
4. Check the calendar yourself.
5. What a short vacation it was!
6. It did go rather quickly.
7. How soon does school start?
8. The first day of school is Tuesday.
9. Get your things ready.
10. I think I have enough clothes.

B. Write each sentence. Underline the simple subject or subjects in each sentence.

11. Luis and I found my book bag.
12. Mom dusted off my lunch box.
13. Pencils and a pen were tossed into the bag.
14. Lunch and snacks went in the box.
15. The weather looked stormy.
16. Dad said to take a raincoat.
17. Freddie met me at the bus stop.
18. Maureen and Sara were there, too.
19. The old yellow bus pulled up.

C. Write the sentence. Underline the one or two verbs in the sentence.

20. We all climbed aboard.
21. The driver smiled and said, "Hello."
22. We answered, "Hello," and sat down.
23. The bus started up again.
24. Soon we reached the school.
25. I looked everywhere for Nancy.
26. She shouted and came over to me.
27. Fred and I waved and smiled.
28. Soon the bell rang.
29. We all walked in together.
30. The principal greeted us.
31. We hurried to our new room.

Unit 2: Nouns   *pages 54–59*

D. Write the plural of each singular noun.

32. deer
33. baby
34. tooth
35. village
36. branch
37. dress
38. tax
39. dish

E. Write each underlined noun. Then write *common* or *proper* after each.

40. This <u>bus</u> goes up <u>Lamar Avenue</u>.
41. <u>Sue</u> and <u>Max</u> ride every <u>Tuesday</u>.
42. The <u>driver</u> is <u>Mr. Freeman</u>.
43. The <u>Community Center</u> is located down the <u>street</u>.
44. <u>People</u> can get <u>lunch</u> there.
45. <u>Dr. Lee</u> stops by every <u>day</u>.

Unit 2: Capital Letters and Periods
pages 60–61

F. Write each proper noun correctly. Use capital letters and periods where they are needed.

46. tuesday   **51.** arbor day
47. i a richards   **52.** august
48. block island   **53.** town hall
49. ohio river   **54.** dr earl reed
50. maple street   **55.** ms owens

Unit 2: Apostrophes   *pages 62–65*

G. Write the possessive form of each noun.

56. children   **60.** grass
57. company   **61.** camel
58. Mark   **62.** windows
59. Mr. Jones   **63.** house

Unit 3: Pronouns   *pages 112–119*

H. Write each sentence. Draw a line under each pronoun.

64. I saw the moon in the sky.
65. Marty was with me.
66. He owns a telescope.
67. We like studying the planets.
68. Saturn has rings around it.
69. Have you ever seen Mars?

I. Write a possessive pronoun for each word or word group.

70. Neil's   **72.** the jet's
71. Rita's   **73.** the Jones's

Units 4 and 5: Verbs
pages 160–163, 166–167, 216–221

J. Write *action verb* or *linking verb* for each underlined word.

74. I hear a fire siren.
75. There is a flashing light outside.
76. Fire trucks are at the corner.
77. People are out on the sidewalk.
78. The neighbors smelled smoke.
79. They were afraid of fire.
80. Mr. Deans pulled the alarm.
81. We were sound asleep.
82. The firefighters found a fire.
83. It was in a trash basket.
84. They extinguished the fire.
85. The trucks rumbled away.
86. The neighborhood is quiet once again.

K. Write each sentence. Draw one line under the main verb. Draw two lines under the helping verb.

87. The Epsteins are moving away.
88. They have lived here many years.
89. First they are going to Maine.
90. They are buying a house there.
91. It is overlooking the ocean.
92. Mr. Epstein has retired.
93. He is planning a garden.
94. Mrs. Epstein is writing a book.
95. She is working each day.
96. Now Mrs. Epstein has finished.
97. They have packed their books.
98. The Epsteins are leaving today.
99. We will miss them.

L. Write each sentence. Use the correct form of the verb in parentheses ( ).

100. My dog (know, knows) it's Sunday.
101. Neighbors (stay, stays) at home.
102. We (take, takes) long walks.
103. Rain (fell, fallen) last night.
104. I (saw, seen) a big puddle.
105. Tish (gone, went) right through.
106. Mud (cover, covers) her feet.
107. We have (run, ran) home together.
108. Tish (track, tracks) mud on the rug.
109. Dad has (saw, seen) the tracks.
110. Trouble has (began, begun) in our house!

Unit 4: Commas   *pages 188–189*

M. Write each sentence. Use commas where they are needed.

111. Move over Tish.
112. Well I'm in trouble.
113. Yes we're both in trouble.
114. No we shouldn't track mud into the house.
115. Well it is fun to walk in puddles.
116. Dad we're very sorry.
117. Tish and I will clean up Mom.
118. Yes I will get the mop.
119. I'm glad you came over Nina.
120. Yes we tracked in all that mud.
121. Nina will you hold the bucket?
122. How does that look now Mom?

N. Write each sentence. Use commas where they are needed.

123. Rick Sue and I went to see Lee.
124. We drove through Boston Belmont and Cambridge.
125. She lives near Mary Stan and Pat.
126. We took flowers fruit and bread.
127. It rained snowed and hailed.
128. We were cold wet and tired.
129. Margaret fixed tea toast and soup.
130. Soon we were warm dry and happy.
131. Then we talked laughed and sang.
132. We put on our coats boots and hats.
133. Then we said goodbye opened the door and ran to the car.
134. We shut the doors started the car and drove away.

Unit 5: Contractions
pages 222–225

O. Write the contractions for the words below.

135. I am
136. you have
137. is not
138. he is
139. does not
140. we have
141. she has
142. could not
143. was not
144. I shall
145. did not
146. will not
147. they will
148. would not
149. have not
150. you would

Unit 6: Adjectives
pages 272–273, 278–283

P. Write each sentence. Then underline the adjective that tells *how many* or *what kind*.

151. We had a surprise party.
152. It was Terri's eleventh birthday.
153. There were a dozen balloons.
154. Mom made a carrot cake.
155. It had yellow candles.
156. Dad took Terri to lunch and a long movie.
157. Then they ran several errands.
158. Ten friends came over.
159. Everyone found hiding places.
160. Some people were in the closet.
161. I was behind the brown chair.

Q. Write each sentence. Use the correct form of the adjective in parentheses ( ).

162. Roger is the (younger, youngest) person in the whole family.
163. He can keep the (straighter, straightest) face of all.
164. He put on his (sadder, saddest) face for Natalie and Dad.
165. He said he had lost his (better, best) gerbil of all.
166. It disappeared when a (bigger, biggest) one chased it.
167. I think Natalie was (sorrier, sorriest) than Dad.
168. She was even (more, most) pleased when they found it.

Unit 7: Adverbs   *pages 326–331*

R. Write each underlined adverb. Then write *how, when,* or *where* to show what question each adverb answers.

169. First the horse walked.
170. Then it galloped.
171. It went everywhere.
172. It trotted briskly.
173. We watched admiringly.
174. It lay down.
175. The horse rolled over.
176. It snorted loudly.
177. Soon it got up again.
178. Grass grew all around.
179. The horse browsed contentedly.
180. Occasionally, it looked at us.
181. It sniffed the air curiously.
182. Then it trotted away.

S. Write each sentence. Use the correct form of the adverb in parentheses ( ).

183. Rex walked (slowly, more slowly) than I to see the young mare.
184. It was watching (more, most) carefully than before.
185. The mare eyed Rex even (more, most) suspiciously than usual.
186. Then it turned and ran off (faster, fastest) than the wind.
187. This mare acted the (more, most) spookily of all the young mares Rex had ever trained.

Alien Activities

Describe the planet Trath by completing the compound subject and compound predicate in each sentence in the paragraph below.

On the planet Trath ___ and ___ often ___ and ___. Sometimes yellow ___ and green ___ suddenly ___ and ___. Then some ___ and ___ usually ___ and ___. All the ___ and ___ on the planet ___ and ___ every day. The ___ and ___ of each creature ___ and ___ strangely.

Animal Alphabet

Complete this animal-alphabet game by writing ten other compound sentences. Follow the pattern in the first three sentences. (Hint: There is an animal for every letter. Use a dictionary if you need ideas.)

1. **A**pes eat bananas, and **b**ears climb trees.
2. **C**ats see in the dark, and **d**ogs like bones.
3. **E**lephants have trunks, and **f**oxes live in forests.
4. **G**...

Unit 8 Extra Practice

1 Reviewing the Parts of Speech

p. 374

A. Write each underlined word. After the word, write *noun*, *pronoun*, *verb*, *adjective*, or *adverb*.

1. <u>Ted</u> likes Be Kind to Animals Week.
2. On Saturdays he <u>works</u> at the animal shelter.
3. <u>He</u> is happy there.
4. A <u>young</u> puppy nips his hand.
5. The gray kitten purrs <u>softly</u>.
6. Lisa's <u>class</u> made a special list.
7. They <u>want</u> people to be kind to animals.
8. The students printed <u>carefully</u>.
9. The principal <u>put</u> the list on the board.
10. Here are the <u>best</u> ideas.
11. Put <u>fresh</u> water in a birdbath on a hot day.
12. You will see birds drink <u>thirstily</u>.
13. Birds like different kinds of <u>foods</u>.
14. <u>They</u> eat cracked corn and seeds.
15. <u>You</u> can care for stray animals.

B. Write the part of speech for each underlined word.

16. <u>Students</u> can raise <u>money</u>.
17. <u>They</u> can work <u>hard</u> for a special cause.
18. A cat <u>often</u> <u>needs</u> a post to scratch.
19. <u>Thoughtful</u> people <u>protect</u> animals.
20. You can save <u>animals</u> from injury.
21. A fence <u>keeps</u> a <u>dog</u> from harm.
22. <u>People</u> must drive <u>carefully</u>.
23. They <u>watch</u> for <u>small</u> animals.
24. Animal lovers <u>show</u> how much <u>they</u> care.
25. <u>You</u> are <u>kind</u>.
26. Animals <u>help</u> <u>people</u>, too.

2 Simple Subjects

p. 376

A. In each sentence below there is a line between the subject and the predicate. Write each subject. Then draw a line under the simple subject.

EXAMPLE: The colorful guide | had pictures of rare birds.
ANSWER: The colorful <u>guide</u>

1. A very interesting person | came to class.
2. Her work | is studying birds.
3. She | is a bird scientist, or ornithologist.
4. Many birds | migrate every year.
5. Scientists | want to know more about the birds.
6. Many birds | fly south in the winter.
7. Springtime | brings them north again.
8. My best friend | watches birds as a hobby.
9. This clever girl | imitates birdcalls.
10. I | am learning to identify birds, too.
11. Migration | is a yearly trip for many birds.
12. Some birds | fly very long distances.
13. They | travel from summer to summer.
14. A goose | can fly from South America to Canada.
15. It | stops in New Jersey or New York along the way.
16. A sudden storm | often confuses birds in flight.
17. Geese | can lose their way in a heavy fog.
18. A powerful hurricane | can carry seabirds more than 2,000 miles off course.
19. Many serious bird-watchers | study birds' habits.
20. They | look for rare or unusual birds.

B. Write the simple subject of each sentence.

21. The tern is the best long-distance flier.
22. It goes from the North Pole to the South Pole.
23. The bobolink covers 7,000 miles on its flight.
24. A few birds stay home in the winter.
25. The chickadee can live through a harsh winter.

3 Compound Subjects
p. 378

A. The subject of each sentence is underlined. Write each subject. Then underline the two simple subjects.

1. <u>Lewis and Clark</u> left St. Louis in 1804.
2. <u>The two men and their group</u> traveled to the Pacific.
3. <u>Woodsmen and hunters</u> joined the party.
4. <u>Lewis and Clark</u> were the leaders.
5. <u>The rivers and streams</u> were their route.
6. <u>Army soldiers and a famous trapper</u> traveled with them.
7. <u>Long hours and hard work</u> went into this journey.
8. <u>A keelboat and two dugouts</u> carried the explorers.
9. <u>Oars and sails</u> powered the keelboat.
10. <u>Flour and salt</u> were part of the supplies.
11. <u>Weapons and some medicines</u> were in their packs.
12. <u>Lewis and Clark</u> made good leaders.
13. <u>The men and boats</u> set out in the spring.
14. <u>Sacagawea and her husband</u> joined the journey.
15. <u>Sacagawea and her baby</u> traveled well together.
16. <u>Many buffalo and beavers</u> roamed the rivers' banks.
17. <u>Horses and supplies</u> were important.

B. Write each sentence. Underline the simple subject or subjects in each.

18. The Western states were wild territory in 1800.
19. The long trip was dangerous.
20. Snow and sleet made the mountain crossings difficult.
21. The strong wind and rough waters slowed them down.
22. The Blackfeet and the Sioux met the explorers.
23. The Shoshones gave them horses and a guide.
24. Sacagawea will long be remembered.
25. We respect this brave woman.
26. She was the first woman to cross the Rocky Mountains.
27. Clark named Pompey's Pillar for Sacagawea's baby.
28. Sacagawea and her friends saw the Pacific Ocean.
29. Idaho and Oregon were finally open to settlers.

4 Simple Predicates   *p. 380*

A. In each sentence below there is a line between the subject and the predicate. Write each predicate. Then draw a line under the simple predicate.

1. Ancient record keepers | wrote on wet clay.
2. The clay | dried.
3. People | collected these clay tablets.
4. Collections of clay tablets | were the first libraries.
5. The Egyptians | had libraries, too.
6. They | wrote their books on papyrus scrolls.
7. Papyrus | is a plant.
8. Very few papyrus books | lasted very long.
9. Ancient Alexandria's library | was famous.
10. These Egyptians | borrowed books all over the world.
11. They | copied the books for their library.
12. The first public libraries | were Greek.
13. Julius Caesar | planned a public library in Rome.
14. The Romans | started many libraries after that.
15. People | used parchment then.
16. Parchment | came in sheets instead of scrolls.
17. Writers | folded the sheets down the middle.
18. They | sewed the sheets together for books.

B. Write each sentence. Underline the simple predicate.

19. Large schools had big libraries in the Middle Ages.
20. Wealthy people owned collections of books.
21. Specially trained workers copied books by hand.
22. The Chinese taught the Arabs something.
23. They showed the Arabs the art of papermaking.
24. This art spread through Europe.
25. Gutenberg invented printing with movable type in 1440.
26. Libraries looked very different after this invention.
27. The shelves held books now instead of scrolls.
28. Public libraries began in America before 1776.
29. Benjamin Franklin started a library in 1731.

5 Compound Predicates *p. 382*

A. Write each sentence. Underline the one or two verbs in each sentence.

   1. I slept and relaxed the first day of summer vacation.
   2. We talked and read on rainy days.
   3. We cooked and ate outdoors every weekend.
   4. Todd fished and swam all day.
   5. He fishes in the evening.
   6. Trudy groomed and watered her pony.
   7. We loved Grandma's ranch!
   8. Sam mixed and baked biscuits early every morning.
   9. The horses bucked and whinnied in the morning air.
  10. Cowhands herded the horses into the corral.
  11. Trudy caught her gray pony.
  12. She saddled and bridled the mare quickly.
  13. Todd called his pinto.
  14. The black and white pony turned and ran.
  15. Todd offered the pony an apple.
  16. He mounted and rode toward the distant hills.
  17. They spent the day on horseback.
  18. They stopped and rested at noon.
  19. The tired horses grazed and stood in the sun.
  20. The weather changed by late afternoon.
  21. The horses shivered and shook in the cold rain.
  22. The riders galloped home.

B. Write each sentence. Add one of these verbs to complete each sentence.

   fed   removed   polished   trotted   barked

  23. The horses walked and ____ around the ring.
  24. A stray dog ____ and nipped at their heels.
  25. Trudy unbuckled and ____ the saddle.
  26. She cleaned and ____ her boots.
  27. Todd brushed and ____ his pony.

6 Compound Sentences   *p. 384*

A.   Write each sentence. Write *simple* or *compound* for each sentence.

1.   Richard Henry Lee thought the colonies should be free, and Congress agreed.
2.   Five men were asked to write a statement of the colonies' reasons for wanting independence.
3.   Jefferson was the main writer, and four others helped.
4.   He finished writing on July 3, and the Declaration was read aloud.
5.   Everyone wanted to make changes.
6.   Thomas Jefferson sat quietly at his desk, and John Adams answered the questions.
7.   The temperature was 68°F at six in the morning, and it rose to almost 80°F in the afternoon.
8.   The room was hot, and the delegates were tired.
9.   Thomas Jefferson wrote 1,817 words, and Congress took out 480 of them.
10.   Congress voted ''yes'' late in the evening of July 4.
11.   July 4, 1776, is America's birthday.
12.   Our town has a parade, and we have fireworks at night.
13.   Some families take a picnic lunch to the parade.
14.   One year a bakery made a huge birthday cake, and the mayor lit the candles.
15.   The fire chief blew out the candles, and everyone had some cake.

B.   Add a simple sentence to each group of words to form a compound sentence. Write the compound sentence.

16.   We brought the hamburgers, and _____ .
17.   Chris built the fire, and _____ .
18.   Our dog stole a hamburger, and _____ .
19.   The Marshes washed the dishes, and _____ .
20.   The fireworks began late, and _____ .
21.   We stayed up late, and _____ .

7 Commas in Compound Sentences

p. 386

A. Write each sentence. Add a comma where it is needed.

1. Some things are counted and others are measured.
2. We count to learn how many and we measure to learn how much.
3. Long ago some people used sticks to measure and some used parts of the body.
4. Romans measured with their thumbs and they also used their feet to measure.
5. A foot is about as long as a person's foot and a yard is about as long as an arm.
6. Today some people measure in yards and others measure in meters.
7. The British pound is a unit of money and the American pound is a unit of weight.
8. Americans use yards to measure cloth and the French use meters.
9. We speak of bushels and they speak of liters.
10. A meter is longer than a yard and a liter holds more than a quart.
11. A millimeter is about the thickness of a dime and a centimeter is about one third of an inch.
12. We buy a pound of peas and we buy a quart of milk.
13. One is a dry measure and one is a liquid measure.
14. Shoe size is one measurement and hat size is another.
15. We can measure inches and we can measure feet.

B. Write each pair of sentences as a compound sentence.

16. Jo wanted a bookcase. She decided to build it.
17. She measured the wall. She drew a design.
18. The height was four feet. The width was three feet.
19. It had six shelves. Each was six inches deep.
20. Jo worked hard. Soon the bookcase was finished.

Acknowledgments continued from page ii.

Permissions: We wish to thank the following authors, publishers, agents, corporations, and individuals for their permission to reprint copyrighted materials. Page 20: *The Best Bad Thing* by Yoshiko Uchida excerpted from *The Best Bad Thing.* Copyright © 1983 Yoshiko Uchida. Reprinted with the permission of Margaret K. McElderry Books, an imprint of Macmillan Publishing Co. Page 74: *Why Don't You Get a Horse, Sam Adams?* Reprinted by permission of Coward, McCann, & Geoghegan from *Why Don't You Get a Horse, Sam Adams?* by Jean Fritz. Text copyright 1974 by Jean Fritz. Page 130: "A lonely sparrow …" from *Flower, Moon, Snow: A Book of Haiku* by Kazue Mizumura, (Thomas Y. Crowell). Copyright © 1977 by Kazue Mizumura. Reprinted by permission of Harper & Row, Publishers, Inc. "Icicles" by John S. Baird. Used by permission of the author. Page 131: "The dark gray clouds…" From *The Sun is a Golden Earring* by Natalia Belting. Copyright © 1962 by Natalia Belting. Reprinted by permission of Henry Holt & Company, Inc. "Under a small, cold…" by Ransetsu from *More Cricket Songs* Japanese haiku translated by Harry Behn. Copyright © 1971 by Harry Behn. All rights reserved. Reprinted by permission of Marian Reiner. Page 132: "Although he never moves house…" by José Juan Tablada. Reprinted with permission of Macmillan Publishing Co. from *The Yellow Canary Whose Eye Is So Black,* edited and translated by Cheli Durán. Copyright © 1977 by Cheli Durán Ryan. "horse" by Valerie Worth. From *Still More Small Poems* by Valerie Worth. Copyright © 1976, 1977, 1978 by Valerie Worth. Reprinted by permission of Farrar, Straus & Giroux, Inc. Page 136: "Trip: San Francisco" by Langston Hughes. Copyright © 1958 by Langston Hughes. Reprinted by permission of Harold Ober Associates Inc. Page 137: "Night Song" from *Whispers and Other Poems* by Myra Cohn Livingston. © 1958 by Myra Cohn Livingston. Reprinted by permission of Marian Reiner for the author. "Running Moon" by Elizabeth Coatsworth reprinted by permission of Grosset & Dunlap, Inc., from *The Sparrow Bush* by Elizabeth Coatsworth, copyright © 1966 by Grosset & Dunlap, Inc. Page 180: "Preparing a Giant Praying Mantis" from *Are Those Animals Real?* by Judy Cutchins and Ginny Johnston. Copyright © 1984 by Ginny Johnston and Judy Cutchins. Reprinted by permission of Morrow Junior Books (a division of William Morrow & Company, Inc.). Page 234: Excerpt from *Mary McLeod Bethune* by Eloise Greenfield, (Thomas Y. Crowell). Copyright © 1977 by Eloise Greenfield. Reprinted by permission of Harper & Row, Publishers, Inc. Page 292: Excerpt from *The Trumpet of the Swan* by E.B. White. Text copyright © 1970 by E.B. White. Reprinted by permission of Harper & Row, Publishers, Inc. Page 342: "The Dragon King" from *A Chinese Zoo,* copyright © 1987 by Demi. Reprinted by permission of Harcourt Brace Jovanovich, Inc., and Curtis Brown, Ltd. Page 344: "The Crow and the Pitcher" from *Aesop's Fables* adapted by Louis Untermeyer. Illustrated by A. and M. Provensen. © 1965 Western Publishing Co. Used by permission. Page 396: Excerpt from *Where the Waves Break: Life at the Edge of the Sea* by Anita Malnig, copyright 1985 by Anita Malnig. Reprinted courtesy Carolrhoda Books, Inc., 241 First Avenue North, Minneapolis, MN 55401.

Study Skills Lessons

Study Habits

1. **Listen in class.** Make sure that you understand exactly what your teacher wants you to do for homework. Write each homework assignment in a notebook.
2. **Have your homework materials ready.** Keep your textbooks, pens, pencils, erasers, rulers, and notebook handy.
3. **Study in the same place every day.** Try to find a quiet and comfortable place where other people will not interrupt you. Do not have the TV or radio on while studying.
4. **Plan your study time.** Make a daily study schedule. First decide on the best time of the day for studying. Then plan exactly when you will study each of your subjects. Also plan time for chores, or household tasks, and recreation. Use the study schedule below as a guide.

Study Schedule
3:30 to 4:00 P.M. — chores
4:00 to 5:00 P.M. — sports, play
5:00 to 5:30 P.M. — study spelling words
5:30 to 6:00 P.M. — study math
6:00 to 7:00 P.M. — dinner and free time
7:00 to 7:30 P.M. — study English
7:30 to 9:00 P.M. — hobbies, reading, TV

Practice

Answer the following questions about study habits.

1. How can you best prepare to do your homework?
2. What kind of place is best for doing homework? What is the best place in your house?
3. How can you improve the way you use your study time?

Test-Taking Tips

1. **Be Prepared.** Have several sharp pencils and an eraser.

2. **Read or listen to the directions carefully.** Be sure you know what you are to do and where and how you are to mark your answers. Below are sample directions.

   Match the synonyms in columns A and B.
   Circle the correct answer.
   Cross out the wrong answer.
   Fill in the circle next to the correct answer.

3. **Answer the easy questions first.** Quickly read all the questions on the page. Then go back to the beginning and answer the questions you are sure you know. Put a light check mark next to those you are not sure of or don't know.

4. **Next, try to answer the questions you are not sure you know.** You may have a choice of answers. If so, narrow your choice. First get rid of all the answers you know are wrong. Try to narrow your choice to two answers. Then mark the answer you think is right.

5. **Answer the hardest questions last.** If you can't answer a question at all, don't waste time worrying about it. Skip the question and go on to the next.

6. **Plan your time.** Don't spend too much time on just one question. Check your watch or a clock from time to time as you take the test. If you spend too much time on one part of the test, you won't have time to finish the rest. You will also need to save some time to check your answers.

Practice

Answer the following questions about taking tests.

1. How can you best prepare to take a test?
2. In what order should you answer the questions on a test?
3. What is the last thing to do before completing a test?

Parts of a Book

Many books have special parts to help you find information easily. The **title page** and **table of contents** are special parts at the beginning of a book. The **index** is at the back. Study the examples below to see what kind of information each book part gives.

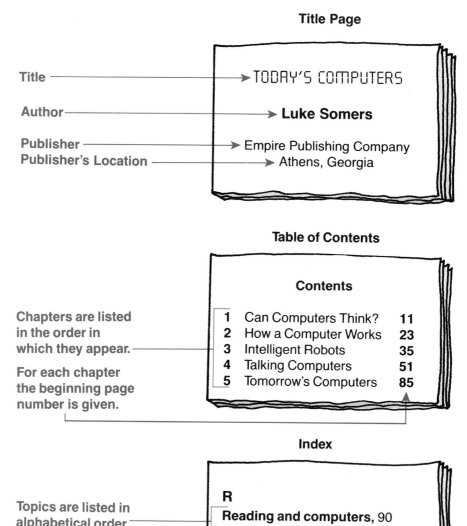

Title Page

Title → TODAY'S COMPUTERS

Author → **Luke Somers**

Publisher → Empire Publishing Company
Publisher's Location → Athens, Georgia

Table of Contents

Contents

Chapters are listed in the order in which they appear.

For each chapter the beginning page number is given.

1	Can Computers Think?	11
2	How a Computer Works	23
3	Intelligent Robots	35
4	Talking Computers	51
5	Tomorrow's Computers	85

Index

Topics are listed in alphabetical order.

A page number is given for every page that has information on the topic.

R
Reading and computers, 90
Robots
    chess and, 14, 37
    human characteristics of,
        35–36, 76, 84
    in industry, 58, 60–61
    in space, 70, 75
Rossum's Universal Robots, 54

Practice

A. Tell if you would use the title page, table of contents, or index to answer these questions about a book. Write each answer.

   1. Who wrote the book?

   2. On what page does Chapter 3 begin?

   3. Which pages give facts about computer language?

   4. Does the book have a chapter on computer games?

   5. What company published the book?

B. Use the title page, table of contents, and index on page 434 to answer questions **6–10**. Write each answer.

   6. On what page does the chapter on robots begin?

   7. What company published the book?

   8. Which pages tell about robots used in industry?

   9. Who is the author of the book?

  10. Which pages tell about robots and chess?

C. Use the table of contents and the index of this book to answer questions **11–15**. Write each answer.

  11. Which unit features the theme ''Artists at Work''?

  12. Which unit has a lesson on homophones?

  13. On what page does Unit 8 begin?

  14. Which pages tell about friendly letters?

  15. Which pages tell about using the library?

Using a Dictionary

Using Alphabetical Order   The words listed in a dictionary appear in alphabetical order. If words begin with the same letter, look at the second letter of each word. If the first and second letters are the same, look at the third letter.

  First letter: **dull, land, marvel, onion**
Second letter: **half, highway, hold, hug**
 Third letter: **creek, crop, crutch, cry**

Practice

A. Write each group of words in alphabetical order.

 1. famous lamb   blank celery
 2. package property poet player
 3. thirteen thought thrill thankful

Finding Words Quickly   To find words quickly, think of a dictionary as having three parts: front, middle, and back.

Middle: h, i, j, k, l, m, n, o, p

Front: a, b, c, d, e, f, g

Back: q, r, s, t, u, v, w, x, y, z

  The word *daisy* is in the front part. You would find *village* in the back and *melon* in the middle.

Practice

B. Write each word. Then write *front, middle,* or *back* to show in which part of a dictionary it is found.

 4. weave **5.** grin **6.** nickel **7.** smoky **8.** invent

Using Guide Words   Two words called guide words appear at the top of each dictionary page. The **guide words** show the first and last entry words on the page. All other words on the page come in alphabetical order between the guide words.

Practice

C. Which words below would you find on the page shown?

margarine   moth
magazine   mask

D. Read each pair of guide words. Write the entry word that would appear on the same page.

9.	**palace—problem**	possible	puzzle
10.	**cabin—cause**	cave	cattle
11.	**eager—exact**	elephant	extra
12.	**sparrow—sport**	sputter	spinach
13.	**lame—legend**	leash	label
14.	**teach—term**	temper	test
15.	**brain—color**	black	care

E. The guide words on a page are **partner** and **pavement**. Write the words below that would appear on that page.

package   patch   patriot   pasture
pause   payment   paprika   patio

F. Find the word *digest* in the Dictionary of Knowledge, which begins on page 440. Write the word that comes after *digest*.

G. Write three words from the Dictionary of Knowledge. Choose words that begin with different letters. Exchange lists with a partner. See how quickly each of you can find the words.

A dictionary gives spellings, pronunciations, and meanings of words. Read the sample dictionary entry below. It is from the Dictionary of Knowledge, which begins on page 440.

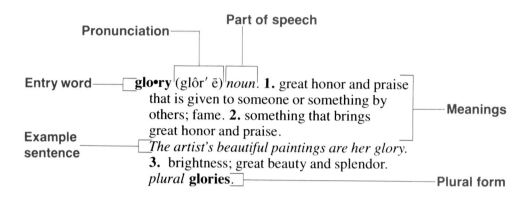

Entry word   This shows how the word is spelled. The entry word has dots between syllables that show how it may be divided at the end of a line of writing.

Pronunciation   This tells how to say the word. It is given in symbols that stand for certain sounds. For example, the symbol ô stands for the vowel sound heard in *off* and *horn,* and ē stands for the long e sound heard in *green.* The Pronunciation Key on page 440 tells the sound for each symbol.

Part of speech   This tells how the word may be used in a sentence.

Meaning   The different meanings of the word are numbered.

Example sentence   This shows how the word is used and helps to make a meaning clear.

Plural forms or **verb forms**   These are shown when the spelling of the base word changes.

Practice

H. Write the answer to each question. Use the dictionary entry on page 438.

    16. What is the entry word?

    17. How many syllables does the entry word contain?

    18. Which of the words below begins with the same sound as the entry word?

    garlic (gär′ lik) or **giant (jī′ ənt)**

    19. How many meanings are given for *glory*?

    20. For which meaning of *glory* is this an example sentence?

    The autumn leaves blazed in all their glory.

I. Read the dictionary entries below. Then write the answer to each question.

    chor•us (kôr′ əs) *noun*. **1.** a group of singers. *The school chorus gave a concert.* **2.** the part of a song that is repeated after each verse. **3.** a saying by many people all at once. *I heard a chorus of "Surprise!" when I opened the door.* *plural* **choruses.**

    gen•er•ous (jen′ər əs) *adjective*. **1.** unselfish; willing to share. *My sister is generous with her clothes.* **2.** large; ample; more than enough.

    21. For which meaning of *chorus* could this be an example sentence?

    I hummed the chorus of "Yankee Doodle."

    22. Which meaning of *generous* does this sentence use?

    I helped myself to a generous serving of salad.

    23. Read the words below. Write the four words that begin with the same sounds as *chorus* and *generous*.

    center   gerbil   garage   cake   kit   jacket

Dictionary of Knowledge

This Dictionary of Knowledge has two kinds of entries, **word entries** and **encyclopedic entries.** Many of the word entries in this dictionary are taken from the literature pieces found in this book. These entries will help you understand the meanings of words. You will use the encyclopedic entries in two "Apply" sections in each unit.

Word Entries ◆ These entries are just like the ones found in ordinary dictionaries. Each entry includes such parts as pronunciation respellings, definitions, and example sentences.

Encyclopedic Entries ◆ These entries are like articles in an encyclopedia. Each entry provides interesting information about a particular topic or person.

Full pronunciation key* The pronunciation of each word is shown just after the word, in this way:
abbreviate (ə brē′ vē āt).
The letters and signs used are pronounced as in the words below.
The mark ′ is placed after a syllable with a primary or heavy accent as in the example above.
The mark ′ after a syllable shows a secondary or lighter accent, as in **abbreviation** (ə brē′ vē ā′ shən).

SYMBOL	KEY WORDS	SYMBOL	KEY WORDS	SYMBOL	KEY WORDS
a	ask, fat	u	up, cut	n	not, ton
ā	ape, date	ʉr	fur, fern	p	put, tap
ä	car, father			r	red, dear
				s	sell, pass
e	elf, ten	ə	a in ago	t	top, hat
er	berry, care		e in agent	v	vat, have
ē	even, meet		e in father	w	will, always
i	is, hit		i in unity	y	yet, yard
ir	mirror, here		o in collect	z	zebra, haze
ī	ice, fire		u in focus		
o	lot, pond			ch	chin, arch
ō	open, go	b	bed, dub	ŋ	ring, singer
ô	law, horn	d	did, had	sh	she, dash
oi	oil, point	f	fall, off	th	thin, truth
ၯ	look, pull	g	get, dog	th	then, father
o͞o	ooze, tool	h	he, ahead	zh	s in pleasure
		j	joy, jump		
yၯ	unite, cure	k	kill, bake		
yo͞o	cute, few	l	let, ball		
ou	out, crowd	m	met, trim	′	as in (ā′ b′l)

*Pronunciation key adapted from *Webster's New World Dictionary, Basic School Edition*, Copyright © 1983 by Simon & Schuster, Inc. Reprinted by permission.

A

ache (āk) *verb*. to have or give a dull, steady pain. *Does your tooth still ache?* **ache, aching.**

am•ble (am′ b'l) *noun*. **1.** the gait of a horse when it raises first the two legs on one side and then the two on the other side. **2.** a slow and easy walking pace. —*verb*. to move or walk at an easy, slow pace. *We ambled along the Paseo del Río.* **ambled, ambling.**

an•gle[1] (añg′ g'l) *verb*. **1.** to move or bend at an angle. *Linda is angling the kite to catch the wind.* **angled, angling.** —*noun*. **1.** a shape made by two straight lines meeting at a point. *The lines formed a right angle.* **2.** the way one looks at something. *She sketched the apple from different angles.*

an•gle[2] (añg′ g'l) *verb*. to fish with a hook and line. *Bill angles in this lake every summer.* **angled, angling.**

Au•du•bon, John (ôd′ ə bon, jon) 1785–1851

John Audubon was an artist who studied and painted American birds. His paintings were so lifelike and natural that he became rich and famous because of them.

As a young man, Audubon had many business failures. While his business partner worked, Audubon roamed the countryside. He searched everywhere for wild birds to observe and paint. Finally, Audubon thought of publishing a collection of his bird paintings. He could not find an American publisher, so he went to England and Scotland. The British people loved Audubon's paintings. His *Birds of America* collection was published there. Later, Audubon returned to the United States where he published more of his work.

B

bi•valve (bī′ valv) *noun*. a water animal whose soft, boneless body is inside a shell with two hinged parts. *Clams and oysters are both bivalves.*

bleach (blēch) *verb*. to lighten or whiten by using chemicals or by the action of the sun. *The sun and salt water bleached my jeans.*

Bos•ton Tea Par•ty (bôs′ t'n tē pär′ tē) Around 1763, the British government started passing laws to tax the colonies. The British put taxes on such items as glass, paint, and tea. The taxes upset the colonists, who wanted a voice in British government. The colonists' motto was, "No taxation without representation." To show their anger, many colonists refused to buy British goods.

a fat	er care	ī bite, fire	oi oil	u up	th thin	ə = a *in* ago
ā ape	ē even	o lot	ᴏᴏ look	ʉr fur	***th*** then	e *in* agent
ä car, father	i hit	ō go	ᴏ̄ᴏ̄ tool	ch chin	zh leisure	i *in* unity
e ten	ir here	ô law, horn	ou out	sh she	ñg ring	o *in* collect
						u *in* focus

By 1770, Britain had ended most of the hated taxes. But the British wanted to prove that they still had the right to tax. They kept a small tax on one item: tea. The colonists, however, still refused to pay the British tea tax. They drank smuggled Dutch tea instead.

As a result of the colonists' boycott, British companies were not selling much tea. In 1773, Britain passed a law saying that only the British East India Company could sell tea in the colonies. But when three ships full of British tea arrived in Boston Harbor, the colonists demanded that the ships return to England immediately. The British refused, and the colonists took action.

On the night of December 16, 1773, a group of colonists led by Samuel Adams boarded the three ships. The group, which called themselves the Sons of Liberty, dumped more than 300 chests of tea into the bay. This event became known as the Boston Tea Party. It is one of the actions that led to the Revolutionary War.

brit•tle star (brit′ ′l stär) *noun*. a kind of starfish with five or more arms arranged like the points of a star. *A brittle star is similar to other types of starfish.*

C

Car•son, Ra•chel (kär′ s'n, rā′ chəl) 1907–1964

Rachel Carson believed that all living things are related. She wrote books about marine biology and science. In *The Sea Around Us,* Carson described everything about the sea and how important it is to the life chain. In *Silent Spring,* she warned about the harmful effects of pesticides and how they poison many fish and animals. She also warned us that pesticides could poison the human food supply as well. Because of Carson's writing and research, several new laws were made governing the use of pesticides.

During much of her adult life, Rachel Carson worked for the U.S. Fish and Wildlife Service. She tried to protect our natural resources.

chaise (shāz) *noun*. **1.** a light carriage, especially one with two wheels and a folding top. *The two horses pulled the chaise down the cobblestone street.* **2.** a couch-like chair.

She sat back in the comfortable chaise and closed her eyes.

chor•al read•ing (kôr′ əl rēd′ iŋ)

    The word choral comes from *chorus*, which is a group of voices. In choral reading or speaking, a chorus reads poetry or prose aloud, usually before an audience. Different voice combinations within the group are used for various tones and contrasts. The effect can be very dramatic although no real acting is done. Choral reading often sounds like spoken music. The voices are grouped according to tone, just as they are in music.

    Sometimes a choral group may be split in half, with the two sides taking turns reading lines. Or, one side can wait until the other side has read the first line before beginning the poem.

    Present a choral reading of the poem "Sea Horse."

Sea horse, sea horse,
come forward do,
make a big bow
to the people before you.
Sea horse, sea horse,
you can come out now,
the lady of the house
has sent for you.
Sea horse, sea horse,
you dance very well,
we might even call you
darling-sweet-boy.
Sea horse, sea horse,
it's time now, it's time,
to drift away slowly
go back to your place.

clutch (kluch) *verb.* **1.** to grasp or hold tightly. *Please clutch the child's hand tightly as you cross the street.* **2.** to reach or grab for; snatch.—*noun.* **1.** the grasp of a hand or claw. **2.** part of a car for shifting gears. *We had to replace the clutch after two years. plural* **clutches.**

com•mon•wealth (kom′ ən welth) *noun.* **1.** the people of a nation or state. **2.** a nation or state in which the people hold the ruling power. *The state of Massachusetts is a commonwealth.* **—the Commonwealth**, a group of independent nations joined together under the British king or queen.

con•ven•ience (kən vēn′ yəns) *noun.* **1.** something that makes things easier. *We appreciate the convenience of the new mall.* **2.** personal comfort or advantage. *The extra buses are for the convenience of townsfolk.*

cro•chet (krō shā′) *noun.* a kind of needlework done with one hooked needle called a crochet hook. —*verb.* to create something by this kind of needlework. *I crocheted a scarf for my grandmother.* **crocheted, crocheting.**

——————— **D** ———————

dan•de•li•on (dan′ də lī ən)

    The dandelion is a bright-yellow wildflower that most gardeners consider to be a pest. It is a weed that is very hard to control. It can overrun a garden.

    The dandelion was brought to America from Europe by early colonists. Its name comes from *dent de lion*, which means

a fat	**er** care	**ī** bite, fire	**oi** oil	**u** up	**th** thin	ə = a *in* ago
ā ape	**ē** even	**o** lot	**oo** look	**ur** fur	**th** then	e *in* agent
ä car, father	**i** hit	**ō** go	**oo** tool	**ch** chin	**zh** leisure	i *in* unity
e ten	**ir** here	**ô** law, horn	**ou** out	**sh** she	**ŋ** ring	o *in* collect
						u *in* focus

"lion's tooth" in French. Its leaves somewhat resemble teeth. Its yellow flower head is really a bunch of smaller flowers. The hollow stem of the dandelion holds a white, milky liquid. Young dandelion leaves can be used in salad or cooked as vegetables. The leaves taste much better if the plant has not yet flowered.

The dandelion is an unusual plant because it can reproduce without being pollinated.

dec•la•ra•tion (dek′ lə rā′ shən) *noun.* **1.** the act of making something known. *The declaration of the new club officers will be tonight.* **2.** a public statement as in the Declaration of Independence.

di•gest (di jest′ *or* dī jest′) *verb.* **1.** to change food in the body to a form that can be used. *It is hard for some people to digest milk.* **2.** to think over in order to understand fully. *Digest the article and then write a report about it.—noun.* (dī′ jest) a summary or short account of a longer story or article. *It is a digest of recent stories.*

dis•card (dis kärd′) *verb.* to throw away or get rid of something unwanted. *I discarded several pairs of shoes yesterday.*

dis•guise (dis gīz′) *verb.* **1.** to change something so as not to be recognized. *The detective disguised himself with a false beard.* **2.** to cover up to keep from being known. *She disguised her feelings from her friends.* **disguised, disguising.** *—noun.* anything to hide what one is or is like. *Please come to the costume party in an unusual disguise.*

dis•pen•ser (dis pen′ sər) *noun.* a container that gives out its contents in handy amounts. *Please take a number from the ticket dispenser.*

dol•phin (dol′ fən) A dolphin is a small, toothed whale. Like other whales it is a mammal. Dolphins are warm-blooded. Many scientists believe that dolphins are among the most intelligent animals.

A close relative of the dolphin is the porpoise. Yet they are different in two main ways: snouts and teeth. Dolphins have a beaklike snout and cone-shaped teeth. Porpoises have rounded snouts and flat teeth.

Two *very* different cousins are the bottle-nosed dolphin and the common porpoise.

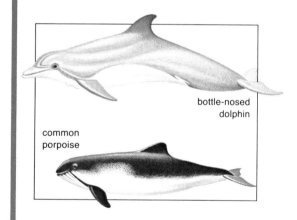

bottle-nosed dolphin

common porpoise

Because of their short beaks, bottle-nosed dolphins always seem to be smiling. They are usually friendly to people. They prefer warm or tropical water and often live within 100 miles of land. Bottle-nosed dolphins are usually the stars of seaquarium shows. They are gray, but their backs are darker than their undersides.

Common porpoises are smaller than bottle-nosed dolphins. They tend to be loners. They usually stay away from people and are not as playful as the bottle-nosed species. They have black backs and white bellies. They tend to live in cool waters and usually stay away from the tropics.

do•mes•ti•cate (də mes′ tə kāt) *verb.* **1.** to tame an animal or cultivate a plant for use by human beings. *Oxen were domesticated by farmers long ago.* **2.** to make happy with home or family life. **domesticated, domesticating**.

E

em•bark (im bärk′) *verb.* **1.** to go on board a ship or to put on a ship. *We embarked at New York for France.* **2.** to start out, begin. *Lynn embarked upon her search for a new job.*

e•merge (i mʉrj′) *verb.* **1.** to appear; to come out so as to be seen. *A lion emerged from the cave.* **2.** to become known. *The truth emerged slowly.* **emerged, emerging**.

F

fa•ble (fā′ b'l)

A fable is a very short story that teaches a lesson, or moral. In most fables, the main character is an animal, a plant, or something else that acts like a person. Most fables have been passed down through generations. Until fairly recently, most fables were told orally. Now they can be found in written collections.

Fables became famous for the truths they told. In "The Boy Who Cried Wolf," for example, a boy kept pretending that a wolf was chasing him. When everyone came running to help, the boy would laugh. Finally, when a wolf actually did chase after him, the boy cried "Wolf!" as usual. This time, no one came to help. The boy had cried "Wolf!" once too often.

The most famous fables were told by Aesop, a Greek slave who lived about 600 B.C. He told wise, witty tales about animals. Two of Aesop's most famous fables are "The Fox and the Grapes," and "The Tortoise and the Hare."

flex•i•ble (flek′ sə b'l) *adjective.* **1.** able to bend easily without breaking. *This hose is very flexible.* **2.** easily changed or managed. *My doctor has flexible office hours.*

a	fat	er	care	ī	bite, fire	oi	oil	u	up	th	thin	ə = a *in* ago
ā	ape	ē	even	o	lot	oo	look	ʉr	fur	*th*	then	e *in* agent
ä	car, father	i	hit	ō	go	ōō	tool	ch	chin	zh	leisure	i *in* unity
e	ten	ir	here	ô	law, horn	ou	out	sh	she	ñg	ring	o *in* collect
												u *in* focus

Frank•lin, Ben•ja•min

(fraṅgk′ lin ben′ jə mən) 1706–1790

Benjamin Franklin was a remarkable man who did many important things in his lifetime. He was a statesman, a printer of books, and a farmer. He was an inventor, a scientist, and a leader in America's move toward independence.

Franklin was one of the first people to experiment with electricity. His most famous experiment took place in Philadelphia in 1752. Franklin wanted to prove that lightning is electricity. First he took a homemade kite and attached a key to the end of the kite string. Next he flew the kite in a thunderstorm. A bolt of lightning struck the kite. The shock then traveled down to the key and caused a spark. Thus, Franklin had proved that lightning is electricity.

Benjamin Franklin was a rare individual. He concerned himself with many things and did them all well.

——————— **G** ———————

glo•ry (glôr′ ē) *noun.* **1.** great honor and praise that is given to someone or something by others; fame. **2.** something that brings great honor and praise. *The artist's beautiful paintings are her glory.* **3.** brightness; great beauty and splendor. *plural* **glories.**

Great Salt Lake (grāt′ sôlt′ lāk′)

This inland sea in Utah is considered one of the natural wonders of the world. Scientists believe that it was once part of a large freshwater lake that dried up.

Great Salt Lake is fed by freshwater streams, yet it is saltier than the ocean. The reason for this is that the waters of the lake do not drain away. Instead, they dry up, leaving salt behind. About 200,000 tons of salt are taken from the lake every year.

Great Salt Lake is about 75 miles long and 50 miles wide. Its size increases and decreases according to season and amount of rainfall.

The shores of the lake often appear white because of mineral deposits. Many wild birds breed on the lake's islands. The largest, Antelope Island, has cattle and wild buffalo on it. There are no fish, but small amounts of brine shrimp do live in the lake.

——————— **H** ———————

horse•man (hôrs′ mən) *noun.* **1.** a person who rides on horseback. **2.** a person skilled in riding or caring for horses. *Is that rider an expert horseman? plural* **horsemen.**

hymn (him) *noun.* a song of praise. *The organist taught us a new hymn.*

———————**I**———————

in•fe•ri•or (in fir′ ē ər) *adjective.* **1.** not as good as someone or something else. *This book is inferior to that other one.* **2.** not very good; below average. **3.** lower in rank. *A major is inferior in rank to a general.*

———————**K**———————

ker•o•sene (ker′ ə sēn) *noun.* a thin oil used as fuel in some lamps, stoves, and so on. *George filled the antique lamp with kerosene. — Another spelling:* **kerosine.**

———————**L**———————

Lib•er•ty Bell (lib′ ər tē bel′)

The Liberty Bell is one of our country's most beloved symbols from the days of the American Revolution. Its inscription reads, "Proclaim Liberty throughout all the land unto all the inhabitants thereof."

The bell was first cast in England in 1752. One year later, it broke and was recast in Philadelphia. It was rung on July 8, 1776, to celebrate the adoption of the Declaration of Independence. Until it cracked in 1835, it was rung every July 8th to celebrate America's independence. The bell became known as the Liberty Bell in 1839. Until then, it

was known as the Old State House Bell, the Bell of the Revolution, or Old Independence.

Because of its crack, the Liberty Bell is no longer rung. It hangs in the Liberty Bell Pavilion, near Independence Hall, in Philadelphia.

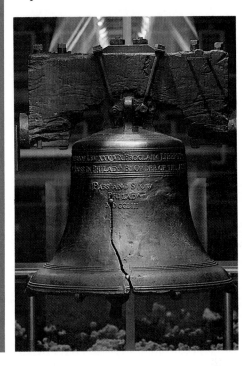

light•weight (līt′ wāt) *noun.* **1.** a person, animal, or thing that weighs less than normal. **2.** a boxer or wrestler who weighs 126 to 135 pounds. *—adjective.* light in weight. *This summer suit is made of lightweight cotton.*

lurch (lʉrch) *verb.* to lean or roll forward suddenly. *The train lurches whenever it starts. —noun.* a lurching movement. *This bus makes a lot of lurches as it moves. plural* **lurches.**

a fat	**er** care	**ī** bite, fire	**oi** oil	**u** up	**th** thin	ə = a *in* ago
ā ape	**ē** even	**o** lot	**ᴏᴏ** look	**ʉr** fur	**th** then	e *in* agent
ä car, father	**i** hit	**ō** go	**ōō** tool	**ch** chin	**zh** leisure	i *in* unity
e ten	**ir** here	**ô** law, horn	**ou** out	**sh** she	**ñg** ring	o *in* collect
						u *in* focus

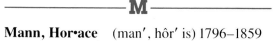

Mann, Hor•ace   (man′, hôr′ is) 1796–1859

   Horace Mann is often referred to as the "Father of Common Schools." In 1837, Mann gave up his law career to become the secretary of the new Massachusetts State Board of Education. He worked to improve public education through several new laws. Schools in almost every state were helped by these laws.
   In 1839, Mann founded the first state teacher's school, called *normal school*, in Lexington, Massachusetts. The normal school produced better public school teachers. Mann also made a long, careful study of European education. His reports told how American schools could learn from the Europeans.
   Mann resigned from the Board of Education to help the antislavery cause. Later, he served as the president of Antioch College in Ohio until his death.

man•u•script   (man′yə skript) *n.* a book, article, etc. that is typewritten or in handwriting; especially, the copy of an author's work that is sent to a publisher or printer.

Mc•Guf•fey's E•clec•tic Read•ers
(mə guf′ fēz i klek′ tik rēd′ ərz)
   William McGuffey was an educator and clergyman. He published reading books for the first six grades of elementary education between 1836 and 1857. Millions of copies of *McGuffey's Eclectic Readers* were sold. For many years the books taught nearly every American schoolchild to read.

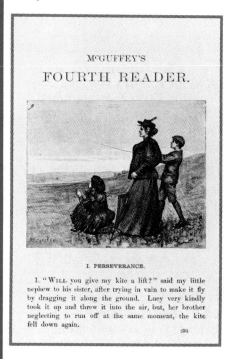

   McGuffey's Readers were different from our present readers in several ways. The readers were printed in black and white only, and contained few pictures. Each reader was divided into lessons. Some of the lessons contained a story or a poem. Other lessons had a theme such as "the way to be happy" or "waste not, want not." These lessons were meant to teach students rules and morals. Definitions were listed at the end of each lesson, rather than in a glossary at the back of the book. *McGuffey's Readers* did have one thing in common with our readers: questions asking students to write about or discuss what they have just read.

mi•cro•scop•ic (mī′ krə skop′ ik) *adjective*. so tiny that it cannot be seen without a microscope. *There are several microscopic animals on this slide.*

Mi•das touch (mī′ dəs tuch)

The term "Midas touch" means someone who makes money in whatever he or she does. The term originally comes from a Greek myth.

To reward King Midas for a good deed, the god Dionysus (dī′ ə ni′ səs) granted Midas one wish. King Midas asked for the touch of gold and Dionysus agreed. At first King Midas loved his power. His wealth became far greater than anyone else's. But then the power became a curse. Soon, everything was changed into gold, including all of Midas's food and even his beloved daughter. Midas grieved deeply for all that he had lost. Finally, the gods took pity on the king. They removed the curse and restored Midas's daughter to him.

mus•sel (mus′ 'l) *noun*. a water animal with a soft body that lives in two shells hinged together. *Mussels are served at many seafood restaurants.*

⎯⎯⎯⎯⎯⎯⎯ ◯ ⎯⎯⎯⎯⎯⎯⎯

o•ri•ga•mi (ôr′ ə gä′ mē)

The term *origami* means "paper folding" in Japanese. Origami is the Japanese art of paper folding. Pieces of colored paper, about 6 inches square, are folded into simple figures. No cutting or pasting is done.

Today there are two kinds of origami. Traditional origami was started in the late 1600s. There are about 100 traditional origami figures including a crane, a dog, and a frog.

Creative origami began in the 1940s. People tried to create original and more

a	fat	er	care	ī	bite, fire	oi	oil	u	up	th	thin	ə = a *in* ago
ā	ape	ē	even	o	lot	oo	look	ur	fur	*th*	then	e *in* agent
ä	car, father	i	hit	ō	go	ōo	tool	ch	chin	zh	leisure	i *in* unity
e	ten	ir	here	ô	law, horn	ou	out	sh	she	ŋ	ring	o *in* collect
												u *in* focus

Dictionary of Knowledge

difficult origami figures. In this kind of origami, some cutting can be done, and odd-shaped paper is often used.

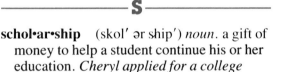

———————— **P** ————————

pray•ing man•tis (prā′ iñg man′ tis) *noun.* an insect that holds its front legs in a praying position and eats other insects. *The praying mantis is helpful to farmers. plural* **praying mantises.**

———————— **R** ————————

raft•er (raf′ tər) *noun.* one of the sloping beams used to hold up a roof. *The rafters are made of wood.*

rasp (rasp) *verb.* **1.** to scrape or rub as with a file. **2.** to speak in a rough, harsh tone. *The coach rasped out his orders.* **3.** to make a rough, grating sound. *That door is rasping unpleasantly on its hinges.* —*noun.* a rough, grating sound.

red al•gae (red′ al′ jē)

Algae can be found in oceans, lakes, rivers, ponds, and damp soil. Algae are simple organisms. Some have one cell and can only be seen under a microscope. Others are large plants. All algae help purify the air and water through the process of photosynthesis. Algae also serve as food for fish

and other water animals.

There are many different kinds of algae. The larger algae are grouped by color—brown, green, or red. Red algae are usually found in subtropical waters where they often grow with coral. Agar comes from certain red algae. This is often used by scientists for growing bacteria. The Japanese eat a kind of red algae called *nori*. It is usually sold in a dry, papery form and needs to be recombined with liquid.

re•pub•lic (ri pub′ lik) *noun.* a state or nation in which the voters choose the leaders who make the laws and run the government. *The Ivory Coast is a republic.*

———————— **S** ————————

schol•ar•ship (skol′ ər ship′) *noun.* a gift of money to help a student continue his or her education. *Cheryl applied for a college scholarship.*

sen•a•tor (sen′ ə tər) *noun.* a member of Congress, specifically of the Senate. *Each state has two U.S. senators.*

slith•er (sli*th*′ ər) *verb.* to slide or glide like a snake. *The snake slithered into the lake.* —*noun.* a slithering motion.

so•cia•ble (sō′ shə b′l) *adjective.* **1.** enjoying the company of others; friendly. *Jeff is a sociable boy.* **2.** full of pleasant talk and friendliness. *We had a sociable afternoon.*

states•man (stāts′ mən) *noun.* a person who is wise and skillful in government. *plural* **statesmen.**

suction cup (suk′ shən kup) *noun.* **1.** a cup-shaped piece of rubber or plastic that can stick to a surface. **2.** an object on an animal's body that allows it to stick to a surface. *Suction cups enable a starfish to move across slippery rocks.*

sum•mon (sum′ ən) *verb.* **1.** to call together; to call or send for. *The counselor summoned all the campers.* **2.** to call forth; to gather. *I am summoning up my strength to deal with the problem.*

T
---

taut (tôt) *adjective.* **1.** tightly stretched, as a rope. **2.** showing strain; tense. *She had a taut smile on her face.*

U
---

up•hol•ster•y (up hōl′ stər ē) *noun.* **1.** the work of putting new springs, padding, and covering on a piece of furniture. **2.** the materials used for this. *The sofa has new upholstery.*

V
---

vein (vān) *noun.* **1.** any blood vessel carrying blood back to the heart. *A vein is usually bluish in color.* **2.** any of the fine lines in a leaf or insect's wing. *Judi closely studied the veins in a moth's wings.* **3.** a layer of mineral formed in another rock. *He discovered a vein of silver in the rock.*

vix•en (vik′ s'n) *noun.* a female fox. *The vixen ran to her den.*

W

Wright broth•ers (rīt′ bru*th*′ ərz)
Wilbur and Orville Wright built the first successful airplane and flew it in 1903. The *Kitty Hawk* flew 120 feet and stayed in the air for 12 seconds.

The Wright brothers' interest in flying started after the death of a glider pilot. The brothers began reading everything they could about aeronautics. They experimented with a 5-foot biplane kite. Wilbur and Orville wanted to learn how wind and air currents affected flight. They built two gliders, but both of them failed. Their third glider was successful; it flew for 600 feet.

By the fall of 1903, the Wrights finished building their first power airplane, the *Kitty Hawk.* On December 17, 1903, the plane had a short but successful flight. At first, the flight was not taken seriously by the U.S. government. By 1908, however, the Wright brothers had received a contract with the Department of War for the first military airplane.

a fat	**er** care	**ī** bite, fire	**oi** oil	**u** up	**th** thin	ə = a *in* ago
ā ape	**ē** even	**o** lot	**oo** look	**ur** fur	**th** then	e *in* agent
ä car, father	**i** hit	**ō** go	**ōo** tool	**ch** chin	**zh** leisure	i *in* unity
e ten	**ir** here	**ô** law, horn	**ou** out	**sh** she	**ng** ring	o *in* collect
						u *in* focus

Dictionary of Knowledge

Thesaurus

A thesaurus contains lists of synonyms and antonyms. You will use this Thesaurus for the thesaurus lesson in Unit 1 and for the Thesaurus Corner in each Reading-Writing Connection in this book. You can also use the Thesaurus to find synonyms to make your writing more interesting.

Sample Entry

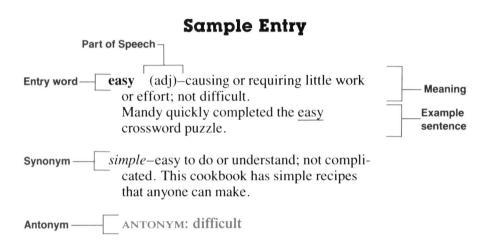

easy (adj)–causing or requiring little work or effort; not difficult.
Mandy quickly completed the easy crossword puzzle.

simple–easy to do or understand; not complicated. This cookbook has simple recipes that anyone can make.

ANTONYM: difficult

How to Use the Thesaurus Index

To find a word, use the Thesaurus Index on pages 453–457. All the entry words, synonyms, and antonyms are listed alphabetically in the Index. Words in dark type are entry words. Words in italic, or slanted, type are synonyms. Words in blue type are antonyms. The page numbers tell you where to find the word you are looking for.

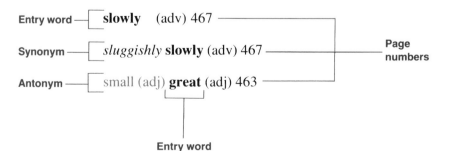

THESAURUS INDEX

A list of all the words in this thesaurus

A

amazing (adj)–causing sudden wonder; surprising. Jenny's haircut made an amazing difference in her appearance.

astonishing–greatly surprising. Mark could not believe the astonishing news that he had won the contest.

extraordinary–beyond the ordinary or usual; remarkable. We saw an extraordinary collection of Egyptian treasures at the museum.

fabulous–not believable. Although everyone knew what had really happened, Adam told a fabulous story about hitting a home run.

incredible–too unusual to be possible; hard to believe. Have you heard about the incredible young girl who is a concert pianist?

marvelous–causing wonder and surprise. The magician performed marvelous tricks to the delight of the children.

spectacular–making an amazing display. The flowers at the garden show are always spectacular.

angry (adj)–feeling or showing great displeasure. We became angry after waiting two hours for the train to arrive.

annoyed–somewhat angry or disturbed; bothered. The annoyed speaker asked the restless audience to settle down.

enraged–fiercely angry. The enraged bull charged into the corral fence.

frantic–wild with excitement and anger. After she calmed down, Gina apologized for her frantic behavior.

furious–full of strong anger. Art was furious when a careless driver crashed into his car.

indignant–feeling angry about something mean or unfair. The indignant workers threatened to go on strike.

irritated–feeling angry or impatient; annoyed. The irritated customer complained to the store manager.

ANTONYMS: calm (adj), content (adj), happy, peaceful, pleasant, satisfied (adj)

answer (n)–words written or spoken in response to a question or problem. Patty will give us her answer tomorrow about joining the club.

rebuttal–an answer that opposes or disproves something. Once Dan made up his mind, he would not listen to my rebuttal.

refusal–an answer given to say no. His refusal came as a surprise, because he usually likes to go to the movies.

reply–words or actions that give an answer. Nina gave her reply by nodding and smiling.

response–a reply to a question; a reaction to some happening. It is best to think about a question before giving a response.

retort–a quick, sharp answer. The angry man shouted a retort as he stormed out of the room.

solution–an answer to a problem or puzzle. Luis wrote the solution to the math problem on the chalkboard.

ANTONYMS: inquiry, problem (n), question (n), request (n)

B

begin (v)–**1** to make or start; to do the first part of something. The president will begin the meeting promptly at 7:00. **2** to bring into being. Should we begin a new committee to do the work?

commence–to formally begin. Following several speeches, the marching band commenced the parade.

establish–to set up or begin on a firm or lasting basis. The town grew as many newcomers established businesses.

initiate–to set up or get started for the first time. The school board initiated many changes to improve the schools.

introduce–to begin; to start. Yoshi always introduces her letters with a funny remark.

launch–to set into action or motion; to initiate. The building company will launch its plans for a new shopping mall.

open–to start or set up; to begin. Should we open the program with a lively song?

ANTONYMS: close (v), complete (v), conclude, end (v), finish (v), stop (v)

brave   (adj)–having no fear. The brave skier sped down the treacherous mountainside.

bold–showing courage. One bold explorer volunteered to go into the cave alone.

courageous–fearless in meeting danger. Only a courageous person would try to tame a cougar.

daring–having the courage to take risks. Amelia Earhart was a daring pioneer of aviation.

hardy–daring and bold. A team of hardy climbers attempted to scale the steep mountain.

heroic–acting with bravery. Everyone praised the heroic woman who risked her life to rescue another swimmer.

valiant–having strength to meet danger with bravery. The valiant fire fighters were unaffected by the raging flames.

ANTONYMS: cowardly (adj), fearful, frightened (adj), scared (adj), timid

break   (v)–to make something suddenly come apart into pieces. If you are careless, you might break that fragile vase.

burst–to suddenly break open or apart. The playful kitten burst the balloon.

crack–to break, but not into pieces; to split apart. Even though Lona cracked the glass on her watch, it still runs.

crush–to grind, pound, or press into fine pieces. The cook crushed walnuts to put into the salad.

destroy–to break and ruin completely. The strong wind destroyed my new kite.

shatter–to break into many small pieces. Tyrone shattered his glasses when he fell from his bicycle.

smash–to break with great force and noise. Whoever smashed Mr. Roth's store window will have to pay for it.

ANTONYMS: fix (v), mend (v), repair (v)

C

calm   (adj)–still and quiet; not excited. It was a calm morning at the pet shop until a

snake got loose.

composed–free from excitement and troubled feelings. The composed dancer was used to performing for large audiences.

cool–not excited or disturbed. The spelling bee champion was cool during the entire contest.

placid–pleasantly peaceful and still. There is a placid spot by the pond where I like to sit and think.

relaxed–at ease; not nervous. Jerry does not fall because he is a relaxed skater.

serene–clear and calm; peaceful. The sailboat silently glided across the serene lake.

tranquil–peaceful and quiet. Some unexpected visitors interrupted our tranquil evening at home.

ANTONYMS: disturbed (adj), excited (adj), nervous, noisy, restless, stormy

clean   (adj)–not dirty, soiled, or stained. After working in the garden all day, Fred changed into clean clothes.

fresh–pure and clear. Open the window so that we can enjoy the fresh air.

immaculate–completely clean. We swept and scrubbed the kitchen floor until it was immaculate.

neat–clean and orderly. My room is neat when I hang my clothes in the closet.

pure–free from dirt, germs, and so on. Brian filled a jar with pure rainwater for his science experiment.

shiny–clean and bright in appearance. The shiny car had just been washed and polished.

spotless–without spots or other markings. This detergent will make the greasy walls spotless again.

ANTONYMS: dirty, filthy, grimy, messy, polluted (adj), soiled (adj)

cold   (adj)–having a low temperature or little heat. In the summer I like to swim in cold water.

bitter–painfully cold. You should wear a warm hat and gloves in this bitter weather.

bleak–cold and cutting. The sky is often gray on a bleak winter morning.

cold (continued)

chilly–somewhat cold; cool. If it gets <u>chilly</u>, put on your sweater.

frigid–extremely cold. Sometimes cars will not start in <u>frigid</u> weather.

frozen–cold and icy. The <u>frozen</u> pond in the park is an ideal place to go ice skating.

icy–covered with ice; like ice. Be careful that you do not fall on this <u>icy</u> sidewalk.

nippy–noticeably chilly. It must be <u>nippy</u> outside, because people are wearing jackets.

ANTONYMS: **hot (adj), mild, scorching (adj), sweltering (adj), torrid, warm (adj)**

crooked (adj)–not straight or even. Use a ruler so that you do not draw <u>crooked</u> lines.

bent–made crooked by bending out of a straight position. The wobbly table must have a <u>bent</u> leg.

curved–shaped like a line that has no straight part. The <u>curved</u> handle on this pot makes it easy to hold.

hooked–shaped like a hook. We can hang the plant on a <u>hooked</u> nail.

twisted–having curves or bends. A telephone has a <u>twisted</u> cord.

winding–bending and turning. The <u>winding</u> river flows in and out of the valley.

zigzag–having short, sharp turns or angles. The shirt I like is decorated with <u>zigzag</u> stitches.

ANTONYMS: **direct (adj), flat (adj), straight (adj)**

cry (v)–to shed tears, sometimes while making sounds, because of pain, sorrow, grief, or another strong feeling. Do you ever <u>cry</u> when you read a sad book?

bawl–to cry loudly. The baby <u>bawled</u> because she was tired and hungry.

snivel–to sniffle and cry. Adrianne <u>sniveled</u> as she apologized to her best friend.

sob–to cry while taking quick, short breaths. Jeremy <u>sobbed</u> as he tried to explain to his father that the puppy was lost.

wail–to cry long and loud. Paco's little brother <u>wailed</u> when he fell off his tricycle.

weep–to show strong feeling by crying. The two friends <u>wept</u> when they had to say good-bye.

whimper–to make low, broken crying sounds. The frightened child <u>whimpered</u> before finally falling asleep.

D

dangerous (adj)–likely to cause hurt or damage. That steep, icy hill is too <u>dangerous</u> for sledding.

critical–full of danger, difficulty, or trouble. Water had to be brought into the town during the <u>critical</u> shortage.

hazardous–full of risk or danger. Signs were posted warning people to stay away from the <u>hazardous</u> area.

menacing–threatening with harm. The ship's captain spotted a <u>menacing</u> storm on his radar screen.

perilous–open to the chance of hurt, loss, or destruction; risky. The bus moved cautiously up the <u>perilous</u> mountain road.

threatening–showing signs of possible harm; endangering. <u>Threatening</u> winds began to toss the small airplane.

treacherous–not as safe as appearance may give; having hidden dangers. Are you sure you want to take this <u>treacherous</u> road in the dark?

ANTONYMS: **harmless, protected (adj), safe (adj), secure (adj)**

dark (adj)–with little or no light; nearly black in color. It is too <u>dark</u> for me to read in this room.

dim–not bright or clear. The glow of the candle cast a <u>dim</u> light.

dismal–dark and gloomy. We did not go to the park because it was a <u>dismal</u>, rainy afternoon.

gloomy–partly or completely dark, making one feel low in spirits. The <u>gloomy</u> old house has been vacant for years.

overcast–dark and cloudy. Sonya took off her sunglasses when the sky became <u>overcast</u>.

shaded–dark because something has cut off part of the light. I like to sit out of the sun on my cool, shaded porch.

somber–having dark shadows. This somber room could use some cheerful colors.

ANTONYMS: bright (adj), brilliant (adj), cheerful, clear (adj), light (adj), sunny

dull (adj)–**1** not bright or clear. This dull floor needs a coat of wax. **2** not exciting or interesting. A paragraph without adjectives might be dull.

boring–tiresome and uninteresting. Pat fell asleep while reading a boring magazine.

drab–dull and lifeless in appearance or quality. My old brown coat is too drab to wear to the banquet.

faded–with less brightness and color than before. The faded curtains had been ruined by the bright sunlight.

lackluster–without brightness; drab. Even though it was a rare antique, no one noticed the lackluster brass lamp.

monotonous–dull because of no variety or change. We were glad when the monotonous drive through the desert ended.

tedious–long and boring. Painting the fence around the pasture was a tedious chore.

ANTONYMS: bright (adj), clear (adj), exciting (adj), interesting (adj), lively (adj), shiny

E

easy (adj)–causing or requiring little work or effort; not difficult. Mandy quickly completed the easy crossword puzzle.

effortless–showing or needing little or no effort. It was an effortless victory for the superior team.

elementary–having to do with the simple, beginning parts of something. The piano teacher showed his new students an elementary exercise.

obvious–easily or clearly seen or understood. Ali laughed at his obvious error on the chalkboard.

plain–marked by its easiness. Susan gave us

plain directions to her apartment building.

simple–easy to do or understand; not complicated. This cookbook has simple recipes that anyone can make.

smooth–without trouble or difficulty. Even with the bad weather, we had a smooth trip to our aunt's house.

ANTONYMS: complex (adj), complicated (adj), difficult, hard (adj), tough (adj), troublesome

eat (v)–to chew and swallow food; to have a meal. We will eat lunch before baseball practice.

consume–to eat or drink. Everyone consumed more food than usual at the annual barbecue.

devour–to eat very hungrily. Michael devoured two hamburgers and asked for a third.

feast–to eat a large rich meal. Our family feasted at a restaurant on Grandmother's birthday.

gobble–to swallow big pieces of food quickly. Lisa gobbled her dinner and rushed outside to play.

nibble–to take quick, small bites of food. My pet rabbit nibbles lettuce and carrots.

snack–to eat lightly between meals. Do you ever snack when you get home from school?

F

fair (adj)–not favoring one more than the others; right according to what is honest and truthful. Evan gave a fair account of how the toy was broken.

equal–treating all things in the same way. The leader divided the campers into two equal teams for the tug-of-war.

honest–acting with honor and fairness; truthful. Beth trusted Ray because he was an honest friend.

impartial–not favoring one person or one side. An impartial person was asked to judge the art projects.

just–fair; right. The jury was asked to make a

fair *(continued)*

just decision.

lawful—permitted by law; rightful. What is the lawful age for driving a car in your state?

objective—free from bias, personal feelings, or opinions. The reporter wrote an objective story about the election.

ANTONYMS: **biased (adj), partial, prejudiced (adj), unfair, unjust**

fat (adj)—having a rounded body with too much flesh; large or larger than usual. We all laughed at Elena's fat guinea pig when it wiggled its nose.

chubby—plump; round. The baby in the picture had dark curls and chubby cheeks.

obese—extremely overweight. The diet and exercise program was very helpful to the obese patient.

plump—slightly fat; round and full. We roasted plump, juicy hot dogs over the fire.

pudgy—short and fat. Katherine gave her nephew a pudgy bulldog puppy for his birthday.

rotund—rounded out. I stuffed the cloth bear with foam rubber so it would have a rotund belly.

stout—large and fat. The stout pig could barely squeeze through the narrow gate.

ANTONYMS: **lean (adj), skinny, slender, slight (adj), thin (adj)**

find (v)—to come upon by chance; to look for and get something that has been lost. Will you help me find my sneakers?

catch—to take hold of or capture, especially after a chase. How many fish did you catch at the lake?

detect—to find something that is hidden or difficult to notice. Colleen knew that spring was coming when she detected tiny buds on the trees.

discover—to find for the first time. Micky lifted up the rock and discovered a turtle.

encounter—to meet or come upon unexpectedly; to be faced with. The mail carrier often encounters new dogs on her route.

locate—to find the exact position of. Air-traffic controllers locate aircraft in flight, using special equipment.

trace—to follow tracks, signs, or marks in order to find something. The scientist traced the animal to its natural habitat in the wilds.

ANTONYMS: **lose, misplace, miss (v), overlook (v)**

fine (adj)—very good or excellent; of high quality. There are many fine paintings and other works of art at the museum downtown.

admirable—worthy of being looked upon with wonder, pleasure, or approval. The students did an admirable job on the scenery for the school play.

impressive—causing a feeling of wonder and pleasure. Cara stopped to photograph the impressive marble monument.

lovely—very beautiful. The lovely blossom had an unusual purple hue.

splendid—excellent; wonderful. Did you see the splendid bird feeder that Noah made?

superior—better than average; higher in quality than others. Amy's supervisor complimented her on her superior work.

valued—thought of highly. I keep my valued items in a special box in my room.

ANTONYMS: **awful (adj), dreadful, inferior (adj), poor (adj), unpleasant, wretched**

full (adj)—having or holding as much as is possible. I still have a full glass of milk to drink.

abundant—having more than enough. We have an abundant supply of canned food stored in the basement.

crowded—uncomfortably full. There were no places left to sit in the crowded theater.

dense—closely packed together. The east side of the city is dense with buildings.

heaping—piled high. Will you please empty the heaping trash can?

overflowing—so full that the excess is spilling over. Water from the overflowing bucket splashed onto the floor.

stuffed—filled with something that has been packed tightly. Rob could not fit another thing into his stuffed suitcase.

ANTONYMS: **blank (adj), empty (adj), hollow (adj), vacant, void (adj)**

G

good (adj)–of high quality; proper, or the way it should be. The polite child has good manners.

excellent–very good; better than others. These excellent pears are ripe and sweet.

pleasant–giving enjoyment or delight; that which pleases. Thank you for your pleasant card and letter.

right–that which is good, fair, or honest. Diana did the right thing by telling her teacher what really happened on the playground.

skilled–able to do things well. Only a skilled weaver could make such a lovely rug.

useful–having a use or giving service; helpful. This book has many useful suggestions for starting a hobby at home.

valuable–being worth something. Nathan keeps his valuable stamps in a special book.

ANTONYMS: **awful (adj), bad (adj), disagreeable, poor (adj), useless, worthless**

great (adj)–**1** large in size, amount, or number. The banquet was held in a great room with a stage for the speakers. **2** important. The leader of a country is a great person.

enormous–unusually large. Have you ever seen such an enormous tree as this redwood?

famous–talked about or written about a lot; very well known. Who would you be if you could be any famous person in the world?

grand–large and fine in appearance. The mayor will ride on a grand float in the Founder's Day parade.

massive–big and heavy; solid. The mountain climber rested his backpack on a massive rock.

prominent–well-known and respected by others. The guest speaker will be a prominent person who works in our community.

vast–very great; huge. The United States is a vast country with many different geographic regions.

ANTONYMS: **infamous, little, slight (adj), small (adj), tiny, unknown**

group (n)–a number of persons, animals, or things together. A group of explorers traveled to the South Pole.

bunch–a group of things of the same kind. Would you like a small bunch of grapes with your lunch?

bundle–a number of objects tied or wrapped together. Scott took a bundle of newspapers to the recycling center.

crew–the people needed to work a ship or an aircraft. The crew greeted the passengers as they boarded the airplane.

crowd–a large group of people collected together. A crowd often forms at the swimming pool on a hot day.

flock–a group of animals of one kind that keep together. The flock of sheep grazed on the hillside.

team–a group of persons joined together in a certain activity, often competitive. Alison plays on her school basketball team.

ANTONYM: **individual (n)**

H

happy (adj)–feeling well and having a good time; showing gladness or pleasure. The happy children played games and sang songs at the party.

cheerful–glad; joyful. Our cheerful neighbor came over to tell us his good news.

contented–happy with the way things are. The contented kitten lapped up the milk I gave her.

delighted–filled with pleasure or gladness. Missy's delighted grandparents were not expecting her visit.

jubilant–showing great joy. Ann Marie was jubilant when she received her pilot's license.

lighthearted–happy and free from worry or trouble. The park was filled with lighthearted people enjoying the warm afternoon.

merry–full of fun and laughter. The merry clowns were my favorite act at the circus.

ANTONYMS: **depressed (adj), downcast, melancholy (adj), sad, sorrowful, unhappy**

Thesaurus

hide (v)–to put or keep out of sight; to keep secret. Our dog always <u>hides</u> her dish in the backyard.

bury–to cover up; to hide from view. The squirrel <u>buried</u> the acorns under the oak tree.

camouflage–to change the appearance of something in order to hide. Many animals <u>camouflage</u> themselves so that they will be protected in the woods.

conceal–to keep secret or out of sight. Please do not <u>conceal</u> the truth when you tell your story.

cover–to hide. Even though Lena was upset, she <u>covered</u> her true feelings.

disguise–to hide what something really is by making it look or seem different. Mark <u>disguised</u> himself by wearing a wig and glasses.

mask–to conceal or disguise. Some honey will <u>mask</u> the sour taste of this drink.

ANTONYMS: **display (v), expose, find (v), reveal, show (v), uncover**

I

idea (n)–a way of seeing or understanding what is formed in the mind. Peter has a good <u>idea</u> of what our clubhouse should look like.

belief–what is accepted as or thought to be true or real. Christopher Columbus's <u>belief</u> was that the world is round.

concept–a general idea. Do you know the <u>concept</u> of this computer game?

impression–a feeling or an idea. My first <u>impression</u> of the new student is that he is friendly and energetic.

opinion–what a person believes to be true, but without certainty or proof. Mary's <u>opinion</u> is that a car wash is the best way to raise money for the school band.

thought–what someone thinks. Before he goes to bed, Andy likes to write his <u>thoughts</u> in a journal.

understanding–a knowledge of the meaning. Erica shared her <u>understanding</u> of the poem with the class.

important (adj)–having worth, value, or meaning; deserving special notice or attention. <u>Important</u> letters and packages are often sent by special delivery mail.

chief–first in importance. The <u>chief</u> crops grown in the north central United States are corn and wheat.

essential–important because it is needed; necessary. What are the <u>essential</u> ingredients in this recipe?

main–the most important and often the largest. There was a traffic jam when the <u>main</u> road was blocked.

major–more important or greater than others. Did you include the <u>major</u> facts about your topic in your outline?

notable–worthy of attention because of importance or excellence. The newspaper story told about a <u>notable</u> local event.

significant–full of meaning or importance; mattering very much. The scientist was honored for making a <u>significant</u> discovery.

ANTONYMS: **insignificant, minor (adj), petty, trivial, unimportant, worthless**

K

kind (adj)–good, friendly, and helpful toward others. We thanked the <u>kind</u> librarian after we checked out our books.

considerate–thoughtful of other people and their feelings. Bob received many get-well cards from his <u>considerate</u> friends.

courteous–polite; thoughtful of others. A <u>courteous</u> woman offered me her seat on the crowded bus.

gentle–kind and friendly. Do not be afraid to pet those <u>gentle</u> dogs.

sympathetic–showing or feeling concern and kind feelings toward others. The <u>sympathetic</u> store manager helped the young child find his parents.

tactful–speaking or behaving kindly so as to not hurt or offend others. The <u>tactful</u> coach did not mention the new player's clumsy fall.

warm–having or showing friendly feelings,

affection, or love. Pilar wrote a warm letter to her favorite cousin.
ANTONYMS: cold (adj), cruel, mean (adj), rude, uncaring, unkind

L

little (adj)–not big or great; small in size. I need a little box for the necklace I made.
compact–having the parts arranged within a small space. This camper even has a compact kitchen.
dwarf–much smaller than usual for its kind. The dwarf trees were not much larger than the bushes in the yard.
fine–very small or thin. The seamstress carefully trimmed off the fine threads.
miniature–made on a small scale. Hai carved a miniature sailboat out of a block of wood.
minute–so small that it may be difficult to see with the eyes alone. The doctor studied the minute cells under a microscope.
tiny–very small. This tiny writing is difficult to read.
ANTONYMS: big (adj), enormous, giant (adj), great, huge, large (adj)

love (v)–to have a strong liking or deep feeling for. Maggie loves horseback riding and hopes to have her own horse someday.
adore–to love and admire greatly. Ted adores his piano teacher and looks forward to his weekly lesson.
cherish–to hold dear; to treat or care for tenderly. My grandparents cherish all ten of their grandchildren.
esteem–to have a very high opinion of. The public esteems the popular artist's work.
fancy–to be fond of; to like very much. On a cold day, I fancy reading a book by the fire.
idolize–to be devoted to a person or thing that is loved or admired. Ginny must idolize her sister because she is always talking about her.
treasure–to value or prize highly. Paul treasures the ribbon he won in his first track meet.

ANTONYMS: abhor, despise, detest, dislike (v), hate (v), loathe (v)

M

mark (n)–something that can be seen on a surface. There were several marks on the table where the children had been coloring.
blotch–a large, uneven spot or stain. This purple blotch in the sink must be from the grape juice.
flaw–a mark that ruins or lessens the beauty of something. I returned my new sweater to the store because the sleeve had a flaw in it.
scratch–a mark made by rubbing or cutting with something rough or sharp. Be careful not to make a scratch on the car when you wash it.
smudge–a dirty mark where something has been smeared. Smudges really stand out on a light-colored wall.
speck–a tiny spot or stain. Those specks of dirt on the carpet barely show.
stain–a spot of dirt that discolors the surface it is on. You will never get that purple paint stain out of your white jacket.

N

neat (adj)–clean and in order. Our room must be neat before we go outside to play.
orderly–having a regular arrangement. Rows of magazines were stacked on the orderly racks in the bookstore.
organized–arranged in some order or pattern. Jeffrey has an organized notebook with dividers for every subject.
tidy–neat and in order. Jo has a place for everything in her tidy closet.
trim–in good condition or order. Larry has a trim yard because he spends many hours taking care of it.
uncluttered–without things scattered all over; not littered. We need an uncluttered place

neat *(continued)*

where we can sit and do our homework.
well-groomed–neat in appearance. The well-groomed children waited in line to have their pictures taken.
ANTONYMS: **cluttered (adj), disorderly, disorganized (adj), messy, sloppy, untidy**

O

old (adj)–having many years of age or use. I have read this old book many times.
ancient–of times long past. We studied the ancient civilization of Rome.
antique–very old but still existing or being used. This antique rocking chair belonged to my great-grandfather.
elderly–somewhat old in age. Both young and elderly persons play on our volleyball team.
obsolete–old and out-of-date. This new typewriter will replace the obsolete model.
outdated–old-fashioned. Hoop skirts are an outdated style of clothing.
worn–much used; tired. Rick's worn jacket is covered with patches.
ANTONYMS: **current (adj), fresh (adj), modern, new, recent, young (adj)**

P

plan (v)–to think out in advance how something is to be made or done. A committee will plan this year's picnic.
arrange–to prepare or form plans for. Meg arranged the sports banquet.
design–to plan something by making a drawing of it. Sheila designs and sews her own clothes.
outline–to make a general plan, usually in writing. Frank outlined his report before writing a first draft.
plot–to make secret plans with others. We plotted to have a surprise party for Lynn's birthday.
program–to make up or prepare instructions for something, especially a computer. Have you ever programmed this type of home computer?

scheme–to plan something, especially something sly or dishonest. The movie was about a thief who schemed to rob a bank.

pretty (adj)–that which is pleasing to the senses; nice-looking. I saw a collection of pretty dolls in the store window.
attractive–drawing interest and liking. Everyone complimented Jan on the attractive pottery she made.
charming–very pleasing, delightful, or attractive. This is my favorite song because it has a charming melody.
graceful–beautiful in form or movement. A pair of graceful swans glided across the still lake.
handsome–pleasing in appearance. Thuy was proud of her handsome new bicycle.
lovely–beautiful in appearance or character. I thought this lovely bouquet of flowers from my garden might cheer you up.
striking–appealing strongly to the eye. The ice skater flashed across the ice in a striking purple costume.
ANTONYMS: **hideous, homely, plain (adj), ugly, unattractive, unsightly**

push (v)–to move something by using force against it. It will be easier if we push our bikes up the hill.
nudge–to push gently. Emily nudged the swinging door with her foot to try to open it.
poke–to push against with something pointed. You can poke the hot coals with this stick to break them into pieces.
press–to push with steady force. I pressed my finger on the picture until it stuck to the cardboard.
propel–to move or cause to move forward or ahead. A sailboat is propelled by the wind.
shove–to move forward by applying force from behind. The painters first shoved the furniture into the center of the living room.
thrust–to push or shove suddenly or with much force. The bulldozer thrust large piles of dirt to the side of the road.
ANTONYMS: **drag (v), jerk (v), pull (v), tow (v), tug (v)**

Q

quietly (adv)–done or said with little or no noise; marked by little movement. No one noticed when Gail quietly left the room.

calmly–in a quiet or still manner. Ramona calmly dialed the telephone as if nothing had happened.

gently–quietly or kindly. The dentist spoke gently to reassure the patient.

peacefully–free from disturbance; calmly. After the disagreement was settled, the friends peacefully continued their discussion.

shyly–quietly and bashfully. The young child shyly answered me when I asked him his name.

silently–with no noise at all. The deer silently darted across the field.

softly–in a manner that is quietly pleasant. Will you be able to read if I play the radio softly?

ANTONYMS: **harshly, loudly, noisily, restlessly, wildly**

R

road (n)–an open way for people or vehicles to travel on. Turn left at the next road to get to the shopping center.

alley–a narrow road behind or between buildings. We took a shortcut through the alley on our way home.

boulevard–a wide, main road, often lined with trees. This boulevard is beautiful when the cherry trees are in blossom.

highway–a long, main road open to the public. The highway goes past several small towns.

path–a narrow way made by people or animals walking. The hikers discovered a path that led them to a clearing in the woods.

street–a road in a city or town, usually with sidewalks and buildings on the side. The post office is on the same street as the library.

trail–a path through an unsettled or wild region. The scouts left markers on the trail so they would not get lost.

S

scared (adj)–feeling fear; suddenly becoming afraid. The scared children ran inside when they heard the thunder rumble.

afraid–full of fear or uneasiness. Some people who are afraid of being alone have pets.

anxious–uneasy from fear of what may happen. Stacey was anxious before her first piano recital.

apprehensive–fearful; worried. Becky's parents became apprehensive when she was not home on time.

frightened–filled with sudden fear. The frightened puppy was startled by the sound of the horn.

terrified–filled with great fear of danger. The terrified crew struggled to keep the sinking boat afloat.

timid–easily frightened; afraid to do something. Jonathan was too timid to ride the huge roller coaster.

ANTONYMS: **bold, brave (adj), courageous, daring (adj), fearless, unafraid**

slowly (adj)–with a low rate of speed; taking a long time or longer than usual. The snow slowly began to melt as the temperature rose.

cautiously–carefully and sometimes slowly. Elaine cautiously climbed the tall ladder.

easily–slowly; without rushing. Mrs. Hill easily talked with each of us in order to get to know us better.

gradually–slowly and in small steps. The apples gradually ripened on the trees.

lazily–in a slow and inactive manner. We watched a giant turtle lazily cross the road.

leisurely–in a relaxed or unhurried manner, taking plenty of time. I like to leisurely read a book when I sit outside in the summer.

sluggishly–slowly and without energy. The water sluggishly drained out of the clogged sink.

slowly (continued)

Thesaurus

ANTONYMS: **hastily, instantly, quickly, rapidly, swiftly, suddenly**

stop   (v)–**1** to come or bring to an end. The umpire stopped the game when it started to rain. **2** to keep from doing something. My tired feet stopped me from walking any farther.

arrest–to stop suddenly. The fire fighters arrested the flames before they could spread.

block–to stop by putting things in the way of. A large truck blocked the driveway in front of our apartment.

discontinue–to stop what has been done regularly. Martha discontinued her visits to the doctor when her broken leg healed.

halt–to make or bring to a complete stop. The crossing guard halted the traffic for the children.

prevent–to keep from happening. Will this toothpaste prevent tooth decay?

quit–to stop or give up something. Julie quit her paper route and took another part-time job.

ANTONYMS: **advance (v), begin, continue, go, proceed, start (v)**

strange   (adj)–differing from what is ordinary or usual; not seen or heard before. Have you ever heard the strange call of a quail?

exotic–strangely different and fascinating. There were many exotic plants at the garden show.

odd–different from what is expected. This mystery story has an odd ending.

peculiar–oddly different from the usual. Spoiled milk has a peculiar odor.

quaint–strange in an interesting or pleasing way. Many tourists visited the quaint waterfront village.

unfamiliar–not well known. We had to ask for directions in the unfamiliar town.

weird–mysteriously strange. The flickering light from the candle made weird shadows on the wall.

ANTONYMS: **common (adj), familiar (adj), known (adj), ordinary, regular (adj), usual**

strong   (adj)–having much strength or power. Only a strong person could move this box of books.

forceful–with much force or power. The candidate spoke in a forceful manner.

hardy–healthy; able to stand against something hard or difficult. Mums are very hardy plants.

mighty–having great strength, force, or power. A mighty storm was brewing.

powerful–having great strength, force, or power. The powerful horses pulled the heavy wagon.

sturdy–firm and strong; not giving way; well made. The sturdy cart did not break under the load.

tough–firm and strong; able to take wear and rough use. Leather for boots must be tough.

ANTONYMS: **feeble, flimsy, frail, weak**

T

teach   (v)–to help to learn or understand; to explain or show how to do something. Will you teach me how to play the guitar?

coach–to help to prepare for a special event, especially an athletic one. Mrs. Brooks will coach the soccer team this season.

demonstrate–to teach or explain by showing how something is done. The salesperson demonstrated the computer.

educate–to develop in knowledge, skill, or ability by study or training. The new business college educates students in many different subjects.

instruct–to give knowledge to. The counselor instructed the campers in first aid and safety.

train–to make skillful by teaching and practice. I trained my dog to sit up and bark.

tutor–to teach, usually privately or individually. The retired teacher still tutors students in the evenings.

throw   (v)–to release and use force to send through the air. Jackie threw the football to her teammate.

cast–to throw forcefully with a jerk. The fisherman cast his line into the water.

fling–to throw with force. Jodi <u>flung</u> her coat on the chair and rushed up the stairs.

heave–to lift and throw. The trash collectors <u>heaved</u> the large bags into the truck.

hurl–to throw powerfully. The strong athlete <u>hurled</u> the shotput.

pitch–to throw something at a target. We <u>pitched</u> horseshoes in the backyard.

toss–to throw lightly with the palm of the hand upward. See if you can <u>toss</u> the bean-bag so it lands in the circle.

ANTONYM: **catch (v)**

W

walk (v)–to go on foot; to advance by steps. Let's <u>walk</u> to the pet shop instead of taking the bus.

lumber–to move along heavily and clumsily. The elephant <u>lumbered</u> back and forth in the grassy area.

march–to walk in rhythm and with even steps. The school band <u>marched</u> in the parade.

shuffle–to walk without lifting the feet completely off the ground. David <u>shuffled</u> across the slippery floor so he would not fall.

stroll–to walk slowly or leisurely for pleasure. We <u>strolled</u> down the street and chatted with some friends.

strut–to walk in a proud or important manner. The winner <u>strutted</u> across the stage to receive her trophy.

trudge–to walk tiredly or with much effort. Russ <u>trudged</u> through several miles of deep snow to get to the cabin.

watch (v)–to look at or pay attention to. We <u>watched</u> the airplane land on the runway.

examine–to look at closely and carefully. Lori <u>examined</u> several pairs of sneakers before choosing her favorite pair.

guard–to watch and protect. Our dog <u>guards</u> our house when we are away.

observe–to watch carefully for a special purpose. Thurman <u>observed</u> the moon through his homemade telescope.

oversee–to watch and direct. The student who is the group leader will <u>oversee</u> the project.

view–to see or look at. Trina <u>viewed</u> the rolling hills from the car window.

witness–to watch something happen. A large crowd <u>witnessed</u> the launching of the space shuttle.

ANTONYMS: **disregard, ignore, miss (v), neglect (v), overlook (v)**

Y

yell (v)–to cry out with a loud, strong sound. Dad <u>yelled</u> to us to come inside for dinner.

cheer–to shout encouragement or praise. Everyone <u>cheered</u> as the runners crossed the finish line.

cry–to call out loudly. The lost child <u>cried</u> for help.

exclaim–to cry out in surprise or with strong feeling. "What a wonderful present!" Carl <u>exclaimed</u> with delight.

howl–to yell or shout. Everyone <u>howled</u> with laughter at the silly chimpanzees.

screech–to cry out sharply and in a high voice; scream. The campers heard blue jays <u>screeching</u> in the morning.

shout–to call or cry out forcefully. I <u>shouted</u> to my friends ahead to wait for me.

ANTONYMS: **murmur (v), mutter (v), whisper (v)**

Reports, Letters, Messages

Book Reports

A **book report** tells what a book is about and gives an opinion of the book. Read Lee's book report.

> <u>The Secret Life of Harold the Bird Watcher</u>
> by Hila Colman
>
> This book is about a boy who spent every day making up secret adventures. Harold always sat by a lake and dreamed about being a hero. His only friends were wild birds and animals. Some bad things happened at his favorite spot. Harold saved the ducks and the lake. He became a hero. His real life and his secret life changed in some surprising ways.
>
> I enjoyed this book because Harold and I are both nine years old. I also make up secret adventures.

Lee began his report with the title of the book and the author's name. He underlined the title and capitalized the important words.

Lee gave us some information about the book, but he did not give away the whole story. Lee also shared his opinion of the book.

Practice

Follow these directions using the book report above. Write a sentence for each direction.

1. Write the title of the book.
2. Write the author's name.
3. Write the name of a character in the book.
4. Tell something that happens in the book.
5. Tell why Lee likes the book.

Business Letters

♦ A **business letter** has six parts: the heading, inside address, greeting, body, closing, and signature.

Business letter

♦ The **heading** gives the writer's address and the date.

Heading

♦ The **inside address** gives the name and address of the person or company to whom the letter is sent. Notice where commas and capital letters are used in the sample below.

Inside address

♦ In a business letter the **greeting** is followed by a colon (:).

Greeting

♦ Only the first word in the **closing** is capitalized. Use one of these closings: *Respectfully, Yours truly, Sincerely.*

Closing

♦ The writer's name is signed under the closing.

Signature

4 Pine Street
Atlanta, Georgia 30308
May 2, 1991

——— Heading

Mr. Frank Kurtz, Director
Hot-Air Balloon Club
29 Fourth Avenue
Amarillo, Texas 79107

——— Inside address

Dear Mr. Kurtz:
    Please send me your booklet on how to start a hot-air balloon club.

——— Greeting
——— Body

Yours truly,
Chim Tran

——— Closing
——— Signature

Practice

Pretend your class wants to take a trip to the police station in your town or neighborhood. Write a business letter to the chief of police, asking when your class could visit.

Thank-You Notes and Invitations

Thank-you note

♦ A **thank-you note** is a short letter of thanks for a gift or favor. It follows the form of a friendly letter.

> 34 Lake Avenue
> Perry, Iowa 50220
> April 23, 1991
>
> Dear Uncle Marty,
>   Thank you very much for the birthday present. How did you know I had been wishing for a fishing rod? I can't wait to use it this weekend.
>
>   Love,
>   Jesse

Invitation

♦ An **invitation** is a note or letter that invites someone to an event. It should answer these questions: *What is happening? Where? When? Who sent the invitation?*

> Please come to _my birthday party_
>
> Place: _7 Hayward Street_
>
> Date and Time: _June 15, 2:30–4:00 P.M._
>
> From: _Your friend, Stephanie Torres_

Practice

Write a thank-you note or an invitation to a real or make-believe person.

Addressing Envelopes

♦ When you address an envelope, you write a return address and the receiver's address.

♦ Write your name and address in the upper left-hand corner. This is the **return address**. It shows where to return the letter if it cannot be delivered.

Return address

♦ In the center of the envelope, write the **receiver's address**. This is the name and address of the person who will receive the letter.

Receiver's address

♦ You may use an abbreviation for the name of a state. There is an official two-letter abbreviation for each state name. You can get a list of these abbreviations from your local post office.

State abbreviations

Return address

Kelly Daly
5 Spring Road
Evansville, IN 47714

NEW MEXICO

USA 25¢

Mr. Brian Dietz
26 Elm Ave.
Bowie, MD 20715

Receiver's address

State abbreviation

Practice

Using a ruler, draw two envelopes like the sample above. Then write this information where it belongs on each envelope.

1. *Return address:*   Ann Kelly   58 Sunset Blvd.   Aiken, SC 29801
   Receiver's address: Ms. Jane Seely   3 Oak St.   Elko, NV 89801

2. *Return address:*   Bob Fox   3 Brook Dr.   Cody, WY 82414
   Receiver's address: Mr. Joe Gómez   4 First Ave.
      Globe, AZ 85501

Telephone Messages

Using the telephone is an important way of communicating with other people. When you use the telephone, speak clearly and listen carefully. When you take a telephone message for someone, write the information correctly and completely.

Dorothy's brother wrote this telephone message.

> Dorothy,
>
> Leslie called at 3:30 on Saturday afternoon. This morning she was shoveling snow. She slipped and broke her arm. Call her at 555-1221.
>
> Danny

Danny included the following important information in his telephone message.

1. person called
2. day and time
3. caller's name
4. caller's message
5. caller's number
6. message taker

When Leslie called about her accident, she was nervous and excited. She talked very fast. Danny listened and then asked her to repeat the message slowly. This way he could be sure he wrote the correct information.

Practice

A. Read the information below. Write a message.
Shelly called today at noon. She wants to borrow Jasper's bike for her paper route tomorrow. She wants Jasper to call her tonight at 555-5966.

B. Write a telephone message for someone in your family. Remember to include all the important information.

A Guide to Spelling

Some useful spelling rules are listed below. Learning them will help you to spell words easily. Remember to use these rules when you write.

1. The suffix *-s* can be added to most nouns and verbs. If the word ends in *s, ss, sh, ch, x*, or *zz*, add *-es*.

NOUNS	gas	gases	**VERBS**	hiss	hisses
	bush	bushes		match	matches
	fox	foxes		buzz	buzzes

2. If a word ends in a consonant and *y*, change the *y* to *i* when you add a suffix, unless the suffix begins with *i*.

NOUNS	cherry	cherries	**VERBS**	study	studies
	baby	babies		try	trying
ADJECTIVES	muddy	muddier	muddiest		

3. If a word ends in a vowel and *y*, keep the *y* when you add a suffix.

NOUNS	turkey	turkeys	**VERBS**	stay	stayed

4. If a one-syllable word ends in one vowel and one consonant, double the last consonant when you add a suffix that begins with a vowel.

NOUNS	swim	swimmer	**VERBS**	stop	stopping
ADJECTIVES	big	bigger	biggest		

5. When you choose between *ie* and *ei*, use *ie* except after *c* or for the long *a* sound.
   (Exceptions: *leisure, neither, seize, weird*)

NOUNS	field	**VERBS**	shriek
	neighbors		receive

6. If a word ends in a single *f* or *fe*, usually change the *f* to *v* when you add *-s* or *-es*.

NOUNS calf calves knife knives

7. If a word ends in *e*, drop the *e* when you add a suffix that begins with a vowel. Keep the *e* when you add a suffix that begins with a consonant.

VERBS drive driving **ADVERBS** sure surely

8. Add an apostrophe and *s* (**'s**) to a singular noun to show possession, but do not add them to a pronoun. Special pronouns show possession.

doctor doctor's Mary Mary's
his hers its ours yours theirs

9. The letter *q* is always followed by the letter *u* in English words. The letter *v* is always followed by another letter; it is never the last letter in a word.

question give

10. Use an apostrophe (**'**) to show where a letter or letters have been left out in a contraction.

is not isn't we are we're you will you'll

Another way to help improve your spelling is to keep a notebook of special words. They may be words you think are interesting or hard to spell. Write them carefully in your spelling notebook. Keeping these words in alphabetical order will make your list of special words easy to find when you need them. If you use a looseleaf binder, you can add pages as your spelling notebook grows.

Words Often Written

The words in the list below came from compositions that were written by students your age. They are the words the students used most often. Are they the words *you* use most often, too?

1. about		**26.** mom
2. after		**27.** not
3. am		**28.** now
4. as		**29.** or
5. back		**30.** our
6. big		**31.** over
7. buy		**32.** people
8. came		**33.** play
9. can		**34.** school
10. could		**35.** see
11. did		**36.** some
12. do		**37.** started
13. don't		**38.** them
14. down		**39.** things
15. from		**40.** think
16. fun		**41.** this
17. going		**42.** time
18. good		**43.** too
19. house		**44.** took
20. if		**45.** us
21. I'm		**46.** very
22. just		**47.** want
23. know		**48.** what
24. little		**49.** will
25. lot		**50.** your

Grammar Handbook

Grammar

▶ **adjective**   An adjective describes a noun or a pronoun.

Ponds are <u>active</u> places.
<u>Several</u> chipmunks run through the <u>wet</u> grass.

adjectives after linking verbs   An adjective that follows a linking verb describes the subject of the sentence.

The swans *are* <u>white</u>.
They *are* <u>beautiful</u>.

adjectives that compare   Adjectives have two different forms that are used to make comparisons.

♦ Use the *-er* form of an adjective to compare two persons, places, or things.

Frogs have <u>smoother</u> skin than toads.

♦ Use the *-est* form of an adjective to compare three or more persons, places, or things.

Snails are the <u>slowest</u> pond creatures.

♦ The words *more* and *most* are often used with adjectives of two or more syllables to make comparisons.

The ducks were <u>more comical</u> than usual.
The goose is the <u>most common</u> bird here.

♦ Some adjectives show comparison in a special way. The correct forms of *good*, *bad*, *much*, and *little* are shown below.

<u>good</u> weather	<u>better</u> weather	<u>best</u> weather
<u>bad</u> storm	<u>worse</u> storm	<u>worst</u> storm
<u>much</u> snow	<u>more</u> snow	<u>most</u> snow
<u>little</u> fog	<u>less</u> fog	<u>least</u> fog

From a writer's point of view...

I use adjectives to add details to my writing, creating vivid word pictures for my readers. Adjectives that compare help me tell how things are alike or different.

articles   The words *a*, *an*, and *the* are a special kind of adjective. They are called articles. *The* is used with both singular and plural nouns. *A* and *an* are used only with singular nouns.

<u>The</u> animals at <u>the</u> pond are very busy.
<u>A</u> friend and I spent <u>an</u> afternoon there.

♦ Use *a* before a word that begins with a consonant sound.

<u>a</u> beaver   <u>a</u> pleasant afternoon

♦ Use *an* before a word that begins with a vowel sound.
<u>an</u> owl   <u>an</u> underwater plant

▶ **adverb**   A word that describes a verb is an adverb.

♦ Some adverbs answer the question "How?"

The fox hides <u>slyly</u> behind the bushes. (how?)

♦ Some adverbs answer the question "Where?"

Aesop wrote fables <u>here</u>. (where?)

♦ Other adverbs answer the question "When?"

<u>Often</u> a fable tells about one event. (when?)

adverbs that compare   Adverbs can be used to compare actions.

♦ Use the *-er* form or *more* to compare two actions. Most adverbs that end in *-ly* use *more*.

The ant worked <u>harder</u> than the cricket.
The tortoise moved <u>more steadily</u> than the hare.

♦ Use the *-est* form or *most* to compare three or more actions. Most adverbs that end in *-ly* use *most*.

The ant worked <u>hardest</u> of all the insects.
The tortoise moved <u>most steadily</u> of all.

From a writer's point of view. . .

Adverbs help me add details to my writing—details about actions and about times and places.

words that mean "no" The word *not* is an adverb. It means "no." Do not use two words that mean "no" in the same sentence.

Wrong: **It <u>wouldn't</u> <u>never</u> matter to me.**
Right: **It <u>wouldn't</u> ever matter to me.**
Right: **It would <u>never</u> matter to me.**

▶ contraction   A contraction is a shortened form of two words. An apostrophe replaces a letter or letters.

♦ Some contractions join a pronoun and a verb.

I have **never been in a dairy shed before.**
<u>I've</u> never been in a dairy shed before.

♦ Some contractions are formed from a verb and the word *not.*

I *cannot* **believe you** *did not* **bring your banjo.**
I <u>can't</u> believe you <u>didn't</u> bring your banjo.

▶ noun   A noun names a person, place, or thing.
The <u>settlers</u> came to <u>America</u> on a <u>ship</u>.
   (person)   (place)   (thing)

singular noun   A singular noun names one person, place, or thing.
The <u>settler</u> kept the <u>cow</u> in the <u>barn</u>.

plural noun   A plural noun names more than one person, place, or thing.
The <u>settlers</u> kept their <u>cows</u> in their <u>barns</u>.

spelling plural nouns   Add *-s* to form the plural of most nouns.
colonist<u>s</u>   river<u>s</u>   pea<u>s</u>   chicken<u>s</u>

♦ Add *-es* to form the plural of nouns that end in *ch, sh, s, ss, x,* or *z.*

bench<u>es</u>   bush<u>es</u>   bus<u>es</u>   box<u>es</u>

♦ If a noun ends in a consonant and *y,* change *y* to *i* and add *-es* to form the plural.

| Singular: | **library** | **city** | **cherry** |
| Plural: | **libraries** | **cities** | **cherries** |

♦ Some plurals are formed by changing the spelling of the singular noun.

| Singular: | **man** | **child** | **foot** | **mouse** |
| Plural: | **men** | **children** | **feet** | **mice** |

♦ A few nouns have the same singular and plural forms.

| Singular: | **elk** | **moose** | **deer** | **sheep** |
| Plural: | **elk** | **moose** | **deer** | **sheep** |

common noun   A common noun names any person, place, or thing.
> **A <u>colonist</u> founded the <u>town</u>.**

proper noun   A proper noun names a particular person, place, or thing.
> **<u>William Penn</u> founded <u>Philadelphia</u>.**

possessive noun   A possessive noun shows ownership.

♦ To form the possessive of a singular noun, add an apostrophe and *s* (**'s**) to the singular noun.
> **<u>Ben Franklin's</u> many talents amazed people.**

♦ To form the possessive of a plural noun ending in *s,* add an apostrophe (**'**).
> **<u>shoemakers'</u> hammers   <u>blacksmiths'</u> forges**

♦ To form the possessive of a plural noun that does not end in *s,* add an apostrophe and *s* (**'s**).
> **<u>men's</u> hats   <u>mice's</u> tails   two <u>deer's</u> tracks**

▶ pronoun   A pronoun takes the place of a noun or nouns.
> Nouns: **<u>Linda</u> writes <u>poems</u>.**
> Pronouns: **<u>She</u> enjoys writing <u>them</u>.**

From a writer's point of view. . .

Pronouns help me avoid repeating the same nouns over and over again.

subject pronoun The pronouns *I*, *you*, *she*, *he*, *it*, *we*, and *they* are subject pronouns. Use these pronouns to replace nouns that are the subjects of your sentences.

> **Robert Frost had been a teacher and a farmer.**
> **He wrote many poems about nature.**

object pronoun The pronouns *me*, *you*, *him*, *her*, *it*, *us*, and *them* are object pronouns. You can use these pronouns to replace nouns in the predicate of a sentence.

> **Paul read *poems* to *Jill*.**
> **Paul read them to her.**

possessive pronoun The pronouns *my*, *your*, *his*, *her*, *its*, *our*, and *their* are possessive pronouns. A possessive pronoun shows ownership. Possessive pronouns can replace possessive nouns.

> **Aileen Fisher's home is in the mountains.**
> **Her poems usually involve nature.**

using *I* and *me*, *we* and *us* Use *I* in the subject of a sentence and *me* in the predicate. Use *we* in the subject of a sentence and *us* in the predicate.

> **My family and I will visit a planetarium soon.**
> **The trip excites Carlos and me.**
> **We wrote a poem about a star.**
> **Dad told us more about the stars.**

▶ **sentence** A sentence is a group of words that expresses a complete thought.

> **People of all ages enjoy hobbies.**

declarative sentence A declarative sentence makes a statement. It ends with a period (**.**).

> **Hobbies are important in people's lives.**

From a writer's point of view...

When I write, I use sentences to express my thoughts clearly. Using different kinds of sentences adds variety to my work.

interrogative sentence   An interrogative sentence asks a question. It ends with a question mark (**?**).

What is your hobby?

imperative sentence   An imperative sentence gives a command or makes a request. It ends with a period (**.**).

Please get your kite ready.

exclamatory sentence   An exclamatory sentence expresses strong feeling. It ends with an exclamation mark (**!**).

That kite will crash!

simple sentence   A simple sentence has one subject and one predicate. It expresses one complete thought.

Kites come in many different shapes.

compound sentence   A compound sentence contains two simple sentences joined by the word *and*. Use a comma in a compound sentence before the word *and*.

The day was cool, and clouds drifted across the sun.

▶ subjects and predicates   The subject is the part of the sentence that names someone or something. The predicate tells what the subject is or does. Both the subject and the predicate may be one word or many words.

Currents move ocean water around the world.
The most common mineral is salt.
Ocean water moves.
Sea water flows in vast streams.

simple subject   The simple subject is the main word in the complete subject.

The five biggest oceans are really one huge ocean.

compound subject   A sentence may have more than one simple subject. The word *and* may be used to join simple subjects. The simple subjects share the same predicate.

> *Spiny <u>crabs</u> and colorful <u>fish</u> scurry along the underwater reef.*

simple predicate   The simple predicate is the main word or words in the complete predicate.

> **Ocean waters <u>*flow*</u> in vast streams.**

compound predicate   A sentence may have more than one simple predicate. The word *and* may be used to join simple predicates. The simple predicates share the same subject.

> **Some worms <u>*live*</u> and <u>*feed*</u> in the ocean.**

▶ verb   A verb is a word that shows action or being.

> **Nina <u>paints</u> in art class. (action)**
> **That painting <u>is</u> beautiful. (being)**

action verb   An action verb shows action. It tells what the subject of a sentence does.

> **The art teacher <u>welcomed</u> the students.**

helping verb and **main verb**   A verb can be more than one word. The main verb is the most important verb. A helping verb works with the main verb.

> **Many people *have <u>admired</u>* Picasso's paintings. (main verb)**
> **His name *<u>is</u> known* all over the world. (helping verb)**

linking verb   A linking verb shows being. It tells what the subject is or was.

> **Grandma Moses <u>was</u> a famous artist.**

From a writer's point of view...

When I write, I use verbs that are colorful and precise. This helps my reader picture exactly what is happening.

♦ **using linking verbs**   When the correct subject and verb are used together, we say they agree. The form of the linking verb *be* that is used depends on the subject of the sentence. Study the chart below.

Using the Forms of *be*	
Use *am* and *was*	with *I*
Use *is* and *was*	with *she*, *he*, *it*, and singular nouns
Use *are* and *were*	with *we*, *you*, *they* and plural nouns

tense   The tense of a verb shows the time of the action.

present tense   A verb in the present tense shows action that happens now.

> **Eli <u>forms</u> the tiles.**

A verb in the present tense must agree with the subject of the sentence.

♦ With *he*, *she*, *it*, or a singular noun, add *-s* or *-es* to the verb.

> **The student learn<u>s</u>.   My cousin teach<u>es</u>.**
> **He walk<u>s</u>.**

♦ With *I*, *you*, *we*, *they*, or a plural noun, do not add *-s* or *-es*.

> **The students learn.   My cousins teach.**
> **They walk.**

♦ If a verb ends in *ch*, *sh*, *s*, *ss*, *x*, or *z*, add *-es*. Notice the word *teaches* above.

future tense   A verb in the future tense shows action that will happen. The future tense is formed with the helping verb *will*.

> **Ann <u>will create</u> a vase.**

past tense   A verb in the past tense shows action that already happened.

> **Lee <u>washed</u> pots.**

From a writer's point of view...

When I proofread my writing, I check to see that all of my subjects and verbs agree.

past tense of irregular verbs   The past tenses of irregular verbs are not formed by adding -*ed*. Some irregular verbs are shown in the chart below.

Verb	Past	Past with *have*, *has*, or *had*
begin	began	begun
bring	brought	brought
come	came	come
do	did	done
eat	ate	eaten
fall	fell	fallen
find	found	found
fly	flew	flown
give	gave	given
go	went	gone
grow	grew	grown
ride	rode	ridden
run	ran	run
say	said	said
see	saw	seen
take	took	taken
throw	threw	thrown
write	wrote	written

spelling verbs correctly   The spelling of some verbs changes when -*es* or -*ed* is added.

♦ If a verb ends in a consonant and *y,* change the *y* to *i* before adding -*es* or -*ed*.

study   studies   studied

♦ If a verb ends in one vowel and one consonant, double the final consonant before adding -*ed*.

trap   trapped   stir   stirred

Capitalization

▶ **first word of a sentence**   Every sentence begins with a capital letter.

> **People enjoy having special projects.**

▶ **proper nouns**   Each important word in a proper noun begins with a capital letter.

♦ Capitalize each word in the name of a person or pet.
> **Patrice Gomez owns a cat named Duke.**

♦ Capitalize an initial in a name. Put a period after the initial.
> **William L. Chen is a doctor in our neighborhood.**

♦ Capitalize a title before a name. If the title is an **abbreviation** (a shortened form of a word), put a period after it.
> **President Jefferson   Dr. Jonas Salk**

♦ Capitalize every important word in the names of particular places or things.
> **Statue of Liberty   Ellis Island   New York Harbor**

♦ Capitalize names of days, months, holidays, and special days.
> **Tuesday   April   Fourth of July**

▶ **pronoun *I***   The pronoun *I* is always capitalized.

> **May I go skating this afternoon?**

▶ **letters**   Capitalize the first word of the greeting and the first word of the closing of a letter.

> **Dear Mother,   Dear Sir: Sincerely yours,**

▶ **titles of books**   Capitalize the first word, the last word, and all of the important words in the title of a book.

> **The Secret Life of Harold the Bird Watcher**

▶ **quotations**   Begin the first word in a quotation with a capital letter.

The Hare asked, "How about a race?"

▶ **state abbreviations**   You may use the United States Postal Service two-letter abbreviations of state names when you write addresses. They have capital letters and no periods.

Alabama	**AL**	Maine	**ME**	Oregon	**OR**
Alaska	**AK**	Maryland	**MD**	Pennsylvania	**PA**
Arizona	**AZ**	Massachusetts	**MA**	Rhode Island	**RI**
Arkansas	**AR**	Michigan	**MI**	South Carolina	**SC**
California	**CA**	Minnesota	**MN**	South Dakota	**SD**
Colorado	**CO**	Mississippi	**MS**	Tennessee	**TN**
Connecticut	**CT**	Missouri	**MO**	Texas	**TX**
Delaware	**DE**	Montana	**MT**	Utah	**UT**
Florida	**FL**	Nebraska	**NE**	Vermont	**VT**
Georgia	**GA**	Nevada	**NV**	Virginia	**VA**
Hawaii	**HI**	New Hampshire	**NH**	Washington	**WA**
Idaho	**ID**	New Jersey	**NJ**	West Virginia	**WV**
Illinois	**IL**	New Mexico	**NM**	Wisconsin	**WI**
Indiana	**IN**	New York	**NY**	Wyoming	**WY**
Iowa	**IA**	North Carolina	**NC**	* * *	
Kansas	**KS**	North Dakota	**ND**	District of	
Kentucky	**KY**	Ohio	**OH**	Columbia	**DC**
Louisiana	**LA**	Oklahoma	**OK**		

Punctuation

▶ **period**   Declarative sentences and imperative sentences end with a period (.).

> **I stood on the corner.   Wait for the signal.**

♦ Put a period after an initial in a name.

> **J.P. Jones   Abigail S. Adams**

♦ Put a period after an abbreviation (a shortened form of a word).

> **Mr.   Mrs.   Ms.   Dr.**

▶ **question mark**   An interrogative sentence ends with a question mark (**?**).

> **Do you have more than one hobby?**

▶ **exclamation mark**   An exclamatory sentence ends with an exclamation mark (**!**).

> **That kite will crash!**

▶ **comma**   A comma (**,**) is a signal that tells a reader to pause.

♦ Use a comma after *yes*, *no*, or *well* at the beginning of a sentence.

> **Yes, I saw the display of Eskimo art.**
> **Well, my favorites were the bears made of silver.**

♦ Use a comma to set off the name of a person spoken to.

> **Your painting is very beautiful, Roberta.**

♦ Use a comma to separate words in a series. A series is made up of three or more items. No comma is used after the last word in the series. The last comma goes before the word *and*.

> **The artists carve, smooth, and polish their work.**

♦ Use a comma to separate the city from the state.

I grew up in Tulsa, Oklahoma.

♦ Use a comma to separate the day and the year.

Pablo was born on February 7, 1984.

♦ Use a comma after the greeting of a friendly letter. Use a comma after the closing of a friendly or a business letter.

Dear Kim,   Your friend,   Yours truly,

♦ Use a comma before the word *and* in a compound sentence.

The merchants crossed central Asia, and they reached China.

▶ quotation marks   A quotation is the exact words someone speaks. Quotation marks (" ") show where a speaker's exact words begin and end.

♦ Use quotation marks before and after a quotation. Begin the first word in a quotation with a capital letter. When the quotation comes last, use a comma to separate the speaker from the quotation.

The Tortoise said, "I'm not going to lose this race."

♦ When the quotation comes first, use a comma, a question mark, or an exclamation mark to separate the quotation from the speaker. The end mark of a quotation always comes just <u>before</u> the second quotation mark. Put a period at the end of the sentence.

Statement: "Let's do something else," replied the Tortoise.
Question: "Are you afraid you'll lose?" teased the Hare.
Exclamation: "I'm not afraid!" snapped the Tortoise.

▶ **apostrophe**   Use an apostrophe (') to show where a letter or letters have been left out in a contraction (a shortened form of a word).

> **we'd (we + had)   wasn't (was + not)**

♦ Use an apostrophe to form the possessive of a noun.

> **man's   James's   men's   workers'**

▶ **colon**   Use a colon (:) after the greeting in a business letter.

> **Dear Mr. Kurtz: Dear Sir or Madam:**

▶ **underlining**   Underline the title of a book.

> **I enjoyed reading <u>A Chinese Zoo</u>.**

Writing and Computers

Along with great ideas, the best friend a writer can have is a computer. It's easy and fun to write using one. You can use it to prewrite, write, revise, and proofread. Then it takes only a few minutes to print a final copy.

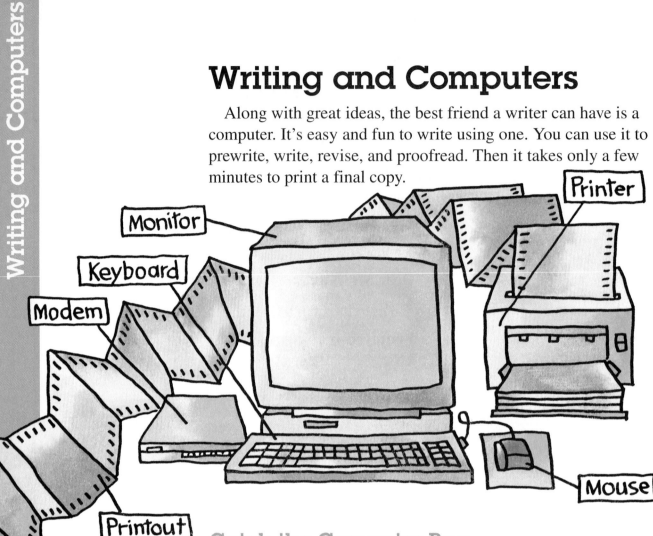

Catch the Computer Bug

If you've never used a computer, you may feel nervous. Many people think that computers are hard to use. Some even think that computers are smart! But a computer is just a machine. The only trick you need to know is how to tell it what to do. You need to know how to put your writing into it. You also need to know how to give it commands. Then the computer can help you revise and proofread your writing.

Every computer is slightly different. But each has a manual, or handbook. The manual tells you how to give the commands. Use the manual for help. This list of computer terms, and the chart of computer commands after it, will help you understand the directions in your manual.

Computer Terms

Backup: a copy of a document that is made to protect the original. The backup is often stored on a floppy disk.

Character: a single letter, numeral, or space. The word *dog* has three characters; so does the number *134*.

Command: an order, such as PRINT or SAVE, that the user gives to the computer.

Computer program: a list of instructions that tells the computer what to do; software.

Cursor: the blinking line or square on the screen that shows where the next typed character will appear.

Disk: a magnetic object on which information is stored (See *floppy disk* and *hard disk*).

Document: one or more pages of your writing, such as a story, a report, or a poem.

Edit: to change what you type into the computer; to revise.

Floppy disk: a small plastic disk used to save and store documents. Sometimes this is called a diskette.

Floppy Disk

Font: any one of various styles of letters that a computer can use in order to print output.

Format: to prepare a blank floppy disk for use (also called *initialize*).

Hard copy: document, or writing, that is printed out from the computer onto paper.

Hard disk: an inside part of the computer where information is stored. This differs from memory, which stores information being used at the moment.

Hardware: the machine, including the monitor, computer, and keyboard.

Input: information—text, numbers, and so on—typed into the computer.

Keyboard: part of the computer used to input information. It looks like a typewriter keyboard.

Load: to take information from an information storage device, such as a disk, and put it into a computer's memory.

Menu: a list on the monitor of things the computer does on command, such as SAVE.

Modem: the device that allows computers to communicate over telephone lines.

Monitor: the television-like screen on which input and output can be viewed.

Output: text that the computer displays, on the screen or in hard copy.

Printer: the device that prints output in hard copy.

Printout: a copy of your writing made by the printer.

Program: a disk that contains a group of instructions that tells the computer what to do.

Software: programs that run on a computer to allow it to do word processing, math calculations, and so on.

Terminal: includes the keyboard, which loads input into the computer, and the monitor, where output is viewed.

Virus: a set of instructions, hidden in a computer system, that leaves copies of itself in other programs or disks and can erase stored information.

Computer Commands

Cut ▶ Tells the computer to take out, or "cut," a piece of text.

Delete ▶ Tells the computer to remove selected text.

Find ▶ Tells the computer to find a certain word in the text.

Open ▶ Tells the computer to open a document.

Paste ▶ Tells the computer to insert text in a certain place in the document.

Print ▶ Tells the computer to print out the document in hard copy.

Quit ▶ Tells the computer to close a document.

Return ▶ Tells the computer to move the cursor to the next line.

Save ▶ Tells the computer to save a document by putting it into permanent storage.

Shift ▶ Tells the computer to use a capital letter.

Tab ▶ Tells the computer to indent a line of text, as for a paragraph indent.

The Key to Typing

The hardest part of writing on a computer can be learning
how to type. The first step is learning which fingers hit which
keys. Use the finger diagram below. Practice typing "The quick
brown fox jumped over the lazy dog." Make sure your fingers
are curved over the keys on the keyboard. It may be slow going
at first, but with practice you'll soon be typing like a pro.

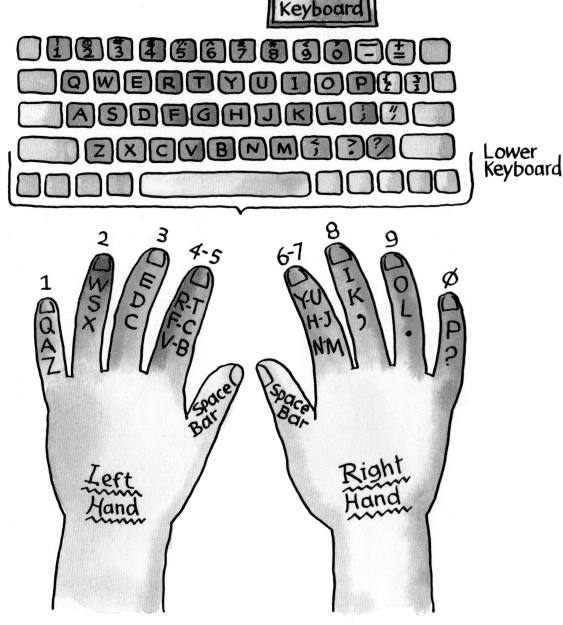

Word Processing

Writing with a computer can make it easier to

- choose topics to write about
- discover your ideas
- organize your ideas
- write your first draft
- revise your writing
- correct your mistakes
- share your writing with others

The word processing program you use will tell you how to use the computer to enter, save, edit, and print your work. Check your manual for special features. Some programs can catch spelling errors. Others have drawing features (called graphics) for adding pictures or borders.

Word processing programs cannot do the following things:

- think
- get ideas
- choose the best words
- organize your work
- spell words as you write
- punctuate correctly

You are still in charge of the writing, and you still need to use all of your language skills.

Ready, Set, Write!

Now you are ready to prewrite, write, revise, and proofread a piece of writing. Follow these steps.

Create a File and First Draft A file is a group of related documents. In a file folder, you might keep such related papers as prewriting ideas, first draft, revision, and final copy of a story. A computer can also keep a file for you.

- Tell the computer to open a new document.
- Give the document a name. Some computers ask you to name a document with words. Others ask for a series of numbers or letters. For example, you might use *STORY.DR1*, meaning "story, draft 1."
- Type a list of ideas, words that describe your topic, or questions about your topic.
- Type your first draft. Tell the computer to SAVE it.

When you have finished, follow the directions in your manual and create a file. Give it a name, such as *STORY.FILE*. Put your draft in the file. Take a break! Then begin to revise.

Revise and Proofread Your Draft You'll have no more messy papers with arrows and cross-outs when you revise on a computer. You do the thinking; let the computer do the work!

- Make a computer document copy of your first draft.
- Label it—for example, *story revision* or *STORY.REV*. Save the original draft. Use the new copy for revising.
- Move the cursor to a place that needs revising. Give the computer a command. You might tell it to CUT a sentence, move it to another place in your paper, and PASTE it in.
- Check your writing for errors and correct them.

Print your document. Decide how to share your writing.

Index

to review a story, 24–25
on the telephone, 474
visualizing, 24–25, 134–135, 184–185,
    296–297, 400–401
to your writing. *See* Revising as a step of the
    writing process.
See also Cooperative learning; Partner, working
    with a; Peer conferencing; Speaking;
    Speaking and Listening; Working Together.
Literature. *See* Fiction; Nonfiction; Stories;
    Poetry.
Literature
bibliographies, 41, 99, 149, 201, 261, 313, 363,
    415
character, setting, plot in, 348–349
listening as a response to, 23, 79, 133, 183, 239,
    295, 345, 399
space order in, 298–299
speaking as a response to, 23, 79, 133, 183, 239,
    295, 345, 399
thinking skills related to, 23, 79, 133, 183, 239,
    295, 345, 399
time order in, 26–27
writing as a response to, 23, 79, 133, 183, 239,
    295, 345, 399
See also Fiction; Nonfiction; Poems; Stories;
    Thinking Skills; Thinking Strategies.
Literature in Your World, Introduction l
Little, less, least, 282–283

Main idea
of outline, 248–249
of paragraph, 82–83, 100, 249, 300–301,
    402–403
Main verbs, 166–167, 202, 211, 419
Malnig, Anita, from *Where the Waves Break*,
    396–399
Mary McLeod Bethune, from, by Greenfield,
    Eloise, 234–239
Mathematics. *See* Writing Across the
    Curriculum.
Messages, telephone, 474
Metacognition, 19, 40, 73, 98, 129, 148,
    179, 200, 233, 260, 291, 312, 341, 362,
    395, 414
Metaphors in poetry, 138–139
Mizumura, Kazue, untitled poem, 130
Mood, 296–297
More and *most*
with adjectives, 280–281
Music. *See* Writing Across the Curriculum.

Narrating, A Strategy for, 18–19
Narrating, Writing Process, 32–39
Negative words, 332–333, 364, 371
No, **using comma after**, 188–189
Nonfiction
important facts, 250–251
interesting facts, 250–251
Nonfiction
from *Are Those Animals Real?*, 180–183
from *Mary McLeod Bethune*, 234–239
from *Where the Waves Break*, 396–399
Nonfiction and fiction in a library, 242–243
Nonstop Writing, 92. *See also* Prewriting
    strategies.
Notes, taking, 135, 246–247
Nouns
common, 58–59, 103, 107, 205, 418
definition of, 52, 374
identifying, 100, 102, 374–375, 416, 423
plural, 54–55, 56–57, 100, 102, 106, 204,
    316, 418
plural possessive, 64–65, 109
proper, 58–59, 60–61, 103, 107, 205, 418
singular, 54–55, 100, 102, 106, 204, 316, 418
singular possessive, 62–63, 108–109
spelling of plural, 56–57, 106–107
writing with, 53, 55, 57, 59, 63, 65, 105

Object pronouns, 116–117, 120–121, 150, 155,
    205–206, 316, 419
Observation Chart, 178–179, 183, 194, 200,
    394–395, 399, 408. *See also* Thinking
    Strategies.
Observing, 178–179, 183, 194, 200, 394–395,
    399, 408, 414. *See also* Thinking Skills.
Onomatopoeia. *See* Echo Words; Imitative Words.
Opinion
in book report, 470
in writing, 80–81
See also Fact and Opinion.
Order. *See* Directions; Space order; Time order in
    stories.
Outlines, making. 248–249

Paragraphs
choosing and narrowing topics for. *See* Topic
    Choosing and Narrowing Strategies.
definition of, 82
descriptive, 298–299, 300–301, 405
detail sentences in, 84–85, 186–187, 249,
    298–299, 300–301, 402–403